THE MANY LIVES OF ANNE FRANK

The Many Lives of Anne Frank

RUTH FRANKLIN

Yale
UNIVERSITY
PRESS
New Haven and London

Yale University Press books may be purchased in quantity for educational, business, or promotional use. For information, please e-mail sales.press@yale.edu (U.S. office) or sales@yaleup.co.uk (U.K. office).

Set in Janson type by Integrated Publishing Solutions.
Printed in the United States of America.

ISBN 978-0-300-24812-8 (hardcover : alk. paper)
Library of Congress Control Number: 2024941662
A catalogue record for this book is available from the British Library.

This paper meets the requirements of ANSI/NISO Z39.48-1992 (Permanence of Paper).

10 9 8 7 6 5 4 3 2 1

Frontispiece: Anne Frank's first diary (*center*) surrounded by some of her other writings: the loose sheets on which she rewrote her diary (*bottom left*), her "Favorite Quotes Notebook" (*right*), and her book of short stories (*top left*). Copyright Anne Frank House, Amsterdam. Photographer: Allard Bovenberg.

For all of Anne's readers

CONTENTS

Introduction: Icon 1

Part 1. Anne Frank

1. Child: From Frankfurt to Amsterdam, 1929–1934 19

2. Refugee: Amsterdam, 1934–1940 32

3. Target: The Holocaust in the Netherlands, 1940–1942 44

4. Witness: The Annex Eight, 1942–1943 76

5. Lover: Anne and Peter van Pels, 1943–1944 105

6. Artist: Anne and the Diary, 1943–1944 129

Interlude: The Raid 157

7. Prisoner: Westerbork and Auschwitz, August–October 1944 165

8. Corpse: Bergen-Belsen, November 1944–February 1945 192

Part 2. "Anne Frank"

9. Author: Otto and the Diary, 1945–1947 207

Interlude: Anne Frank in Ethiopia 238

10. Celebrity: The Diary in America, 1951–1952 241

Interlude: Ghostly Muse 268

11. Ambassador: Into the Infinite, 1955–1959 273

Interlude: Surrogate Father 295

12. Survivor: Anne in Fiction 299

Interlude: Family Secret 318

13. Pawn: Anne in the Political World 323

Notes 343

Selected Bibliography 399

Acknowledgments 409

Index 413

THE MANY LIVES OF ANNE FRANK

INTRODUCTION

Icon

THEY CONGREGATE ON THE PLAZA outside the entrance to Prinsengracht 263, beside a kiosk selling tickets for tours of Amsterdam and another offering traditional Dutch pancakes: children with school groups, teenagers sulking beside their parents, college students on a backpacking adventure, older couples who have saved up for a long-awaited European vacation. They come from just about everywhere: the United States, Canada, Puerto Rico; England, Wales, Ireland, Portugal, Italy, Spain, France, Denmark, Norway, Sweden, Finland, Estonia, the Czech Republic, Slovakia, Ukraine; Brazil, the Dominican Republic, Peru, Argentina; the Philippines, South Korea, Sierra Leone, Israel, Tunisia; Germany, so many from Germany. They wear jeans and crop tops, tank tops and sun hats, T-shirts that say Levi's or Led Zeppelin or the names of their schools. Some take photos by the front door, striking a sexy or silly pose, and post the results on Instagram. If they happen to be there at the top of the hour, when the bells on the Westertoren clock, above the plaza, play their melancholy tune, they may look up in recognition, remembering what Anne wrote about that sound: *I loved it from the start, and especially in the night it's like a faithful friend.*[1]

Many of them have come because of the *Diary*. They read it in school or on their own, once or many times over. They tried to picture Anne's hiding place: the swinging bookcase, the steep stairs, the darkened rooms where she and her parents—together with the Van Pels family and the dentist Fritz Pfeffer—cooked and slept and studied and used the toilet and argued and listened to the radio and did everything that people do, twenty-four hours a day, seven days a week, for 760 days straight, never stepping outdoors, never seeing the sun. (In the first published version of the *Diary*, Anne used pseudonyms for some people. The Van Pels family was called by the name Van Daan; Pfeffer was called Dussel. I use their real names, as later editions of the *Diary* also do.)

The experience of visiting these rooms can be profoundly emotional. Taking photos or video is prohibited; no screen can mediate between the visitors and the space. Many people comment on how much smaller it is than they expected. I first visited at age eight, after reading the *Diary* for the first time; little as I was, I found it impossibly cramped. Returning forty years later, now well into middle age, my body registered how rickety and steep the staircases were, set at such a narrow angle that I banged my knee while climbing up.

The *Diary* is one of the best-selling nonfiction books of all time. Still, many of the visitors haven't read it. They're here because they're visiting Amsterdam and the Anne Frank House is a must-see, along with the Rijksmuseum and the red-light district. In 1952, after the *Diary* became a surprise best-seller in the United States, Otto Frank, Anne's father, found that tourists spontaneously appeared at Prinsengracht 263, which then still housed his business, wanting to see Anne's "Secret Annex." Johannes Kleiman and Victor Kugler, longtime employees of Otto who helped to sustain the family in hiding, showed them around; visitors often greeted them as "Koophuis" and "Kraler," Anne's pseudonyms for them. Otto used the proceeds from the enormously successful Broadway adaptation of the *Diary* and the movie version that followed to purchase and restore the building, which had been in danger of collapse owing to disrepair. He imagined it not as "a dead monument" but as an international youth center. In 1960, the year it opened, 6,000 people came. Within thirty years, that number had climbed to 300,000.[2]

Now, along with Madame Tussaud's and the Louvre, the Anne Frank House is one of the most popular museums in Europe, admitting some seventy tourists every fifteen minutes, from nine in the morning until ten o'clock at night every day, including Christmas and New Year's: nearly 1.3 million people per year. Tickets sell out weeks in advance. At least as much as the *Diary*, this building represents Anne to the world: a living monument in her name. But in the decades since her death, Anne Frank herself has become not just a person who once lived, breathed, and wrote but a symbol: a secret door that opens into a kaleidoscope of meanings, most of which her legions of fans understand incompletely, if at all.

* * *

Anne's chronicle of the period she spent in hiding, now with more than thirty million copies in print in seventy languages, is the most famous work of literature to arise from the Holocaust. Since it first appeared in the Netherlands more than seventy-five years ago, Anne—who, had she survived the camps, would be nearly one hundred years old—has become an icon. *Time* magazine included her on a list of the most important people of the twentieth century. An asteroid discovered in 1942, the year she went into hiding, has been named after her. The horse chestnut tree in the courtyard behind the Annex, which Anne loved to gaze at through the attic window, died in 2010, but its saplings live on at museums and memorials around the world, including Manhattan's Ground Zero. Her name is synonymous with courage, with resistance to persecution, with optimism; in Japan, it has also been used as a euphemism for a woman's period.[3] (Translated into Japanese in 1952, the *Diary* was one of the first books in that language explicitly to address menstruation.)

Anne's face, smiling enigmatically from billboards worldwide and often accompanied by the most famous line from the *Diary*—*In spite of everything, I still believe that people are really good at heart*—has been compared to "a present-day Mona Lisa."[4] Statues of her have been erected in Canada, Argentina, Great Britain, Idaho, and Hiroshima, as well as in the park across the street from the South Amsterdam apartment building where she grew up. Her name and image have been used to sell everything from makeup to hot dogs. In 2017, Deutsche Bahn, the German national railway company, included her, as a Frankfurt native, on a list of German luminaries whose names would adorn a new fleet of high-speed trains. In the era of social media, when her name "trends," it's usually not good news: an Anne Frank Halloween costume that resurfaces every few years; a Rhode Island restaurant that tweeted an offensive meme with her image; Italian soccer fans who made stickers depicting her wearing the colors of a rival team, in an attempt to insult them by associating them with a Jew.[5]

Documentaries track the memories of Anne's friends and the tragedy of her last seven months, after the Gestapo raided the Annex and deported her and the other residents to concentration camps.[6] Artworks created in her name range from images of her face by the German artist Gerhard Richter to a poster listing all the items mentioned in her diary (margarine, strawberries, the Oscar Wilde play *An Ideal Husband*).[7] She has inspired a Grammy-winning orchestral work by the American composer Michael Tilson Thomas, an opera, a ballet, even a "puppet show for adults."[8] And poetry: by Yevgeny Yevtushenko, C. K. Williams, and countless others.

As with the Mona Lisa, Anne's image evokes endless interpretations. Some see her as a little girl who dreamed of becoming a movie star and whose scribbled diary radiates goodness and hope amid one of the darkest periods in human history. Others, including myself, have come to understand her as an accomplished and sophisticated writer—a deliberate, literary witness to Nazi persecution who revised her original diary into a brilliant work of testimony in response to a Dutch government minister's call for documents of the war years. To the novelist and journalist Meyer Levin, whose desire to adapt the *Diary* for the stage turned into a hubristic conviction that only he could represent Anne's true message to the world, she was "the voice of six million vanished Jewish souls," a prophet whose words reached him like a revelation and turned him into a proselytizer for the *Diary*.[9] "What she wrote privately has now been interpreted by so many admirers and emulators that the bright, saucy Anne Frank has become a blur of images," write Hyman A. Enzer and Sandra Solotaroff-Enzer, the editors of one of the many collections of scholarly essays about Anne. "She is no longer just a young girl budding into womanhood, writing to make sense out of a cruel confinement, but has become a patron saint of adolescence, an ardent feminist, a literary prodigy, a champion of religious and racial equality, and an embattled literary property."[10]

The story of Anne's life and death evokes meaning on the deepest symbolic levels. Some hear Judeo-Christian—mostly Christian—martyrological undertones: she is Moses (a hidden child), Mary (a virgin), Jesus (a person betrayed who then undergoes a "resurrection through words"), the murdered holy virgin Saint Ursula, Joan of Arc, Saint Thérèse of Lisieux. As a writer, she is compared to the Roman philosopher Boethius, who wrote *The Consolation of Philosophy* while imprisoned for political reasons, and to medieval monks such as Thomas à Kempis, who wrote spiritual works under a vow of seclusion. "Anne Frank is the only Jewish saint," writes Jenny Diski, a British journalist, imagining her as a friendly intercessor to the intimidating, unapproachable Jewish God. Others liken her to Cleopatra, Antigone, Juliet, Goethe's Marguerite, or Tolstoy's Natasha.[11] Locked in a tower, she is a heroine from a fairy tale, waiting for a prince who will never come to save her.

At the same time, Anne has often been a lightning rod for controversy. Some contemporary Holocaust educators believe that by virtue of its extreme popularity as a text—often the only text—from which children learn about the Holocaust, the *Diary* has crowded out other, more representative stories; more than once my offers to speak to students about Anne have been politely rebuffed by teachers who view her book as pedagogically passé. Meanwhile, right-wing activists in America regularly try to pull versions of the *Diary* from public school libraries, objecting primarily to a passage in which Anne expresses attraction to another girl.[12]

Critics have attacked the Broadway play and the movie based on it for downplaying Anne's Jewishness and emphasizing the humanism in her writing. The play implies that the *Diary* concludes with her reflections on people being "good at heart." But Anne wrote the famous line in July 1944, setting it just before a bleak passage that imagines *the world gradually being turned into a wilderness . . . I hear the ever approaching thunder, which will destroy us too.*[13] "It is not enough to identify oneself with Anne Frank," wrote the Austrian critic Alfred Werner in 1958, disturbed by the spectacle of West Germans who seemed to equate viewing the play—which was received with near universal silence by German audiences, who felt that applause would desecrate the seriousness of the occasion—to genuinely reckoning with the nation's past. "It is one thing to find 'catharsis' in the theater and quite a different thing to admit, 'Yes, I am guilty,' and to go on living with this feeling of guilt," Werner continued. "There is a danger of equating the sorrows of little Anne, who suffered in an Amsterdam garret, with the anxiety of a German boy or girl, who heard from an air raid shelter the Allied bombs crash on the city."[14] Indeed, in the intervening decades Anne's name has been invoked in service of a bewildering range of political causes, from the U.S. civil rights movement to the boycott campaign against Israel. An op-ed essay by the *New York Times* columnist Nicholas Kristof in 2016, which drew a comparison between the Frank family's efforts to escape Nazi-occupied Holland and the Syrian refugee crisis, was headlined "Anne Frank Today Is a Syrian Girl."[15]

Some have argued that all these interpretations and reinterpretations constitute a betrayal of Anne, crowding out the essential aspect of her identity, namely that of a Jew persecuted by Hitler. Anne's story, the novelist Cynthia Ozick writes, has been "bowdlerized, distorted, transmuted, traduced, reduced; it has been infantilized, Americanized, homogenized, sentimentalized; falsified, kitschified, and, in fact, blatantly and arrogantly denied"—by its many adapters and would-be adapters; by Americans and other privileged teenagers who "identify" with Anne because they, too, quarrel with their mothers; and by Otto Frank himself. Many critics and readers have attacked Anne's father for the way he edited the *Diary*, claiming that he censored her criticisms of her mother and her feelings about her body. Ozick judges him complicit in promoting a "shallowly upbeat view" of his daughter, emphasizing her idealism while downplaying the antisemitism that destroyed her world and her life.[16]

As the Holocaust scholar Alvin Rosenfeld has pointed out, the *Diary*—which, of course, does not chronicle Anne's miserable death from typhus at Bergen-Belsen—allows readers to feel they are accessing a Holocaust story without forcing them to confront its brutal reality. "The image of the emaciated, disease-ridden girl lying dead amidst the human waste of the camp latrine, then dumped into a huge hole that serves as a mass grave, forms no part of the cherished 'legacy' of Anne Frank," Rosenfeld argues. Instead, Anne has become a "symbol of moral and intellectual convenience," with her affirmation of humanity's goodness allowing her to be seen as an emblem of forgiveness and consolation rather than a tragic figure.[17]

It is precisely this chameleon-like quality that has made Anne's story uniquely enduring. The *Diary* is multifaceted and multi-perspectival; as demonstrated by the comments that visitors to the Anne Frank House leave in the guest books—spontaneous, heartfelt, and not particularly thoughtful—there is truly something in it for everyone. Some find a contemporary political message in Anne's story. "Just like Anne wrote, we don't have to wait, we can start to gradually change the world now, to fight for marginalized people and against the climate crisis," a note from a visitor from Alaska reads. Some address her directly: "Thank you for writing about things that are painful but must be remembered so it does not happen again." Visitors from Israel often write the Hebrew phrase *Am yisrael chai*—"the people of Israel live." Someone else has written, in Arabic, "I truly feel sorry for what happened to Anne Frank and her family, but what the Jews (Zionists) are doing to the Palestinians is much worse." Another puts it simply, if crassly: "Great experience RIP Anne Frank."[18]

In Nathan Englander's short story "What We Talk About When We Talk About Anne Frank," an American Jewish couple and a pair of friends play what they call "the Anne Frank game." In the event of another Holocaust, they ask, which of their non-Jewish friends and acquaintances would hide them? The story isn't actually about Anne or the Holocaust—it's about the differences between American Jewish life and Israeli Jewish life, and between secular Jews and Orthodox Jews; in a larger sense, it's about how people define being Jewish in the post-Holocaust world. "It's just what we talk about when we talk about Anne Frank," one character explains.[19] In the story, the "Anne Frank game" becomes emblematic of the fissures that exist in even the closest relationships and the complicated dynamics of trust and betrayal within a marriage.

The idea of "Anne Frank," too, has become a mirror of broader cultural and political preoccupations. The title of Englander's story is a play on Raymond Carver's "What We Talk About When We Talk About Love," another story about marital betrayal. As that phrase implies, when we talk about love, we may be talking about many things, but we're not talking about love. Likewise, when we talk about "Anne Frank," we're not talking about Anne as a person, but about the constellation of ideas that swirls around her image. Anne's transformation into an icon has had the effect of obscuring who she really was. She becomes whoever and whatever we need her to be.

* * *

The title of this book, *The Many Lives of Anne Frank*, refers to the multiplicity of ways in which Anne has been understood and misunderstood, both as a person and as an idea. Drawing on the *Diary* in all its versions as well as her fiction and other writings, I strive to return Anne to herself, restoring her as a human being rather than an icon. Writing alongside Anne rather than over her and allowing her words to punctuate the narrative, I chronicle and interpret her brief life while offering social and historical context to help the reader understand the world around her, specifically regarding the circumstances of the Holocaust in the Netherlands. In a scattering of experimental sections, I reflect directly on the problems inherent in writing a biography of Anne, owing to the lack of sources for some aspects of her life and the contradictions in those that exist.

Part 1, Anne Frank, attempts a biographical treatment. The chapters titled "Child" and "Refugee" explore the earliest years of her life, starting with her birth in Frankfurt am Main and continuing through her elementary school days in Amsterdam. "Target" chronicles her early adolescence alongside the German occupation of the Netherlands, which began when she was ten and affected every aspect of her life: family, friendships, education. "Witness" follows her into the Annex, where she struggled to adapt to the situation around her and to narrate it in her diary. "Lover" charts her relationship with Peter van Pels and considers her as a sexual being. "Artist" analyzes the ways in which Anne methodically and self-consciously revised her diary for publication, intending it to appear after the war as a book called *Het Achterhuis*—literally "The House Behind" or "The Annex." (*Het Achterhuis* was rendered poetically but inexactly by Barbara Mooyart-Doubleday, the first English translator of the *Diary*, as "the Secret Annex." In this book, I refer to the hiding place as the Annex.) Finally, "Prisoner" follows her from the Annex to the transit camp Westerbork, and from there to Auschwitz; "Corpse" describes her death at Bergen-Belsen. We do not have the benefit of an account written by Anne of the final seven months of her life, but testimony has emerged from people who encountered her in each of these places, and what happened to her in the camps can be extrapolated from the experiences of other girls and women who survived to tell about them.

The second part of the book, "Anne Frank," is a cultural history of the idea of Anne as it has developed since 1947, when the *Diary* first appeared in Dutch. "Author" describes Otto Frank's experience of reading Anne's diary, recognizing it as a literary work, and preparing it to go out into the world, with a close look at both what he changed in it and what he preserved. "Celebrity" tells the story of the publication of the *Diary* in America; "Ambassador" discusses the stage and screen adaptations, which disseminated Anne's story worldwide but have often been accused of misrepresenting her ideas and deemphasizing her Jewish identity. "Survivor" charts the numerous works of fiction that imagine Anne's life had she survived, from *The Ghost Writer* by Philip Roth, in which she appears as an attractive assistant to a famous Jewish novelist, to more recent novels by Shalom Auslander, David Gillham, and others. Finally, "Pawn" takes on the vexed question of the ways Anne's image and words have been used in the service of political causes by people who incorporate her into a pantheon of social justice icons ranging from the civil rights leader Malcolm X to the student activist Greta Thunberg. Throughout, I have included brief profiles of people whom Anne has influenced in unusual ways.

* * *

The most important misconception about Anne, with the longest lasting repercussions, has to do with the diary itself. In the form in which it was published, her book was not in fact a diary in the way we generally understand the term: a dated record of the writer's thoughts, emotions, and activities, entered concurrently with the events that it documents.[20] Anne's rough draft fits this definition, but the published version of the *Diary*, the one that nearly all her readers know, does not.

Anne's diary exists in three versions, which can be compared in *The Diary of Anne Frank: The Critical Edition*, an 851-page tome published by the Dutch Institute for War Documentation in 1986 and revised in 2001. (Translations into English appeared in 1989 and 2003, respectively.) There is Version A, Anne's rough draft, which survives in three notebooks: "Diary 1," the red-checkered notebook she received for her thirteenth birthday, which covers the period from June 12 to December 5, 1942, with brief additions in 1943 and 1944; "Diary 2," starting December 22, 1943, and ending April 17, 1944; and "Diary 3," from April 17 until August 1, 1944. At least one missing notebook presumably chronicled the period from December 6, 1942, to December 21, 1943. There are also a few loose pages with later dates that Anne inserted into her notebooks.

Anne began rewriting her diary in May 1944. (Throughout this book, I use "diary" when discussing Anne's original manuscript and "*Diary*" for the published text.) Version B, the draft she planned to publish, begins on June 20, 1942, and ends on March 29, 1944. Scholars assume that Anne's arrest interrupted her work on the book before she could complete it.

Version C is the first published version of Anne's diary, which appeared in Dutch as *Het Achterhuis: Dagboekbrieven, 1942–1944* (The Annex: Diary Letters, 1942–1944) and in English as *Anne Frank: The Diary of a Young Girl;* it was assembled and edited by Otto after Anne's death. Miep Gies and Bep Voskuijl, two of the Dutch gentiles who supported the Franks in hiding, found Anne's papers in the Annex after it was raided and kept them in the hope that she would return. (Bep's pseudonym was Elli Vossen. Miep appeared in the diary under her real name, but Anne called her husband, Jan, by the pseudonym Henk.) When Otto learned of Anne's death, Miep gave the papers to him. Otto based his version on Anne's Version B, but he cut some material and added material from Version A that Anne had removed. I will explore in depth the ways in which Anne chose to represent herself as well as how the editing by Otto and others affected her representation.

The versions conflict in small details—for instance, the dates on which certain events take place. It is impossible to know whether those discrepancies exist because Anne corrected a previous mistake or because she chose to make adjustments for literary purposes. Assuming that the majority of her changes were motivated by stylistic rather than factual concerns, I rely here primarily on Version A, while incorporating material from the other versions as necessary. This does not imply that the other versions are less authentic—only that, as Anne's biographer, I prefer to remain as close as possible to her original words.

The fact that Anne edited her own diary has been well known to English readers at least since 1995, when Mirjam Pressler, the first translator of the *Diary* into German, produced a new text, sometimes called Version D, that adds material from Version A to Version C, expanding the text by nearly a hundred pages. The Anne Frank Foundation, an organization founded by Otto Frank and based in Switzerland, which owns the copyright to the *Diary*, calls this "the Definitive Edition." Because of the incomplete and unfinished nature of the texts she left behind, I don't believe it's possible to establish a "definitive" version of Anne's diary. But the desire to do so is itself revealing of the way Anne is understood.

If Anne, as the journalist and historian Ian Buruma has written, has become "a ready-made icon for those who have turned the Holocaust into a kind of secular religion," then her diary is akin to a saint's relic: a text almost holy, not to be tampered with. This special aura around the diary conflicts with the messiness of its reality. It's simpler to imagine Anne's diary as a child's "found object," as the Dutch novelist Harry Mulisch called it—"a work of art made by life itself"—than to grapple with what it really was: a carefully conceived and largely realized work of testimony to the persecution of the Dutch Jews.[21] Recognizing and respecting Anne's intentions as an author is a crucial first step in reclaiming her as a human being rather than a symbol.

In *The Heroine with 1,001 Faces*, the critic and scholar Maria Tatar brilliantly rewrites Joseph Campbell's myth of the hero's journey by asking how that framework might change if the archetypes it was based on were female instead of male. She notes that women, historically deprived of the weapons that gave men power, sought strength in storytelling. "Women have relied on the domestic crafts and their verbal analogues—spinning tales, weaving plots, and telling yarns—to make things right, not just getting even but also securing social justice," Tatar argues.[22] Think of Penelope waiting faithfully for Odysseus, all the while weaving her cloth and unraveling it again. But we are conditioned to see these women as passive victims, not as heroes; as objects acted upon rather than the authors of their own narratives.

Tatar considers Anne Frank as an example of the war heroine redefined, emphasizing how different her immortality is from that earned in battle by Achilles and other classic war heroes, as well as Anne's use of "words and stories not just as a therapeutic outlet for herself but also as a public platform for securing justice." She insightfully notices the number of times Anne's entries refer to acts of heroism in preserving "decency, integrity, and hope" and credits her as a literary prodigy, putting her in the company of Mary Shelley, who wrote *Frankenstein* in her late teens, as well as the teenage poet Arthur Rimbaud.[23]

But I'm also struck by the way Anne's story reenacts another of the mythological archetypes Tatar identifies: the woman who defies silencing. Its roots are found in the Greek myth of Philomela, a princess who is raped by her sister's husband, Tereus. As Ovid recounts in the *Metamorphoses*, Tereus cut out Philomela's tongue to prevent her from telling anyone what he did to her; she then brilliantly took revenge by weaving a tapestry that revealed his crimes. In some versions of the story, Zeus took pity on her and turned her into a nightingale, giving voice to her mournful song.

Anne, too, might have been silenced by the Gestapo officers who invaded the Annex, arrested her and the seven other residents, and scattered her papers on the floor. But her story was preserved—first by the two women who gathered those papers, then by her devoted father—and disseminated far and wide, almost miraculously, as an account of trauma and persecution. This powerful mythological resonance helps to explain the indelible imprint Anne's diary has left on generations of readers.

But it also contributes to the difficulty in seeing Anne as the agent of her story rather than the object, the actor rather than the acted upon.

Anne Frank was not a princess hidden away in an attic begging for rescue, but a brilliant young woman who seized control of her own narrative. Reimagining her that way requires a willingness to reconsider not just the facts of her life but also the way we understand heroism, both in her time and in ours.

Part 1

Anne Frank

1

Child
From Frankfurt to Amsterdam, 1929–1934

Daddy was born in Frankfurt am Main, his parents were immensely rich, Michael Frank owned a bank and became a millionaire . . .

The photograph, from spring 1933, depicts a square in the center of Frankfurt. A statue of Friedrich Schiller, the eighteenth-century poet, playwright, and philosopher, stands there, along with the baroque Hauptwache, or guard house, one of the city's most famous landmarks. But the photographer must be a local, because he has chosen to focus not on the sights but on a mother and two daughters. The woman's coat is plain, her shoes sensible, but the girls are dressed for an outing. The elder sister, who just turned seven, wears a wool coat with a fur collar and shiny Mary Janes; her knees are visible in the gap between her skirt and her high socks, a sign that the weather is starting to warm up. She looks straight at the camera, her expression serious, her gloved hand resting in the crook of her mother's elbow. The younger girl, nearly four, is swathed in a fluffy white coat that might be made of rabbit fur and a matching white hat that allows a curl to escape over her forehead; white spats cover her shoes. She scowls at the camera with the expression of a child who's been made to stand still. Only the mother manages a smile.[1]

They look as if they belong there, and they do. Margot and Anne Frank are the newest generation of a family with deep roots in the region. Alice Stern Frank, Otto's mother, could trace her ancestors in Frankfurt back to the seventeenth century. Michael Frank, Otto's father, came from Landau in der Pfalz, a town in the countryside about eighty miles south of Frankfurt, where the Jewish community was also centuries old. He *worked his way up*, Anne would explain, establishing himself as a banker and stockbroker.[2]

The Franks raised their children in the style of upper-class Germans, which they were. When Otto was born—on May 12, 1889, less than a month after Hitler—the family was living in an apartment in the elegant Westend, walking distance from Michael's office in central Frankfurt, near the stock exchange; the mayor lived on the same block.[3] In 1901, the year Otto turned twelve, the family moved into their own multistory home, welcoming Alice's widowed mother into the household. They vacationed at a resort in the Black Forest and had their own box at the opera; in 1907, the year before he graduated from high school, Otto traveled to Spain for Easter break. Otto attended the Lessing-Gymnasium, one of the oldest and best high schools in Frankfurt, where he was the only Jewish student in his class. In his free time, he learned to play the cello and ride horses. The Franks hosted costume balls and other fancy parties: Milly Stanfield, a younger cousin who visited as a child, recalled that the Franks served "an enormous ice cream gateau decorated with fairytale figures" and invited her to the circus.[4] It became a tradition for family members to write poems in honor of one another's birthdays as well as their own, a custom the adult Otto continued with his wife and children.

Edith, too, came from a wealthy family. Born Edith Holländer in Aachen, near the Dutch border, she later impressed Anne with *stories of engagement parties of two hundred and fifty people, private balls and dinners.*[5] Her early life was marked by tragedy, with the death of her older sister from appendicitis at age sixteen. Nonetheless, she enjoyed the privileges of a woman of her class: playing tennis, swimming in the sea. As a young woman, she wore flapper dresses, cut her hair in a bob, and danced the Charleston.[6]

The Franks were assimilated Jews. Alice's great-uncle Moritz was said to have once concealed a copy of *Faust* underneath his prayer shawl in synagogue; her mother was named Cornelia, after Goethe's sister.[7] In addition to their German upbringing, Alice and Michael gave their children German names: Otto's siblings were Robert, Herbert, and Helene (Leni). Otto did not have a bar mitzvah and never learned to read or speak Hebrew. When Edith came into the family, she was by far its most religious member. Her parents kept kosher and attended synagogue regularly, a practice she maintained after her marriage to Otto, in 1925.[8]

Otto and Edith were clearly eager to become parents. Margot (pronounced in the German way, with the "t" audible) Betti, nicknamed "Mutz," was born on February 16, 1926, barely nine months after her parents' wedding. Annelies Marie—her nickname, Anne, also pronounced German-style, AH-na—followed on June 12, 1929. It was a difficult delivery, and she initially had trouble gaining weight; Edith had to stop breastfeeding her within a few months. Margot would be athletic, playing tennis and rowing.[9] But health problems plagued Anne throughout her childhood: a tendency to dislocate her joints that some researchers have speculated was a symptom of Ehlers-Danlos syndrome, a connective-tissue disorder that causes hypermobility; a bout of measles followed by heart trouble. Sometimes she was bedridden for weeks at a time. The family called her by the nickname *Zärtlein*, "tender one."[10] An avid photographer, Otto lovingly recorded her childhood with his treasured Leica camera, one of the first to be commercially available.

Anne's illnesses did not impede her spirit. Those who knew her as a child recalled her as outgoing, bright, and full of personality. "You have eyes like a cat," she told an adult neighbor in Frankfurt. The Franks' housekeeper at the time, Kathi Stilgenbauer, who attended the births of both girls, remembered that for Margot, "dirt did not exist," while Anne, who liked to play out on the balcony in the rain, could go through multiple changes of clothes in a day.[11] When their cousin Buddy made trading cards with illustrations of family members, he captioned Anne's card "Anne the rascal"; Anne "clapped her hands and hopped all around" with delight at the moniker. The tagline on Margot's card was more decorous: "Doesn't allow kisses."[12] For her fifteenth birthday, Otto and Edith gave Margot printed "visiting cards," with a poem explaining that they could be used in lieu of "the loathsome task / Of speaking your name in public out loud."[13] That same year, Anne, age twelve, talked so much in class that she was made to write essays on the theme of being a chatterbox.

Even as a young child, Margot was studious, serious, and obedient. "She radiated a calm, quiet kindness and liked to help people in need," remembered Anne's friend Hannah Goslar, who wished she had a big sister like Margot. Anne, by contrast, was rambunctious and imaginative. The nursery featured a lamp painted with animals—"a regular zoo," according to Stilgenbauer—that Anne liked to tell stories about.[14]

Otto, too, liked to tell the girls stories, which often revolved around two sisters, both named Paula: one good and one bad.[15] In the Annex, he told Anne stories to comfort her during nighttime air raids. In her "Book of Tales," a volume of fiction and comic sketches that she wrote in addition to her diary, she recorded one of them: "Paula's Flight," in which bad Paula stows away on a plane and winds up getting adopted by a Russian family.[16]

Were good Paula and bad Paula stand-ins for Margot and Anne? There is no evidence that Otto intended this. But others, including Edith, did compare the two girls—often to Anne's detriment. Margot's grades were excellent, but Anne struggled to focus, Edith wrote to a friend after the family moved to Amsterdam. In grade school, Margot was already thinking about college, while Anne was "less industrious, but very droll . . . witty and amusing." In the Annex, Margot served as Dutch proofreader for the adults, all of whom were native German speakers. "We thought Margot terribly talented and capable of anything," Hannah Goslar later remembered; Anne was more of a "social butterfly." The mother of another friend recalled Margot as "*summa cum laude*, all through school, all through life." When Miep Gies and her husband visited the Franks' apartment for dinner, Anne came running to greet them, her voice "rapid" and "high-pitched." Margot, shy and quiet, sat at the table with perfect posture, her hands folded. As Miep observed, "Margot seemed to be Mommy's little girl, and Anne was very much Daddy's."[17]

This won't surprise readers of the *Diary*, in which Anne often complains that Edith favors Margot and expresses her own preference for her father. Otto may have deleted some of Anne's criticisms of her mother, but he had little need to perform similar edits regarding himself. Almost invariably, Anne writes of him with warmth and love, using her nickname for him, "Pim." He's *the only one who understands me*, never angry for more than a few minutes. When she seeks comfort at night, it's his bed she crawls into. She even cuts his hair: *Pim swears that I do such a good job he'll never go to another barber after the war.* The worst she can say about him—in spring 1944, after nearly two years in hiding—is that he's *different lately . . . much too cool.*[18]

Still, like most adolescents, Anne went through periods of feeling alienated from her family. *I don't fit in with them and that's something I've been feeling very much, especially lately,* she complained after only a week in hiding. *I'm not at all keen on a narrow cramped existence like Mummy and Margot,* she insisted later. While Margot hoped to immigrate to Palestine and become a midwife, Anne envisioned a more sophisticated future for herself—a year each in Paris and London to *learn the languages and study the history of art,* with *beautiful dresses and interesting people.* She rebelled when her parents and the Van Pelses encouraged her to be more like her sister. *I don't want to be in the least like Margot. She is much too soft and passive for my liking, and allows everyone to talk her around. I want to be a stronger character!*[19]

Despite their differences, the sisters had moments of great intimacy. There are far more photographs of them together in childhood than apart: whether at the beach, at home, or with family, they came as a pair. Miep noticed the ten-year-old Anne's obvious admiration for her sister: "Anything Margot did or said was sponged up by Anne's darting eyes and quick mind."[20] One night a few years later, as they lay in bed together in the Annex—*it was a frightful squash, but that was just the fun of it*—Margot asked to read Anne's diary. *I said yes at least bits of it, and then I asked if I could read hers.* She didn't record Margot's response.[21]

This is the only time Anne mentions—tantalizingly—that Margot, too, kept a diary. In its absence, we can only imagine whether Margot suffered from her parents' elevated expectations for her or her own perfectionism; if she resented having to be the "good" sister, the one who always behaved, while Anne rebelled and spoke her mind; if she envied Anne's close relationship with fun-loving, good-natured Pim. Alison Leslie Gold, who collaborated with Miep on her memoir, recalled that Miep only "shook her head" when asked about Margot. She and her husband, Jan, explained that "the only reason they had a relationship with Anne was because Anne had defied social convention, had sought them out, been curious and bold, gregarious and friendly . . . whereas Margot, though polite, had always hung back." To her regret, Gold said, she was never able to portray Margot as "anything more than the shadow she was to the Gieses."[22]

At Auschwitz, according to survivors who knew them there, Anne and Margot stayed as close to Edith's side as possible. After being transferred to Bergen-Belsen without their mother, the sisters were inseparable. Lien Brilleslijper, a Dutch-Jewish Resistance worker who was deported to the camp with her own sister, Marianne (Janny), recognized Margot and Anne there: "two thin, shaven-headed figures that looked like freezing little birds."[23] The two pairs of sisters formed a group, looking out for one another as best they could. When Lien and Janny were assigned to a new barrack, they asked Margot and Anne to come with them, but Margot was ill with severe diarrhea and had to remain behind. Anne stayed to take care of her.

Lien and Janny visited periodically, bringing food when they could, and eventually found Margot and Anne in the sick barracks. Margot was too ill to speak. "Here we can both lie on one bunk, we are together, and it's peaceful," Anne told them. Returning the next day, they found Margot barely conscious, having fallen on the floor. A few days later, both were dead.[24]

Did they remember, in those horrible last days together, the times in the Annex when they snuggled in the same bed, sharing confidences? If Lien Brilleslijper's testimony is accurate, Anne had an opportunity to save herself, but chose to stay with Margot. She may have contracted the disease that killed her by caring for her sister.

* * *

Monday, February 7, 1944: Day 582 in hiding. Margot, getting ready for bed, is poked by a pin that Edith has accidentally left in her blanket after mending it. Otto shakes his head and comments to the girls on Edith's "slipshod ways." *You're a real Rabenmutter*, Anne says to Edith—in German, "raven mother," shorthand for a woman who neglects her children. (It was once believed that raven fledglings were kicked out of the nest too early.) She means it as a joke, or so she claims. But Edith yells at Anne for her own lack of tidiness and criticizes her for leaving out a manicure case, even after Margot admits that she was the last to use it. *It's always me who gets into trouble when someone else does something wrong!* Anne complains.[25]

At this point in the entry, *The Diary of Anne Frank: The Critical Edition*—which purports to be a complete reproduction of Anne's diary in all its versions—offers a series of ellipses and a footnote explaining that forty-seven lines in which Anne Frank "gave an extremely unkind and partly unfair picture of her parents' marriage" have been deleted "at the request of the Frank family." But the truth will out, most of the time, and in 1998 it was revealed that Otto not only had omitted this passage from Version C but had taken the extra step of removing the pages containing the forty-seven lines from the manuscript of the *Diary* and entrusting them to a friend for safekeeping—thus enabling him to state, truthfully, that he no longer had in his possession any materials relating to Anne's diary.[26] The pages that Otto had gone to such lengths to protect, and which his friend gave to the Austrian journalist Melissa Müller when she was researching her biography of Anne, were then published by *Het Parool*, a major Dutch newspaper, for the world to see.

What does Anne say about the marriage that merited such a cover-up? She alludes to a love affair that Otto had in his youth and which he continues to idealize, or so she claims: *It can't be easy for a loving wife to know she'll never be first in her husband's affections.*[27] Anne assesses the marriage as essentially a business arrangement that Otto entered into at a time when his *ideals had been shattered and he was no longer young.*[28] Sounding every bit like the fourteen-year-old that she is, Anne writes that Otto loves Edith but isn't *in love* with her: *He kisses her the way he kisses us.* He doesn't consider her a role model for the children; *he looks at her teasingly, or mockingly, but never lovingly.* Edith, for her part, is *crumbling away* from the long-term effects of unrequited love. Anne asks herself if she should have more sympathy for her mother, considering the pain Edith must endure, and admits that she is unable to. *I can't talk to her, I can't look lovingly into those cold eyes.*[29]

In 1908, when he was eighteen, two formative events took place in Otto's life. He became engaged to a woman whose identity remains unknown—the love affair Anne refers to in her diary. And, during a summer at the University of Heidelberg, he met Nathan Straus Jr., who remained a lifelong friend. American Jews of German origin, Straus's family had lived in the United States for more than fifty years, working their way up from selling dry goods in the South to owning Macy's department store. Soon after meeting Nathan, Otto left to spend a year in the United States, where Nathan Straus Sr. took a fatherly interest in him and taught him the inner workings of the business. While he was away, his fiancée married someone else, breaking his heart.[30]

"A man alone is an incomplete half-being," Otto wrote to his sister Leni from the front in June 1918.[31] He and his brothers were among the 100,000 German Jews to enlist, demonstrating their patriotism; for Otto, the army may have served as a useful distraction. Nearly seven years passed between the end of the war and his engagement to Edith, at age thirty-six. During that period, the Michael Frank Bank foundered, partly because Alice, who had taken it over after her husband's death, in 1909, invested in war bonds that proved worthless.[32] The bank failed in December 1924. Four months later, Otto proposed to Edith, who was eleven years younger and brought with her a substantial dowry. The marriage may have been arranged, either by a relative's introduction or by a professional matchmaker.[33]

Although a teenager may regard as unromantic a marriage based on anything other than (or in addition to) love, it's not known whether Otto concurred with Anne's assessment of the relationship. Still, there is some evidence that she was right. In a letter written to Edith on May 12, 1939, their fourteenth anniversary and his fiftieth birthday, he reflected on their years of happy and successful partnership, a source of stability amid the mounting chaos around them, without using the word "love." Their joint goal, he wrote, was "to transmit to our children that same sense of solidarity, feeling of comfort, and sense of mutual responsibility." The letter also refers to an understanding between the two of them, but does not explain what it is: "If we stick to our tested agreement, nothing can go wrong."[34] After the war, Otto admitted that he missed Margot and Anne much more than he missed Edith.[35]

About six feet tall, with a salt-and-pepper mustache and sparkling eyes, Otto was considered a kind, deeply principled, and attractive man.[36] Still, he reached middle age without finding a wife. Edith was shy and appeared standoffish to those who did not know her, but she had many friends—in her youth, among the circle of German Jews that coalesced in Amsterdam, and even in Westerbork, according to survivors who remembered her fondly. Despite her traditional upbringing, she was open-minded and liberal; in the Annex, the Van Pelses criticized her modern attitude toward education, which included letting Margot and Anne read books that the Van Pelses thought inappropriate for teenagers. Her pride in her family is evident in that picture taken on the Hauptwache square, in which she's the only one who's smiling.

Her intimacy with the children is even more apparent in another photograph taken the same day, this one at a photo booth in the Tietz department store. Margot leans her forehead on Edith's left cheek in an open gesture of affection. Anne cuddles against her mother's right shoulder, her face a blur—she must have moved as the shutter snapped. Edith's beaming face is centered in the frame, her dark hair parted, her brown eyes vivid. With a high forehead and a long nose, she is not conventionally beautiful. But her joy in the girls radiates.[37]

* * *

On January 30, 1933, the day Hitler came to power, the Franks visited a friend. On the radio, they listened to the shouts and cheers of Stormtroopers parading in Berlin. "Let's see what the man can do," their host suggested. Otto and Edith were silent.[38]

Though the Frankfurt Jewish community dated back to the 1300s, Jews hadn't always been welcome there. Starting in 1462, they were confined to a cramped and crowded ghetto outside the city walls. In 1811 that decree was lifted, and in 1864, a year before Alice was born, the city granted full civil rights to Jews, many of whom later counted among its most influential figures. Leopold Sonnemann was a co-founder of the German People's Party (Deutsche Volkspartei), a liberal party popular in southern Germany, and served as its delegate to the Reichstag in Berlin; he also ran a local newspaper. Theodor Creizenach, a poet and historian, is credited with the quotation adorning the façade of the city's Renaissance-style opera house, inscribed in stone amid Corinthian columns and intricately carved marble sculptures: *Dem Wahren Schönen Guten* ("To the true, the beautiful, the good").[39]

In national elections held on March 5, a week after the Reichstag fire, the National Socialists won 288 of 648 seats—a slight majority when counted together with the German National People's Party (Deutschnationale Folkspartei), not the landslide that Nazi propaganda made it out to be, but a majority nonetheless. Otto recalled hearing Nazi gangs marching on the street outside the family home, singing the "Horst Wessel Lied," the infamous Nazi anthem: "When Jewish blood spurts from the knife / Oh, how we love to see it."[40]

March 10, 1933, when Edith and the girls visited the Tietz department store, was a Friday. Hitler had been chancellor for thirty-nine days. In local elections, held that Sunday, the National Socialists won forty-two out of eighty-five seats, and Frankfurt's liberal Jewish mayor, Ludwig Landmann, was replaced by a Nazi.[41]

The first concentration camps in Germany, including Dachau, were created for political prisoners in mid-March. On March 31, under the new Aryanization rules for businesses, the Tietz brothers, who were Jewish, were forced to sell their shares in the company. A non-Jew replaced them and changed the name of the store to Hertie, which was for decades a popular German department store. The Tietzes fled to America; they lost everything, but they survived.[42]

As of April 1, schools were required to separate Jewish students from the rest of the class. Margot, along with a few other Jewish children, was told to sit on a bench in the back of the room. Their teacher, known for her liberal politics, didn't return to school after the Easter break.[43]

A few months earlier, to save money, Otto, Edith, and the children had moved back into the Frank family home with Alice. The house was now much emptier. Leni and her husband, Erich Elias, had moved to Basel to set up a Swiss office for Opekta, the pectin company that later played a major role in Otto's life. Robert had left to open an art gallery in England; Herbert was living in Paris. Otto was the last of the Frank brothers still in Germany. In September 1933, Alice, age sixty-eight, joined Leni and Erich in Basel, bringing a three-page inventory of all her furniture. Thanks to Switzerland's neutral status, their entire household would survive the war.[44]

The Franks considered trying to immigrate to Palestine but quickly dismissed the idea. Following the imprisonment of Alfred Dreyfus, a French army captain falsely convicted of spying, the nascent Zionist movement was gaining new momentum. Arguing that Jews could be free from antisemitism only in a land they governed themselves, Theodor Herzl and other early Zionist leaders were seeking to establish a Jewish homeland in the biblical land of Israel where Jews could escape the persecution they suffered throughout Europe. Like many other Jews of their class, the Franks supported the idea of a Jewish state in principle, but they still believed they could be safe in western Europe. In addition, they saw Palestine as a "desert": inhospitable, primitive, and lacking the cultural life to which they were accustomed. As assimilated Germans, they felt they belonged in Europe, or possibly America, but not in the Middle East. In any event, it was difficult to immigrate to what was then called Mandatory Palestine—it was controlled by the British, who enforced strict visa requirements—and tensions between Arabs and Jews were already brewing there.[45]

Otto and Edith decided to take a chance on the Netherlands, where Otto had friends from an earlier effort to open a branch of the Michael Frank Bank in Amsterdam. The decision was made for them in part by Opekta, which hired him, at his brother-in-law's recommendation, to open a Dutch office for the company in Amsterdam, a city whose nicknames included "Mokum Aleph" (Hebrew for "first town") and "the Jerusalem of the West"—signs that Jews felt at home there. Edith stayed with the children at her parents' house in Aachen while Otto traveled ahead to set things up. By early 1934, the family was reunited in their new home.[46]

2

Refugee
Amsterdam, 1934–1940

If I think back to the [Merwedeplein], my girl friends, school, fun, it is just as if another person lived it all, not me.

Built in the 1920s, Amsterdam's Revierenbuurt, or "River District," was (and still is) a bright, well-kept neighborhood. Named after rivers that flow through the Netherlands, the streets are lined with brick apartment blocks with sloping orange roofs, which were quite modern when Anne and her family moved in. "We were all quite proud of this forward-looking treatment of ordinary working people: comfortable housing, indoor plumbing, tree-filled gardens in the rear of each block," Miep Gies, who moved to the neighborhood as a teenager and lived there for years, later remembered. Fresh and clean, it was "an ideal spot for uprooted people, a blank slate."[1]

Bordered to the east by the Amstel River and to the south by Zuider Amstellaan, a poplar-lined boulevard served by the No. 8 tram, the neighborhood was full of children: riding scooters, pushing hoops with a stick, and playing *binkelen* (a game like hopscotch) on the sidewalks or hide and seek on the Merwedeplein, an attractive square with a park.[2] The Franks' apartment, at Merwedeplein 37, overlooked the square. Children called to their friends by whistling through their apartments' letterbox slits. Anne, who couldn't whistle, sang a melody instead.[3]

The Franks furnished their five-room duplex with antiques, brought from Frankfurt, in polished dark wood that looked dramatic against the light-blue patterned wallpaper. There was a delicate nineteenth-century French secretary desk, veneered with mahogany; a grandfather clock made in Frankfurt that ticked as softly as a heartbeat and required winding every few weeks; a large, round oak dining table. On the wall was a framed charcoal sketch of a mother cat nursing two kittens, a token of the family's fondness for cats.[4] Anne would write sadly in her diary of missing her own cat, Moortje, *every moment of the day* after the family went into hiding.[5] Green velvet curtains and Persian rugs in red tones added to the elegant mood. "The apartment smelled like vanilla and books," one of Anne's friends remembered.[6] Decades later, Bep Voskuijl, who worked as a secretary at Opekta as a teenager, remembered the pleasures of lunch at the Franks' apartment: rolls with cream cheese and sprinkles, a typical Dutch treat; lemonade to drink. The food was served on a lazy Susan, "so you could spin the platter and take whatever you wished"—a stark contrast to her own home, where, as the eldest of eight siblings, she never had quite enough to eat.[7]

The Franks sent Margot to a traditional public school, but for Anne, who they clearly thought would benefit from a less conventional education, they chose a Montessori school. Founded in the early twentieth century by Maria Montessori, an innovative Italian educator, this pedagogical method, popular in the Netherlands starting in the 1920s and 1930s (and forbidden in Nazi Germany), encourages children's independence and imagination. The school Anne attended—on Niersstraat, a ten-minute walk from home—was a place that was tolerant of her tendency to speak out of turn, and where her freedom of thought was encouraged rather than tamped down. One of Anne's teachers, who sometimes walked with her to school in the morning, remembered her as "no prodigy . . . in many things she was very mature, but on the other hand, in other things she was unusually childish."[8] She wanted to be a writer early on, he remembered, and often recounted to him stories and poems that she and her father had invented together. Putting on plays, both at school and with her friends, also appealed to her: she enjoyed performing in front of an audience and was a natural mimic, reproducing a cat's meow or the voices of friends and teachers. The school principal recalled her as "rather small among her schoolmates, but when she played the queen or the princess she suddenly seemed a good bit taller than the others."[9]

Anne attended school with Hannah Goslar, five months older than she, whose family came to the Netherlands from Germany at around the same time as the Franks and lived nearby on the Merwedeplein. The families became friendly after Hannah's mother, Ruth Goslar, and Edith met in the supermarket, both struggling to speak Dutch, which Ruth called "a throat condition, not a language." A few days later, on the first day of school, Hannah came into the classroom and recognized Anne, who was playing music on silver bells. The girls raced into each other's arms and were best friends for the next six years.

Hannah's father, Hans Goslar, had been a deputy cabinet member during the Weimar Republic; after Hitler came to power, he lost his job. The Goslars kept kosher and observed the Sabbath; the Franks often joined them for holidays like Purim (for which the Goslars hosted an annual costume party) and Passover, as well as Friday night dinners featuring traditional German-Jewish foods like roast chicken and noodle kugel. Otto, always an involved father who took an interest in his daughters' friends, tried to teach Hannah to ride a bike, holding on to the back as he raced alongside her. When Hannah's baby sister, Gabi (born in October 1940), proved to be a picky eater, Otto—his eyes twinkling above his salt-and-pepper mustache—was the only one who could coax her to open her mouth for the spoon.[10]

The girls collected picture postcards featuring movie stars—Anne's favorites were Shirley Temple and Deanna Durbin—and the British and Dutch royal families, "swooning over their clothes and wondering which eligible royals might marry who," Hannah remembered.[11] She could play Parcheesi or Monopoly for hours, but Anne sometimes lost patience before the game was over. By age eleven, they were spending weekends at the ice-skating rink.[12] Anne and Margot both loved to help care for little Gabi, taking her out for walks in her carriage. "She was like pepper," Hannah once said. "My mother always said, 'God knows everything, but Anne knows everything better.'"[13] While this quality struck some as abrasive, Anne's family and friends mostly found it endearing.

Hannah and Anne grew apart after the girls entered the Jewish Lyceum a few years later. Hannah, whose grandfather had once worked with Theodor Herzl, began spending more time with friends from the Zionist youth group that met at her synagogue, including Alfred Bloch, who became her boyfriend. He gave her a picture he had painted of the Western Wall in Jerusalem, an emblem of their dream of a more secure future in an autonomous Jewish state.[14] Around the same time, Anne quickly attached herself to the more sophisticated Jacqueline van Maarsen: before the war, her mother, a dressmaker, had run a fashion atelier out of their home. As Jacqueline was cycling home from school along the Amstel dike, Anne drew up next to her and asked if she was also going toward the River District. When Jacqueline said she lived there too, Anne announced, "Then the two of us will ride home together from now on." She had noticed Jacqueline in class and invited her new friend to her apartment. "She told me everything there was to know about her girlfriends and her former school, and wanted to know everything about me in turn," Jacqueline remembered. They did their homework together, and Anne insisted that Jacqueline stay for dinner and meet her father; the next day she went home with Jacqueline. "From that day on we were inseparable," Jacqueline remembered. Anne wanted company all the time. "She just *had* to have someone to talk to or play with, or she would get dreadfully bored."[15]

The girls copied each other's habits: Jacqueline imitated the way Anne held her pen, and Anne sometimes wrote in print rather than cursive, as Jacqueline did. They also read the same books—their favorite was the Joop ter Heul series by Cissy van Marxveldt, about a spunky Dutch teenager and her group of girlfriends. Jacqueline and Anne read their favorite scenes aloud, acting them out, and established their own ping-pong club (as Joop does), meeting at the home of a friend whose mother let them stretch a net across a table in the living room. "Not only were the adventures of the books' spirited gang of heroines vividly drawn; we also liked to compare ourselves to those girls, who lived in such a free and untroubled world," Jacqueline later wrote.[16] The two girls had frequent sleepovers, for which Anne would arrive with a suitcase and a toiletry bag containing a hairbrush and curlers. Jacqueline remembered her brushing her hair for a long time every night to make it shiny. The night before Jacqueline's birthday, Anne insisted on sleeping over, so that she could be the first person to wish her friend happy birthday in the morning.[17]

"Anne was very vivacious," remembered Nanette Blitz, who also went to the Jewish Lyceum with Anne and Jacqueline. "She always wanted to be the center of attention—she loved that." Petite, with "lovely, very expressive" gray-green eyes—Miep called them "electric"—she wasn't the most beautiful girl in the room. At one point she had to wear braces that made her face appear broader, which she was self-conscious about. But she had a quality that attracted people. "She could see things—and how!"

Jacqueline's mother remembered. "She saw everything exactly as it was, and sometimes she would make a remark—sharp as a needle. Only it did not hurt, because she always hit exactly to the point."[18]

* * *

As antisemitism mounted in Germany, the population of German-Jewish refugees in the River District grew. The refugees included Anne's maternal grandmother, Rosa Holländer, who came from Aachen to live with the family. People joked that the ticket-taker on the No. 8 tram "also speaks Dutch" (as well as German). Miep noted that the refugees, many of whom were wealthier than the Dutch workers in the neighborhood, "created a stir when seen in furs or with other fancy possessions"—perhaps hinting at an animosity toward the Jews on behalf of the Dutch, with their reputation for practicality and frugality. (In her memoir, Miep, whose idea of a wedding-day luxury was to take the streetcar rather than walk, never misses a chance to remind the reader that her bicycle was secondhand.)[19]

"There was a big change in our standard of living," remembered Barbara Ledermann, whose family emigrated from Germany at around the same time as the Franks and the Goslars.[20] In Berlin, where her father had worked as a lawyer, the Ledermanns had household help and all the luxuries: English and French lessons, horseback riding, two grand pianos. When they moved to Holland, her father went back to law school, this time in Dutch, to restart his career. He and Hans Goslar created an impromptu refugee agency in the Goslars' apartment, with Ruth Goslar, who could type, serving as secretary.[21]

Barbara was in the same class as Margot; Susanne (Sanne), her sister, was Anne's age. According to Barbara, Margot was "an absolute genius," as well as "very calm . . . very deliberate, very beautiful," with "great big brown eyes. A very serious person. She would have made a real mark in the world." Barbara, who wanted to become a dancer, was less academically inclined. "Margot dragged me through school . . . Without her saying, 'Today we study,' I wouldn't have been able to get through."[22] Sanne became close to Hannah and Anne, the three of them, with their rhyming names, forming a trio.

Around the same time, Jacqueline was noticing the arrival of new children at the elementary school she attended, which was on Corellistraat, just west of the River District: "I knew that they had come from Germany, but I didn't realize they were all Jewish." Her mother was not Jewish, and her father's side of the family considered Judaism "a tradition rather than a religious calling."[23] Still, at one point her father had registered his wife and their children as official members of the Dutch-Jewish community. This caused problems later. Nazi regulations in the Netherlands normally defined a Jew as any person whose grandparents included three or more Jews. But someone with only two Jewish grandparents, like Jacqueline, would be considered (and persecuted as) a Jew if they were a member of the Jewish community as of May 9, 1940, or were married to a Jew on or after that date.[24]

Theo Coster, another of Anne's classmates, remembered having to ask special permission to invite Anne to his house, such was "the divide between Dutch Jews and Jews who came from the east." The German children greeted others with a handshake or a curtsy and leaped to their feet when responding to a teacher's question, a custom the Dutch children found hilarious.[25] Barbara Ledermann remembered how inappropriate she looked in her fashionable Berlin clothing, which included an embroidered Russian-style coat and hat, next to the Dutch children. They were "more 'peasanty,' more plain, even in Amsterdam."[26]

The Franks began to hold regular get-togethers on Saturday afternoons, at which new arrivals from Germany gathered over coffee and cake to meet Dutch people who were concerned about the situation for the Jews. Margot and Anne would join the adults for a snack before disappearing again, Anne often with her cat in her arms: she was so small, and the cat was so large, that its body dangled almost to the floor.[27] Among the guests were the Van Pels family, who had Dutch ancestry but considered themselves German; they emigrated from Osnabrück in 1937.[28] Hermann van Pels, who had worked in Germany selling butchering supplies, found employment at Pectacon, a spice business that Otto started. "With one sniff of his nose he could name any spice," Miep remembered.[29] Peter Schiff, Anne's first crush, emigrated from Berlin with his family in 1939.[30] He and Anne dated briefly, but then he rejected her; in the Annex, she remembered him as the one who got away.

Edith, still nostalgic for her homeland, spoke with melancholy of the family life the Franks had enjoyed there, as well as the quality of German clothing and pastries. Margot, too, confided to a friend that "we miss hills and woods."[31] "Some of [the German Jews] had become so assimilated that they seemed to behave in a more German manner than the 'Aryan' Germans themselves, and felt the need to tell everybody how much better everything had been *bei uns in Deutschland*—before Hitler, of course," one historian writes.[32] Even so, they could hardly ignore the ominous news from Germany. In 1937, Kathi Stilgenbauer's husband was arrested and sent to prison for membership in a "seditious workers' group." "We think often of you and your grief," Edith wrote to her.[33]

In response to the influx of refugees, the Dutch Ministry for the Interior created Westerbork in 1939 as a refugee camp for Jews from Germany. The land was made available by the Department of Economic Affairs, but the Relief Committee for Jewish Refugees, funded by the Jewish communities of the Netherlands, was required to reimburse the government for the cost of constructing and equipping the camp. The ministry initially selected an area in the Veluwe nature preserve, seven miles from Queen Wilhelmina's hunting lodge. The queen objected:

it wouldn't do, she said, for the camp to be so close to her summer residence.[34] The camp was established instead in the northeastern Drenthe region, "one of the most depressing stretches to be found anywhere in our country," as a Dutch member of parliament described it at the time. The site of the camp was a "wind-swept plain, little better than a peat-bog . . . one of the very few places in the Netherlands before the war where you could feel truly 'God-forsaken,'" according to Jacob Presser, a Dutch-Jewish historian who survived the war in hiding and became one of the first chroniclers of the Holocaust in the Netherlands.[35] Within a few years, Westerbork became notorious as the transit camp to which Dutch Jews were deported before being sent on to camps in the east.

In April 1940, when the Germans invaded Denmark, Jacqueline made a little clay doll and pretended it had magic powers that would keep the Nazis away. A month later, on the day after the Dutch surrender, she took a detour on the way to school. The direct route was only a five-minute walk, but instead she headed several blocks down Beethovenstraat, a busy commercial boulevard, until she reached the Reijnier Vinkeles Quay canal. There, she tossed her doll into the water.[36]

The Nazis tried to requisition the Montessori school that Anne and Hannah attended, but when they learned that it lacked central heating, they set up their headquarters in a school for girls at Euterpestraat 99, around the corner from Jacqueline's home. After the war, the name of the street was changed to honor Gerrit van der Veen, a Resistance fighter.[37]

* * *

On April 29, 1940, eleven days before the Nazi invasion, Anne wrote a letter to a new pen pal. Juanita Wagner, age eleven, lived on a farm in Danville, Iowa, population 309, in the southeastern part of the state. Somehow—either while traveling in Europe the previous year or while taking classes in New York

City—her teacher, Birdie Mathews, had encountered teachers from the Montessori school on Niersstraat and collected names and addresses for a "program of international correspondence." Anne Frank, Merwedeplein 37-II, was among them.[38]

Juanita's letter to Anne has been lost, but Anne's response survives. Writing in English, almost certainly with Otto's help, Anne enclosed a postcard depicting the canals of Amsterdam—a postcard collector herself, she already had "about 800"—and described her life. She and Margot were the only children in the household, which by now also included Edith's mother. Her father worked in an office and her mother was "busy at home." At her school, the students "may do whatever we prefer" and received little homework: "Your mother will certainly know this system, it is called Montessori." Ever the social connector, Anne included the address of Sanne Ledermann, who was also interested in an American pen pal. She signed the letter, "Hoping to hear from you, I remain your Dutch friend, Annelies Marie Frank."[39]

Anne's letter made no reference to the political situation. But Margot, writing to Juanita's fourteen-year-old sister, Betty Ann, noted that "we often listen to the radio as times are very exciting." Since the Netherlands was a small country that shared a border with Germany, "we never feel safe." Hitler had attacked Denmark and Norway just a few weeks earlier; Czechoslovakia and Poland had already fallen under his control. The Franks were no longer able to visit their family in Basel, since to reach Switzerland, "we have to travel through Germany which we cannot do or through Belgium and France and . . . that we cannot either. It is war and no visas are given."[40] Neither she nor Anne mentioned that the family was Jewish.

In the early hours of May 10, Hannah Goslar awakened to what she thought was thunder; at daybreak, she realized it was the sound of bombers.[41] Her father, fearing that he would be targeted as an enemy of the Nazi Party, began tearing up copies of articles he had written that were critical of Hitler; it was Hannah's job to flush the little pieces down the toilet. Outside, the sidewalks filled with piles of destroyed papers and discarded books. All the neighbors "were pouring out of their apartments and onto the streets with armfuls of whatever they thought might get them into trouble," Hannah later remembered. Around the city, clouds of smoke rose from chimneys as people burned antifascist periodicals and books by Jewish writers.[42]

On the radio the morning of the invasion, Queen Wilhelmina, who had ruled the Netherlands for forty-two years, vowed that the country wouldn't give up without a fight. Three days later, she and her cabinet were evacuated on British destroyers. "It felt like a betrayal," Hannah remembered, thinking of all her trading cards with pictures of the royal family.[43] The Dutch announced their surrender on the evening of May 14, after the Nazis threatened to bomb Rotterdam and Utrecht. Perhaps owing to a communications failure, they bombed Rotterdam anyway, destroying most of the historic center and leaving almost 80,000 people homeless.[44] The bombardment was audible in Amsterdam, fifty miles away.

The official surrender took place the next day. Clocks were set to Berlin time, one hour ahead.[45] Barbara Ledermann, then age fifteen, watched from the window as columns of German soldiers marched through the River District, flags aloft, singing "Deutschland, Deutschland Über Alles." "Take care of your mother," her father told her. "They'll come for me tomorrow."[46] Did the Franks watch too? Or did they close the curtains and occupy themselves with books, needlework, games—anything to shut out the sound of the chants they had heard on the streets outside their home seven years earlier, when the Nazis took control of Frankfurt?

Juanita and Betty Ann wrote back, but the Frank sisters never answered. Birdie Mathews explained that communication with the Netherlands had been cut off. As the war progressed, the Wagner girls worried about their pen pals as young men from Danville shipped out to fight. "Were bombs dropping nearby? What was it like to live in a war-torn country?" Betty Ann wondered. The largest number of American POWs from any state would come from Iowa, among them the boyfriend of one of Betty's friends.[47]

In August 1945, after Japan surrendered, Betty Ann wrote again. By then, she was a teacher herself, in charge of twenty-eight children in a one-room schoolhouse in Milan, Illinois, a town on the Rock River just across the border from Iowa, halfway between Chicago and Des Moines. Otto replied with a handwritten letter of four or five pages, telling her about the family's time in the Annex, their deportation and imprisonment, and Anne and Margot's deaths. After she received it, she "just sat and cried," she later told the *New York Times*.[48] Until then, she hadn't realized the Frank girls were Jewish.

Later, Betty Ann shared the letter with her students. "I wanted them to know what they had missed by living in America during the worst war anyone had ever known."[49]

3

Target
The Holocaust in the Netherlands, 1940–1942

Jews must wear a yellow star; Jews must hand in their bicycles; Jews are banned from trams and are forbidden to use any car, even a private one; Jews are only allowed to do their shopping between three and five o'clock, and then only in shops which bear the placard Jewish Shop; Jews may only use Jewish barbers; Jews must be indoors from eight o'clock in the evening until 6 o'clock in the morning; Jews are forbidden to visit Theatres, cinemas and other places of entertainment; Jews may not go to swimming baths, nor to tennis, hockey or other sports grounds; Jews may not go rowing; Jews may not take part in public sports. Jews must not sit in their own or their friends' gardens after 8 o'clock in the evening; Jews may not visit Christians; Jews must go to Jewish schools. . . . But life went on in spite of it all.

THE GERMAN INVASION OF the Netherlands, one historian has written, "came as a shock to the whole population."[1] Owing to their longstanding policy of neutrality, the Dutch were unequipped for war, materially or mentally. With the surrounding borders closed—Germany to the east, Belgium to the south—

around 30,000 people fled to Ijmuiden, the major port thirty miles from Amsterdam, offering jewelry and cash in exchange for passage to England. People abandoned bicycles and cars on the beach even as German aircraft fired on boats in the harbor. Conditions at the port became so overcrowded that the Dutch authorities closed access to it within several days, forcing refugees into a park outside town.

Only a few hundred Jews managed to escape by sea, including seventy-five German and Austrian children from the Amsterdam Municipal Orphanage, who had been brought to the Netherlands as part of the *Kindertransport* by Gertruida (Truus) Wijsmuller-Meijer, a social worker. Although the port was already closed when the children arrived, Wijsmuller-Meijer persuaded the Dutch commander to allow the buses carrying them into the dock area. The children departed on the SS *Bodegraven*, the last passenger ship to leave Ijmuiden. After getting them settled in England, Wijsmuller-Meijer returned to the Netherlands and worked for the Resistance. Also on board was the Amsterdam art dealer Jacques Goudstikker, who left behind a collection of more than 1,000 paintings by Old Masters that were subsequently sold to Hermann Göring. Goudstikker fell to his death on the ship after it left the port.[2]

Looking out her window on the eve of the Dutch capitulation, Etty Hillesum, a young Dutch-Jewish teacher and scholar whose deeply spiritual diary of the war years has become a classic, saw Willem Adriaan Bonger, one of her former professors at the University of Amsterdam, on the street. Impulsively, she ran after him. "Do you think democracy can win?" she asked him. "It's bound to win, but it's going to cost us several generations," he replied. Once "the college tyrant," he now appeared to her "a broken man . . . all the passion and fire in him had been doused." The next day, she learned that he had shot himself an hour after their encounter.[3]

"Jews started jumping out of windows," Barbara Ledermann

recalled. Jacob Presser wrote of an "epidemic of suicides" in the days after the Dutch capitulation, perhaps prompted by rumors that a pogrom was about to take place. The suicide rate in May 1940 was more than five times as high as in previous months. Those who died by suicide included several prominent politicians as well as a German-Jewish family who were acquaintances of the Van Maarsens. Abel Herzberg, a legal scholar and journalist who survived Bergen-Belsen, argued that Jewish deaths from suicide in the early days of the war should be counted among the deaths attributed to the Nazis, since their arrival "engendered such fear" even before persecution began. Not surprisingly, foreign-born Jews, many of them refugees from the Nazis, were initially more likely to die by suicide than Dutch Jews.[4]

Suicide attempts also increased by at least threefold. Presser observed anecdotally that "many who applied for exit permits appeared at the relevant offices with bandaged wrists and throats." Barbara and Sanne Ledermann watched from their window as a neighbor was evacuated from his apartment after trying to gas himself.[5]

The threatened pogrom did not materialize. Many later recalled that for the first six months or so after the invasion, not much changed. Indeed, the State Security Headquarters (Reichssicherheitshauptamt) Section B4 Bureau IV, the department ultimately responsible for implementing the Final Solution, did not begin operating in the Netherlands until March 1941, when Adolf Eichmann was appointed head of the division. The department, abbreviated IV B4, was directed locally by Wilhelm Harster, commander of the Security Police (Sicherheitspolizei) and Intelligence Service (Sicherheitsdienst) in the Netherlands. His immediate boss was Wilhelm Zöpf, who took orders directly from Eichmann.[6]

The Jews, for their part, were represented by the Jewish Council (Joodse Raad), also created in early 1941, which took direction from the Central Office for Jewish Emigration (Zentralstelle für Jüdische Auswanderung). (Nazi organizations used German terminology; Dutch organizations, including the Jewish Council, used the Dutch language.) "Emigration" here is a Nazi euphemism: this was the office responsible for deportation. Created by the occupiers in February 1941, the Amsterdam Jewish Council, like its better-known counterparts in Warsaw, Łódź, and elsewhere, was ostensibly meant to serve as a liaison between the Jewish community and the occupiers. The council's twenty initial members saw their work, according to the minutes of their first meeting, as "predominantly executive and mediatory." They declined responsibility for the orders they had to pass on, though they claimed they would not accept orders "dishonorable to the Jews."[7] One person who was initially asked to join refused, presciently, on the grounds that the council would inevitably be a pawn of the Germans.

As a teenager, David Cohen, a classics professor who served as co-chairman of the council, waited with friends at the local train station to pass hot tea through the windows to refugees fleeing pogroms in Russia—an experience he later credited for his desire to advocate for Jews. Later he became secretary of the Dutch Zionist League as well as chairman of the Committee for Jewish Refugees. Cohen's co-chairman was Abraham Asscher, heir to his family's diamond business and a prominent liberal politician who also had a long record of dedication to the Jewish community.[8]

The council provided services that the Dutch government was no longer permitted to offer to Jews, such as education and health care. It also created the *Jewish Weekly* (Joodsche Weekblad), a newspaper that served as a central organ to disseminate information about new Nazi regulations, from the surrender of businesses and property to the prohibition on using swimming pools and sports facilities. But its primary role—evidenced by the Nazi department to which it reported, known to all simply as the "Zentralstelle"—would be to draw up lists of Jews eligible for deportation. In his memoirs, Cohen wrote that he hoped the Jewish Council would set up a barrier between the Jews and the Germans. But in hindsight many have come to see its role in much darker terms. "The Jewish Councils were nothing more than burial societies," Herzberg wrote in his memoir of the war years. "They imagined the undertaker could come to a compromise with death."[9]

In his inaugural address, on May 29, 1940, Reichskommissar Arthur Seyss-Inquart, the incoming head of the Nazi civil regime in the Netherlands, made no reference to the persecution of the Jews. A German official assured the mayor of The Hague that Dutch Jews would be treated just the same as the rest of the population. Nonetheless, smaller measures targeting Jews—German Jews in particular—began almost at once. In June, all Jews who had immigrated to the Netherlands between January 1, 1933, and March 1, 1938—a group that included the Franks—were made to register. In September, German Jews were ordered to leave The Hague and all coastal areas. Jews in general were restricted from holding public office; Jewish businesses and shops were required to be marked as such.[10]

In November, all Jewish civil servants, including teachers, were fired. Writing to her grandmother Alice in Basel in December 1940, Margot reported that her French teacher and math teacher had disappeared; classes were now shorter, as was the school day. Anne, in a letter around the same time, lamented having to put up blackout curtains, wooden frames covered with thick black cardboard: "these are *the concerns* right now." At night, residents were required to black out their windows before sunset; guards patrolled neighborhoods after eight o'clock and tapped on the windows if any light was visible. Obedient Margot, Anne complained, had put up the curtains earlier than necessary that day. After she left the room, Anne took them down again.[11]

* * *

In January 1941, Jews were excluded from the cinema—a blow for eleven-year-old Anne, who loved going to the movies. In the Annex, she would memorize movie magazines; if one of the helpers mentioned wanting to see a film—any film—she could list the cast members and summarize the reviews. She distracted herself with ice-skating lessons, learning how to "waltz, jump and everything else," she wrote to her grandmother. By her next letter, two months later, there was no more ice skating: Jews were no longer allowed to play sports in public. Anne put a positive spin on the situation: "I need to have a little patience until the war is over, if Papa can still afford it, then I'll get skating lessons again."[12]

Anne must have been concerned about Otto's business situation. She was a well-known presence in the Opekta office, which moved in December 1940 from smaller quarters to Prinsengracht 263. The narrow, gabled eighteenth-century brick building, which faced a large canal, also housed Pectacon, Opekta's spice division, led by Hermann van Pels. When the spice grinders were operating, the entire house smelled of cinnamon, pepper, or whatever else might be in production. Anne often joined her father at the office after school or on Sundays, watching him experiment with different ways to make jam. When Hannah joined her, the girls played with the telephone and threw water out the windows on passersby.[13]

Anne may have heard that, starting in fall 1940, the Nazis required businesses with more than 25 percent Jewish ownership or at least one Jewish director to register with the authorities—Opekta included. She also knew that the Franks were economizing by renting out one of their larger bedrooms. *When times are hard and the rent is badly needed, you have to put aside your pride*, she wrote more than two years later, from the Annex, in a reminiscence in which she amusingly described the Franks' travails in finding a suitable occupant for the space. One tenant was a kindly man who bought chocolate for the children and cigarettes for the adults, but eventually he moved out. The next, a woman, had a drunk fiancé who appeared at the door in the middle of the night; the one after that kept his electric heater on all day. *One day my fearless mother took the fuse out of the box and disappeared for the rest of the afternoon*, Anne wrote, describing a resourcefulness in Edith that she rarely gave her mother credit for. *The young man was obliged to sit in the cold.* The story ends with a cheery remark that can only be read ironically, considering the circumstances: *Just about then we moved and finally got rid of our lodgers (hopefully once and for all)!*[14]

Anne likely did not know that Otto, showing ingenuity at least equal to his wife's, had managed to protect the business from "Aryanization"—that is, plunder. Opekta's parent company, the Frankfurt-based Pomosin-Werke, founded by two half-Jews, had already been taken over by the state. The day after the Nazis announced that Jewish businesses had to register, Victor Kugler, Otto's second in command, together with Jan Gies, Miep's husband, registered "Gies and Co.," a new firm to "manufacture and trade in chemical and pharmaceutical products, foodstuffs, and table luxuries": a legal Aryan business, albeit with initial capital supplied by Otto. The following spring, after the Nazis demanded that Jews transfer all their assets to Lippmann, Rosenthal and Co., a Jewish bank that the Nazis had commandeered, Otto was able to continue supporting his family via this "new" business at a time when many Jews were out of work.[15]

On February 19, 1941, a month after Anne's letter about ice skating, someone booby-trapped the Koco ice cream parlor, run by a pair of Jewish refugees from Germany, with a bottle of ammonia that sprayed German police when they entered. The police opened fire and arrested the owners and several other Jews. The following weekend, Nazis descended on Amsterdam's Jewish quarter and arrested around four hundred "hostages"—older teenage boys and young men, mostly poor and working class, taken at random while returning from a birthday party, shopping for groceries, picking up unemployment checks.[16] Among them was a family friend of the Van Maarsens, a teenager named David who had been studying to become a teacher in Palestine.[17]

In response, the Dutch staged a three-day general strike, including transportation, industry, and dockworkers. "Perfectly ordinary Amsterdam citizens . . . all went on strike over what was happening to us," Anne's classmate Theo Coster later marveled.[18] But the strike did not help the hostages, who were transported to Buchenwald, a concentration camp in eastern Germany near Weimar, home of Goethe. Of the several hundred who were still alive in May, the Nazis moved all but a few to Mauthausen, established three years earlier on the sloping green hills above a charming market town in southern Austria near Linz, Hitler's birthplace, with the Alps visible in the distance.[19]

The stories of Mauthausen are less familiar than those from Auschwitz or Bergen-Belsen, because almost no one survived to tell about it. The level of brutality, even by Nazi standards, was extraordinary: it was a place where the commandant gave his son fifty Jews to execute as a birthday present. The camp, which the Dutch nicknamed "Moordhuizen" (murder houses), was set above a granite quarry that had once supplied rocks to pave the streets of Vienna. One hundred eighty-six "Stairs of Death" led to the base of the quarry. Prisoners, lined up in columns, were forced to haul blocks of granite, often weighing more than a hundred pounds, up the stairs. When a prisoner near the head of the line collapsed from exhaustion, the men beneath him fell like dominos.[20]

Only two of the initial group of Dutch prisoners survived. Many of them, once they were able to work no longer, became victims of some of the Nazis' first experiments with poison gas, which took place at nearby Hartheim Castle.[21] The families of the dead were informed that their loved ones had perished of ailments such as heart failure or sunstroke. Jacqueline van Maarsen, visiting David's mother just after she received the news of his death, found her sobbing on the sofa—an image of grief that stayed with Jacqueline for the rest of her life.

After the parents of some of those deportees published death notices in the newspapers, the Nazis told the Jewish Council to make them stop. The council wrote to the Dutch Red Cross to ask for the address of the camp and the procedure for sending packages there with food and supplies.[22] In retrospect, it is hard to know whether to judge this as optimism or naïveté. It's likely best not to judge it at all.

* * *

Sixty years after its publication, Jacob Presser's book *The Destruction of the Dutch Jews*, a hybrid historical chronicle and memoir, is still an essential source on the Holocaust in the Netherlands.[23] It is hard to convey how moving this remarkable book is. Presser attempts to make sense of history as it is taking place, watching as his friends, his students, and his wife are deported. His book incorporates the testimony of other eyewitnesses as well as a vast quantity of archival material that he gained access to after the war, including the minutes of the Jewish Council. There are small errors of fact—he writes that there were 149 stairs at Mauthausen—and things he simply couldn't know. But the overall impression is of the almost unbearable freshness of his recollections.

Before the Nazi invasion, the Jewish population of the Netherlands stood at around 140,000. Of the 107,000 who were deported to camps—primarily Auschwitz and Sobibór—around 5,500 returned. Another 25,000 or so survived in hiding. By most estimates, the Nazis murdered around 106,000 Dutch Jews, or 75 percent, including almost all children and elderly people—the highest rate of Jewish death in western Europe.[24] The success, so to speak, with which the Nazis carried out their mission in the Netherlands suggests an efficient operation.

Not so, Presser argues. He depicts the Nazi administration as bumbling, improvisational, and redundant; officials had trouble acting in concert and often contradicted one another's orders. When conflicts arose between different Nazi factions, he says, those who favored harsher measures generally prevailed; but this was "the only constant . . . in a [system] that was, in reality, more planless and improvised than its horrifying results would lead one to suppose."[25]

Along with Presser, many of the historians who have followed in his footsteps have attempted to account for the almost complete destruction of the Dutch Jews. The Netherlands—literally "the Low Countries"—is a small, flat, low-lying nation without the dense forests in which partisans and others were able to hide elsewhere in Europe.[26] Since Dutch society was relatively segregated, Jews were unlikely to have close non-Jewish friends who would help them find hiding places or support them in hiding. (This was not true for the residents of the Annex, who were sustained by Otto's employees.) And the queen and the government relocated to London, leaving behind an organized system of civil servants who largely cooperated with the occupation. But the most significant factor seems to have been the general Dutch propensity—among Jews as well as non-Jews—to comply with the law. When they were told to register their names and addresses, to surrender their firearms and radios, they did.[27]

And the Amsterdam Jewish Council, too, behaved in a largely credulous manner, at least initially. They dutifully circulated the news of Nazi regulations in the *Jewish Weekly*, which offered the Germans a ready audience for reports about their new prohibitions while at the same time shielding the non-Jewish population from knowledge of the threats against their neighbors. When the first transports to Dutch labor camps began in January 1942, the Jewish Council ran an article urging people to comply with the call-ups and reassuring them that all was normal: "Do not fail to catch the train . . . What you are asked to do is ordinary relief work in ordinary Dutch camps."[28]

In the aftermath of the war, some argued that the council's willingness to cooperate with the Nazis amounted to collaboration. In the face of Nazi demands for greater and greater numbers of Jews to deport, they "played for time" rather than resisting outright.[29] They haggled over how many Jews needed to report for deportation on any given date and tried to finagle as many deportation exemptions as possible, particularly for council employees and their families. In retrospect, many have seen the council's desire to protect their own as reflecting poorly on them. If they had instead urged Jews in Amsterdam to go into hiding, as a local Jewish council in the city of Enschede did, many more Dutch Jews might have been saved.[30] (Initially, multiple Jewish councils were set up in different cities, but the Amsterdam Jewish Council was the central organizing body.)

Others have made the case that the Amsterdam Jewish Council was in an untenable position. Their decision to cooperate with the Nazis was a fatal gamble, made with the hope that they could mitigate the worst effects of persecution and buy extra time for the Jewish population. Rumors of mass extermination in Poland—the gas trucks that were running at Chełmno and Bełżec—were still only rumors. Auschwitz, established in May 1940 as a labor camp for Polish prisoners as well as others, was converted into an extermination camp primarily for Jews only in summer 1942. Earlier letters coming from prisoners at Auschwitz described the hygiene there as "satisfactory" and even mentioned "magnificent shower arrangements with hot and cold water."[31] And going into hiding required a great deal of money for food, rent, and bribes; it also brought its own risks, which were considered potentially even more severe than deportation. "The reality of Auschwitz and Sobibór was beyond the imagination of the vast majority of Dutch people," historian Bart van der Boom has written. "It was conceivable that the slow death that deportation threatened was less risky than the quick death that would follow if one went into hiding and got caught."[32] Many also believed that the Germans would be defeated within a few months.

Abraham Asscher—who, along with his Jewish Council co-president, David Cohen, was investigated after the war for collaboration and cleared—later said that an anonymous German soldier told him as early as 1941 that "the boys" transported to Mauthausen were all murdered. He claimed that he passed that information on to "all Jews" and advised them to go into hiding. Presser, who generally keeps his voice out of the narrative but allows himself interjections in the third person at some of the most emotional moments, comments here: "The writer could, however, find no evidence in support of this claim; rather the opposite."[33]

* * *

"I am forced to look out for emigration and as far as I can see U.S.A. is the only country we could go to," Otto wrote on April 30, 1941, to his old friend Nathan Straus Jr.[34] The men had last seen each other more than ten years earlier, when they vacationed together with their spouses at a villa in Switzerland owned by a cousin of Otto's. Straus too had served in World War I, in the U.S. Army; afterward he worked briefly as a journalist and then entered politics. He also owned Nathan Straus & Sons, a producer and importer of china and glassware. When Otto's letter reached him, he was serving as administrator of the U.S. Housing Authority, an agency created by President Franklin Delano Roosevelt in 1937 as part of the New Deal, lending money to states to build low-cost housing. He was a public servant, albeit one with a vast family fortune. Helen, his wife, also came from a distinguished background; her father was Bernard Sachs, a neurologist who was one of the first to describe the genetic disease now known as Tay-Sachs.

In late 1938, after Kristallnacht, Edith's brother Walter Holländer had been arrested and briefly imprisoned in a concentration camp. After his release, he and his brother Julius immigrated to the United States, and their mother, Rosa Holländer, moved to Amsterdam to live with the Franks. That same year, at the U.S. consulate in Rotterdam, Otto filed an immigration application on behalf of the whole family—including Rosa Holländer—but the consulate, along with its records, was destroyed in the Nazi bombing of the city in May 1940. The Van Pelses, too, tried to immigrate to the United States in 1939.[35]

Otto's cousin in London, Milly Stanfield, suggested that Margot and Anne live with her until the war was over, but Otto and Edith wanted to keep the family together. The Swiss borders were closed: a brother of Erich Elias, Otto's brother-in-law, had been trying to get a Swiss visa since spring 1939 without success.[36] The United States seemed to be the only option.

Initially, Otto believed the main difficulty was financial. "Everyone who has an effective affidavit from a family member and who can pay his passage may leave," he assured Straus. Julius Holländer was living in Canton, Massachusetts, outside Boston, and earning $28 a week tending furnaces at night for the Canton Japanning Company. Walter Holländer, some fifty miles away in Leominster, earned $20 a week at the E. F. Dodge Paper Box Company.[37] They had managed to save nearly $3,000. But Otto worried that this wouldn't be enough. "Would it be possible for you to give a deposit in my favor?" he asked Straus. He thought $5,000—the equivalent of about $100,000 in 2024—might be sufficient for the family.[38]

Over the previous few years, just as Jews were growing more and more desperate to leave Germany and its territories—"I think every German Jew must be combing the world in search of a refuge and not finding one anywhere," Edith Frank wrote to a friend who had made it to Buenos Aires—many countries had proved unwilling to relax their immigration policy.[39] Some, including the United States, had even introduced new restrictions. "The bar was set so high for visas to the U.S. in the 1930s that those who made it were like entrants to an elite university," one journalist writes.[40] In July 1938, on Roosevelt's initiative, delegates from thirty-two countries met at the French resort Evian to discuss the refugee problem. Many of those attending argued that Jews were "undesirable" refugees and expressed concern that taking in additional refugees would increase economic hardship for their own citizens. Only the Dominican Republic agreed to admit a meaningful number of Jewish refugees.

As German Jews living in the Netherlands, the Franks were included under the U.S. quota for German immigrants. By early 1939, the waiting list included around 300,000 names—likely the reason no action was taken on the Frank family applications originally filed in Rotterdam. As Germany's victories in western Europe mounted, U.S. politicians expressed fear that a "Fifth Column" of German loyalists in the United States might act as spies or worse. As the U.S. ambassador to Cuba, George Messersmith, put it, under the right circumstances German nationals "would become willing and dangerous elements, being so widely scattered over our country and employed in all kinds of key industries in all kinds of capacities."[41]

In an attempt to work around this, Senator Robert Wagner and Representative Edith Rogers introduced legislation in 1939 intended to provide refuge for 20,000 German children. But President Roosevelt refused to support the bill, and it died in subcommittee. "Twenty thousand charming children will all too soon grow up into 20,000 ugly adults," one opponent of the bill commented.[42]

As a result of such political pressure, the State Department tightened visa controls in June 1940. It was no longer enough for applicants to have a reason for leaving Europe; they had to supply a reason for entering the United States and avow that they would not engage in subversive activities. Meanwhile, the application procedure was confusing, varying from consulate to consulate. Some demanded only affidavits; others required proof of material support.

The Strauses wanted to help the Franks, but they were unsure exactly how to do so. "After all the letters + requests for help we've had from people we hardly know, the enclosed one . . . is from my husband's best friend during their university years—an extraordinarily fine man," Helen Straus wrote on May 28 to Augusta Mayerson, the acting director of the Migration Department of the National Refugee Service, a refugee aid organization in New York.[43] The Strauses were willing to sponsor the Franks but were concerned that the family was too large for a single sponsor. Helen worried as well that even if the Strauses put up the money, the authorities might not be satisfied. Mayerson advised her to focus on preparing affidavits of support to send to the American consul in Amsterdam; if the affidavits were sufficient, perhaps no financial support would be necessary. She also promised to contact the Holländer brothers to find out what they had been able to accomplish and to look into making steamship reservations, as visas could be issued only after passage was booked.

The brothers had already sent four affidavits to the Netherlands. Julius and Walter vouched for Otto, Edith, and their mother; in a gesture that the family found deeply moving, two American Jews unacquainted with the Franks—Walter's employer, Jack Hiatt, and Hiatt's friend Harry Levine—sent affidavits for Margot and Anne. Beneath the formality of the letters sent on their behalf, the Holländers' anxiety is palpable. "Mr. Holländer is quite eager for your office to encourage Mr. Straus in arranging for the transportation of this group and to assure him that the Holländers have always cared for their relatives and that he should not fear about being repaid for the passage money," the executive secretary of the Boston Committee for Refugees, who interviewed Julius, wrote to the National Refugee Service. The Holländers also hoped that Straus would use his political influence in persuading the German consul in Rotterdam to let the Franks out. Otto, an English speaker and a successful businessman, would certainly be able to support his family in the United States; the Holländers pledged to support their mother "in accordance with their own financial means."

"I am afraid . . . the news is not good news," Nathan Straus reported to Otto in July.[44] He had learned from the National Refugee Service as well as from officials in the State Department that unless Otto could get to a country where a U.S. consulate was still operating—Portugal, Spain, Free France, or Switzerland—it would be impossible to arrange a visa. In mid-June, the United States had required Germany to close its U.S. consulates; in retaliation, Germany expelled all U.S. consuls on German territory. If Otto could reach a U.S. consulate in a neutral country, Straus could help him. But such a trip was effectively impossible. You could travel to a neutral country only if you already had an exit permit—that is, a visa for the country you wanted to immigrate to. But the only way to get the visa was to appear in person at a consulate in a neutral country. And the entire family would have to come: no one with relatives remaining in German territory could qualify for a visa.

Apparently undiscouraged, Otto wrote in September 1941 with a new idea. It might be possible to enter a neutral country with a visa for Cuba, which people he knew had managed to get. The problem was the cost. According to Otto's calculations, this plan would require a security deposit in an American bank in Cuba as well as fees to the Cuban immigration service, transport from Cuba, and the cost of the visas—around $6,000. "Edith urges me to leave alone or with the children," he wrote—a tacit acknowledgment that his mother-in-law might be too infirm for this journey. The sense was that older women would not be deported, so it would be safe for Edith to stay behind with Rosa. But Otto was afraid to leave the Netherlands without the girls, particularly Margot, who in six months would turn sixteen and be eligible for deportation. They had pledged to keep the family together, but "there might be situations in which one tries everything." Julius Holländer wrote to Straus himself offering to share Otto's expenses.

Meanwhile, Augusta Mayerson cabled the Jewish Council in Amsterdam for advice. The response—when it finally arrived, more than a month later—only reiterated the same information. A visa for Cuba would allow the Franks to leave the Netherlands for a neutral country, but someone would have to pay for it. Otto, too, received a letter from the Jewish Council directing him to a law firm in Amsterdam that explained the procedure for leaving the Netherlands. "Cuba is the only country giving order to their Representatives that visas can be given to certain people at Bilbao and Berlin and I have seen telegrams to this respect coming from New York," Otto wrote to Straus. Only after receiving such a telegram was it possible to apply for an exit visa from Holland; after receiving the exit visa, you could then get a transit visa to Spain. "It is all much more difficult [than] one can imagine and is getting more complicated every day," he wrote.

It wasn't clear whether this plan could work either. Mayerson had learned that it was becoming harder to negotiate with the German authorities for an exit permit, even with a Cuban visa in hand. If the Germans denied the request, the visa money would be lost. And the Strauses now seemed hesitant to commit to backing the Franks. "Mr. and Mrs. Nathan Straus are very much interested in helping Otto Frank and his family, but this is only one of many cases that the Strauses are interested in and they are not prepared to invest the large sum of money that is indicated," Mayerson wrote to her colleague in Boston, asking him to ascertain that the Holländers were "able to carry the good part of the financial burden." Julius appeared personally at the office of the Boston Committee for Refugees to promise that he would pay $1,500. When no response from Straus was forthcoming, Julius increased his offer: he and his brother would "repay every amount given," on a monthly basis, starting immediately.

Something changed the Strauses' minds. "I shall never be able to leave here without your help," Otto pleaded in October. Writing to Mayerson on November 12, Helen Straus mentioned receiving a letter from Otto that sounded "urgent," adding, "I think we should act as quickly as possible." The same day, Mayerson wrote to Julius that the Strauses were willing to cover the refundable bank deposits and bonds and offered an additional $1,500. The night oven man and the box maker would be responsible for the remainder. A flurry of letters and cables followed, hammering out the details: Cuban visas for the whole family? Or just for Otto, to test whether an exit permit would be forthcoming? Julius hired a New York travel agency to arrange for the Cuban visa and paid $250 for it—nearly ten weeks' salary. The visa was sent to Otto on December 1.

The situation was more urgent than Helen Straus imagined. On December 7, the Japanese attacked Pearl Harbor. On December 11, when the United States entered the war, all communication with occupied Europe was cut off and Otto's Cuban visa was canceled. Julius Holländer had lost both his money and his chance to save his family.

On June 22, 1945, Julius—who had since moved to New York City—visited the National Refugee Service again. An "intense middle aged man," he "manifested a great deal of interest and concern for his sister's family," the agent who met with him reported. Was it possible, Julius wanted to know, to pick up on the "threads of activity" from 1941? He had sent a cable to Otto and Edith, but no one had answered it.

The refugee service made inquiries. Otto, they learned, had

returned to Prinsengracht 263. Edith was dead. The girls were missing. The file does not record who gave this information to Julius or what his reaction was.

* * *

As Otto's and Nathan's letters crossed the Atlantic, the pressure on the Dutch Jews was mounting. In summer 1941, as the weather grew warmer, the Nazis issued new prohibitions: Jews were barred from parks, spas, and hotels, as well as public beaches and swimming pools. "Playing outdoors soon became difficult because everything was taboo for us quite early on," Anne's classmate Theo Coster remembered.[45] Later that summer, the Nazis forbade Jews to visit libraries, theaters, museums, restaurants, coffee houses, playing fields, or zoos. On September 15, 1941, signs reading "Forbidden to Jews" were installed on park benches. Theo particularly missed being a boy scout. A troop was created for Jewish children, but it lasted only a year before that too was forbidden.

Despite the prohibitions, in early September Otto took Anne, now twelve, on a father-daughter getaway to the countryside. "I wanted to have some peace again and not go all by myself. Anne is always good and dear company and she was easily able to get a few days off school," he wrote to his mother.[46] In fact, school hadn't started yet for Anne or Margot. In early August 1941, just before the school year was supposed to begin, the Nazis announced that Jewish children must attend separate schools. In retrospect, there had been signs that this was coming, including a census of Jewish children conducted in February and the order, a few months later, that heads of schools must count and report the number of Jewish students enrolled. At Jacqueline van Maarsen's school, Jewish students were called to the headmaster's office before the start of summer vacation. Those who were graduating—including Jacqueline—were told that the new schools in which they had enrolled were no longer allowed to accept them. "After school, as I and two other girls who'd been told the same thing were standing around trying to figure out what this meant, some boys sneaked up behind us chanting softly, 'Ju-huws, Ju-huws,'" Jacqueline wrote later.[47] It was her first direct experience with antisemitism.

Since most parents sent their children to public schools, Amsterdam had only a few small Jewish schools, geared toward Orthodox children. Half of the students in Anne's class at the Montessori school were Jewish. The Franks had been planning to keep her there for an additional year, since she was behind in math after having been sick so often. Hendrika Kuperus, the principal, was also anxious for Anne to stay: "She was still very young for the class, and very frail also."[48] Kuperus cried as she said goodbye to the Jewish children. Out of the students who left the school—around ninety children—fewer than a quarter survived.[49]

The Jewish Council rallied: twenty-five public schools for Jewish children opened on October 1. Among them was the Jewish Lyceum, housed in an empty school building on Stadstimmertuinen, an alley between the Amstel River and Weesperstraat, in the Jewish quarter. The No. 8 tram, known as the "Jewish line," connected the neighborhood with the River District. The same route would be used by the Nazis to take Jews to the train station for deportation.[50]

Anne and Margot were among the nearly five hundred students to enter the Jewish Lyceum in fall 1941: Anne in class 1L2, the equivalent of American seventh grade, and Margot in 4B2, or tenth grade. In her diary, Anne gives the impression that she was always surrounded by friends and admirers, but in fact she wasn't uniformly popular at school. Those who weren't close to her found her unremarkable. One teacher remembered Margot much more clearly: she "stood out . . . [for] her beautiful intellect, her feeling for posture and style." Jaap Meijer, Anne's history teacher, later wrote a poem about Anne that included the lines "nobody saw / anything special / in her."[51] Anne saw herself as an undistinguished student who *surprised everyone* by getting accepted to the Lyceum along with Margot, whose grades were always much better than hers.[52] When her teachers took notice of her, it was often because she was talking in class.

The teachers and administration resolved to make the Jewish Lyceum feel as normal as possible for the students. Cohen, who taught history at the school in addition to his Jewish Council duties, instructed the teachers to avoid overemphasizing the budding Zionist movement or other Jewish topics. The atmosphere was nonetheless quite different from what they were used to. Many of the students, who had previously been in mixed classes, were anxious about being singled out as Jewish: "You were together in a group and they [the Nazis] could come to remove you just like that," one girl remembered.[53]

Anne was initially anxious, too, but for different reasons. Looking at the *big crowd* of kids gathered outside to register, she recognized only one: her friend Hannah Goslar. On the first day of school, she *felt quite forlorn, all by myself in my assigned seat in the back row, behind a group of tall girls.*[54] Ever assertive, she raised her hand and asked if she could move. Later, in gym class with a sympathetic teacher, Anne dared to ask if Hannah could be transferred into her class. Hannah joined her before the end of the day.

Students remembered that despite the "constant fear," the circumstances contributed to a sense of school spirit and an intimacy not only among the students but also between students and faculty. The teachers, many of them newly fired from universities or other high schools, were an unusually talented cohort; students later remembered the "special teachers that came from everywhere." The faculty was a cordial and tight-knit group. "We were all in the same situation," remembered Yakov Arnon, an economics teacher.[55] Many of them took a special interest in the well-being of their students, developing close relationships with them and spending time with them outside of school. "It was as if there was an unwritten pact between us to make the best of the situation now that we'd all been thrown into this experience together," Hannah remembered.[56] Students gave Presser, who taught history, fish scraps for his cats—a special treat at a time when Jews could buy fish only on the black market.[57] During summer 1942, the teachers set up a library so that students could borrow books from one another.

That one year in the Lyceum was heaven to me: the teachers, the things I learned, the jokes, the prestige, the crushes, the admirers, Anne wrote in an undated sketch during her time in hiding. Her classes included biology, English, math, history, and French, but her memories focused mostly on the admirers: a boy who gave her a brooch, signing the card only "*un ami*, R"; a boy who complimented her looks; another who *always followed me on his bicycle and wanted to walk arm in arm with me*. In other sketches, she remembered Miss Biegel, the biology teacher: *a tiny woman with a big nose, blue-grey eyes and grey hair, with the face of a mouse*, constantly wringing her hands. Anne enjoyed Miss Biegel's class: *She tells a good story, about everything from fish to reindeer, but most of all . . . she likes to talk and ask questions about reproduction*.[58] Her classmate Albert Gomes de Mesquita later remembered Miss Biegel telling the students that "when you put a horse and a donkey in the stable together, you'll end up with a mule." When he expressed confusion about how this worked, "Anne Frank was quite prepared to explain it . . . but I really wasn't so keen on that—to the great amusement of the class."[59]

Anne's math teacher was Aaron Keesing, *an impressive figure: tall, old, always in the same gray suit with a wing collar, a bald head with a wreath of gray hair.* She found him *fun to talk to after the lesson*, but he was unamused by her tendency to talk to her friends in class and assigned her numerous essays as punishment. In the first, "A Chatterbox," she argued that talking was *a hereditary disease* passed down by her mother. Keesing proved able to take a joke, she said, and *laughed heartily*. The extra assignments finally ended after Anne submitted an essay in verse, written with the help of Sanne Ledermann, which used her own nickname, "Miss Quack-Quack," as the inspiration for a story about a mother duck and her ducklings.[60]

In the Annex, Anne wrote that having to use a glass jar as a toilet during visits from the plumber wasn't as bad as *having to sit still and not talk the whole day. You can't imagine what a trial that was for "Miss Quack-Quack."*[61]

* * *

In April 1942, the Nazis announced that all Jews were to wear a black six-pointed star printed on a palm-sized piece of yellow material, "clearly visible and affixed to the outer clothing over the left breast," with the black inscription *Jood*.[62] The Jewish Council was given 569,355 stars to distribute over a period of three days, which included the weekend—a standard power play by the Nazi administration, which got a kick out of forcing the council to break the Sabbath. Jews were entitled to a maximum of four stars apiece, in exchange for one clothing ration coupon. The council's presidents, Asscher and Cohen, were again shocked. "This is a terrible day in the history of Dutch Jewry," Cohen told Hauptsturmführer Ferdinand aus der Fünten, head of the Zentralstelle. Asscher insisted that the war would be over within a few months. The *Jewish Weekly* ran an article with tips for keeping the stars colorfast in the laundry.[63]

One teacher at the Jewish Lyceum declined to wear the star, telling his students he refused "because I do not recognize [the Nazis'] authority, because I will not let them humiliate me, because I will not be led as a lamb to the slaughter." But most of the other staff agreed to communicate to the students that although the star was intended as a humiliation, they should wear it as "a badge of honor." Some Dutch chose to call the star "orange," the national color of the Netherlands, instead of yellow. Non-Jewish students at an agricultural school put on stars bearing the words "Protestant" or "Roman Catholic" and were sent for two weeks to a Dutch labor camp.[64]

The war made its presence felt at the Jewish Lyceum in other ways. One of Anne's classmates, a Polish refugee named Danka, spread the news that the Nazis were killing Jews in Poland by asphyxiating them inside trucks outfitted with poison gas. "Such a weird story that I couldn't even believe it," Nanette Blitz recalled later.[65] Did Anne believe it? She found Danka *petty* and *horribly affected*, a girl who *cries at the slightest little thing.*[66] Perhaps what Anne saw as annoying behavior was the result of trauma.

The first graduation and promotion ceremony for the Jewish Lyceum—it would also be the last—took place on the evening of July 3 in the Dutch Theater (Hollandse Schouwburg), a grand theater on the east side of the city center, near the botanic gardens. As of the previous fall, it had been renamed the Jewish Theater (Joodse Schouwburg). Within a few weeks, it became a transit camp within the city of Amsterdam, a holding pen for deportees waiting for their trains.[67] Margot's grades were *brilliant as usual.* Anne's were undistinguished—mostly Bs, with a C minus in algebra and one D—but her parents cared more about whether she was *well and happy, and not too cheeky* than about her grades.[68]

Rumors circulated about the impending mass deportations. Still, the celebration went on as planned. Students played music; a choir sang Hebrew songs. There were "many dignified and serious speeches," recalled Jaap (Jakob) Hemelrijk, a classics professor.[69] Cohen arrived very late. After his speech, he turned to Presser and said, "This war grows worse with every hour it continues." Presser was surprised by the remark, "which, from a man usually so impassive, was highly charged with emotion." Later he learned that Cohen had just been informed that the deportations were about to begin in earnest.[70]

When students and faculty reconvened in the fall for the Jewish Lyceum's second year in operation, both populations were considerably smaller. Of the thirty students who had been in Anne's class the previous year, only thirteen remained. None of Margot's classmates returned. "Fewer children came to class every day," Hannah Goslar said later. Students abandoned their assigned seats, moving closer to one another rather than spread out among empty chairs. By May 1943, only four students were left in one of Presser's classes. "The writer will never forget the look on his pupils' faces when names were called from the register and there was once again no voice to answer," he wrote. If students were absent, everyone wondered: had they been deported, did they go into hiding? Or could they just be sick? Students who knew the fate of others used one gesture to signify "caught," another to indicate "hiding."[71]

As both teachers and students dwindled in number, classes were combined. Liberated from the demands of the curriculum, teachers taught whatever they liked. One of the math teachers worried aloud that his students would not have time to prepare for their summer exams, then realized that most of them would be unlikely to be there for the test. In early 1943, eight Friday afternoons were devoted to a series of lectures on the Romantic movement. At one of the sessions, a group of musicians dared to play a forbidden quintet by Schumann, an Aryan composer.[72]

One of Presser's students was pulled out of class after both of his parents were arrested: "Now Freddy had to come along because—and the writer remembers the precise words—'we like to keep families together.'" The boy was allowed to go home to retrieve his coat, with the understanding that if he did not return, the headmaster would be deported instead. One of the last children to be taken was "little Carla G.," part of a group of students who walked home with Presser every afternoon. When he left school early one day, he noticed a police car parked outside her house. He went back to the Lyceum immediately to try to warn her, but she had already left. He never saw her again.[73]

In March 1943, Presser's wife was arrested. The next day, he read aloud in class the episode of Dante's *Paradiso* in which the poet and his love are reunited in heaven. Jacqueline and Hannah watched as he broke down in tears in the classroom. Even after he saw his wife's name on the list of those who had been gassed at Sobibór, "he continued to hope for a miracle," Jacqueline remembered.[74] Miss Biegel, the hand-wringing biology teacher who reminded Anne of a little mouse, died by suicide at Westerbork in June 1943.[75] Mr. Keesing's fate is unknown.

* * *

July 5, 1942, 3 p.m. The doorbell rings at Merwedeplein 37-II. Anne is expecting her new boyfriend, Hello Silberberg. They've already spent the morning together, sitting in the sun—the parks may be off limits, but Anne's apartment has a balcony. Like her, Hello was born in Germany—his real name is Helmuth—but he's been living in Amsterdam with his grandparents since 1938, after his father's clothing store was destroyed during Kristallnacht.[76] He's sixteen, and at first he preferred Margot, but she was "completely unapproachable."[77] When he met Anne at a friend's house, she made an impression on him, despite being three years younger. Quickly he became "fascinated with her."[78] The two of them have been going out only for a week or so, but they've spent a lot of time together. He walks her to the Jewish Lyceum in the mornings; after school, they go to the Oasis ice cream parlor or hang out at each other's homes. They speak Dutch together, not German. He loves to hear her talk. She asks him about his family, how he came to the Netherlands, what happened to his parents. (They fled to Belgium; he's had barely any contact with them for four years.) His grandmother thinks Anne is too young for him, but he doesn't care. Like many Jewish teenagers in their circles, he also goes to meetings of a Zionist club. His grandparents don't approve of that either, so he's used to asserting himself.[79] Perhaps this is part of what Anne finds attractive in him. Or perhaps it's just that he's older and clearly interested in her.

But it's not Hello at the door. A man's voice calls: "Miss Margot Frank."[80] Edith goes down to answer. The man gives her an envelope containing a single sheet of paper. At the top, in large capital letters, it reads: "Summons!"[81]

> You are hereby ordered to participate in the
> police-supervised work relief program currently taking
> place in Germany, and are therefore to appear on
> July 15, 1942 at 1:50 a.m.
> at Amsterdam Central Station.
> The following may be taken as baggage:
>
> 1 valise or rucksack
> 1 pair of work boots
> 2 pairs of stockings
> 2 pairs of underpants
> 2 waistcoats
> 1 pair of overalls
> 2 sets of bedclothes (cover and sheet)
> 1 bowl
> 1 drinking cup
> 1 spoon and
> 1 cardigan
>
> as well as provisions for a 3-day march and the ration
> coupons valid for that period.
> The following items may not be taken:
> stock and share certificates, currency, bankbooks, etc.,
> objects of value of all kinds (gold, silver, platinum—with
> the exception of wedding rings) and domestic animals.
> Should you fail to give heed to this summons,

> you will be punished with measures to be taken by the *Sicherheitspolizei.*
> This document serves as your travel permit, and also provides you with the right to make use of abovementioned train, free of charge.

Impossible to imagine what goes through Edith's mind at this moment. *Mummy was terribly upset.* Otto is out visiting residents at a home for elderly and indigent Jews. Edith leaves the girls together in the apartment and returns with Mr. van Pels. Anne is told that the summons is for Otto, not Margot. Considering how close Anne is to her father, it's not clear why Edith thinks she will find this less frightening. *Of course I started to cry terribly.*[82] The doors are locked; the Franks prepare to go into hiding immediately. Anne finds an excuse to drop off a few things with the neighbors' daughter, Toosje Kupers: a book, a tin of marbles, a tea set.[83] She will not say goodbye to Hello.

The order originated with Eichmann on June 22, 1942: Starting in mid-July, thousands of Jews were to be taken in special trains for "labor service" at Auschwitz. The camp, which soon became the largest Nazi concentration camp, was located in a humid, swampy valley between the Polish mining town of Katowice and Kraków, home to the Jagiellonian University and a jewel-box medieval town square. The site initially included more than a dozen army barracks housing 1,200 Polish prisoners, who were evicted to make room for the new inmates. As the camp grew steadily, some residents of the neighboring town and surrounding districts were displaced to create an empty region measuring about fifteen square miles. What we now know as "Auschwitz" was actually three camps in one: a concentration camp, Auschwitz I, located on the first site; a killing center and women's camp, Auschwitz II/Birkenau, built in spring 1942 and expanded in 1943; and a constellation of slave labor camps, Auschwitz III/Monowitz—an industrial complex created by the chemical and pharmaceutical manufacturer IG Farben, a subsidiary of which manufactured Zyklon B, the poison used in the gas chambers at Auschwitz/Birkenau. The satellite camps were spread throughout the surrounding area, serving the war effort as well as the company's bottom line.[84]

In the second half of 1941, Heinrich Himmler, one of Hitler's top deputies, charged the Auschwitz authorities to prepare for the mass annihilation of European Jews. In early 1942, following the formalization of the "Final Solution" at the Wannsee Conference, the Nazis evicted the residents of local peasant cottages and renovated them into provisional gas chambers that could hold about 2,000 people at a time.[85] The first sectors of Birkenau, which was designed to hold prisoners as well as functioning as a death camp, were built soon afterward. The first transports of Polish Jews probably arrived in early 1942. In March 1942, Jews began to arrive from France and Slovakia.

Eichmann demanded 90,000 *Stücke* ("pieces," as he referred to his victims): 40,000 from France, 40,000 from the Netherlands, and 10,000 from Belgium. In the Netherlands, rumors circulated that foreign-born Jews would be among the first to be deported. On June 26, a Friday, members of the Jewish Council were summoned at ten o'clock at night—another Sabbath violation—and told that "police-supervised labor contingents" of men and women, ages sixteen to forty, were to be sent to camps in Germany.[86]

A few hundred randomly chosen deportees to Mauthausen was one thing, but this was clearly on a different scale. A debate ensued within the council over whether it would be better in the long run to cooperate or resist. The possibility of asking for exemptions from deportation for council members and others—a matter that would prove extremely controversial in the future—was also raised. Some members rejected any thought of either cooperating or requesting special favors, arguing that to do so suggested that the council was more interested in taking care of its own than in protecting all Jews. Others believed that the council, by remaining in place, could potentially delay the imposition of further anti-Jewish measures. This position dominated.[87]

The next step was to figure out how many people could reasonably be deported at a time. The Nazis called for 600 per day, which Asscher and Cohen haggled down to 350. On the morning of July 5, after the first notices had already gone out—they were sent by registered mail on July 4 and delivered by the Dutch postal service the following day—the Germans insisted that a total of 4,000 Jews be deported between July 14 and 17: 1,000 per day. Members of the council were to be exempted, since they were "essential to the life of the Jewish community in the Netherlands."[88]

The staff of the Jewish Council was tasked with typing up the notices. Mirjam Levie, a secretary for the council who kept a diary in the form of letters to her fiancé, who had already immigrated to Palestine, could not bring herself to do it. "I know there's no fundamental difference between typing call-ups and compiling the card index for the exempt, and yet I couldn't type the call-ups," she confessed.[89]

On July 14, one day before the first deportees were due to report, the Nazis seized 700 Jews off the street in the Jewish quarter and brought them to Gestapo headquarters to be held as hostages until the first 4,000 deportees answered their summonses. Presser was among them. Acting under the assumption that the 700 hostages could be sent to Mauthausen, from which they probably would not return, whereas the 4,000 deportees were supposed to do "labor service" and therefore might, the Jewish Council pressured those who had been called up to report for duty, telling them, "The fate of 700 fellow Jews is at stake." Most of the hostages were released two days later, after the first transport left, but a few were held behind, including one of Presser's students. The first thing the teacher did after being released was to visit the boy's parents "in a vain effort to console them." Both the student and his parents were deported soon afterward.[90]

The call-up notices stated that the deportees would be put to work. Nonetheless, there was a general sense among the families of those called up—if perhaps not yet among the Jewish Council—that no one who got on those trains would ever be seen again. In retrospect, the Nazis' refusal to grant exemptions for disabled people should have demonstrated that they were lying about the fate that awaited the deportees at their destination. One man with an amputated leg who applied for an exemption from "labor service" was rejected by a Wehrmacht commander who wrote on his notice, "A Jew is a Jew, legs or no legs."[91]

Hannah Goslar's boyfriend, Alfred, also received a notice. The two of them speculated about what lay in store for those who were called up. It might be a kind of adventure; some of the girls were even bringing things like lipstick and hair curlers. They couldn't be gone for more than a few weeks. The war would surely be over soon. Alfred promised to write. "You'll wait for me?" he asked, and Hannah agreed. Because her father and grandfather worked for the Jewish Council, her family was temporarily exempt from deportation.[92]

Between midnight and two in the morning on July 15, under a moonless sky, tram cars brought the deportees to Amsterdam's Central Station. They clattered through the sleeping city, heading northeast from the quiet streets of the River District along Zuider Amstellaan, across the Amstel River and the Herengracht before zigzagging back toward the Old Town, where the windows of the Royal Palace were dark. Across from the station, they might have raised their eyes for a last glimpse of the medieval Schreierstoren. A barrel-shaped brick defense tower with a sharply pitched roof, it was the site from which countless Netherlanders—Henry Hudson among them—set out to sea, leaving their homes forever.

The first train—run, like the others, by Dutch Railways—left at 2:16 a.m. Another followed twenty minutes later. Altogether, 962 people reported for deportation. The Nazis made up the difference with detainees from Westerbork, en route from Amsterdam to Auschwitz. "Henceforth the inmates in that camp went in fear and trembling lest Amsterdam 'failed them' again in this matter," Presser wrote.[93]

Heinz Geiringer, one of Margot's classmates, took comfort in the fact that she and two of his other friends had also been called up. "I'm sure the Nazis will not harm me if I work hard," he told his mother.[94]

But Margot did not present herself at the station. Her place on the train would be filled by someone else, someone whose name remains unknown.

4

Witness
The Annex Eight, 1942–1943

We would be going to Daddy's office and over it a floor had been made ready for us . . . We have things to read . . . and we are going to buy all sorts of games.

Of course we are not allowed to look out of the window at all or to go outside. Also we have to do everything softly in case they hear us below.

The wood paneling was dark green, the wallpaper already yellowed and peeling, the rooms narrow, the stairs steep and rickety. The whole place was constantly damp and leaned slightly to one side. Still, they made it into a home: coverlets on the beds, books on the shelves, curtains on the windows. In the kitchen, a hook with a colander, the ever-present Dutch coffee pot, a colorful tablecloth. Anne pasted pictures on her wall: the movie stars she loved, like Greta Garbo and Ginger Rogers; Princess Elizabeth of York; postcards from her collection, including one with a photo of chimpanzees having a tea party; images of adorable curly-haired children; even a brightly colored advertisement for the house product, depicting fruits and the slogan "Now Make Your Own Jam with Opekta!"[1]

The potential need for a hideout may have been on Otto's mind as early as December 1940, when he moved the office to Prinsengracht 263.[2] By some accounts, it was Johannes Kleiman, one of Otto's first employees—before bringing him to Opekta, Otto had hired him in the early 1920s to work in the Amsterdam branch of the Michael Frank Bank—who came up with the idea of using the building as a hiding place.[3] Regardless, Otto and Kleiman thought the plan through together before bringing Hermann van Pels in on it. Like many such structures in Amsterdam, the tall, narrow house was two buildings in one, with a front section and another, equally large but separate, in back: the *achterhuis*, or "back house." The front had a warehouse on the ground floor, offices on the second floor, and storage on the third and fourth floors. The upper two floors in the back, already outfitted with plumbing and electricity, were connected to the main building by a staircase. Otto had been subletting part of the space to a German-Jewish pharmacist for use as a laboratory, but the pharmacist moved out after Nazi regulations forbade him to practice his profession.

Shortly after the pharmacist left—more than a year before the Franks and Van Pelses moved in—Otto, Kleiman, and Kugler began moving food, bedding, and furniture into the space. Jacqueline van Maarsen, who often visited the Franks' apartment, once noticed that all the dining room chairs were missing—they were being reupholstered, the Franks explained, unconvincingly.[4] Miep would be amazed by how much they had concealed without attracting the attention of any of the other workers, including herself. On the weekends, Kleiman's brother used a van owned by his business to move in furniture and other larger items.[5] Otto even managed to bring Anne's collection of film star photographs without her noticing.

Move-in day was Monday, July 6, 1942. Miep and Jan came to the Franks' apartment at eleven the night before to collect some clothes and other belongings. Anne was still up, her eyes "like saucers, a mixture of excitement and terrible fright."[6] At daybreak, Miep returned to escort Margot to Prinsengracht 263. The family watched, Anne still in her nightgown, as they bicycled off through pouring rain. Anne and her parents set off on foot shortly thereafter. A close observer might have noticed that her slender frame looked a little puffier than usual: she had on two undershirts, three pairs of underpants, a dress, a skirt, a wool cardigan, and a coat. *No Jew in our situation would have dreamed of going out with a suitcase full of clothing.*[7] Whatever they wanted to bring, they had to wear.

It was about an hour's walk to the office from the River District, much of it a straight line north on Ferdinand Bolstraat, a major commercial artery, where bakeries and newsstands would have been getting ready for the morning rush. Did the Franks turn left at the Singel canal to take a picturesque cobblestone path that winds among the weeping willows? Did they pause for a last look across the canal at the ornate Rijksmuseum, now occupied by the Nazis, part of its collection transferred to a bunker nearby? Did they check the time on the Westertoren, with its famous black-and-gold clock? Or did they trudge through the rain with their heads down, sparing no glance for the city from which they were about to disappear? How do you say goodbye to the place where you've made your life, not knowing when you'll be able to return? The Dutch word for going into hiding, *onderduiken*, translates literally as "diving under." The Franks would vanish like the periscope of a submarine slowly disappearing beneath the ocean's surface, gradually and then all at once.

Once they arrived at Prinsengracht 263, Miep hurried them all to the Annex. The Franks took the two rooms on the building's third floor—the lower level of the Annex. The Van Pelses, who joined them a week later, got the big room on the upper level, which they had to share with the rest of the residents during the day; it also served as the kitchen and the living room. Peter carved out space for himself on the landing to the attic. A few months later, when Fritz Pfeffer arrived, they reshuffled: the dentist roomed with Anne, while Margot moved into Otto and Edith's bedroom. The bathroom, with a toilet and a sink but no tub, was next to the landing on the lower level. According to the daily schedule—a necessity with eight people sharing the facilities—Anne was permitted to use it between 9 and 9:30 p.m. The next person often had to call her back to remove *the gracefully curved but unsightly hairs* remaining in the sink.[8]

The rooms, Miep and Bep both remembered, were in "total disorder" when the Franks arrived, with everything that had been brought there—"sacks and boxes and furnishings"—in piles. Margot and Edith, "like lost people," collapsed on the beds. Otto and Anne got to work making order, "pushing, carrying, clearing." Edith's mood remained low, but Otto was composed and calm. "Always a nervous man before, he now displayed a veneer of total control," Miep remembered. The place soon looked to her like a home, with schoolbooks or a hairbrush lying on the table and "the old, trusty coffeepot" on the stove.[9]

Later that morning, Ruth Goslar sent Hannah over to the Franks' apartment: she was making jam—Otto kept the Goslars supplied with pectin—and wanted to borrow a kitchen scale. The Franks' subletter, Mr. Goudsmit, answered the door. He told her the Franks had apparently departed in a hurry, leaving breakfast dishes on the table and a note with a scribbled address in Maastricht, near the Belgian border; they must have fled from there to Switzerland, he speculated.[10] Hello Silberberg, too, knocked on the door, but no one answered.[11] Gossip about the family's departure began to circulate almost immediately. One neighbor claimed to have seen the Franks leave on bicycles; another spread the rumor that a military car had come to pick them up during the night.

Hannah and Jacqueline returned together later. Jacqueline's emotions were mixed: she was glad that the Franks had made it out, but her best friend's sudden disappearance left her feeling "empty." She and Anne had promised to leave a farewell letter if either of them had to go away. Now, Jacqueline looked for the letter but found nothing. She thought about taking a board game called Variété, which Anne had just gotten for her birthday; they had played it often in the past few weeks. But Nazi regulations forbade removing anything that the owners of a home had left behind, so the girls left the Franks' apartment untouched. Anne's bed was unmade, and a new pair of shoes she had recently bought were next to it, "as if she had just kicked them off."[12]

A week or so later, Otto's sister Leni in Basel received a letter with birthday greetings—a surprise, since her birthday was in September. The envelope, postmarked July 6, was stamped with the eagle and swastika symbol of the Wehrmacht High Command (Oberkommando). Otto wrote that the family wanted to be sure that she received their birthday wishes in time, since "we won't have a chance to send them later." They were "healthy and together, that's the main thing. Everything is hard for us these days, but sometimes you just have to take what comes. . . . We can't correspond with [Alice] and with you all anymore, which is regrettable, but there's nothing we can do about it."[13] The family did not hear from Otto again until after the liberation of Auschwitz.

* * *

Although the vast majority of Dutch Jews were deported between July 1942 and September 1943 to Auschwitz or Sobibór and gassed immediately, around 28,000 went into hiding, of whom around two-thirds survived.[14] Those who were lucky enough to become *onderduikers* usually did so under circumstances very different from Anne's. Whereas many people had to abandon their homes in haste, the Franks and Van Pelses had the wherewithal—both financial and practical—to outfit their hiding place in advance with food and furniture. Unlike most Dutch Jews, who had relationships only within their own community, the two families had close non-Jewish friends who took on the responsibility of sustaining them in hiding. Many *onderduikers* went to farms or homes in country villages, but the Annex Eight—as Anne dubbed them—hid virtually in plain sight in the center of Amsterdam, with access, through their protectors, to whatever supplies and services remained in the war-wracked city. Very few Jews had their own hiding place; most had to change their addresses at least three or four times.[15]

Finally, the Franks were unusual because they stayed together. In most cases, parents had to make the agonizing decision to send their children into hiding alone. "To hide one person was an enormous undertaking; it required space and food as well as constant vigilance and luck," writes the historian Debórah Dwork. "The more people hidden in one place, the greater the risk and the more onerous the task."[16] It was easier to hide children than adults: with so many families displaced, few people would be suspicious if a new "niece" or "nephew" joined a neighbor's household. Anne's classmate Albert Gomes de Mesquita and his sister spent time with a family in a town near Amsterdam, where they felt safe enough to help outside in the vegetable garden and even to go on errands: "We had blond hair and fairly light eyes, so we weren't very conspicuous."[17] Together with his family, the farmer Johannes Boogaard created a rescue network that succeeded in hiding hundreds of Jews, both on the family's own farmstead and elsewhere in the countryside. The children knew him as "Oom Hannis," Uncle Hannis.[18] Children unprotected by their parents were in a uniquely vulnerable situation. Many were abused, sexually or otherwise, by their so-called guardians.[19]

In contrast to the closets or spaces beneath trapdoors where others hid, the *superpractical exquisite little* Annex was relatively spacious.[20] The residents could do their own cooking and set their own schedule, as long as they made as little noise as possible during the workdays, when the warehouse employees were on the premises. They occupied their minds with reading, schoolwork, sewing, even board games. The "house guidelines," drawn up by the Van Pelses before Pfeffer's arrival, made the situation sound like being *on vacation in a very peculiar boardinghouse:* "Open all the year round . . . Special fat-free diet. Running water in the bathroom (alas, no bath) and down various inside and outside walls. . . . Own radio center, direct communication with London, New York, Tel Aviv and numerous other stations. . . . Speak softly at all times, by order! All civilized languages are permitted, therefore no German!"[21]

Most unusually, the Annex residents had a variety of companions. Miep came daily to visit and take requests for food or other items. "So Miep, what's the news?" Anne invariably greeted her.[22] Jan, who often joined her for lunch at the office, was another frequent visitor, supplying Mr. van Pels with black-market cigarettes; Peter's cat, Mouschi, liked to jump into his arms. Kleiman, Kugler, and Bep also came regularly with supplies or just to offer moral support. Anne called them *the soup eaters* because of their habit of showing up at lunchtime for a cup of soup.[23] At twenty-one, Bep was closer in age to Margot, but she became intimate friends with Anne, who was always glad to listen to her romantic problems. She spent so much time in the Annex that Anne, in a description of the residents at table, called her *Number 9*.[24] When Otto came up with the idea of using a bookcase to conceal the entrance to the Annex, Johan Voskuijl, Bep's father, who served as warehouse supervisor and also happened to be a talented carpenter, built it in his home workshop and created the hinge mechanism that allowed it to open and close from either side.[25]

At Anne's request, Miep and Jan even spent a night in the Annex, sleeping in Anne and Margot's room while the girls bunked with their parents. Bep later slept over as well. Lying in Anne's "hard little bed," Miep was conscious of every sound in the rooms around her—someone dropping a shoe, the cat's footfalls—and then, later, of the terrifying silence:

> The quietness of the place was overwhelming. The fright of these people who were locked up here was so thick I could feel it pressing down on me. It was like a thread of terror pulled taut. It was so terrible it never let me close my eyes.
>
> For the first time I knew what it was like to be a Jew in hiding.[26]

In the weeks after the Franks went into hiding, the situation for Jews in Amsterdam transformed utterly. With the Nazis demanding ever increasing numbers of deportees, raids—the Dutch called them *razzias*—took place without warning in the Jewish quarter and elsewhere, sometimes lasting all day and into the night. The Nazis appropriated the elegant Jewish Theater and transformed it into a transit station for deportees waiting to be taken to Westerbork. As many as 1,400 people were held in a building designed for 800, possibly for days or even weeks. "At night, it could be terrible, particularly when there were screaming children everywhere—in the corridors, foyers, balconies, the pit, the staircases, the stalls," Presser wrote.[27] Trucks from the moving company Puls, which emptied the apartments of deported Jews and delivered their belongings to the Nazis, circled the streets. As fall turned to winter, Anne could hardly believe it when she spotted two Jews through the curtain one evening: how many of them still dared to walk on the street?

"Suddenly, with so much frightfulness going on outside in the streets of Amsterdam, going into the hiding place was almost like entering the safety and the sanctuary of a church," Miep recalled. "It was secure and our friends were safe." She was fully committed to her role as provider and protector. "Every time I pulled the bookcase aside, I had to set a smile on my face, and disguise the bitter feeling that burned in my heart. I would take a breath, pull the bookcase closed, and put on an air of calm and good cheer that it was otherwise impossible to feel anywhere in Amsterdam anymore."[28]

* * *

Miep's "calm and good cheer" weren't always shared by those in hiding. From a historical perspective, Anne was lucky to be in hiding with her parents, but it didn't feel that way to her. *A month ago today they were all being so nice to me because it was my birthday, but I have the feeling that I'm getting more estranged from Mummy and Margot*, she wrote soon after the move. Edith was constantly snapping at her and comparing her to her sister. She missed her cat. Even Otto's kind words were falling flat. *They say how nice it is for the four of us to be together, and that we get on so well, but it never occurs to them for one moment that I mightn't feel like that at all.*[29]

Anne's descriptions of her mother's behavior throughout the two years in hiding suggest that Edith may have suffered from depression. Immigrating to the Netherlands from Germany eight years earlier had profoundly destabilized her, requiring her to create a new social life and learn a new language, which she did with difficulty. Otto was outside the home in a Dutch-speaking environment daily, forging new relationships with his colleagues, while the children learned the language at school. Edith's life, by contrast, revolved around the home; she had fewer opportunities to practice Dutch and socialized mainly with fellow German-Jewish émigrés. Now, ripped from that close circle, she frequently took to her bed with headaches or malaise. She worried constantly: about the children getting sick, the possibility of discovery, the war never ending. She sought comfort in religion, urging Anne (against her will) to pray with her. In fall 1942, Ruth Goslar, one of her closest friends, died after giving birth to a stillborn baby, which must have been an enormous blow. Otto asked Anne to help her mother out more when she wasn't feeling well, which Anne generally resisted doing. Later, Edith confessed her despair to Miep, who would remember that no matter how encouraging the news from the outside world was, Edith "saw no light at the end of the tunnel."[30]

The arrival of the Van Pelses, on July 13—they had been planning to move in on July 14, but the Germans had begun calling up people *right and left*, so they figured *better a day too early than a day too late*—increased the tension. The families were already acquainted through their business relationship, but they don't seem to have known each other well enough to predict the personality conflicts that soon arose. Anne wrote that *after three days it was just as if we 7 were one large family*, but it quickly became a dysfunctional one.[31] Hermann van Pels seems to have cared mainly for his cigarettes and his food; over the previous few months, he had brought Miep regularly to visit his butcher, to ensure that the man would remember her later and provide extra meat.[32] Auguste, his wife, is perhaps the most memorable figure in Anne's diary, stealing every scene in which she appears with her sudden swings from flirtatiousness to rage. She criticized Anne's picky eating (Anne rejected most forms of meat) and her reluctance to perform chores like peeling potatoes or shelling peas. She clashed with Edith over the use of dishes and linens (*she wants to make sure that all our sheets are getting torn to shreds by being washed and used, while her ladyship keeps her own nice and neat for after the war*) and over her permissiveness in allowing Margot to read books intended for adults.[33] She and her husband had screaming fights that shocked the soft-spoken Franks; sometimes their arguments were audible in the office or even the warehouse, two stories below, and Johan Voskuijl had to yell at the workers to distract them.[34] (The office workers were all in on the secret, but the crew in the warehouse were not.) Anne was particularly offended by what she perceived as Mrs. van Pels's efforts to flirt with Otto, which made her jealous.

Despite his gift of a chocolate bar for her thirteenth birthday, Peter doesn't seem to have struck Anne as worthy of her attention prior to the move. Miep described him as "a good-looking, stocky boy with thick dark hair, dreamy eyes, and a sweet nature," but to Anne he seemed dull and hypochondriacal: *one day he has lumbago, next day he has a blue tongue and itches.*[35] He must have found her more appealing, since she complained about his tendency to stroke her cheek: *I don't like being pawed by boys.* The Van Pelses suggested early on that she might *get fond of him,* to her horror. *I thought oh dear, and said, no I can't.*[36]

The families devised a daily routine to manage tension and establish order. Wake-up was at seven in the morning, followed by scheduled slots in the bathroom before breakfast at nine. Daytime hours were devoted to chores and study: Anne gave herself a few weeks off in the summer, but starting in September 1942, she reported working on French grammar, algebra, and geometry. She kept a list of vocabulary words in foreign languages and read books in French, English, and German. (By contrast, Anne's classmate Albert later claimed that during the three years he spent in hiding, he never opened a book.) Otto made sure all the teenagers kept up with their schoolwork; of the three of them, Peter was the weakest student, so Otto spent extra time tutoring him. Margot, ever industrious, taught herself Latin using a mail-order curriculum that Bep sent away for, completing grammar and vocabulary exercises that Bep then mailed back to a teacher to correct; Margot, Anne, and Peter all learned shorthand via this method as well. "Every time I silently walked into the hiding place, I'd see each person engaged in activity," Miep later recalled. "They looked like living cameos: a head lowered intently over a book; hands poised over a pile of potato peelings; a dreamy look on a face whose hands were mindlessly knitting; a tender hand poised over Mouschi's silky back, stroking and touching; a pen scratching across blank paper, pausing as its owner chewed over a thought, then scratching again. All of them silent."[37]

During the lunch break or in the evenings, once all the workers had gone home, the residents were freer to make noise. They exercised, ran the vacuum cleaner, or went downstairs to the main office to listen to the radio. Anne and Margot, whom Miep called "night fairies," assisted the office employees with filing and other light work.[38]

Time was set aside for reading from 8:30 to 9:30 a.m., 2:30 to 3:45 p.m., and 7:30 to 8:30 p.m., with new library books brought every Saturday by one of the helpers and passed among the residents. Kleiman, *the one who always cheers us up*, brought books for Anne that his youngest daughter, two years older than she, no longer read; on Mondays, Kugler—a dapper dresser whose slender form reminded Bep of a character in an Egon Schiele painting—delivered *Cinema & Theater*, an entertainment magazine.[39] In an interview many years later, he recalled how Anne watched him expectantly until he presented her with it; sometimes, he said, he hid it in a pocket "so that I could watch those questioning eyes for longer."[40] Otto read aloud from the works of Dickens, Goethe, Schiller, and others, and urged the girls to keep a list of the books they had read. By the end of the period in hiding, Anne's list became impressive in both length and sophistication: European and Middle Eastern history; literature by Thackeray (which Anne studied, in English, with Peter) and Oscar Wilde; biographies of Maria Theresa, Franz Liszt, and Carl Linnaeus; a five-volume history of art (a gift for her fifteenth birthday); Greek and Roman mythology; and various popular novels, including *The Forsyte Saga* by John

Galsworthy.[41] But in the early days, Anne's reading consisted mainly of fairy tales by Hans Christian Andersen and the Brothers Grimm, as well as Dutch young-adult novels such as Nico van Suchtelen's *Eva's Youth*, a romantic story that includes discussion of menstruation—a topic of great interest to Anne, who was wondering when she would get her first period—as well as prostitution (*I'd die of shame if anything like that happened to me*).[42]

And, of course, Anne passed the time by writing in her diary. People often have the idea that she wrote every day, or at least most days. That wasn't the case, especially early on. Her initial entries from the Annex are sparse: three in July 1942, three in August, and then nothing until late September. She often sounds listless. *Something happens every day, but I am too lazy and too tired to write everything down.* She comments on the household routines, on the food (*we had barley soup which I don't like*), on the hot weather, on her parents' and the Van Pelses' complaints about her, and on her situation. *The reality is that we have to stick it [out] here until the war is over, we are not allowed to go out and we are only allowed to be visited by Miep Gies-Santroschits, Jan Gies her husband, Bep Voskuyl, Mr Voskuyl, Mr Kugler, Mr Kleymann and Mrs Kleymann, but she doesn't come because she thinks it's too risky.*[43] (Though Anne's Dutch was excellent, the spelling of some of those names defeated her.) Looking back later on these early pages, she remarked that she *found it so hard to write in my diary.*[44]

But on September 21—Day 78—Anne had a new idea. *I would just love to correspond with somebody, so that is what I intend to do in future with my diary. I shall write it from now on in letter form.*[45] The pace of entries increased and their tone became more energized. Anne went back to the beginning of her diary and inserted photographs of herself with her comments on them as well as photos of family members—her father, her grandmother, Margot, even one of Edith. She wrote the farewell letter that she had promised to Jacqueline, although it was now too late to send it: *When you telephoned me on Sunday afternoon* [July 5] *I couldn't say anything, for my mother had told me not to, the whole house was upside down. . . . I hope we'll meet again soon, but it probably won't be before the end of the war.* She immediately wrote a reply to an imagined response from her friend. Even when pretending, she remembered to be cautious: *I forgot to tell you in my last letter that you must not keep these letters from me, because no one must find them.* And she began to speak to the diary itself: *I am, Oh, so glad that I took you along.*[46]

What happened to galvanize Anne's writing? Was it the strain of living with her parents? The squabbling between the Franks and the Van Pelses? Her increasing loneliness as the separation from her friends grew longer? Her realization, as the weather grew *damp and chilly* and the school year began without her, that her Annex time would be measured in months or years, not weeks? *The war still goes on, and we get almost no butter now on our bread. . . . It has turned terribly cold here already, and I have just woken up to the disturbing fact that I have only one long-sleeved dress and 3 cardigans here.*[47]

Any or all of these factors may have contributed to the new interest Anne took in her diary. But one thing is certain to have had an impact: she was reunited with her favorite author.

* * *

Readers know Anne's diary in the form of letters to an imaginary friend named "Kitty." But Anne's unedited diary shows that after she came up with the idea of writing her diary in letters, she initially addressed them to various other figures, including "Jettje," "Pop," "Pien," and "Conny." The editors of the Critical Edition initially passed over these names silently, offering no explanation. While preparing the German translation, Mirjam Pressler, a German-Jewish translator and author of children's books, recognized them as characters in the *Joop ter Heul* series by Cissy van Marxveldt—Anne's favorite books.[48] Anne had first read the series at least a year earlier. In late September, Kleiman brought his daughter's copies to the Annex for her.

Cissy van Marxveldt was the pen name of Setske de Haan, a Dutch writer born in 1889 who published more than two dozen novels for girls and women. Anne was hardly alone in her fondness for these books, which were popular reading for many Dutch girls, then and later, and even inspired a form of fan fiction.[49] But certain elements may have appealed especially to her. Joop is an untraditional girl: a tomboy who delights in playing pranks, slacks off on her homework, and sneaks cigarettes behind the bike shed at school. Her older siblings are sanctimonious; her mother, self-absorbed; her father, secretly loving but silent and stern—he refuses to let her see her friends and puts her under "house arrest" for disobeying his strict rules. Her life revolves around her girlfriends; like Anne, she is often scolded for talking to them in class and even made to write an essay as punishment. Also like Anne, she is fascinated by romantic relationships, whether other people's or her own.

The novels are written in casual, direct language that incorporates slang and local references to the wealthy Amsterdam neighborhood where the Ter Heul family lives. And much of the first novel in the series, *The High School Times of Joop ter Heul* (first published in 1919 and still in print in Dutch), is written in diary form, a technique that makes it seem to be taking place in "real, measurable time," as one critic writes.[50] After Joop's father forbids her to correspond with her friends because he believes it interferes with her school work, she begins to keep a diary—her "paper confidante." Writing in it, she says, is like "an evening chat" with "no one other than yourself" and helps her calm down when she is upset. It may be "a silly whim of mine," she continues, but "everything I experience ends up in my diary."[51]

Now Anne, following Joop's lead, began to write regularly

in her diary. Separated from her own friends, she pretended she was Joop, writing to each of the girls who figure in the books—sometimes several in a day—and apologizing when she felt she had neglected one or another. So deeply did she imagine herself into the world of the novel that she mentioned events in the characters' lives as if they were real, asking one about her boyfriend and another about the progress of a pregnancy.[52] Later on, she settled on a single addressee: Kitty, the name of one of Joop's friends.

It's not clear why Anne chose this name rather than any of the other girls'. She may have felt a certain kinship with the character: Kitty in *Joop ter Heul* is often rambunctious in class, at one point making her classmates laugh so hard that the teacher loses control entirely. A story in Anne's "Book of Tales" describes a character named "Kaatje," a Dutch version of the name Kitty: she is Christian, with blond hair and blue eyes, a loving mother and a dead father, and six brothers and sisters. This story, one critic argues, demonstrates that Anne "has fully appropriated Kitty from Cissy van Marxveldt," making the character her own.[53] It also situates Kitty as an ideal correspondent for Anne: since she exists "somewhere outside the reality of occupied Europe," it makes sense for Anne to explain her circumstances.[54] But Anne addresses her diary in Dutch using the English name "Kitty," not Kaatje, so it's possible she didn't intend the characters to be identical. Most likely she developed an image of Kitty as a sort of generic figure: the "paper confidante" of the diary personified.

The lighthearted tone Anne borrowed from Van Marxveldt jars in contrast with her subject matter. While the problems Joop faces are mainly limited to bad grades and misunderstandings, Anne reported the details of her circumstances—that is, her persecution. She wrote of the Franks' former tenant, Mr. Goudsmit, who they feared had stolen the belongings they left behind. She described the cumbersome process of bathing in the Annex: she had to carry a washtub downstairs to the office kitchen to get hot water and then bring it back upstairs, full, to the bathroom. Workmen periodically came to the building, requiring all the residents to crowd into the top floor of the Annex and refrain from flushing the toilet; a carpenter working downstairs once rattled the bookcase, terrifying them all.

Meanwhile, the reports from outside grew worse. Miep was reluctant to relay news that might frighten the Annex inhabitants, but Anne "would have made a great detective. She'd sense that something was being withheld and she'd pull and squeeze, probe and stare me down, until I'd hear myself revealing just what I had decided not to reveal."[55] Radio Orange had already reported that the Nazis were using gas to murder Polish Jews, warning, "Our own Jewish citizens will fare no better."[56] On October 2, which would be known as "Black Friday," huge roundups took place. *Last night they were dragging Jews from house after house again in South Amsterdam. Horrible. God knows which of our acquaintances are left.* Anne heard the Nazi leader Hermann Göring on the radio *cursing the Jews something awful.*[57]

Miep did relay a report from a man who escaped from Westerbork, which was understood by then to be "a kind of holding camp" for deportees: *if it's so bad there what can it be like in Poland? People get hardly anything to eat let alone drink. . . . They all sleep mixed up together men and women and the latter + children often have their hair cut off so that everyone can recognize them if they escape.*[58] Despite all the annoyances, Anne was grateful to be safe in the Annex.

* * *

In November, Fritz Pfeffer, Miep's dentist, joined the Annex crew: now they were eight. Another German-Jewish émigré, he was in his early fifties, the same age as Otto: "a handsome man, a charmer who resembled the romantic French singer Maurice Chevalier," in Miep's words.[59] She had met him at one of the

Franks' gatherings for refugees and started seeing him as a patient, which she continued to do even after the Nazi laws forbade her to visit a Jewish dentist. He asked her—perhaps guessing, correctly, that Jan was involved with the Resistance—if she knew of a place he could hide. *We had been saying once more that we really ought to take in another person and fate pointed to Mr. Pfeffer, for he doesn't have much family.*[60] The published version of Anne's diary states that his wife was away from the Netherlands when the Germans invaded. In fact, as Anne writes in Version B, Pfeffer was in a long-term relationship with Charlotte Kaletta, a non-Jewish Dutch woman. If they had been married, Pfeffer could likely have obtained at least a temporary exemption from deportation, but since they were not, the relationship offered him no protection.[61]

When Miep brought Pfeffer to the Annex, the Franks and Van Pelses greeted him with coffee and cognac. Pfeffer couldn't hide his surprise—he thought they'd escaped to Switzerland! Yet here they were in the center of Amsterdam.[62]

It was useful to have a dentist around: he was pressed into service right away to fill a cavity for Mrs. van Pels. (Later, he performed *some really horrible nerve-treatment*, presumably without anesthesia, on Anne.)[63] But he, too, soon became an annoyance. Though she claims that *there was quite enough room and food for one more*, in fact it was a strain for her to share a bedroom with him—the room was so narrow that a person standing in the middle could touch the walls on either side.[64] Otto and Edith must have been aware that it was nearly as inappropriate for thirteen-year-old Anne to bunk with an adult man as it would have been for sixteen-year-old Margot—her breasts were developing, and her period would begin within months. The imperative of squeezing a fellow Jew into their tight quarters must have outweighed such concerns.

Under the best of circumstances, Anne would have found Pfeffer uncongenial: he had a tendency toward pomposity and was unsympathetic to the needs of a teenager. (In contrast to the Van Pelses, whom she always refers to as Mr. and Mrs., Anne calls Pfeffer by his last name only.) The close contact turned irritation to contempt. She quickly came to despise everything about him: his snoring, the amount of time he spent in the bathroom, his way of speaking and eating. He doesn't seem to have liked her any more than she liked him. *Just as if I didn't hear enough sh-sh during the day, for making "too much" noise, my gentleman bedroom companion now repeatedly calls out sh to me at night too.*[65] They nearly came to blows when Anne asked him to extend the hours during which she could use the desk in their room. At first he dismissed her work as unserious: "If your sister Margot, who has more right to work space than you, had come to me with the same request, I'd never even thought of refusing, but you . . ."[66] He agreed to compromise only after Otto intervened.

Pfeffer's arrival was disruptive in another way as well. After initially upsetting the residents by telling them about the deportations of friends and neighbors, Miep and Bep had decided to shield them from the worst news.[67] Now, from Pfeffer, they learned the truth about the transports leaving for Westerbork and beyond. The Jewish Council negotiated with the Nazis over the number of people to be deported as if discussing cattle: Would they take 275? 280? Or did it have to be 300? Decisions were based on the most arbitrary criteria: one night a drunk German commandant inspected the feet of everyone waiting in the Jewish Theater and allowed those with clean soles to go home. Via a nursery across the street from the theater, hundreds of children were smuggled to hiding places. One of them was Ed van Thijn, who later became the mayor of Amsterdam.[68]

Among the deported were two of Anne's classmates, Betty Bloemendal and Nanette van Praag-Sigaar, both of whom were murdered in Auschwitz in the fall of 1942. *Countless friends and acquaintances have gone to a terrible end. Evening after evening the green and gray army lorries trundle past and ring at every front door to inquire if there are any Jews living in the house, if there are, then the whole family has to go at once. . . . Nobody is spared, old people, children, babies, expectant mothers, the sick[,] each and all join in the march of death.* Fear for her friends continually occupied Anne's thoughts in hiding. *I feel wicked sleeping in a warm bed, while my dearest friends have been knocked down or have fallen into a gutter somewhere out in the cold night.*[69]

The Annex residents were shocked. *The news about the Jews had not really penetrated through to us until now. . . . The stories [Pfeffer] told us were so gruesome and dreadful that one can't get them out of one's mind.*[70] Still, Anne philosophized, it was best to try to keep up their spirits. Her next entry describes the entertainments devised by the Annex Eight to conserve electricity after dark, including her own favorite: peering with binoculars into the lighted rooms of the houses on the other side of the courtyard, hoping for a glimpse of ordinary life.

Frances Goodrich and Albert Hackett, who adapted the *Diary* for Broadway, have been criticized for the comedic tone their play took, but Anne relished the lighter moments: board games, reading aloud, baking gingerbread for a special occasion. She often tried to amuse the others. One night when they were celebrating Mrs. van Pels's birthday, she put a fur collar around her father's neck, *which made him look so divine you could have died laughing;* Mr. van Pels joined in the clowning.[71] Sometimes she felt an unexpected intimacy with Margot or even Edith. She and Peter listened to comedy programs on the radio and she recorded the dirty jokes in her diary, even when she didn't understand them.

Less a religious event than an excuse to dote on children, St. Nicholas Eve (Sinterklaas) is celebrated throughout the Netherlands on December 5 with gifts and sweets, which parents traditionally put in their children's shoes. Miep and Bep threw a party for the Annex Eight, writing poems and coming up with gifts: a baby cupid doll, flowers, sewing boxes and other items made out of wood by Johan Voskuijl. For Chanukah, which had begun the day before—Day 152 in hiding—the residents *didn't make much fuss . . . just gave each other a few trifles and then we had the candle*, which they could burn for only ten minutes, owing to a shortage.[72] The men put on hats—not yarmulkes, apparently—for the candle-lighting; Anne stood next to Otto and afterward joined in singing the traditional song "Maoz Tzur," a liturgical poem that thanks God for the Jews' victories over their enemies.[73] "Bare your holy arm," the song exhorts,

> and hasten the End for salvation . . .
> For the triumph is too long delayed for us
> and there is no end to days of evil.

* * *

"I don't want people saying later on that Anne Frank failed her exams because Mr. Pfeffer refused to relinquish his table!" Pfeffer told Anne during their dispute about the desk.[74] The remark betrays an assumption that seems futile only in retrospect: that someday the Annex Eight would re-emerge into daylight and resume normal life in *the inhabited world*, as Anne once called it.[75] The physical torments of hiding were obvious—the close quarters, the need to be quiet, the stench of a toilet not flushed for long stretches, the restricted diet. But not knowing how long the situation would last was one of the major psychological torments, perhaps second only to the fear of discovery. A few months into hiding, Anne made an offhand comment about something that would happen after the war, provoking a *big bust-up* with her mother: *she said that I'm always carrying on about "later."*[76] Edith, hopeless about the future, may have found her daughter's optimism unbearable.

No one knows for how long the Franks initially thought they would be in hiding, but judging from the way Anne describes their conversations, my best guess is a year at most. In May 1943, after nine months in the Annex, Mr. van Pels predicted that the families would remain there through December. *That's a terribly long time, though we'll make it*, Anne reassured herself.[77] In fact, it was August 1944 before they saw the sky again, under the worst possible circumstances.

Thinking ahead to the time after seems a healthy impulse, a way of staving off despair. About a year in, the residents daydreamed together about what they would do first when they got out. Margot and Mr. van Pels wanted a long, hot bath; Mrs. van Pels pictured herself eating cream cakes; Peter would go to the movies; Edith wanted a real cup of coffee. Otto would visit Bep's father, who had just received a diagnosis of terminal cancer and was no longer able to work. Pfeffer longed only for Charlotte, to whom he wrote letters every week. Anne says she would be *so blissful, I shouldn't know where to start! Most of all*, she added later, *I long for a home of our own, to be able to move freely and to have some help with my work again at last—in other words, back to school!*[78] Further down the road, she pictured her future children someday reading the *Joop ter Heul* books and calling her "Mams," an affectionate Dutch word for mother that she refused to use for Edith.

More practical plans for the future show up in some of Anne's earlier entries. Edith talked about adopting Hannah Goslar's younger sister, then a toddler, after the war.[79] When the Van Pelses ran out of money, requiring Mrs. van Pels to sell her prized rabbit fur coat, she hoped to keep the proceeds to buy new clothes later, prompting another fight with her husband. Anne initially worried most about keeping up with her studies—*I certainly don't want to still be in the first form* [seventh grade] *when I'm 14 or 15*.[80] Later, perhaps looking back on her own fantasies about a new wardrobe, she castigated herself: *we really ought to save every penny, to help other people, and save what is left from the wreckage after the war,* she wrote in a passage about the poverty and hunger Dutch children were currently enduring. Peter at one point imagines taking off to live on a rubber plantation in the East Indies, which had been colonized by the Dutch in the early seventeenth century.[81] (The spices that were ground and packaged in the building were imports from the colonies.) Anne's real first wish, she wrote later, was someday to become a Dutch citizen: *I love the Dutch, I love this country, I love the language . . . even if I have to write to the Queen myself, I will not give up until I have reached my goal!* She also longed to surpass her mother in professional achievement. *If God lets me live . . . I shall not remain insignificant, I shall work in the world for mankind!*[82]

These lines appear in an entry from April 1944, when the nerves of everyone in the Annex had reached a breaking point. There are earlier indications that Anne had trouble maintaining an optimistic outlook. *I do talk about: "After the war," but then it is only a castle in the air, something that will never really happen.* Her former life—her neighborhood, her girlfriends, her school—felt as though it belonged to someone else. She pictured the Annex Eight standing on a little piece of blue sky, with storm clouds closing in around them. *The round, clearly defined spot where we stand is still safe but the clouds gather more closely about us and the circle which separates us from the approaching dangers closes more and more tightly.*[83]

This striking image expresses not only the precariousness of the Annex residents' position but also Anne's increasing fears about the ways in which the experience of isolation had intangibly marked them. Looking through the crack between the office curtains, as she sometimes allowed herself to do after dark, she stared down at the people walking freely on the street: was it their way of living that was mad, or hers? She worried about the decline in her family's manners: the oilcloth on the table was dirty, the sheets couldn't be laundered, her father's clothes looked worn, her mother's corsets had split. (The contemporary reader can only marvel that Edith wore corsets in hiding.) Would she be able to return to life as she remembered it, seamlessly integrated with friends, neighbors, classmates? Or would she be forever changed by her time in hiding, however long it turned out to be?

* * *

Anne's fourteenth birthday—June 12, 1943—marked the anniversary of her diary, which meant that she had been in hiding for almost an entire year. Thanks to Miep and Bep, she was able to celebrate with "little sweets and goodies"; she also received a *fat book* on her new favorite subject, Greek and Roman mythology.[84] (Later that summer she compared Peter's appetite to a *danaïdean vessel, which is never full.*)[85] As per Frank family tradition, there were poems. "Though youngest here, you are no longer small," Otto wrote, continuing with a candid account of the criticisms Anne had to put up with:

> But life is very hard, since one and all
> Aspire to be your teacher, thus and thus:
> "We have experience, take a tip from us." . . .
> Please bear with us, your parents, for we try
> To judge you fairly and with sympathy.
> Corrections sometimes take against your will,
> Though it's like swallowing a bitter pill;
> Which *must* be done if we're to keep the peace,
> While time goes by till all this suffering cease.[86]

What Anne needed most—new clothes—wasn't among her birthday presents. Despite the poor diet, she had grown several inches in the past year and gained nearly twenty pounds. She had to use chairs to extend her bed so that her feet wouldn't dangle off at night. When she tried on her fall clothes, imagining what she would wear to go back to school, her sweaters reached only to her forearms; Margot called her nightgown "indecent."

Miep couldn't help but notice that "her shape had changed so much that it was impossible even to try to make buttons meet. . . . Little Anne . . . was turning into not-so-little Anne before our very eyes."[87] The only shoes that fit her were ski boots. ("To put on shoes would mean to cut off toes," Otto wrote in his birthday poem.) Nonetheless, Anne tried out new hairstyles and experimented with her clothes, trying to make herself look older, or perhaps just different. At one point Bep rustled up new skirts for Anne and Margot, but the best material she could find was like burlap, and they didn't fit, either. One of Bep's sisters was given Anne's hand-me-downs, including a velvet dress in cobalt blue, embroidered with roses, that the little girl adored.[88]

There were shortages of everything. Bep bicycled to farms outside the city in search of food for sale; once a Nazi stopped her on the way back and followed her home. She flirted with a local milkman, telling him about her seven hungry younger siblings, so that he would give her extra milk. Miep felt like "a kind of hunter, ever hunting for my always-hungry brood."[89] The grocery lines were longer and longer, and sometimes the only food she was able to buy was of such poor quality that it made the Annex residents sick or gave them digestive problems. Miep was under five feet tall, but Anne compared her to a *pack mule, she fetches and carries so much*.[90]

There was no shampoo, only sticky green soap for washing hair and everything else. So little cloth and thread was available that before darning a sock, the ever frugal Miep asked herself whether the thread could be used for a better purpose or if a friend might need it more. Unbeknown to the Annex Eight, she and Jan were concealing a ninth *onderduiker* in their apartment: the college-aged son of their landlady. The Nazis had required all Dutch students to sign a loyalty pledge to the German Reich—which he had refused to do—or risk deportation to a labor camp. At one point Miep and Jan also found hiding places for two Jewish children whose parents had been arrested.

In late summer 1943, the Nazis began rounding up non-Jewish Dutch men for "labor service" in Germany, and Miep worried that Jan would be taken.

Determined to find something that would make Anne feel both grown-up and attractive, somehow Miep came up with a pair of secondhand red pumps. Anne put them on instantly. "She got very quiet then: she had never felt herself on high heels before," Miep wrote. "She wobbled slightly, but with determination, chewing on her upper lip, she walked across the room and back, and then did it again. Just walking back and forth, up and back, more and more steadily each time."[91]

Anne was also having trouble with her eyes. Margot had been wearing thick glasses for years, and now Anne needed them as well. There was talk of taking her to an eye doctor. Though excited at the idea of going out, Anne was "white around the mouth with fear"—not without reason.[92] Roundups of Jews were continuing. On Sunday, June 20, one of the most beautiful days of the season, the Nazis staged a huge *razzia* of the Jews remaining in the River District. They blocked off the streets and stood guard at bridges and intersections so that no one could get away. As in much of Amsterdam, the apartment buildings in the River District are set close together; in many buildings half a dozen apartment doors open off a single landing. When the Nazis knocked on one of the doors, everyone in the building would have heard.

In a now famous photograph, two teacups sit on a windowsill; just outside, the camera lens observes a crowd of Jews with luggage, waiting to be deported. "One could look out the window, while drinking tea, and see their neighbors, marked, forced into public squares, beaten, humiliated, deported," the journalist Nina Siegal writes in *The Diary Keepers*, her book about the Holocaust in the Netherlands.[93] Cornelis Komen, a salesman who happened to be heading to the countryside for the day to pick cherries, witnessed the *razzia* from the window of a tram.

"The Jews are herded together like cattle," he wrote in his diary. "Carrying their bundles on their backs. . . . Parting from their familiar living rooms, their friends and acquaintances. While we are eating cherries, one basket after another."[94]

Barbara Ledermann, the older sister of Anne's friend Sanne, was passing as a non-Jew outside Amsterdam, using false papers, but had chosen that weekend to visit her family. When the roundup began, her parents insisted that she leave. She went from bridge to bridge, trying to cajole a policeman into letting her out, until she finally found one willing to look the other way for an attractive teenage girl in the wrong place at the wrong time. On the other side of the bridge, Barbara remembered, it looked like any other Sunday; people were going to church, apparently oblivious to what was happening two streets away. The Nazis picked up her parents and Sanne, deported them to Auschwitz, and gassed them.[95] Hannah Goslar, together with her father and her sister, was also picked up in this *razzia;* her family remained in Westerbork for months before being transported to Bergen-Belsen.

The Franks decided that it was too dangerous to go out. The glasses would have to wait. In the meantime, Anne gave up learning shorthand, fearing the strain on her eyes.

Anne's eye problems may also have been caused by the unusual amount of reading and writing she was doing. In addition to her diary, she had started writing "sketches" of life in the Annex: lighthearted descriptions of the daily routines around waking up, dinner, chores; a page-long diatribe titled "Villains!" about the Van Pelses' negligence in controlling their cat's fleas, which were making it impossible for the residents to sleep; a set piece in which each resident's style of peeling potatoes becomes a referendum on his or her character:

> *Mr. Pfeffer begins. He may not always peel them very well, but he does peel non-stop, glancing left and right to see if everyone is doing*

> *it the way he does. . . . To Father, peeling potatoes is not a chore, but precision work. When he reads, he has a deep wrinkle in the back of his head. But when he's preparing potatoes, beans or vegetables, he seems to be totally absorbed in his task. He puts on his potato-peeling face, and when it's set in that particular way, it would be impossible for him to turn out anything less than a perfectly peeled potato.*[96]

Anne wrote many of these sketches on separate pages and copied them into a notebook she titled "Book of Tales," complete with a table of contents and a date for each one.

In addition, she wrote reminiscences of life in the *inhabited world.* Perhaps thinking about how another September was about to come and go without her return to school, she chronicled her anxiety two years earlier about the first day at the Jewish Lyceum, her delight at getting Hannah switched into her class, the time she tattled on her classmates for cheating on a French test. She devoted a sketch to Miss Biegel, the hand-wringing biology teacher who had reminded her of a little mouse, and another to Mr. Keesing, who had made her write all those essays as punishment for talking in math class.[97] Was she unconsciously memorializing her teachers or simply remembering a happier time?

Anne was writing fiction, too, from character sketches to fables and fairy tales. *My pen-children are now piling up*, she wrote in August 1943.[98] She had started as early as the previous fall; on the night Bep spent in the Annex, Margot read one of Anne's fairy tales aloud. "I can still see Margot's face: 'Yes, Anne wrote these all by herself,'" Bep later remembered.[99] Anne asked Bep for help getting the stories published, but Bep had no idea how to go about it. Later Anne asked Kleiman to submit them to *The Prince*, a weekly magazine, but he thought it was too risky, even under a pseudonym.[100]

One of Anne's favorites, "Eva's Dream"—*my best fairy tale*, *and the queer thing about it is that I don't know where it comes from*— can be read as a fable about maturation.[101] A girl named Eva falls asleep wishing that she could be as "calm and friendly" as the moon outside her window. In her dream, an elf takes her to a beautiful park and describes the flowers as if they were human. The bluebell is "simple and kind," while the rose is "like a spoiled child . . . beautiful, sweet-smelling and elegant, but if things aren't going her way, she shows her thorns." Eva gets the message and resolves to be less like a rose and more like a bluebell; eventually she realizes the elf was her own conscience. When Mrs. van Pels asked to hear some of Anne's tales, "Eva's Dream" was one of the ones Anne chose to read. Mrs. van Pels *thought that was very nice.*[102]

Some of the stories have obvious parallels to Anne's situation: isolated girls, sometimes with one or both parents dead, suffer through miserable circumstances but try to make the best of things, often by finding comfort in faith and in the natural world. In "Fear," a sketch of a family living in a city under siege, the narrator runs away during an air raid, reaches a field, and falls asleep under the sky, where she wakes up feeling that "God is much closer than most people think." "The Flower Girl" tells of twelve-year-old Krista, who lives alone with her sister and has to walk two and a half hours each way to the market every day to sell flowers. When she gets home, chores await, but finally, at sunset, she can relax in a meadow, which makes all her labors worthwhile. "There in the meadow, among the flowers and the grass, beneath the wide-open sky, Krista is content. Gone is her exhaustion, gone are the market and the people; she thinks and dreams only of the present . . . alone with God and Nature."[103]

Anne wrote in her diary of her own joy in nature, but with an important difference. Unlike Krista, she wasn't content to enjoy it alone. More than anything, she longed to share it with a beloved person.

5

Lover
Anne and Peter van Pels, 1943–1944

My longing to talk to someone became so intense that somehow or other I decided to speak to Peter.

THE *DIARY* IS A STUDY OF human psychology under extreme stress. As the novelty of the situation wore off and the months stretched endlessly on, the adults responded to their straitened circumstances by picking fights with one another. The teens turned inward, sublimating their repressed energy in intellectual activity. *One day we laugh and see the comical side of the situation, but the next we are afraid, fear, suspense and despair staring from our faces.*[1]

By fall 1943, after more than a year in hiding, the mood in the Annex had reached a new low. The *inhabited world* was no longer inhabited by Dutch Jews. Amsterdam was officially *Judenrein:* all the Jews living openly in the city, including members of the Jewish Council and their families—several thousand people—had been deported to Westerbork on the eve of Rosh Hashanah.[2] No exemptions were given anymore. The only Jews who remained in the city were in hiding. The silence about what was happening to friends and neighbors may have been worse than the news had been. On New Year's Eve 1943, Queen Wilhelmina stated in a speech—broadcast on Radio Orange and published in an underground newspaper—that the destruction of the Jewish community in the Netherlands had "unfortunately become almost a fact."[3] Meanwhile, air-raid warnings in response to Allied bombers brought hope, but also fear: what if the Annex were hit?

You've probably noticed I'm going through a spell of being depressed, Anne confided to Kitty. She lost her appetite and began taking valerian pills for anxiety. *All this quarreling and weeping and nervous tension are so unsettling that in the evening I drop into my bed crying, thanking heaven that I sometimes have half an hour to myself.* The other residents, too, were starting to crack, engaging in arguments so bitter that they could no longer be concealed from the helpers. When Pfeffer complained that he was treated like an outcast, Edith snapped that they all found him a great disappointment. He started referring to Mrs. van Pels as "that old heifer"; she, in turn, called him an "old maid." More than once, Bep had to run up from the office to tell them all to be quieter.[4]

Anne's temper, too, was "explosive," Bep later said. Once, while she was visiting, Otto spoke sharply to Anne, who ran to her room in tears. Neither Edith nor Margot made a move to comfort her, so Bep went in. To her surprise, when she saw Anne crying, she too began to weep. Then she put her arms around Anne and spontaneously began to dance, twirling her around the little room. They both burst out laughing.[5]

The previous year, Miep and Bep had thrilled Anne, Margot, and Peter with their first St. Nicholas Day festivities. Now, as December approached, Kleiman was hospitalized multiple times for abdominal problems, possibly ulcers. Then Bep had to quarantine for six weeks with diphtheria. With shortages still rampant and two of their protectors out of commission, Anne and Otto came up with a modest plan to cheer up the others. With little in the way of gifts to share, they filled the other residents' shoes with lighthearted poems:

> St. Nicholas has come once more
> Though not quite as he came before.
> We can't celebrate his day
> In last year's fine and pleasant way. . . .[6]

The humor could not disguise an evidently grim occasion. Anne ("Little Anne, the youngest child / With fear she sometimes grows quite wild") got a valerian tablet. For Edith, there was a radish.

In a sign of how low Anne was feeling, the pace of her diary entries slowed down to only a handful each month.[7] *The atmosphere is so oppressive, and sleepy and as heavy as lead; you don't hear a single bird singing outside, and a deadly sultry silence hangs everywhere, catching hold of me as if it would drag me down deep into an underworld.* Despite—or perhaps because of—being among others day and night, she was lonely for a real friend. In her dreams, her grandmother appeared to her as a kind of guardian angel. She dreamed, too, about Hannah, picturing her friend *clothed in rags, her face thin and worn*, and regretted having neglected their friendship during their year together at the Jewish Lyceum.[8]

And in early January 1944, she dreamed about Peter Schiff, whom she had a crush on when she was around ten and he was thirteen. *I can still see us walking hand in hand through the streets together.* A friend convinced him that she was too childish for him, and he broke up with her, as she now told Kitty. *I adored him so that I didn't want to face it.* She realized that chasing him would do no good, so she resigned herself to the loss, but she continued to hope he would change his mind. The last time she had seen him was at the end of June 1942, on an evening when she was out with Hello Silberberg; she was pleased that he noticed her in the company of another boy. Now, she dreamed that they were sitting together, looking at a book, when he gazed at her and said, "If I had only known, I would have come to you long before . . . !" When she awoke, she could still feel the softness of his cheek against hers.[9]

Who has not had a dream like this, in which a beloved person, now lost, appears so vividly that we can feel their touch? Imagine waking from such a dream as a teenager in hiding, hungry, without privacy, surrounded by uncomprehending adults. For a year and a half in the Annex, Anne realized, she had been longing, *often consciously but much more often unconsciously, for trust, love and caresses.* In the beginning, she thought this meant she missed her cat. Now she recognized it as a longing for love. *I long for every boy, even for Peter [van Pels]—here. I want to shout at him: "Oh say something to me, don't just smile all the time, touch me, so that I can again get that delicious feeling inside me that I first had in my dream."*[10] The two Peters began to blur into one.

Until this time Anne hadn't taken much notice of Peter van Pels, except to complain about how boring he was. *He flops lazily on his bed half the time, does a bit of carpentry and then goes back for another snooze. What a fool!*[11] Perhaps he, too, was overwhelmed and depressed. He may also have been intimidated by Anne. His talents were vocational rather than intellectual: furniture making, carpentry, upholstery. Later he told her that before the Annex, whenever he had seen her, she was "always surrounded by 2 or more boys and a whole troupe of girls . . . always laughing and always the center of everything!"[12] Miep found both him and Margot difficult to read: unlike Anne, the older teenagers "made no requests, let me know no needs, [shared] nothing of themselves."[13] By the end of 1943, she worried they were growing even more remote.

People who write about Anne tend to view Peter from the perspective of her published *Diary:* sweet, a little dull, and ultimately not ambitious or thoughtful enough for her—a *disappointment*, as she would say in May 1944.[14] In her book about Anne, Francine Prose judges him to be "moody, mercurial, restless, not especially perceptive . . . a scrim on which the isolated girl can project her loneliness and longing."[15] In the Broadway adaptation, when they're not kissing, he serves mainly as an audience for Anne's lectures about the oppression of minorities.

Her complaints about him notwithstanding, Anne's depiction of Peter, even before she becomes infatuated with him, is actually kinder than this. She noticed that he could be *quite funny* when he came out of his shell. Like her, he enjoyed dressing up, which they did to entertain the others. *He appeared in one of Mrs. VP's very narrow dresses and I in his suit [and] we topped it all off with a hat and a cap. The grownups were doubled up with laughter and we enjoyed ourselves as much as they did.*[16] Anne looked down on him as something of an ignoramus, but she also described his room as overflowing with books, albeit ones *covered—with a boy's typical disregard of elegance—with brown paper.*[17] Though he was only fifteen when he went into hiding—his sixteenth and seventeenth birthdays took place in the Annex, and his eighteenth at Auschwitz—the men trusted him to make evening rounds of the premises and to accompany them downstairs when they feared that someone had broken in. *He's always been modest and helpful, but I have the feeling that he's much more sensitive than people realize or would ever suspect.*[18] The Broadway play and film portray him as lazy, but he apparently did chores without complaint, including hard labor like chopping wood and hauling heavy items to the attic. His poem for St. Nicholas Day 1943, likely written by either Anne or Otto, attests to his many responsibilities:

> Who keeps the attic spick and span?
> Peter is the very man.
> Who gets the spuds, the coals for heat,
> Creeps downstairs in his stockinged feet?

Feeds the cats downstairs, you bet
Peter never will forget.
Who fetches wood, who cleans the grate,
Washes clothes when it's late?
Piet does that and much much more
That's what St. Nick likes him for.[19]

* * *

The beginning of 1944 saw something of a change in Anne. After an impatient wait—probably extended by her poor nutrition in the Annex—she had finally gotten her period a few months earlier, to her delight. She felt a new maturity, which contributed to her longing for love. For the first time, she found herself able to rise above the petty remarks made by the Van Pelses and Pfeffer. She also felt newly spiritual. One night, despite the risk of an air raid, she went down to the warehouse alone. *I realized that I was a-person-to-myself, not needing to rely on the support of others. My fear vanished, I looked up at the sky and trusted in God.*[20]

As with many teenagers, the changes in Anne brought a desire for privacy that drove a wedge between her and the adults. *I am not prudish, Kitty, but when they keep talking here about what they've been doing in the lavatory, I feel my whole body rise up in revolt against it.*[21] At the same time, her parents refused to talk with her about sex. Edith's idea of advice on the subject was "Never speak of such things to boys and don't reply if they begin about it!"[22] When Anne once asked her what the clitoris was for, she said she didn't know. Otto, too, answered her questions evasively. Anne had learned most of what she knew about sex from Jacqueline van Maarsen. The two girls examined the instruction manual from a box of Edith's tampons and looked at an explicit book at the home of another classmate.[23] At one of their sleepovers, Anne, whose breasts had then not yet begun to develop—she sometimes stuffed cotton in one of Margot's bras—

suggested to Jacqueline that they touch each other's breasts. Jacqueline refused, though she did allow Anne to kiss her on the cheek.[24]

One day in January, this new Anne—desperately lonely, keenly aware of her own physicality, dreaming of her past crush—decided Peter van Pels wasn't as boring as she had thought. The two of them were engaged in the daily chore of peeling potatoes when he mentioned that Boche, a cat in the warehouse they had thought was pregnant, was actually male. (The residents called the cat Boche—a derogatory nickname for the Germans—because he picked fights with the attic cat and always lost. The attic cat, naturally, was named Tommy, after the British.) Anne asked how he knew, and Peter admitted that he had watched the cat "having intercourse."[25] She was embarrassed, but also fascinated.

Later the two of them went down to the warehouse to check out Boche together. Peter picked him up and gave her a matter-of-fact tour of the cat's genitalia. He didn't know the Dutch word for penis, so he called it "the male organ." Anne volunteered that the female counterpart was called a vagina. To her astonishment, Peter informed her that when he had questions about sex, he asked his parents, who "had more experience."[26] Well! Here is a different perspective on the loudmouth Van Pelses. Perhaps their lack of a filter had certain advantages over the Franks' reserve. Later, Anne wanted to ask Peter if he knew what female genitalia looked like but wondered *how in heaven's name . . . to explain the setup to him* if he didn't.[27]

I'm longing—so longing—for everything, Anne confided to Kitty on February 12. Two days later, she started to notice Peter noticing her. *I made a special effort not to look at him too much, because whenever I did, he kept on looking too and then—yes, then—it gave me a lovely feeling inside.* When she went up to the attic to get some books for Pfeffer, Peter followed her, but they were interrupted by his father. Later, he sought her out alone and *unburdened himself.* He hated to talk, he told her, because he so easily got "tongue-tied," stuttering and becoming confused. He admired Anne for being "never at a loss for a word, you say exactly what you want to say to people." She assured him that often her words didn't come out exactly the way she intended, but Peter wasn't dissuaded. As he fulminated about Pfeffer—a subject on which she could deeply empathize—Anne looked at him and saw something new. *Something was burning inside him just as it burns in me.*[28]

* * *

Something's holding me back here. It's one of Anne's elves—that is to say, my conscience. Didn't I promise to write alongside her rather than over her? When I look up from my desk, she's watching me from the sofa across the room, her legs curled under her. "How could you?" I hear her say. "You know I didn't want to publish all that."

I do know it. This is the biggest change made by Otto—and everyone else who has edited, adapted, or otherwise worked on the diary in his wake. In her revision, Anne took out most of her feelings for Peter. Otto put them back in.

Why did Anne edit her romance with Peter out of her diary? We can't know, just as we can't know for certain why, a couple of months after her infatuation peaked—*I believe I'm pretty near to being in love with him . . . Oh Peter, just say something at last, don't let me drift on between hope and dejection*—her feelings seem to have cooled.[29] Maybe, like many adults as well as teenagers, she enjoyed the thrill of the chase ("conquest" is the word she uses) more than its satisfaction, with the corresponding decrease in excitement. Maybe she realized they didn't have enough to talk about, and that the romance was driven by circumstances rather than real affinity. Maybe the daily contact hastened the relationship's progress toward an inevitable conclusion. Maybe she simply found the details of her first love too personal to publish. (Would you like to publish your private romantic ramblings for the world to read?) She also took out other things of an extremely intimate nature, such as her descriptions of her body, her desire to touch Jacqueline's breasts, and her dreams.

And why, if we can speculate, did Otto put the love story back in? He died, at the age of ninety-one, in 1980, six years before the Critical Edition was first published, so he was never asked explicitly about the editorial choices that he made—very few people were aware of them. Try to put yourself in his position: as a parent, but also as an editor—in certain ways, one could even say a co-author—who was trying to create a book at once true to Anne's vision as well as capable of finding a wide audience. He must have had some instinct to protect his daughter's privacy, to respect her wish that this aspect of her experience not be laid out on the page for the titillation of the reading public. But, as the French critic Philippe Lejeune observes in a brilliant essay examining the edits to the diary, Otto's work was predicated on the knowledge that Anne had died.[30] The dead do not require the same protection as the living. The deaths of Anne and Peter gave Otto tacit permission to lift Anne's censorship of their love story.

The editing decisions Otto made in this section of Anne's diary—not just the reinstatement of the entries but some of the small changes he made to them—may also reflect the ways his own relationship with Peter changed while they were imprisoned together at Auschwitz. In the Annex, we already see Otto behaving in a fatherly way toward Peter, helping him with his studies together with Anne and Margot. After the Annex residents were deported to Auschwitz, Peter managed to get a plum work assignment in the camp post office (SS soldiers and non-Jewish prisoners were allowed to receive mail and packages). This job spared him the hardest labor and allowed him extra rations, which he shared with his father and Otto.[31]

Hermann van Pels was selected for gassing in early October

1944 after injuring himself while digging a trench. Peter and Otto watched as he was marched away; later, they saw the gassed prisoners' clothing in a truck. Afterward, Peter treated Otto as a surrogate father. When Otto was admitted to the hospital barracks for severe diarrhea in November, Peter visited him every day, bringing food. In Otto's recollection, they never talked about Anne.[32]

On January 18, 1945, as the Russian army approached Auschwitz, the Nazis announced that they would evacuate the camp and force prisoners to march on foot toward Germany. A doctor friend told Otto it would be safer for him to remain in the hospital, and Otto tried to persuade Peter to stay there with him. "Peter, hide yourself," Otto begged him. "You can hide yourself here in the hospital upstairs or somewhere."[33] Peter refused. According to Otto, he believed he had a chance of surviving the march because he was young, reasonably well fed, and still fairly strong. But perhaps he simply couldn't bear the idea of any more hiding.

* * *

I also imagine that Otto's desire to complete Anne's edits in the way she might have wanted—remember, she left Version B unfinished—was overruled by the experience of reading her love story. Otto was a reader; in the Annex, his favorite form of recreation was an hour with his Dickens. And as a reader, he must have been enchanted by Anne's genuine, emotional, real-time narration of her budding romance. It lightens the gloomy atmosphere of the Annex and brings new momentum to the endless succession of days in hiding. An adolescent reading it will sigh along with each of Anne's vicissitudes; for an adult, it poignantly recalls the memory of first love. And if what Anne says about Otto and Edith is true, we know that his own marriage may have been a romantic disappointment.

Not long after Otto published the *Diary*, he embarked upon a new love. His second wife was Elfriede (Fritzi) Geiringer, a Jew from Austria who had sought refuge in the Netherlands and knew Otto through the community of German Jews there. Together with her husband and children, Heinz and Eva (the same ages as Margot and Anne), Fritzi too had been in Auschwitz; her husband and her son did not survive. She recognized Otto in occupied Poland, "a man with a small head who was shepherding some of his sick and weakened comrades and lovingly taking care of them"; they encountered each other again on the transport back to the Netherlands.[34] In Amsterdam, Otto made a practice of trying to support other Jews who had returned from the camps or come out of hiding, including Fritzi and Eva.

Seven years later, they were married. Fritzi became Otto's partner on all matters related to the diary, often joining him in meetings with publishers and adapters and helping with his extensive correspondence. Otto sometimes accompanied her to work, Fritzi on the tram, he riding alongside on his bike. At each stop, they blew each other kisses.[35]

When Otto—widowed, without a family—read Anne's lines about her growing love, *that which is still embryonic and impressionable and which we neither of us dare to name or touch*, he may have wondered if he would ever experience that again. *Love is understanding someone, caring for someone, sharing their ups and downs. And in the long run that also means physical love, you have shared something, given something away and received something . . . someone will stand by you, will understand you for the rest of your life.*[36] Perhaps those lines were in his head as he looked at Fritzi, as he imagined his new life with her.

One thing is certain: Otto knew that love makes for good reading. Had Anne lived to finish editing her diary and gained perspective on her relationship with Peter, she might have realized that and changed her mind. She, too, cared about a good story.

* * *

One more thing before we continue. Some contemporary readers view the entry for January 6, 1944, in which Anne describes wanting to touch Jacqueline van Maarsen's breasts, as evidence that she was attracted to girls. Let's look at it in full.

> *Sometimes, when I lie in bed at night, I have a terrible desire to feel my breasts and to listen to the quiet rhythmic beat of my heart.*
>
> *I already had these kinds of feelings subconsciously before I came here, because I remember one night when I slept with Jacque I could not contain myself, I was so curious to see her body, which she always kept hidden from me and which I had never seen. I asked Jacque whether as a proof of our friendship we might feel one another's breasts. Jacque refused. I also had a terrible desire to kiss Jacque and that I did. I go into ecstasies every time I see the naked figure of a woman, such as Venus in the Springer History of Art, for example. It strikes me sometimes as so wonderful and exquisite that I have difficulty not letting the tears roll down my cheeks.*
>
> *If only I had a girl friend!*[37]

Many readers who come upon this passage in the Definitive Edition of Anne's diary—the version incorporating material from Version A, which was published in English translation in 1995 and is now the best-selling version of the *Diary* in America—believe that it was not included in the originally published edition. Some express anger at what they perceive as the censoring of Anne's bisexuality. "When I was just discovering I liked both girls and boys, there was an actual, real life person who could have told me those feelings were natural?" one critic writes. "Representation matters, and to discover I was denied that representation when I needed it most was all too painful." Another comments, "Let's face it, if her sexual orientation hadn't been erased, the diaries wouldn't have been widely published."[38]

At the same time, social conservatives have attacked this passage as inappropriate for children. They target especially the graphic adaptation of Anne's diary, which incorporates both the sleepover with Jacqueline and Anne's ecstasy at the sight of a female nude, illustrated with an image of her walking through a garden filled with classical statues. A Republican representative from Florida has said that the graphic adaptation constitutes "Anne Frank pornography." In September 2023, a teacher in Texas was fired for using it in the classroom. Jennifer Pippin, a spokesperson for a group called Moms for Liberty, told journalists that the graphic adaptation is "not the actual work . . . It chooses to offer a different view on the subject."[39]

So many people have alleged that this passage appears only in later versions of the *Diary* that I have trouble trusting my own eyes, which clearly show that Otto included it in the first U.S. edition, albeit with some minor alterations. Here is the passage as it was originally published in English:

> *Sometimes, when I lie in bed at night, I have a terrible desire to feel my breasts and to listen to the quiet rhythmic beat of my heart.*
>
> *I already had these kinds of feelings subconsciously before I came here, because I remember that once when I slept with a girl friend I had a strong desire to kiss her, and that I did do so. I could not help being terribly inquisitive over her body, for she had always kept it hidden from me. I asked her whether, as a proof of our friendship, we should feel one another's breasts, but she refused. I go into ecstasies every time I see the naked figure of a woman, such as Venus, for example. It strikes me [sometimes] as so wonderful and exquisite that I have difficulty in stopping the tears rolling down my cheeks.*
>
> *If only I had a girl friend!*[40]

These changes are typical of the way Otto edited the *Diary*. He rearranged things, he condensed a little, and he took out details he regarded as extraneous. In this case, as with many of the later entries about Peter, his editing also involved reinstating an entry that Anne had deleted in Version B.

Yes: Anne removed almost all of the January 6 entry—a multi-page meditation on Edith's insensitivity toward her, her feelings about going through puberty and getting her period, and her desire to kiss Jacqueline and touch her breasts—from the version of her diary that she wished to publish. Otto put the material back in. He removed Jacqueline's name: in the first published version of the *Diary*, she appears under the pseudonym Jopie, but here he chose to omit even that identifier. Still, he kept the substance of the entry. To say that he "censored" Anne, as many readers have done, is wrong.[41]

Where does this misconception come from? In an article for the *New York Times* about the publication of the Critical Edition, the journalist Herbert Mitgang stated that Otto deleted Anne's references to menstruation, "together with the reference to two girls touching each other's breasts."[42] (Note that the reference was actually to two girls *not* touching each other's breasts.) As best I can tell, this comes from a misreading of the Dutch historian Gerrold van der Stroom's essay "The Diaries, *Het Achterhuis*, and the Translations," which appears in the Critical Edition and summarizes the changes made by Otto as well as by the book's publishers. Mitgang's sentence about (unidentified) girls touching each other's breasts is an unattributed quote from this essay. Van der Stroom explains that the Dutch publisher of the *Diary* removed the reference.[43]

But Mitgang apparently did not read further, because if he had, he would have seen that the omission troubled Otto. Although the first French translation of *Het Achterhuis* seems to have been based on the Dutch version, Otto saw a new opportunity with the English-language version. In July 1951, he personally brought the text of the passages that the Dutch publisher had deleted to the London offices of Vallentine, Mitchell, the *Diary*'s British publisher. As an editor there explained to Barbara Mooyaart-Doubleday, the first translator of the *Diary* into English, the passages had been cut "because they were either too long, or were likely to offend Dutch Puritan or Catholic susceptibilities. . . . We think the English edition definitely ought to contain them."[44] The passages were reinstated and appeared in the first English-language edition of the *Diary* as well as in every later edition. As Van der Stroom's account makes clear, not only did Otto *not* censor the passage about Anne and Jacqueline (though Anne did that herself), he insisted that it be restored.

Why? Likely because he didn't find it remarkable. Anne's interest in another girl's breasts was of a piece with her interest in sex more generally. At the time of this sleepover, Anne was twelve years old. Many adolescents are curious about their friends' bodies in a way that may or may not have implications for their adult sexual orientation. As one contemporary journalist writes, "Speculating over a minor's sexuality—no matter who they are!—is predatory behavior, especially when said minor is in no position to comment. Labeling Anne without her consent is disgracing her memory."[45] Although "predatory" goes too far, it seems presumptuous to impose a label on Anne's developing sexuality.

Still, Jacqueline's memoir does depict Anne's behavior toward her as having something of a romantic quality. On the first day of school, Anne pursues her as the girls are bicycling and insists that they ride home together—not only on that day, but "from now on." "I hadn't noticed her in class, and felt a little awkward to have to ask for her name," Jacqueline wrote. She liked Anne right away and was happy to spend time with her but also found her possessive. "After a few days, Anne firmly declared that I was her best friend and she mine. . . . It wasn't always easy being Anne's best friend. She was very demanding and quickly jealous." Among the scenes from *Joop ter Heul* that they enjoyed acting out together was a marriage proposal: "We'd burst out laughing every time Leo made an ardent attempt to kiss Joop, only to be fobbed off with a cherry bonbon."[46] Anne also doesn't seem to have been as physically attracted to Peter as she expected to be—another possible sign of interest in girls.

There is no way to know what the adult Anne's sexual orientation would have been. But once she settled on Peter van Pels as her love interest, she doesn't seem to have been distracted by thoughts of Jacqueline or any other girl. Later on in the same entry, in a passage that has attracted less attention, Anne insists, *You mustn't think I'm in love with Peter—not a bit of it! If the v.P.'s had had a girl instead of a boy, I should have tried to tell her something about myself and to let her tell me things as well.*[47] Before long, she changed her mind. *I'm glad after all that the v.P.'s have a son and not a daughter, my conquest could never have been so difficult, so beautiful, so good, if I had not happened to hit on someone of the opposite sex.*[48]

* * *

April 15, 1944: Day 650 in hiding. Anne and Peter are together in his room, the smallest in the Annex, crowded with items from *the inhabited world:* a cardboard armoire stuffed with the Van Pelses' clothes, Peter's bicycle wrapped in packing paper and suspended from the ceiling, three genuine Persian carpets on the floor. Sheets of cardboard line the ceiling, to keep rain and cat pee (one of the cats has been missing the litter box) from leaking from the attic. Like Anne, Peter has decorated the walls with photos of movie stars. As they sit on the divan, he puts his arm around her, pulling her close, and she lies with her head against his chest as he strokes her hair. When they get up to go downstairs, he kisses her. Mostly through her hair, but she still regards it as her *first kiss.*[49]

It took them almost two months—two months of evenings

spent confessing their secrets by the attic window; two months of near daily diary entries chronicling Anne's delight in their intimacy, her impatience at the slow pace of its unfolding, her agony when he ignored her—to get here. Those months were particularly difficult ones. Miep, Bep, and Kleiman all fell ill. In addition, their source for ration coupons was arrested, resulting in a precipitous decline in the already poor quality of the food. In March, the residents' diet was reduced to porridge, milk, and a hash made from old kale, which smelled like *a mixture of W.C., bad plums, preservatives + 10 rotten eggs.* Things improved when the protectors returned, though not by much. The Annex Eight typically went through "food cycles," periods in which there was only one primary food available. In April, it was potatoes, sometimes accompanied by kidney beans (which Anne could no longer stomach), pea soup, or—*by the grace of God*—turnip tops or rotten carrots. *The greatest attraction each week is a slice of liver sausage, and jam on dry bread.* Anne continued to worry about the effects of deprivation on the residents' ability to live in polite society again. After Miep described a sumptuous meal at the wedding of a wealthy couple, she mused, *If we had been at the party we should undoubtedly have snatched up the whole lot and left not even the furniture in place!*[50]

On the night before Easter, the residents had their worst scare yet. Peter knocked on the Franks' bedroom door late at night and asked Otto for help with an English translation. Anne instantly knew it was a ruse: something was going on downstairs. The men went down to the warehouse while the women waited in the Annex. *Four frightened women just have to talk, so talk we did, until we heard a bang.*

Otto and Mr. van Pels reappeared, *white and nervous.* The men had frightened off burglars in the act of raiding the warehouse, but the would-be thieves had broken a plank on the front door. What if the police noticed the damage and came to investigate? They tried to cover the hole, but a couple walking past shone a flashlight inside, and they retreated upstairs, fearing discovery.

There was nothing to do but wait in silence. *It turned half past 10, 11, but not a sound. . . . Then, a quarter past 11, a bustle and noise downstairs.* They heard footsteps moving through the office, the downstairs kitchen, then to the staircase leading to the Annex. The bookcase rattled. *"Now we are lost!" I said and could see all fifteen of us being carried off by the Gestapo that very night.* (Anne included the protectors among the fifteen.)

The bookcase did its job to conceal the Annex, and the footsteps retreated. But could someone still be lying in wait outside? The residents, huddled in the larger room on the upper level—at that hour, normally the Van Pelses' bedroom—stayed put all night. In whispers they wondered if they should destroy their radio before the police arrived, or Anne's diary, which Mrs. van Pels suggested burning to protect their helpers from incrimination. *This, and when the police rattled the cupboard door, were my worst moments; not my diary, if my diary goes I go with it!* But nothing happened. *Four o'clock, five o'clock, half past 5.* Anne went to sit beside Peter, *so close that we could feel the quivering of each other's bodies.* By morning, they deemed it safe enough to go down to the office and phone Kleiman for help. Miep and Jan finally arrived a few hours later. "At the sight of us, Anne ran and threw her arms around my neck," Miep wrote. "She was in tears. The others gathered round us, almost as though they could be reassured only by a touch, by some contact with us."[51]

The tension must have worn on Peter, too. A few days after the break-in, he forgot to unbolt the front door one morning, forcing Kugler and the warehouse men to enter through a window when they arrived for work. Both cats, to whom he was greatly attached, got sick. He can't have enjoyed the Annex food any more than Anne did. Perhaps all these factors combined to give him the courage to bring their relationship to the next level. Or perhaps—he was, after all, a seventeen-year-old boy—he just needed the physical comfort of holding a girl in his arms.

Anne was ecstatic about the kiss. By the next day, however, she was already starting to feel the pricking of her conscience. For weeks, the adults had been nervous about the amount of time she was spending in Peter's room. "Can I really trust the two of you up there?" Mrs. van Pels teased. Pfeffer lectured Peter that "it's not right to receive young girls in your room so late at night." For the sake of propriety, Anne asked Peter to start coming downstairs to invite her up rather than waiting for her to initiate the visit, but he didn't always remember. A few weeks after the first kiss, she confessed to Otto that the two of them didn't "sit miles apart" when they were together. "Do you think it's wrong?" she asked him.[52]

Did she think it was wrong? Recording her fantasies about Peter Schiff, Anne insisted that she understood sexual desire: *with all my heart and soul, I give myself completely!* But her definition of "completely" reveals how strictly she adhered to the conventional morality of her time: *he may touch my face, but no more.*[53] Now, she worried about her honor. Margot, she was certain, would never kiss a boy unless marriage was imminent. *What would my girl friends or Jacque say about it if they knew that I lay in Peter's arms, my heart against his chest, my head on his shoulder and with his head and face against mine! . . . Is it right that I should have yielded so soon, that I am so ardent, just as ardent and eager as Peter himself?*[54]

Anne decided that under the circumstances, the normal rules didn't apply. Otto seems initially to have agreed, though he told her to try to avoid seeing too much of Peter—as if that were possible. Though he was too delicate to say so, his concerns were likely practical as well as moral. The Annex could not accommodate an infant. The Goslars had been unable to go into hiding when the Franks did because Ruth Goslar had been pregnant; they also had a two-year-old. It was hard enough for adults and teenagers to be silent and still for most of their waking hours, but for a baby or a small child, it would be impossible. And how could they handle another mouth to feed?[55] After thinking about it overnight, he all but ordered her to end the physical relationship. "Don't go upstairs so often, don't encourage him more than you can help," he cautioned. "It is the man who is always the active one in these things; the woman can hold him back."[56]

Anne didn't want to give Peter up, but she also didn't want to sneak around, even if she could have. She responded to Otto with anger: how dare he tell her what to do? Perhaps drawing new confidence from her relationship with Peter, she lashed out at her father in a letter. She was not the little girl he thought she was. *I have now reached the stage that I can live entirely on my own, without Mummy's support or anyone else's for that matter.* (She must have meant emotional support rather than material, since they were all dependent on the helpers.) Any teenager might have felt this way, but in Anne's case it was more defensible. *You can't and mustn't regard me as fourteen, for all these troubles have made me older.* Her father would have to either forbid her to see Peter (which he could not do) or trust her to do the right thing. To her dismay, her letter prompted a sorrowful response from Otto, who was particularly hurt by her insistence that she didn't *feel in the least bit responsible to any of you.*[57] His willingness to forgive her only compounded her remorse.

Anne also worried about Margot's feelings. Her sister, who had just turned eighteen, was less than a year older than Peter, and she had wondered if Margot might be interested in him. Now that it was clear Peter preferred her, she knew that if she were Margot, she would be jealous. "I think it's so rotten that you should be the odd one out," she told her sister. "I'm used to that," Margot replied *somewhat bitterly*—a rare moment in which we see her as anything other than even-keeled.[58] Did she envy

Anne's close relationship with Otto? Anne doesn't speculate, and we can't know.

Within hours, Margot had regained her composure, reassuring Anne that she wasn't jealous. Though she was "a bit sorry that I haven't found anyone yet . . . with whom I can discuss my thoughts and feelings," she didn't begrudge Anne the fact that she had: "one misses enough here anyway." Margot added that she would want her boyfriend to be "someone whom I felt to be my superior intellectually, and that is not the case with Peter. But I can imagine it being so with you and Peter."[59] Francine Prose reads this line as a little dig at Anne's intellect. But Margot may simply have meant that the age gap between Anne and Peter was more appropriate.

Anne asked Peter not to let their physical relationship progress further, and he agreed. Nonetheless, the two of them continued their attic meetings. *All goes well*, Anne wrote in May. At last she had someone other than Kitty to listen to her. Though he had *the greatest difficulty in saying anything about himself*, he could be *very gradually drawn out.*[60] They shared complaints about their families' quarrels and about the estrangement between themselves and their parents. They talked about male and female anatomy in some detail, although the only anatomical terms Peter knew were German—apparently he did get all his information from his parents. She told him about her ambition to be a writer; he responded that he wanted to take care of her. She felt a new confidence in herself and the world, knowing that she could rely on him.

Anne's relationship with Peter also seems to have altered her feelings about his mother, for a long time second only to Pfeffer as the Annex resident she most despised. After listening to her mother and Mrs. van Pels giving Bep romantic advice, she had to admit that Peter's mother might understand young people better than Edith did. On the night of the break-in,

Anne comforted the terrified Mrs. van Pels, even after the older woman suggested burning her diary. A few weeks later, she tended to Mrs. van Pels after Peter accidentally injured her wrists. The grudges she had accumulated against Mrs. van Pels during nearly two years in the Annex seem to have faded once Anne came to see the woman she had once called *unspeakably disagreeable* as the mother of the boy she was involved with.[61]

Still, within a couple of months, Anne recognized that Peter wasn't living up to her fantasies of a boyfriend. *I don't get any satisfaction out of lying in each other's arms day in, day out, and would so like to feel that he's the same.* It was becoming apparent that he wasn't the same. Anne longed to be able to share her thoughts about God and nature, the ecstasy she felt when she gazed at the horse chestnut tree in bloom or looked deep into the night sky. In her diary, she recorded "A thought for Peter": *As long as you can look fearlessly at the heavens, as long as you know that you are pure within . . . you will still find happiness.* But she struggled to find a way to say it aloud. Peter hadn't broken through her *concrete armor* after all.[62]

She thought about reading to him from her "Favorite Quotes Notebook," a commonplace book she had started keeping at Otto's suggestion but which had become a deeply personal repository of ideas and sayings that resonated with her. Many of the quotations are religious in nature. Anne recorded lengthy passages from *I Begin Again*, a now-obscure memoir by an American woman named Alice Bretz, who lost her sight in midlife and espoused a "simple faith" based on gratitude and friendship with God. ("Alice Bretz wrote this book after she had gone blind," Anne noted to herself.) From a biography of Franz Liszt, she copied these lines: "To study the world and acknowledge it as God's creation, that is science. To depict the world in all its parts as God's creation, that is art."[63] But she must have sensed that this wasn't the way to reach Peter, and anyway it wasn't what she wanted. *I like it much better if he explains something to me than when I have to teach him, I would really adore him to be my superior in almost everything!*[64] Perhaps Margot's words had made an impression on her.

We talked about the most private things and yet up till now we have never touched on those things that filled, and still fill, my heart and soul, Anne ruminated in a long entry written on July 15, a few weeks before the raid on the Annex. *I still don't quite know what to make of Peter, is he superficial, or does he feel shy, even of me?*[65] Anne's reader also doesn't know what to make of Peter. As with so many things, we have little to go on other than her word.

One thing we do know is that Anne was not easy to get along with. She was smart, funny, and vivacious, but also moody and critical. Speaking her own mind came more naturally to her than listening to others. An unintentionally hilarious piece in her "Book of Tales" that purports to be an interview with Peter contains barely a word from him.[66] He apparently tolerated with good cheer her many efforts to improve him. ("I believe that you have good qualities, and that you'll get on in the world," she lectured him at one point.)[67] He was kind and supportive, and he respected the limits she set on the relationship. For her fifteenth birthday, he presented her with a bouquet of peonies, thanks to Miep.

Most readers assume that Anne ended the relationship in the Annex, but no breakup takes place in her diary. As of that July 15 entry, they were still meeting on intimate terms. At least one person who knew Anne and Peter later, at Westerbork, remembered that the two of them were inseparable there. Perhaps their changed circumstances brought them closer once more.

The final entry in Anne's "Favorite Quotes Notebook" is a passage from Oscar Wilde's play *An Ideal Husband,* in which the morally rigid Lady Gertrude Chiltern struggles to reconcile herself with a deception her husband committed in the past. "We women worship when we love; and when we lose our worship, we lose everything," she tells him. In Lord Robert's response, Anne may well have heard Peter's voice:

> Why can't you women love us, faults and all? Why do you place us on monstrous pedestals? We all have feet of clay, women as well as men; but when we men love women, we love them knowing their weaknesses, their follies, their imperfections, love them all the more, it may be, for that reason. It is not the perfect, but the imperfect, who have need of love.[68]

Whatever their differences, Peter and Anne had something extremely important in common. Both spent their *most meditative years* in the Annex.[69]

6

Artist
Anne and the Diary, 1943–1944

In a true book, the writer writes himself free.
—Frida de Clercq Zubli, *The Eternal Song*, quoted in Anne's "Favorite Quotes Notebook"

Once upon a time, there was an elf named Dora and a gnome named Peldron. Cheerful Dora smiled all day long; Peldron spent his days wailing at "all the misery in the world." One day a wise old gnome locked them up in a cottage together. They weren't allowed to go out or even to argue; all day long they had to do chores. Dora cooked and cleaned and spun thread; Peldron chopped wood, worked in the garden, and repaired shoes. Every night the gnome made sure they were following the rules.

As time went on, Dora's outlook rubbed off on Peldron. He became less gloomy and even laughed at her jokes. Meanwhile, she began to take life more seriously and to appreciate the value of hard work and struggle.

After a few months, the wise old gnome told them they

could go home. "Do you understand that being here has done you good?" he asked. They did not. "I brought you here so that you would learn that there is more to life than your own pleasure and sorrow," the gnome explained. "You'll now be able to deal with life much better than you did before. Dora has become a bit more serious and Peldron a bit more cheerful, precisely because you were forced to make the best of the situation in which you found yourselves."

And Dora and Peldron lived happily ever after.[1]

"The Wise Old Gnome" is probably one of the last stories Anne wrote: she copied it into her "Book of Tales" on April 18, 1944—Day 653 in hiding. It's part of a group of fairy tales that also include "Blurry the Explorer," about a teddy bear who thinks he wants to leave home but has all sorts of unpleasant experiences when he does, and "The Fairy," a moralistic fable about a fairy who travels the world helping people, which Anne presented to Otto as a gift on May 12, 1944, his fifty-fifth birthday. Scholars and readers have paid little attention to Anne's fiction, generally viewing it as charming but not up to the level of her diary and unworthy of analysis.[2] But the fairy tales clearly "parallel life in hiding," as Otto later said, and each of them can be read, in different ways, as representing Anne's desire to find meaning in her situation.[3]

The writer Carson McCullers, who was deeply affected by the *Diary* and at one point considered adapting it for the stage, was especially taken with "The Wise Old Gnome." In a short essay on Anne's fiction that she wrote in 1953 to help Otto get some of the stories published in America, she called it "a curious mingling of the conscious mind and the unconscious." The wise gnome, she believed, was a stand-in for "the father Anne loved so much," who served as peacekeeper in the Annex, helping the others to overcome their conflicts.[4]

That's possible, but another interpretation also comes to

mind. Like "Eva's Dream," Anne's fable about the rose and the bluebell, "The Wise Old Gnome" is a story about maturing—about learning to overcome one's limitations and grow into a better, more accepting person. The Annex, like the cottage in the story, was a crucible from which Anne, like the carefree elf Dora, emerged with a more nuanced understanding of the world around her. Any number of things contributed to that transformation: her persecution by the Nazis, the exigencies of life in hiding, her father's education and support, the experience of falling in love. But I believe the greatest catalyst of her change was her diary.

* * *

March 28, 1944: Day 632. The Annex Eight are listening to Radio Orange, the broadcast service of the Dutch government-in-exile in London. They used to listen to the evening news down in the office, after the employees had gone home. But after a spate of burglaries, they no longer leave their quarters at night. Instead, they all crowd around the table in the Annex kitchen/living room, at night the Van Pelses' bedroom.

At around 7:30 p.m., Gerrit Bolkestein, minister of education, arts and sciences, comes on to make a special address announcing the planned creation of a national archive of material relating to the war years.

"My fellow countrymen," Bolkestein begins, "I believe I am expressing what many among you must be feeling when I say that the struggle and the suffering of our people since May 10, 1940, constitutes a period of crisis in our existence as an independent nation—a crisis comparable in its significance only to those years in the sixteenth century when our people fought for and established that nation's independence."[5]

When Bolkestein says "our people," it's doubtful he means Dutch Jews, although Jews seeking refuge from persecution in

Spain and Portugal had already begun to arrive in the Netherlands by the late sixteenth century, attracted by the promise of a nation with freedom of religious practice. Still, those inclusive words must cheer the hearts of his listeners in the Annex, especially Anne, who hopes after the war to become a Dutch citizen. As Jewish refugees from Germany, her family has been officially stateless ever since Hitler's invasion of the Netherlands.

"But consider how poorly and how incompletely we are informed about the Eighty Years' War!" Bolkestein continues. "How painful the realization that we must do without—to take only a single example—the diary of an average citizen from the days of the siege and liberation of Leiden."

Are those the words that pique Anne's attention?

After the war, Bolkestein continues, the government plans to establish a national center to collect, edit, and publish "all historical material relating to these years": personal documents as well as copies of Dutch underground magazines, records of the Resistance, and so forth. Bolkestein acknowledges that some citizens might wish to keep their papers private. But in order for this center to become a "truly national" institution, all possible materials must be gathered in one place. "That is why I am calling on all listeners," he says.

> History cannot be written on the basis of official decisions and documents alone. If our descendants are to understand fully what we as a nation have had to endure and overcome during these years, then what we really need are ordinary documents—a diary, letters from a worker in Germany, a collection of sermons given by a parson or a priest. Not until we succeed in bringing together vast quantities of this simple, everyday material will the picture of our struggle for freedom be painted in its full depth and glory.

Imagine Anne, hearing these words. Nearly fifteen years old, she is no longer the "short, skinny girl with shiny black hair and rather sharp features" whom Jacqueline van Maarsen remembered from the Jewish Lyceum, whose schoolgirl photo—her hair tucked behind her right ear, her eyes gazing upward, her mouth serious—would become an unlikely icon.[6] She now stands five feet six inches tall, with breasts and hips that long ago burst the seams of the clothes in which she had arrived at the Annex. Miep later recalled that she was "spontaneous and still childish sometimes, but she had gradually acquired a new coyness and new maturity. She had arrived a girl, but she would leave a woman."[7]

Of course they all made a rush at my diary immediately, Anne records the next day. Her thoughts go immediately to its revision as *a romance*—that is to say, a novel—*of the "Secret Annex,"* although she worries that people will think that it's a detective story.[8] *But, seriously, it would be quite funny 10 years after the war if people were told how we Jews lived and what we ate and talked about here.*[9]

"If people were told"—that's Version A. Returning to it a few months later, Anne makes a small but significant revision: *But, seriously, it would be quite funny 10 years after the war if we Jews were to tell how we lived and what we ate and talked about here.*[10] The story of persecution can't be told by others. Those who lived it need to tell it themselves.

Although I tell you a lot, still, even so, you only know very little of our lives, Anne reflects, addressing her diary in the second person. The idea that others might read what she had written has made her conscious of all the things she has failed to communicate, such as how frightened the women in the house are during the air raids: when the British drop bombs on the port town of Ijmuiden, thirty miles away, windows rattle in Amsterdam. Or the epidemics raging in the city; the long lines for vegetables and other necessities; the rampant thefts and burglaries, even by children. *I would need to keep on writing the whole day if I were to tell you everything in detail.*[11]

* * *

At long last after a great deal of reflection I have started my "Achterhuis," Anne wrote at the end of May 1944. Nearly two months had passed since she and the other Annex residents had heard Bolkestein's call for documents. *In my head it is as good as finished, although it won't go as quickly as that really, if it ever comes off at all.*[12]

The time Anne spent puzzling over how to transform her personal diary into a publishable text speaks to the immense difficulty of the undertaking. To start with, a diary conveys meaning in ways other than its content. Literary critic Philippe Lejeune, one of the few to study diary-writing systematically, argues that the nontextual signifiers of a diary—all the methods by which it communicates information about itself and its subject, including type of notebook, paper, ink, handwriting style, spelling, and collaging of other items such as photographs or mementos—must be considered alongside the content. For Anne's diary, those nontextual signifiers include the shape, size, and color of her notebooks (the red-checkered one she started with as well as others she was able to finagle while in hiding, one of which started out as Margot's chemistry exercise book); her writing in print, cursive, and shorthand; the photographs she pasted on blank pages and the captions she wrote for them; and her later notes to herself scattered throughout the text. "To publish a journal, then, is like trying to fit a sponge into a matchbox," Lejeune writes.[13]

Even if the manuscript of a diary is relatively straightforward—like Anne's Version B, which she rewrote by hand onto loose vellum pages, similar to onionskin or carbon paper—the route to making it comprehensible to others is still not obvious.[14] As another scholar writes, a diary "is best read not as a book with a beginning and an end, but as a process."[15] While it shares characteristics with memoir, it is another genre entirely, one that is fragmentary, disorderly, and resistant to neat summation.

The problems of publishing a diary are inherent to its genre. There are different ways of defining that genre, but a diary is generally considered to be a text written as life is happening, "the daily recording of the thoughts, feelings, and activities of the writer, entered frequently and regularly,"as one critic describes it.[16] Whereas an autobiography or memoir is assumed to have a beginning, a middle, and an end, and to have been written by "a later self that derives from a former self," a diary isn't driven by plot but instead responds to events as they happen; it has no perspective on itself.[17] It may look back upon the past and ahead toward the future, but it doesn't know where its narrative will lead. A diary is always in process and can be considered finished only if circumstances prevent the writer from continuing the diary or if they decide to give it up: We know how Anne's diary ends, but she did not. It may be addressed to someone other than the diarist, either real or imaginary, as Anne's diary is addressed to "Kitty," but more often it is written for the diarist's eyes alone. A diary is personal: it may treat other topics, but its primary subject is the self. Because of this, a diary is almost always considered to be private—so much so that it may be kept locked.

Anne's diary was many things to her—a confidante for her emotions about her parents and Peter, an outlet for blowing off steam at Pfeffer and Mrs. van Pels, a safe place to work out her most deeply held beliefs—but it was not the coherent testimonial narrative she now wanted to write. If the idea, as Bolkestein had suggested, was to help others "understand fully what we as a nation have had to endure and overcome during these years," then she must have realized, as she flipped back to the first pages of her red-checkered notebook, that her diary was too focused on her personal life to fulfill that purpose.

That problem is most evident at the start. Anne receives the diary in June 1942, she spends a few happy weeks with her friends, and then—boom!—the door of the Annex shuts behind her. The entries she wrote during that time were lengthy but sparse: she might cover the events of an entire week in a single writing session. She hadn't yet decided to write her diary in the form of letters, so the first pages were conventional diary entries. And their tone was all wrong, preoccupied with gossip about her classmates and her would-be boyfriends. *When I look over my diary today, 1½ years on, I cannot believe I was ever such an innocent young thing*, she mused in January 1944.[18] Those early entries might have come from the pen of Joop ter Heul, but not from the pen of Anne Frank, as we now know her.

Anne came up with a bold solution. She rewrote the first months of her diary almost from scratch, using her first draft as a scaffold. At the start of Version A, she celebrates her thirteenth birthday at the center of a group of friends, surrounded by gifts (including the diary) and admirers. She lists her classmates, with sharp, catty descriptions of their personalities. She pastes in photographs and letters, including one sent by her father a few years earlier. She provides what appears to be a word-for-word transcription of a conversation with Hello Silberberg in which he confides that he's broken up with his girlfriend because he's interested in her. And she gives a brief summary of her life to date, from her birth in Frankfurt to the family's flight to the Netherlands, although it doesn't include—as the revision does—a list of the anti-Jewish regulations that affected her most, such as wearing a yellow star and being forbidden to participate in any public entertainment. Anne does not mention the persecution of the Jews at all until after her move to the Annex, when she writes the list of restrictions but describes her feelings about them indirectly. *Jacque used to say to me: "You're scared to do anything because it may be forbidden."*[19]

Almost none of what Anne discusses early on appears in Version B, which includes both more and less information about the crucial period between June 12 and July 5, delivered in a tightly written sequence of entries jam-packed with all the background information necessary for the reader to appreciate what a blow the move to the Annex will be. She instinctively understood the challenges of making the text publishable and tried to compensate for them, getting rid of those class lists—perhaps she was thinking more fondly of her former classmates from her new vantage point—and condensing the conversation with Hello into a few sentences. And she cleverly seeded her accounts of what appears to be a normal teenager's life with hints about the mounting persecution of the Jews. In the first letter to Kitty, she casually drops the key detail that she and her friends hang out at the ice-cream shops Oasis or Delphi because those are the ones *where Jews are allowed.* Then she carries breezily on: *among our large circle of friends we always manage to find some kindhearted gentleman or boy friend, who presents us with more ice cream than we could devour in a week.*[20] (In Version A, Mr. van Pels, whom she knows at this point only as her father's colleague, is the "gentleman" who treats her and her friends to ice cream. The Anne of Version B wasn't yet ready to introduce this major figure into her text.) After an entry devoted to her worries about her grades and a description of her troubles with Mr. Keesing, the math teacher—drawn from the "remembrance" of him she had written at what would have been the start of the 1943–1944 school year, that is, more than a year after the date she attaches to it in the *Diary*—she describes a visit to the dentist and how the new Nazi prohibitions on Jews using public transport have made it difficult to get around the city during a heat wave. *Now I can fully appreciate how nice a tram is, but that is a forbidden luxury for Jews.*[21]

Most notably, in an entry dated July 1, Anne recounts a conversation with Otto about going into hiding.

> *When we walked across our little square together a few days ago Daddy began to talk of us going into hiding, he is very worried*

that it will be very difficult for us to live completely cut off from the world. I asked him why on earth he was beginning to talk of that already. "Yes Anne," he said, "you know that we have been taking food, clothes, furniture to other people for more than a year now, we don't want our belongings to be seized by the Germans, but we most certainly don't want to fall into their clutches ourselves. So we shall disappear of our own accord and not wait until they come and fetch us."

"But Daddy, when would it be?"

He spoke so seriously that I grew very anxious.

"Don't you worry about it, we shall arrange everything. Make the most of your carefree young life while you can."

That was all. Oh, may the fulfilment of these sombre words remain far distant yet.[22]

As a biographer, I'm uncertain how to treat this material, all of which appears on pages written nearly two years after the fact and with a specific purpose: to transform the private text of Anne's diary into a public work that could be published, read, and understood by strangers. The task of fitting the sponge into the matchbox here involves, paradoxically, expanding the sponge. That visit to the dentist, for instance: did she really go on that day, or some other time during those weeks? Or did she invent the visit as an illustration of the hardships Jews were facing at that time? In other words, is it a biographical fact or a literary device?

All this is quite normal for someone writing a memoir—essentially what Anne was now doing, perhaps inspired by the memoir of Alice Bretz, which she had just read. As Francine Prose has succinctly put it, the revised version of her diary is understood better as a "memoir in the form of diary entries" rather than as a diary proper.[23] We trust memoirists not to make up major events, but otherwise they have quite a bit of leeway to dramatize scenes or recount dialogue that they may not remember word for word. Of course, it doesn't matter in the long run whether Anne went to the dentist on that day; what matters is the heat and the hardship, which there's no doubt she experienced.

But what about this conversation with Otto? There are three possibilities. It happened when Anne says it did—"a few days" before her entry of July 1, 1942, which is the date she assigned to it in Version B; it happened on a different date; or it didn't happen at all. If it happened when Anne says it did, why is it absent from Version A? Could it not have seemed significant enough to record? Or was the idea of going into hiding too frightening for her to dwell on, and she preferred, understandably, to focus on her girlfriends and Hello?

Perhaps it doesn't appear in Version A because it took place earlier in the year, before Anne's birthday and the inauguration of her diary. Looking back in May 1944, Anne would have realized that some anticipation of the events that were about to happen would make internal sense for Version B while providing some good literary drama. And so she added from memory an account of a conversation that had happened several months before; or she imagined one. Regardless, the small prayer at the end—*Oh, may the fulfilment of these sombre words remain far distant yet*—rings hollow. It doesn't sound like the voice of thirteen-year-old Anne innocently looking forward, because it's not. It's the mature, polished voice of nearly fifteen-year-old Anne looking back.

* * *

The gulf in tone between Version A and Version B, in these early months, cannot be overstated. In the first, Anne's voice is the voice of a little girl, one who is still young enough to play with dolls. She reports that Kleiman needs an operation for what she calls "Hemorites" (hemorrhoids). She sketches out a daydream about going to Switzerland, just her and Otto, where she goes shopping for clothes, attends school, and figure skates with her cousin Buddy. After three months in hiding, she records each family member's weight and notices with surprise how much her own has increased: *I eat an enormous amount, so much so that everyone is astounded.*[24] She is growing before the reader's eyes.

Version B, by contrast, lays out the important events of the first few months in hiding with remarkable sophistication and control. *Years seem to have passed between Sunday and now*, Anne sighs in the first line of what purports to be her first entry written in the Annex, on Wednesday, July 8. Whereas Version A for the same date begins, self-consciously, with *I still have a whole lot to write in my diary* and continues chronologically with an account of the previous Sunday—from Anne's visit with Hello to the delivery of the call-up notice—her revision deftly emphasizes the important points while leaving other details for color. She gives the reader an almost too-knowing hint of what the call-up notice signifies (*I picture concentration camps and lonely cells*). She can't bring many clothes to the Annex, but *memories mean more to me than dresses.* Though the Franks' neighbors don't know where they're going, they watch in pity as the family walks through the rain: *You could see by their faces how sorry they were they couldn't offer us a lift, the gaudy yellow star spoke for itself.*[25] In any event, the Franks could hardly have accepted a "lift" to their hiding spot.

Throughout, Anne writes with a self-possession that was understandably absent from her real-time account. Thirteen-year-old Anne was so discombobulated by the move that in one entry she seems uncertain about whether she's mentioned it already, apparently forgetting that she could look back through her diary to check. Nearly-fifteen-year-old Anne neatly parcels out the walk in the rain to the Annex, the division and organization of the space, and the arrival of the Van Pelses over the course of several entries, deftly paced and determinedly upbeat. Anne proudly showed Bep the entry about Margot's call-up as she revised the journal; much later, Bep vividly remembered its effect on her.[26] On at least one later entry Anne left a note for the reader that she had accidentally skipped a page—evidence that she was either sharing her writing with someone (Bep and/or Margot) or that she imagined a future reader.[27]

While the testimonial impulse is largely absent from the early days of Version A, Anne's revisions to the entries for fall 1942 consistently offer more and clearer information about the persecution of the Jews as well as her commentary on it—essential to her new vision of her diary as a public document. The younger Anne mentions news of the war that hits her the hardest, such as a classmate's deportation or the fates of other people she knows. One expects a diary's focus to be on the self; even so, the juxtaposition of shocking events in the outside world and quotidian life in the Annex is whiplash-inducing. On October 20, 1942 (Day 107), Anne writes of the shootings of hostages accused of sabotage in the same entry in which she complains that a new skirt doesn't fit.[28] The mass roundups in Amsterdam—*Every night people are being picked up without warning. . . . The poor old people are taken outside at night and then they have to walk . . . in a whole procession with children and everything*—receive the same amount of space as Kleiman's "Hemorites."[29]

Returning to the events of that fall a year and a half later, Anne streamlines the entries and adds some explanatory information—with unintended consequences. She puts the roundups in an entry about Westerbork and moves the whole thing up a couple of weeks. It's worth taking a close look at the two passages:

> Version A: *Miep told us about a man who escaped from Westerbork, and if it's so bad there what can it be like in Poland? People get hardly anything to eat let alone drink, for they have water for only 1 hour a day and 1 w.c. and 1 washstand for a few 1000 people. They all sleep mixed up together men and women and the latter + children often have their hair cut off so that everyone can recognize them if they escape.*

> Version B: *Our many Jewish friends are being rounded up by the dozen. These people are treated by the Gestapo without a shred of decency, being loaded into cattle trucks and sent to Westerbork, the big Jewish camp in Drente. Westerborg* [sic] *sounds terrible, only 1 washstand for thousands of people, 1 w.c. and there is no separate sleeping accommodation. Men, women and children all sleep together. One hears of frightful immorality because of this, and a lot of the women and even girls who stay there any length of time are expecting babies.*
>
> *It is almost impossible to escape, the people in the camp are all branded as inmates by their shorn heads and many also by their Jewish appearance.*
>
> *If it is as bad as this in Holland, whatever will it be like in the distant and barbarous regions they are sent to? We assume that most of them are murdered. The English radio speaks of their being gassed; perhaps that is the quickest way to die.*[30]

Looking at this, one wonders if the "frightful immorality" of Version B was information deemed inappropriate for sharing with thirteen-year-old Anne, who would have probably included it. (Other entries in Version A refer to prostitution.) It is not just the shaved heads but the "Jewish appearance" of the inmates that betrays them—a fear more vivid to Anne after her time in hiding than to her earlier self, who mixed easily with friends in public without anyone remarking on her Jewishness. But the most important change is the added paragraph speculating about what happens to the deportees after they leave Westerbork—a speculation absent from the 1942 diary. Perhaps Anne knew that Jews were being gassed but couldn't bring herself to write about it. But it seems more likely that she and the other residents weren't yet aware of what was taking place. The question of what Jews in the Netherlands knew about the extermination camps and when they knew it has been intensely debated among historians, some of whom have pointed to this entry as evidence that the gas chambers were already public knowledge in the

Netherlands in fall 1942.[31] But—as no one reading the *Diary* could know until the publication of the Critical Edition—Anne wrote those lines in spring 1944, a year and a half after first hearing about the conditions in Westerbork. Thus they offer no evidence whatsoever about the state of knowledge among the Dutch public a few months after deportations began.

Perhaps even more important to Anne's testimony than the facts of persecution was her careful chronicle of the physical and psychological effects of life in hiding—on herself and on the others. While her early entries were simple reports on the daily life of the household, as she matured she began to contemplate the larger significance of being in hiding. In the entry in which Anne considers the decline in living standards among the Annex residents, she moves with ease from objective descriptions of their reduced quality of life to a more philosophical reflection on their situation: *I sometimes wonder with a shock, how are we, now going about in worn-out things, from my pants down to Daddy's shaving brush, ever going to get back to our prewar standards?*[32] The question feels existential as well as material.

Even Anne's most lighthearted accounts of the Annex routine have a point to make about the problems of life in hiding. Consider her description of taking a bath: since the bathroom lacked a tub, anyone who wanted to bathe had to carry a washtub downstairs to the hot water heater, fill it, then lug it to a private spot. In the first version, she writes only of her own experience: *of course it all splashes everywhere and later when I'm clean, I have to wipe everything up with the dirty mop.* In her revision, she creates a set piece that uses household members' bathing routines to exemplify their personal quirks. Though the office kitchen has a glass door, that's Peter's chosen spot; he simply tells everyone to avoid the area while he is bathing. Mr. van Pels carries the washtub upstairs for greater privacy. Mrs. van Pels has postponed her baths entirely until she can determine the most advantageous location. Otto uses the private office, where he once managed his business; Edith finds a spot in the kitchen. Anne and Margot initially bathe together in the front office, where one of them can peek out through the curtains while the other washes herself, but later Anne chooses her own spot in the office bathroom.[33] In the Annex, even taking a bath becomes a microcosm of life under the Nazis.

* * *

Anne seems to have initially envisioned *Het Achterhuis*—the book she intended to publish after the war, based on her diary—as a work of fiction about the Annex. *Whether I shall succeed or not, I cannot say, but my diary will be a great help.*[34] In spring 1944, Anne also started a novel called *Cady's Life*, inspired in part by her father's first romance. But she abandoned it and threw her creative energies into the revision of her diary. While her embryonic fiction only suggests her potential as a novelist, Version B of the diary—which may or may not be the "novel" titled *Het Achterhuis* that she hoped to write—demonstrates enormous novelistic skill. I don't mean that the work is fiction, in the sense of being imaginary; as one critic puts it, the differences between Version A and Version B are "mostly strategic" rather than factual or matters of substance.[35] But when an editor of the Critical Edition writes that the revised diary is "a literary work by Anne Frank rather than . . . an autobiographical document *sensu strictu*," he is paying her a compliment.[36]

As we know, Anne started off by modeling her literary strategies on those of Cissy van Marxveldt, author of the *Joop ter Heul* series. As Van Marxveldt does with Joop's diary, Anne introduces tension into Version B by interrupting her entries: "Someone is calling me," she might write before ending abruptly, a device that seems calculated both to keep the reader turning the pages and to introduce verisimilitude.[37] Similarly, in another device borrowed from Van Marxveldt, she appends a postscript to some of her letters to introduce information apparently acquired later. Though her tone in Version B is not as casual as that of the first draft, she still speaks in a chatty, colloquial voice, addressing Kitty by name and asking for her opinion.

Another likely influence on Anne's writing—as yet unacknowledged by scholars—was the correspondence of Liselotte von der Pfalz, a German noblewoman sent to France at age nineteen to marry the brother of King Louis XIV. Anne was reading a collection of Liselotte's letters in May 1944, as she began revising her diary.[38] Despite Liselotte's high rank, she was all but a prisoner in the court, her movement restricted by the whims of the king, which she described as "tyranny": he forbade her to travel on her own to visit her family elsewhere in France or in Germany, or even to seek medical treatment. Her letters to family and friends, which discuss daily events at court as well as literature and the theater, are filled with literary imagery and sensory descriptions as well as homesickness and nostalgia for her previous freedom. Writing was Liselotte's "whole life, her way of mastering a destiny that was forced upon her by transforming her loneliness, her frustrations, and her anger into literature," writes the editor of an English edition of her letters. It is easy to imagine why Anne found her voice congenial.[39]

The novelization of the diary is also informed by Anne's sense of narrative structure and dramatic irony. We might imagine that Anne, revisiting her first impressions of Pfeffer, would present him as a villain from the start. Instead, she revises her initial neutral description—*we had been saying once more that we really ought to take in another person and fate pointed to Mr. Pfeffer, for he doesn't have much family*—into one that is ironic only in retrospect: *Great news—we want to take in an 8th person. . . . [Pfeffer] is known to be quiet and refined and so far as we and Mr. v.P. can judge from a superficial acquaintance both families think he is a congenial person.*[40] The reader will be surprised by the mismatch between expectations and reality, just as Anne was.

The most frequent changes are stylistic. Since at least one

notebook belonging to Version A has been lost, we can't pinpoint exactly when the enormous development in Anne's writing skill took place, but it happened sometime between December 5, 1942, when the first notebook ends, and December 22, 1943, when the second begins. A handful of surviving entries from the intervening period, written on loose sheets of paper and inserted into the first notebook, suggest that the voice we know as characteristic of the mature Anne—articulate, intelligent, questioning, funny—was present as early as May 1943, shortly before her fourteenth birthday.[41] Throughout Version B, the new writerly Anne improves on her earlier language. Consider this passage and its revision:

> Version A, October 15, 1942: *Yesterday we had another terrible fright. The carpenter was working in front of our cupboard. . . . We hadn't been warned and were calling blithely to one another all through the house. Suddenly after lunch, Bep had just decided to go downstairs, I heard some hammering and I said psst upstairs, but we thought it was Mummy who was just coming down the attic stairs. . . . I heard it again, and the others did too, that's when we realized the carpenter was there. . . . Suddenly we heard terrible rattling, at our door. We thought it had to be the carpenter wanting to come and have a look here. It was absolutely terrifying.*

> Version B, October 20, 1942: *My hand still shakes although it's two hours since we had the shock. I should explain that there are five fire extinguishers in the house. Downstairs they are such geniuses that they didn't warn us when the carpenter, or whatever the fellow is called, was coming to fill them. The result was that we weren't making any attempt to be silent until I heard hammering outside on the landing opposite our cupboard door. . . . Daddy and I posted ourselves at the door, so as to hear when the man left. After he'd been working for a quarter of an hour, he laid his hammer and tools down on top of our cupboard (as we thought!) and knocked at our door. We turned absolutely white. Perhaps he had heard something after all and wanted to investigate our secret den.*[42]

The entry's date has changed, but that's the least of it. In addition to condensing her language, Anne has added a dramatic opening flourish (her hand couldn't still be shaking—the shock took place a year and a half earlier) and a note of sarcasm in calling their protectors "genuises" (loyal Otto took it out in Version C). And she has absorbed the writing maxim of "Show, don't tell," illustrating the fear of the Annex residents at the knock on the door rather than informing the reader of it.

Often, Anne adds descriptive language, simile, or metaphor. In the entry about the carpenter's visit, she uses an image to illustrate her fear: *In my imagination the man who I thought was trying to get in had been growing and growing in size until in the end he appeared to be a giant.* Elsewhere, the adults' criticisms of her *find their mark, like shafts from a tightly strung bow, and . . . are just as hard to draw from my body;* later she hopes that *the rain of rebukes dies down to a light summer drizzle.* These are all improvements Anne made in Version B. But by the last few months in hiding, her first drafts too showed a high level of polish. Contemplating her mythology work to be done, she wrote, *Theseus, Oidipus, Peleus, Orpheus, Jason and Hercules are awaiting their turn to be arranged, as their different deeds lie crisscross in my mind like fancy threads in a dress.*[43]

Anne's two main strategies, as critic Nigel Caplan writes, were "to make the *Diary* both more vivid (pleasurable) and more public (useful)."[44] At its most effective, her prose combines the two modes in a text that works simultaneously on the literary and testimonial levels, as in this often-quoted passage in Version B, which expresses both her physical and mental claustrophobia in an unforgettable metaphor: *I wander from one room to another, downstairs and up again, feeling like a songbird who has had his wings clipped and who is hurling himself in utter darkness against the bars of his cage.*[45]

People who keep a diary often note that it allows them to detach psychologically from their emotions. The playwright and poet Claude Fredericks, who kept a journal from age eight until his death at age eighty-nine, compared the practice to watching himself crying in the mirror: it helped him realize that "there is suddenly an 'I' who is separated from that 'me' who is suffering," he wrote.[46] For Fredericks, this was the detachment of the Buddhist. For Anne, it was the detachment of the novelist, who must step outside herself to experience and portray the perspectives of others.

* * *

After the *Diary* was published, Hannah Goslar returned to visit the Montessori school she and Anne had attended. Hendrika Kuperus, the principal and their former teacher, was still there, and Hannah asked her if she had seen anything special in Anne. Kuperus suggested Anne's talents had yet to emerge. "When a girl at that age is removed from friends, plants, animals—from everything, really—and you put her in a home with only adults, everything develops much faster," she remarked. "Who knows—if there had been no war, she might not have become a great writer until she was thirty."[47] Anne herself believed the war had hastened her maturation. *Am I really still a silly little schoolgirl?* she asked her diary shortly before her fifteenth birthday. *I have more experience than most; I have been through things that hardly anyone of my age has undergone.*[48]

But the war seems only a partial explanation. It wasn't just being in hiding that matured Anne so quickly; it was the act of using her diary to process the experience. At once text and practice, document and activity, a diary can serve multiple functions, many of which resonate with Anne's situation.[49] The most common of these, of course, is as a repository for private thoughts and feelings. Miep, too, kept a diary as a teenager, "jotting endlessly . . . in secret, for myself only"; perhaps this was part of the reason for her deep sympathy with Anne.[50] For anyone experiencing distress or conflict, recording and interpreting it in a diary can be a way of asserting control over the experience. For prisoners, a diary is a way to track the passage of time, the mounting days and hours tangible in the pile of paper. By transforming "life into text," as critic Irina Paperno writes, a diary creates a monument in one's own image, "a lasting trace of one's being—an effective defense against annihilation."[51] No reader of the *Diary* can forget Anne's cry: *I want to go on living even after my death!*[52]

A diary can serve as a laboratory for self-improvement, particularly from a religious perspective; a seventeenth-century diary by the English clergyman John Beadle, who insisted that Christians ought to keep a record of their acts and ways and reread it periodically to judge how they measure up to Christian standards, can be read as a manual of how to keep such a diary. In the eighteenth and nineteenth centuries, the diaries of young upper-class European women were often monitored by a governess, who made certain that the practice served a moral and instructive purpose.[53] Anne, too, had a mania for personal improvement, regarding both herself and others—Peter being her favorite target. (Margot was already perfect.) *When I realized he could not be a friend for my understanding, I thought I would at least try to lift him up out of his narrow-mindedness and make him do something with his youth.*[54] In an essay titled "Why?," about asking questions, she encourages parents to teach children to think for themselves and urges her reader *never to pass up an opportunity for self-examination.*[55] Writing a diary, as Samuel Pepys noted, can also be a form of recreation and a way of enhancing one's enjoyment of life; Boswell, too, found "the writing up of the day's events . . . one of the pleasures of the day."[56]

But for a writer, a diary can have a particularly meaningful purpose: it is a chrysalis from which the creative self emerges. This doesn't mean just that a diary provides good writing practice, although it does—one need only look at the differences in style between Version A and Version B to appreciate Anne's technical improvement. Its function is more existential than that. By the nineteenth century, diarists—including Virginia Woolf, who referred to her journal as a "capacious hold-all, in which one flings a mass of odds & ends without looking them through"—increasingly viewed diary-keeping as a literary act.[57] Through the practice of writing a diary, Anne proved to herself, and to those around her, that she was a writer and that her writing was worth taking seriously.

The very act of taking up the pen and writing down thoughts is an assertion of value. The process is self-reinforcing: the more the writer claims the title of "diary writer," the more she feels she deserves it and the more deeply she becomes invested in her identity as a writer. "The theme of the diary is always the personal, but it does not mean only a personal story: it means a personal relation to all things and people. The personal, if it is deep enough, becomes universal, mythical, symbolic," wrote Anaïs Nin, whose detailed record of her self-discovery is one of the most important twentieth-century diaries by a woman.[58] Susan Sontag, another writer who used her diary as a site of intellectual transformation, wrote that it is "superficial to understand the journal as just a receptacle for one's private, secret thoughts—like a confidante who is deaf, dumb, and illiterate. In the journal I do not just express myself more openly than I could do to any person; I create myself."[59]

One afternoon in July 1944, only a few weeks before the raid on the Annex, Miep paid an unexpected visit upstairs. She had finished her work early and thought she'd see if anyone wanted to chat. Anne was sitting at the table in her parents' bedroom, "writing intently." She heard Miep and looked up. "I saw a look on her face at this moment that I'd never seen before," Miep remembered later. "It was a look of dark concentration, as if she had a throbbing headache. This look pierced me, and I was speechless. She was suddenly another person there writing at the table."[60]

* * *

By the end of her time in the Annex, Anne was deeply invested in her autonomy. Remember the letter she wrote to Otto that hurt him so deeply, in which she asserted her emotional independence from him and Edith. Rewriting her diary gave her an opportunity to present herself to the world exactly as she wished. The young woman who was writing *Het Achterhuis* wasn't the little girl who had received a diary for her thirteenth birthday—how could she be? A lifetime of experiences had taken place in the interim.

Anne's vision of herself as *quite alone in the world* begins with a preface of sorts she placed before the first entry in Version B. She knows that she is fortunate and lacks for nothing: *darling parents*, an older sister, a circle of admiring acquaintances, *strings of boyfriends*. Still, she has no one with whom she can truly share her thoughts; if she had such a friend, she wouldn't need to keep a diary.[61] The reader familiar with Version A will find this preface especially poignant: however much it might have been true of the Anne of June 1942, jealous and possessive of Jacqueline's friendship, it is far more true of the Anne who wrote this preface in spring or summer 1944, who tried to find such a friend in Peter and failed.

In contrast with the relaxed, loving Pim, Anne describes Edith as oblivious to her needs or simply unable to meet them: her protectiveness is intrusive, her manners annoying. I have already wondered if depression contributed to Edith's moods in the Annex. Others have suggested that Anne's portrayal of her mother was exaggerated. Bep, who spent a great deal of time with Edith and Mrs. van Pels, remembered both women as much more sympathetic than the way Anne depicted them and thought of Edith in particular as a "kind and nurturing mother."[62]

Indeed, a careful reader will notice Edith repeatedly asserting herself on her daughter's behalf. During the first days in the Annex, when Anne is too scared to venture down to the office with the others to listen to the radio at night, Edith sympathizes with her anxiety and stays upstairs with her. When Anne seeks solace in her parents' bedroom (and in Otto's bed) during the air raids, Otto—a stickler for the rules—insists on keeping the candle in the room unlit; defying him, Edith gets up and lights it to comfort Anne. She also stands up to the Van Pelses, insisting at one point that the children receive extra butter while the adults go without.[63] Nonetheless, Anne writes of her in almost entirely critical terms. Otto removed a little of her cruelest language, as well as the entry in which Anne speculated that the marriage had always been loveless. But he retained the substance of Anne's complaints.

In the context of her self-creation, Anne's depiction of Edith makes more sense. In order to represent herself as fully alone, Anne must somehow explain away the presence of her mother, just as fairy tales do away with children's parents in order to start them on their adventures. Anne gets rid of Edith by rejecting her. As her writing grows more sophisticated through spring 1944, so do her complaints, which start off as personal and become political. *I can't imagine that I would have to lead the same sort of life as Mummy and Mrs. v.P. and all the women who do their work and are then forgotten, I must have something besides a husband and children, something that I can devote myself to!*[64] As scholar Berteke Waaldijk puts it, "Anne's wish to lead the life of a writer coincides with her desire to lead a better life than that of her mother."[65]

Though Anne won't erase her language about Edith, she does attempt to rectify it. In her lengthy first entry for January 1944 (Version A), Anne says she must confess *three things:* her realization that she does not respect her mother, her feelings about her period and her body (including the episode involving Jacqueline's breasts), and her hope that Peter might be the confidant for whom she longs.[66] Revisiting this entry a few months later, after her relationship with Peter has progressed, she saw in it an opportunity. And so she created an entirely new entry dated several days earlier, in which she depicts herself rereading her diary and feeling dismay at her representation of Edith. How, she asks, could she have been so *full of hate?* Now she claims she has reached a new understanding of their relationship in which she too is at fault. *She did love me very much and she was tender, but as she landed in so many unpleasant situations through me and as she was nervous and irritable because of other worries and difficulties, it is certainly understandable that she snapped at me. I took it much too seriously, was offended and was rude and irritating to Mummy, which, in turn, made her unhappy.* Still, she concludes, *I can't really love Mummy in a dependent childlike way.*[67] As Caplan writes, this entry is "either fictitious or an afterthought, as it does not appear in [Version A]. It foregrounds the fiction of the narrative persona."[68] The conclusion Anne draws from it, however, rings true. She values her diary as *a book of memoirs . . . but on a good many pages I could certainly put "past and done with."*[69]

Critics have suggested that Anne played down her relationship with Peter in Version B for the same reason as she cut some of her references to menstruation, her descriptions of her genitalia, and her dreams about her grandmother and about Peter Schiff, among other things: it was too personal. This may well be accurate. But if Anne saw giving Edith any credit for supporting her or influencing her as a threat to her depiction of herself as *sui generis*, her numerous entries chronicling her longing for Peter pose a similar problem. From January through March 1944, she wrote about him nearly every day. *Oh, it's so terribly difficult never to say anything to Peter, but I know that the first to begin must be he . . . Everything would be all right, and I would make light of everything else, if only I had Peter . . . if he looks at me with those eyes that laugh and wink, then it's just as if a little light goes on inside me.*[70] How excruciating she must have found all this in retrospect! She removed ten entries in February and March describing their meetings in the attic, which Otto, as we know, reinstated. That may be a greater betrayal of Anne's legacy than anything else. She made it clear that she did not want her romance with Peter to define her, yet it occupies at least one-third of her published *Diary* and forms much of the basis for the play and movie adapted from it.

But it's possible to imagine that even if Anne's feelings for Peter had remained as intense, she still would have rewritten or removed the entries about him. Her emendations, writes Caplan, form "a more coherent text which does not descend into a sentimental teenage love-story . . . but retains its dual focus on Anne's personal development and her life in hiding."[71] It's true that Anne's disappointment in Peter propelled her into a more fervent declaration of her independence than she might otherwise have reached. But even before she developed feelings for him, the pressures of the Annex combined with puberty to create a more confident, more mature Anne. *I became a young woman, an adult in body and my mind underwent a great, a very great change, I came to know God!* she wrote in early March 1944, describing herself at the end of the previous year. *I started to think, to write and I discovered myself.*[72]

It is not unusual for a writer to revise her journal with an eye toward what she is becoming rather than what she was. The British novelist Fanny Burney, who addressed her diary to "Nobody," edited it at least twice.[73] At age twelve or thirteen, Elizabeth Barrett Browning edited journal entries she had written several years before, "collecting her own archives for a later history of her childhood genius," in the words of one scholar, "so that all her 'past days [might] appear as a bright star.'"[74] Anne used the act of writing the journal to create herself as a diarist, but in the act of revising it she was reborn as an artist.

* * *

In late spring and summer 1944, Anne turned her focus to her writing as never before. Even as she revised her earlier work at an extraordinary pace—up to a dozen pages a day—she composed new entries that display a greater complexity of thought than anything she had previously written. In her last few months in hiding, she reflected at length on the war (*There's in people simply an urge to destroy, an urge to kill, to murder and rage*), on the price that the period in hiding had exacted on both the residents and their helpers (*would it not have been better for us all if we had not gone into hiding, and if we were dead now and not going through all this misery, especially as we should be sparing the others*), on women's equality (*I believe that the idea that a woman's duty is simply to bear children will change over the centuries to come*).[75] She speculated that life in wartime was even more difficult for the teenagers in the Annex than for the adults, because young people are naturally idealistic and suffer more greatly the pain of having their beliefs crushed. *I simply can't build up my hopes on a foundation consisting of confusion, misery, and death*, she wrote in July 1944, just after the famous line about people being *really good at heart*.

> *I see the world gradually being turned into a wilderness, I hear the ever approaching thunder, which will destroy us too, I can feel the sufferings of millions and yet, if I look up into the heavens, I think that it will all come right, that this cruelty too will end, and that peace and tranquility will return again. In the meantime, I must uphold my ideals, for perhaps the day will come when I'll be able to carry them out!*[76]

Part of what sustained Anne, though it has rarely been acknowledged, was her belief in God. Her relationship with religion was personal and idiosyncratic: she writes of saying her nightly prayers (in German, her first language) and of feeling God's comforting presence in nature.[77] Many of the passages she copied into her "Favorite Quotes Notebook" are about religion, emphasizing the role of the individual worshipper: "There is no worthier work for the person who has been graced with the ability to see even a small part of God's mercy than to serve Him and to keep vigil and to pray for those people whose sight is still clouded by the shadow of worldly matters" (Sigrid Undset, *Kristin Lavransdatter*); "Love can be perfect, but not disillusionment, because there's always consolation in God" (Zsolt Harsányi, *The Star-Gazer*).[78]

But what one feels most strongly in Anne's writing, particularly in the last few months, is the extent to which the diary itself was sustaining her. *I am grateful to God for giving me this gift, this possibility of developing myself and of writing, of expressing all that is in me!*[79] "Her diary had become her life," Miep recalled.[80] Her writing was not just the record but also the instrument of her day-to-day survival. This, I believe, is part of the reason it has fascinated readers so intensely and for so long. One feels that it is no ordinary document but a kind of talisman. There were days when it may have literally kept her alive.[81]

During the raid on the Annex, the Gestapo officer Karl Silberbauer asked where the valuables were kept, and Otto gestured toward a small wooden box. Looking for a place to store its contents, the officer picked up Anne's briefcase and dumped out her diary—the original notebooks and the loose sheets on which she had been reworking them. Anne, Otto said later, did not even cast an eye at the papers lying on the floor.[82] She would have to manage without her diary from now on.

INTERLUDE

The Raid

DAY 761: FRIDAY, AUGUST 4, 1944. The morning is bright and warm. Miep arrives at the office and comes up for her daily check-in. Afterward, Otto works with Peter on his English. Anne and Margot are in the Franks' room, probably reading or studying. On the ground floor, the warehouse doors stand open to the sun.[1]

At the Gestapo headquarters on Euterpestraat, across the city, the phone rings at the desk of SS Sergeant Karl Josef Silberbauer, a member of the "Jew-hunting unit." His superior, Lieutenant Joseph Dettmann, tells him a call has just come in with the information that Jews are hiding at Prinsengracht 263. Several Dutch policemen, as well as a detective, will join in the raid. Silberbauer later remembered his annoyance: he had been about to have lunch.[2]

Reports conflict regarding just about every aspect of the betrayal of the Annex Eight and the subsequent raid on the Annex.

Otto is the only person who survived to give an account of what happened from the perspective of the residents. The memories of Miep, Bep, Kleiman, and Kugler, all of whom were in the office at the time, diverge on minor points—not surprising, considering the shock.

The only account from the perspective of the SS comes from Silberbauer, who was tracked down in Vienna by the Nazi hunter Simon Wiesenthal in 1963 and was later questioned by police in Austria and the Netherlands. He is the one who said the betrayal came in the form of a tip to Dettmann, although he didn't know who the source was. (Dettmann committed suicide shortly after the German surrender.)

Silberbauer seems to have been an extremely boorish and insensitive man, even for a Nazi. Interviewed by a Dutch journalist, Jules Huf, shortly after Wiesenthal found him, he emphasized that he had "done nothing wrong" and was distressed to learn that Jews in hiding knew about the gassings, since the Nazis had intended to keep them in ignorance. "He seems to care more about the flaw in the system than about the fact that Jews were gassed," Huf observed. Silberbauer also told Huf he had bought the *Diary* "because I wanted to know if I was in it. But it ends just before the arrest."[3] In his interview with Huf, he took pains to present himself in the best possible light. He may well have fabricated details about the raid to protect himself or others.

Over the years, numerous theories about the betrayal have been proposed. Anne, along with the rest of the household and the office staff, worried that Willem van Maaren, who replaced Bep's father, Johan Voskuijl, as warehouse manager after Voskuijl's diagnosis with cancer, might be untrustworthy. She described him as *the man with the dark past,* perhaps a reference to a previously failed business venture; the staff suspected him of stealing food and other goods from the warehouse.[4] In turn, Van

Maaren had his own suspicions about nighttime activity in the warehouse, setting traps that the Annex residents had to be careful not to disturb: *he places books and bits of paper on the very edges of things in the warehouse so that if anyone walks by they fall off.*[5] In his interview with Huf, Silberbauer claimed that Van Maaren had been the tipster: he knew it, he said, because the warehouse clerk had silently gestured with his thumb toward the upper floors when the police arrived, before they had even stated their business. This seems like a false assumption: Van Maaren might have simply been directing the police to the people in charge. An inquiry into the betrayal conducted by the Amsterdam police in 1948—following a letter from Kleiman outlining the case against Van Maaren and a personal visit to the police from Otto—focused on him but turned up nothing conclusive.

Carol Ann Lee, the author of biographies of both Anne and Otto Frank, uses much of her book about Otto to build a case against Tonny Ahlers, a Dutch Nazi and petty criminal who blackmailed Otto in 1941 for making a negative comment about Germany's chances in the war. Melissa Müller, the author of another biography of Anne, suspected Lena Hartog, the wife of one of Van Maaren's assistants. According to at least one account, the phone call to Dettmann was made by a woman; Lee thinks it could have been Ahlers's wife.[6]

Bep's son Joop van Wijk-Voskuijl has accused his aunt, Bep's sister Nelly, who had close connections with soldiers in the Wehrmacht and suspected that Bep and Johan Voskuijl were involved in hiding Jews. Family members remember Nelly screaming "Go to your Jews!" after an argument with them. When she came home for dinner the day after the raid, Johan—Otto's close friend—beat her violently.[7]

In 2016 the filmmaker Thijs Bayens and the journalist Pieter van Twisk opened a new inquiry, building a team that included some two dozen Dutch investigators, historians, and researchers, as well as a former FBI special agent. The "Cold Case Team," as they called themselves, used artificial intelligence together with old-fashioned detective work and research to hunt for clues that other investigators might have overlooked. Their efforts and conclusion were chronicled by Rosemary Sullivan, the Canadian author of a well-received biography of Stalin's daughter and numerous other best-selling books. *The Betrayal of Anne Frank: A Cold Case Investigation* was published simultaneously to great fanfare in the United States and the Netherlands in January 2022. The likely betrayer, the team concluded, was Arnold van den Bergh, a wealthy Jewish notary who was a member of the Amsterdam Jewish Council.

Sullivan's book came under immediate and intense attack from Dutch historians and others who argued that the team had made unjustified assumptions and relied too heavily on circumstantial evidence, a key piece of which was the theory that the Jewish Council had access to lists of addresses of people in hiding. As the historians demonstrated, the evidence that such lists existed is extremely flimsy; even if the lists did exist, it's unthinkable that the inhabitants of the Annex or their protectors would have revealed their address to anyone. Remember those letters Anne wrote to Jacqueline in her first months in hiding: she knew she couldn't send them. Pfeffer did exchange letters with his fiancée, but Miep served as courier.[8] In the wake of a sixty-nine-page "refutation" of the book, written by a group of prominent Dutch historians and published on the website of NIOD (the Dutch Institute for War, Holocaust, and Genocide Studies), Sullivan's Dutch and German publishers took *The Betrayal of Anne Frank* out of distribution. It is still for sale in the United States and elsewhere.[9]

"It is no longer possible to reconstruct exactly what happened," concludes Harry Paape, one of the editors of the Critical Edition, in an essay on the betrayal.[10] One scenario proposed by researchers at the Anne Frank House is that the SS were expecting to find stolen goods and discovered the people in hiding by chance.[11] This seems to presume that Silberbauer's testimony is unreliable or that he misunderstood what Dettmann told him.

Regardless of whether the identity of a "betrayer" is ever conclusively determined, ultimately only the Nazis can be held responsible for the death of Anne Frank: from Hitler and Eichmann all the way down to the lowly functionary Silberbauer and his henchmen.

* * *

Miep, Bep, and Kleiman were at work in the main office when an SS man holding a pistol—probably Silberbauer—opened the door. He had a "long, dried-up, yellowish face," Bep remembered.[12] Kugler, in the next room, identified himself as the person in charge. The police ordered him to lead them around the building. After a look at the storerooms—Silberbauer later remembered the strong, pleasant smell of the spices—they went back into the hallway and demanded that Kugler move the bookcase. He refused, so they did it themselves.[13]

Only one person at a time could climb the narrow staircase. Kugler went first, the police holding their pistols to his back. At the sight of Edith, sitting in the Franks' room, he felt too emotional to speak. "The Gestapo is here," he whispered.[14]

Otto, upstairs, heard footsteps. The door to Peter's room opened and the two of them came face to face with a plainclothes policeman pointing a gun at them. By the time they descended the stairs, the other residents had already assembled with their hands up. "Pack your things—you can't stay here any longer," Silberbauer told them. Margot was silently crying; the others betrayed none of their terror. A few months earlier, during the agonizing Easter weekend break-in, Anne had exhorted Mrs. van Pels to be brave if they were caught. *We must simply behave like soldiers, Mrs. v.P. If all is up now, then let's go for Queen and Country, for freedom, truth and right, just what the Dutch news from England keeps telling us.*[15] Now they followed through.

The residents packed a few belongings. After dumping the papers in Anne's briefcase on the floor, Silberbauer noticed the insignia on Otto's army trunk, signifying his rank as an officer—a distinction earned by only 2,000 Jews. "At once, Silberbauer's attitude changed. He even looked for a moment as if he was going to snap to attention in front of me," Otto later recalled. The Nazi asked why Otto hadn't reported his service to the Gestapo, which, Silberbauer claimed, would have treated the family more leniently as a result—perhaps by deporting them to Theresienstadt (Terezín), the "family camp" that was a destination for certain privileged Jews, where the conditions were known to be somewhat less horrific than those at Auschwitz and other extermination camps. But at that point, the best Silberbauer could do was to give them a few extra minutes to gather their belongings. "Perhaps he would have spared us if he had been by himself," Otto later wondered.[16]

In his interview with Huf, Silberbauer mentions none of this, claiming instead that Otto introduced himself as a former reserve officer in the German army. Curious, Silberbauer asked him how long the families had been in hiding. "Twenty-five months," Otto replied. When Silberbauer responded incredulously, Otto took Anne by the hand and led her to a wall where he had made height markings for her and Margot. Anne stood against the wall to show Silberbauer how much she had grown; perhaps Margot did as well. "Your daughters are very attractive," Silberbauer apparently said to the man he was about to arrest.

Meanwhile, Jan Gies arrived at the office for lunch. Miep sent him away quickly, saying under her breath, "It's wrong here."[17] Kleiman told Bep to take his wallet, stuffed with illegal ration coupons, to a nearby pharmacist, who alerted his wife.

Before long, Miep, still in the office, heard the Annex Eight coming down the stairs "like beaten dogs."[18] Was Anne first, leading the way, or at the rear of the procession, her head down? Did she hold Margot's hand, or Peter's? Again, there were no goodbyes. Across the canal, on the other side of the street, Jan watched with Kleiman's brother as a windowless police van pulled up outside Prinsengracht 263. Kleiman, Kugler, and the residents exited the building and got into it. Then they were gone.[19]

Bep—resident "Number 9," Anne's closest friend and confidante among the protectors—stayed at the pharmacy for a while, then spent the day wandering around the city before finally meeting her boyfriend. They had been together, on and off, for most of the previous two years, but she had never revealed the secret to him. Sometimes on Sundays she would stop by Prinsengracht 263 to "feed the cat," instructing him to wait in the front office so as not to frighten it. Now she told him everything. Though he had sensed the immense tension radiating from her—so intense that she occasionally fainted or collapsed in fits of weeping—he was astounded to learn the source.[20]

Bep's father had been bedridden with stomach cancer for more than a year. When she told him what had happened, he got on his bicycle and rode across the city to the Annex. He told her later that he wanted to get rid of any remaining evidence that might incriminate her or the others, but she thought it was his way of saying goodbye.[21]

The next day, Bep and her boyfriend went to the Annex together, checking the silent rooms for anything valuable left behind. On a later visit, Bep found a pile of papers with Anne's handwriting—likely the revised version of her diary—and gave them to Miep.[22]

For the rest of her life, Miep had a recurring dream that the arrest had not taken place. Instead, the war ended and she threw open the door to the Annex, gesturing to the occupants that they were free and announcing, "Now go home!" Invited to countless productions of *The Diary of Anne Frank*, she found herself wondering each time, as the curtain was about to rise, if the story might somehow end differently.[23]

7

Prisoner
Westerbork and Auschwitz, August–October 1944

> *When the birds sing outside and you see the trees changing to green, the sun invites one to be out in the open air, when the sky is so blue, then—oh, then I wish for so much!*

"All roads lead through Westerbork," SS-Hauptsturmführer Ferdinand aus der Fünten announced during a roundup in Amsterdam.[1] In all of Nazi-occupied Europe, there was no other place like this camp. Part clearinghouse, part dumping ground, part insane asylum, it was the first stop on the route to the east for almost all Jews deported from the Netherlands. Prisoners might spend less than a day there before being put on a transport—usually to Auschwitz, sometimes to Sobibór. The luckiest, those with passports or privileges that made them eligible for exchange with German prisoners of war, might end up at Terezín (Theresienstadt) or Bergen-Belsen, which were comparatively less lethal, at least for some prisoners, earlier in the war. Or they might remain in Westerbork for months, even years.

In July 1942 the Nazis took control of the camp, which the

Dutch had created in 1939 on a half-square-kilometer of land on the Drenthe heath to hold the influx of Jews fleeing Germany, and formally designated it a "police transit camp." Yet Jews continued to run the daily operations. Westerbork's administration largely consisted of German Jews who had been there since the camp's inception and were known as "long-term residents," augmented with (largely Dutch) employees of the Amsterdam Jewish Council. In some cases Jews were even responsible for security: the *Ordendienst* (OD), or "special service," consisted of mostly Jewish former soldiers and other young men who enforced order in the camp and guarded the *Strafbarracke*, the "S-barracks" or "punishment barracks," the destination for those deemed guilty of some crime when they entered the camp, other than just being Jewish. Philip Mechanicus, a well-known journalist, was arrested in Amsterdam for not wearing a star in public and imprisoned for two months in Amersfoort, a Dutch concentration camp, before coming to Westerbork as an "S-detainee" in November 1942. He spent much of his time in the camp writing a meticulous chronicle of his own experience and the operations of Westerbork in general.[2] Jews caught in hiding, including children and babies, were also automatically designated S-detainees.[3]

From summer to fall 1942, as roundups in Amsterdam and elsewhere increased, the population of the camp grew from 1,000 to more than 10,000. Initially, ten or more prisoners were crowded into small huts that had previously held one family each.[4] As deportees poured in—as many as thousands within a few days—the camp expanded with larger barracks, some constructed out of wood plundered from destroyed Jewish communities.[5] By September 1943, when the legal scholar and journalist Abel Herzberg was deported to Westerbork, as many as 1,000 prisoners might be crowded into a single barrack; disease was rampant. "The wash-houses were dingy, the barracks lugubrious and overcrowded, the sleeping accommodations unsalubrious and rudimentary; the lavatories and latrines were disgusting, the overcrowding unbearable . . . and the camp as a whole was hideous, hideous beyond description, just like every camp run by the Germans," Herzberg wrote.[6]

Westerbork shared many features with the better-known concentration camps. The day began with roll call, which could last for more than an hour. As the prisoners stood in rows, Rosa de Winter, who met the Franks on their first day in Westerbork and later was with Edith at Auschwitz, observed their footwear. Wooden shoes were given out upon arrival with no consideration as to size, so that everyone wound up with sore feet; newcomers' shoes were in good shape, but the shoes of those who had been there for six months or longer were "mere rags held together with string." Misery, she concluded, "creeps up from below."[7] Work started at five in the morning and lasted from eight to ten hours. The diet was meager and unappealing, often just bread and watery soup.

But prisoners at Westerbork were not murdered through back-breaking labor, as they were at concentration camps such as Buchenwald, Dachau, and Mauthausen; they were not gassed, as they were at Auschwitz, Bełżec, Chełmno, Majdanek, Sobibór, and Treblinka. They did not die en masse of disease and malnutrition, as in the ghettos in Warsaw, Łódź, and elsewhere. They were not shot at random or beaten to death by deranged guards; the camp commandant, Albert Gemmeker, whom Mechanicus describes as "an enigmatic character with iron hands covered in velvet," seems to have been among the least sadistic of such figures. "He likes music and . . . is a gentleman," wrote diarist Etty Hillesum, who volunteered to work in Westerbork in summer 1942 as an employee of the Jewish Council and remained there, on and off, until she was deported to Auschwitz in September 1943.[8]

Instead, the prisoners were permitted to exist—albeit temporarily. New arrivals were registered by the reception department and the housing bureau. There was a post office and a canteen that sold household items and special food, including powdered lemonade. The hospital, where Mechanicus spent more than nine months recovering from injuries he had sustained at Amersfoort, had a capacity of nearly 2,000 patients at its peak; they were cared for by 120 doctors and a nursing staff of over 1,000.[9] There were workshops for locksmiths, furniture makers, blacksmiths, watchmakers, and other tradespeople; a tailoring department and a dressmaking shop with designated employees who worked full-time for Elisabeth Hassel, Gemmeker's mistress. An agricultural detail took care of the farmland outside the camp. The industrial department was devoted to salvaging scrap metal and other materials. The S-detainees were given the dirtiest work, dismantling old batteries and extracting manganese from them. Instead of their regular clothes, they were made to wear blue overalls with red shoulder patches and wooden clogs; men's heads were shaved and women's hair was cut short. They also received less food than other prisoners.[10]

The camp had a unique culture and social life. There was a school for children aged six through fourteen and an orphanage for younger children. After the Goslars were picked up in the general roundup of June 1943—"every Jew from South Amsterdam, with papers, without," as Hannah described it—and deported to Westerbork, the orphanage director, a German Jew whom Hannah's father had known in Berlin, brought her and her little sister there. Hannah helped care for the small children and volunteered to clean the toilets; since they were located near the door, the job enabled her to talk to her father if he happened to pass by.[11] Anne's classmate Nanette Blitz arrived in Westerbork a few months later, in September 1943, and joined Hannah at work in the orphanage: "We used to sing and play with [the children], adding a little bit of fantasy to such a colorless environment."[12] Ed van Thijn, who came to Westerbork at age eight in March 1943 and survived to eventually become mayor of Amsterdam, recalled taking Hebrew lessons in the camp school.[13] Jewish history and ritual was taught by Max Kormann, a German Jew who had been in Westerbork since 1939, after a journey on the ill-fated SS *St. Louis*, the ship that sailed from Europe to Havana and back again after Cuba, the United States, and Canada all denied entry to the refugees aboard.[14]

With the exception of the punishment detail, work at Westerbork consisted largely of camp maintenance and administrative tasks, which left the inmates with both time and energy for leisure activities. On summer evenings, couples strolled hand in hand down the central road of the camp, nicknamed the Boulevard des Misères. There were soccer matches, boxing, basketball, track, gymnastics, jujitsu. The camp orchestra at one point included "half of the pre-war members of the Amsterdam Concertgebouw."[15] In defiance of Nazi restrictions, they were initially allowed to perform Aryan music—one concert Mechanicus attended featured Schubert's Unfinished Symphony and Sibelius's "Valse Triste"—but soon, like all other Jewish musicians, they were limited to music by Jewish composers. Finally Gemmeker deemed classical music "too tiring" and permitted only popular tunes.[16]

By day, Barrack 9, built partly out of wood from a destroyed synagogue in the nearby town of Assen, served as the registration hall for new arrivals. At night, it periodically transformed into what some called "the best cabaret in Europe," with six revues performed between 1942 and 1944, written and directed by Max Ehrlich, Willy Rosen, and Erich Ziegler, cabaret stars famous in Berlin in the 1920s. At one show, two performers with a guitar sang "jazzy songs in Dutch with a mock American accent."[17] Gemmeker particularly enjoyed "Bei mir bist du schön," a song forbidden in Germany owing to its Yiddish origins. Children also performed songs in Hebrew, including "Hatikvah," the Zionist hymn that became the Israeli anthem, for Gemmeker as well as the camp residents. The commandant served as "our artistic patron," Hillesum wrote, inviting performers to drink and socialize at his house after hours. "One night not so long ago he escorted an actress back home, and when he took his leave of her he offered her his hand; just imagine, his hand!"[18]

Even religious services had a place in Westerbork. Mechanicus recorded the "bright and joyous atmosphere" when prisoners observed Shabbat in the hospital: "candles are lit and a prayer-leader comes forward and, together with the congregation who have gathered round him, he stands with prayer-book open and intones a prayer with a well-marked flowing rhythm that sings of the joys of the Sabbath. . . . Patients in their beds join in." He also noted a celebration of Simchat Torah and a Jewish wedding.[19] Etty Hillesum enjoyed "the Hanukkah lights in the big barracks"; in 1942, Gemmeker attended a Hanukkah celebration, though he forbade the inmates to observe either Hanukkah or Christmas the following year.[20]

All this was provisional. If prisoners at Westerbork were not physically broken in the ways more typical of a concentration camp, they were tormented mentally by the ever present threat of deportation: "a sense of impending doom," in Nanette's words.[21] Nearly every Monday for more than two years, from July 1942 until August 1944, a train with as many as fifty-one cattle cars—Mechanicus called it "a long mangy snake"—pulled up on the tracks that ran the length of the Boulevard des Misères, splitting the camp in two.[22] It stood there for the entire day, its cars empty except for a toilet bucket in the middle and paper mattresses on the floor for the sick. Other than a handful that went to Sobibór, Terezín, and Bergen-Belsen, all of the trains were destined for Auschwitz.

As late as summer 1943, prisoners at Westerbork seem to have had almost no knowledge of where they were being deported or what would happen there. The word "Auschwitz" does not appear in Mechanicus's diary until winter 1944; until then, he refers to the destination of the deportees only as "Poland." "People still know practically nothing about Poland," Mechanicus wrote in August 1943. He also quoted a prisoner transferred from Vught, a Dutch concentration camp, as saying, "Things surely can't be as bad in Poland as they are at Vught."[23] But even if they didn't know where the trains were going, the prisoners knew it was better to stay at Westerbork.

The week's deportees might learn they were "on the list" several days earlier, or they might not find out till the morning of the transport. Mechanicus recalled the house physician going quietly from bed to bed in the Tuesday dawn hours, waking the soon-to-be-deported. Those with advance warning did all they could to avoid having to board the train. As in Amsterdam, where the Jewish Council managed exemptions for those with connections or money, prisoners in Westerbork could buy or beg their way onto various lists of Jews considered either too useful or too privileged to deport—for the moment. The "Palestine List," which included both Hannah's and Nanette's families, was for Jews with certificates allowing them to settle in Palestine; the Nazis considered exchanging them for German prisoners of war in England. There were also lists for baptized Jews, Jews with dual nationality, the partners of mixed marriages (with or without half-Aryan children), Jews with economic value to the regime, and others. Some prisoners were given the option of deportation to Terezín or to "Celle," in northwestern Germany (Bergen-Belsen). Since no one knew whether the lists would prove effective, many tried to hedge their bets by getting their names on more than one. Mechanicus compared it to roulette: "It is as if we are all sitting together at a gaming table and have put our money on different numbers and are waiting to see which number will come up."[24]

In the end, the house always won. Each of these lists, Mechanicus wrote in July 1943, was only "a collection of Jews who will one day be deported."[25] Those who were not put on the transport one week would be sent away the following week, month, year. The "exiles" went to the train with a bag of bread tied to their shoulder and a rolled-up blanket hanging down their backs. Mechanicus observed

> quiet men with tense faces and women bursting into frequent sobs. Elderly folk, hobbling along, stumbling over the poor road surface under their load and sometimes going through pools of muddy water. Invalids on stretchers carried by OD men. On the platform the Commandant with his retinue. . . . Any who dawdle or hesitate are assisted. They are driven into the train, or pushed, or struck, or pummeled, or persuaded with a boot, and kicked on board. . . . Noise and nervous outbursts are not allowed, but they do occur. . . . Men and women, old and young, sick and healthy, together with children and babies, are all packed together into the same wagon. Healthy men and women are put in amongst others who suffer from the complaints associated with old age and are in need of constant care, men and women who have lost control over certain primary physical functions, cripples, the deaf, the blind, folk with stomach disorders, imbeciles, lunatics. They all go on the bare floor, in amongst the baggage and on top of it, crammed tightly together.[26]

On a warm summer day, Hillesum noted the contrast between the beauty of the landscape, complete with blooming wildflowers, and the catastrophe unfolding:

> The engine gives a piercing shriek. The whole camp holds its breath; another three thousand Jews are about to leave. There are babies with pneumonia lying in the freight cars. . . . The sky is full of birds, the purple lupins stand up so regally and peacefully, two little old women have sat down on the box for a chat, the sun is shining on my face—and right before our eyes, mass murder.[27]

Then everything went back to normal until the following week. "You could manage if you adapted yourself to the circumstances," said Bloeme Emden, who attended school with Margot and Anne and met them again in Westerbork. The work was tolerable, and the prisoners could enjoy their free time. "There was a cabaret, and there was laughter. Only those transports were terrible—over and over again."[28]

* * *

By the time the Annex Eight were captured, Amsterdam had been officially *Judenrein* for nearly a year. There were no more mass roundups; no more days-long assemblages; no more nights spent in the darkness of the Jewish Theater, children screaming amid packed aisles. The Annex residents were taken first to Gestapo headquarters, where they were separated from Kugler and Kleiman; then to the prison for political prisoners, a gray brick building on the Weteringschans, across the canal from the Rijksmuseum. On August 8, they boarded a regular passenger train at Amsterdam's Central Station for Westerbork. Anne and Margot were wearing "sporty clothes, with sweatsuits and backpacks, as if they were going on a winter vacation," recalled Janny Brilleslijper, a young Dutch-Jewish Resistance worker who was arrested around the same time and who (together with her sister, Lien) became close to the Frank sisters at Westerbork and in Bergen-Belsen.[29]

Indeed, it may have felt something like a vacation. For the first time in more than two years, Anne could turn her face to the sun. She spent the journey by the window, unable to tear herself away from the Dutch countryside she had gone so long without seeing: meadows, villages, telephone wires.[30] Otto later remembered the mood on the train as cheerful. The Annex residents had been closely following the Allied progress all summer, tracking the troop movements on a map of Europe: by now, the Soviets had taken Ukraine and Belarus and were already deep into eastern Poland, while the English and Americans were fighting their way north through France. *I may yet be able to go back to school in September or October*, Anne mused after D-Day. Otto had predicted that the war would end by October 10.[31] Perhaps the remaining Dutch Jews could wait it out in Westerbork.

Upon arrival, the Franks were composed and dignified, remembered Vera Cohn, the reception employee who registered them in the camp. More than a decade later, she could still see Anne's "bright, young, eager eyes." None of the Franks, Cohn said, "showed any signs of despair over their plight."[32]

That sanguinity may have been short-lived. As people who had been in hiding, the Annex Eight were designated S-detainees and assigned to Barrack 67, one of three punishment blocks; they were forced to wear the regulation blue overalls with red patches and had their hair cut short. This must have been a source of particular pain for Anne, who adored her thick, shiny hair and typically combed it several times a day in the Annex, tying a special "combing shawl" under her chin—beige cotton, with pink, light green, and blue roses—to catch the strands that fell out.[33] While most families at Westerbork stayed together, those in the punishment block were separated by sex; the women and the men could see each other only at night. But even there, people could receive food packages from friends and relatives elsewhere and shared the contents. "There was a very good atmosphere of solidarity in the punishment barracks at Westerbork," one former prisoner remembered.[34]

The Franks had to work on the punishment detail. This meant the industrial department, where the work consisted of chiseling open old airplane batteries and taking them apart. "We had to . . . throw the tar in one basket and the carbon bars, which we had to remove, into another basket; we had to take off the metal caps with a screwdriver, and they went into a third basket," Janny Brilleslijper remembered. The work was filthy, and the dust from the batteries made them all cough. Otto went to Rachel Frankfoorder, who served in the camp administration, and asked if she could get Anne a better job. Anne was "so sweet, a little older than she was in the photo that we've all seen, gay and cheerful," Rachel recalled. "She said, 'I can do everything; I am very handy.'"[35] Unfortunately, Rachel was powerless to help.

Ronnie van Cleef, who also met the Franks at Westerbork, remembered the family in general as "pretty depressed. . . . They were very close to each other. They always walked together."[36] Rosa de Winter, too, recalled Edith as "numbed." She spent her evenings washing the family's underclothes: "The water was murky and there was no soap, but she went on washing, all the time."[37] (S-detainees, unlike other prisoners, did not receive soap.) But others had a different experience of Edith. Lenie van Naarden, whose husband became good friends with Otto, found Edith "a very special woman," if somewhat formal: "I never called her by her first name."[38] (This was typical for German Jews of their era. In all the time they spent together in the Annex, Anne never used first names for the Van Pelses or Pfeffer.) "She was a friendly, intelligent person of warm feelings," Janny Brilleslijper remembered. Her sister, Lien, recalled Edith in similar terms: "We had the feeling that now she had a chance to get things off her chest." Both sisters saw Anne and Margot as very attached to their mother. "Anne wrote in the diary that her mother didn't understand her, but I think that was just an adolescent mood. She clung to her mother in the camp," Janny said.[39] Anne remained close to Otto as well. When she fell sick, he came to the women's barracks every night to visit her, standing beside her bed and talking to her for hours.

At work, the prisoners sat together at long tables; though the guards might yell at them to work faster, they were allowed to socialize. Especially for the teenagers, it was a "relief," Otto said later, "to no longer be locked away and to be able to talk with other people."[40] In the evenings after work, Anne and Peter were "always together," Rosa said. Anne was "so lovely, so radiant that her beauty flowed over into Peter. . . . Her movements, her looks, had such a lilt to them that I often asked myself, Can she possibly be happy?"[41] The cabaret had been shut down by then, but Anne and Peter, like other young people in the camp, may have enjoyed watching the sunset on summer evenings. Men and women sat on the grass as if "on their summer holiday," Mechanicus observed, oblivious to the barbed-wire fence and the guard towers, gazing "into the limitless distance where in the quivering twilight the purple heather merges with the flaming sky"—an improvement on the small patch of sky Anne and Peter had been able to see from the Annex attic.[42]

Just as Anne did in the Annex, Mechanicus and Hillesum both found consolation in the act of writing their chronicles. The two writers, who were friends, sometimes worked alongside each other, offering encouragement in the insurmountable task of explaining Westerbork to the world. "It's too much," Mechanicus once said to Hillesum. "I know I can write, but here I am face to face with an abyss—or a mountain." Hillesum strived to be both "the thinking heart of these barracks" and "the ears and eyes of a piece of Jewish history."[43] For Mechanicus, who filled notebooks from the camp school with his observations, writing was at once "a diversion which often helped me to forget the disgust" and the fulfillment of a larger journalistic obligation.[44] But if Anne kept a diary in the camp, it has been lost. Anything we know about her life in Westerbork comes solely from others' observations of her.

Considering the way Anne wrote about nature and God during her final months in the Annex, she may indeed have been happier in the camp than she was in hiding.[45] People who had been in hiding "viewed Westerbork as a kind of freedom," said Eva Geiringer, whose mother, Fritzi, became Otto's second wife; their family was taken to Westerbork at around the same time as the Franks after also being betrayed in hiding.[46] Hillesum, a deeply spiritual writer whose ideas about God are strikingly similar to Anne's, found a new inner strength in the camp. "The misery here is quite terrible; and yet, late at night when the day has slunk away into the depths behind me, I often walk with a spring in my step along the barbed wire. And then time and again, it soars straight from my heart—I can't help it, that's just the way it is, like some elementary force—the feeling that life is glorious and magnificent, and that one day we shall be building a whole new world," she wrote in summer 1943.[47] Anne spent time in Westerbork talking about religion with an Orthodox Jewish boy a few years younger than she.[48]

Mechanicus, less spiritually inclined, found strength in his role as a reporter in the camp, developing sources and making careful notes. "It was a means of survival," his granddaughter later said. From his first entry (May 28, 1943) until his last (February 28, 1944), he neglected to write on only twenty-eight days.[49] "Anyone who can hold out at Westerbork and evade the transports can do more with his positive captivity than the Jew in Amsterdam with his relative freedom or the Jew who has gone into hiding and sits between four walls and is every minute in terror of being picked up," he wrote, adding:

> Captivity means the barbed wire and the discipline of hut life, but with a little imagination and a sense of humor and a love of nature you can create a world of your own in which it is possible to forget the captivity of the material body. . . . The sky is so delightful here and there is color on the moor. The sunsets are enchanting. Flocks of seagulls with white bodies and black heads, perhaps a thousand of them together, spend their lives cavorting on the air. I can stand and look at the gulls for long periods on end—they are the symbol of true freedom.[50]

* * *

By late summer 1944, the mood in the camp was more hopeful than perhaps ever before. The Allies liberated Paris on August 25 and were heading toward Brussels; Soviet troops continued to advance into Poland. Otto's prediction may have seemed about to come true.

Before dawn on Sunday, September 3, the mangy snake pulled into the camp once again. Although no one knew it then, the train was making its final journey: no more transports would leave Westerbork for Auschwitz.[51] As the Allies approached, Gemmeker had decided to empty out the camp as quickly as possible. He kept four hundred inmates to keep things running; the rest were deported.[52]

When the train departed later that morning, the Annex Eight were on it. So were Rachel Frankfoorder, the Brilleslijper sisters, Ronnie van Cleef, Rosa de Winter and her daughter Judy, and the Geiringer family. Of the 1,019 people on board, 45 men and 82 women survived the war.[53]

In the cattle cars, people jostled for position by the airholes to take a breath of fresh air and get a glimpse of the cornfields passing by. Frieda Brommet, who had just celebrated her nineteenth birthday in Westerbork, stayed next to a man she knew from the camp, and felt guilty for decades afterward for not having spent the journey with her father instead.[54] In the Franks' car, a young man stood by the little barred window by the ceiling and tried to determine the train's location, calling out the names of towns and villages to the other passengers. *If it is as bad as this in Holland, whatever will it be like in the distant and barbarous regions they are sent to?* People in a different car managed to saw a hole in the bottom and escape. Though some lost limbs in the process, they survived. Once, the train stopped and the SS opened the doors to ask if anyone still had any jewelry; whatever they had was taken by force. Ronnie threw her fountain pen through a crack in the boards rather than surrender it.[55]

There wasn't enough room in the cars for everyone to sit or lie down at once, so people took turns. Young men gave up their places for women and the elderly. Anne and Margot slept by leaning against their parents. Edith spent much of the journey trying to remove from her overalls the red patch that designated her as an S-detainee.[56]

After nearly three days of darkness in the closed car, of pushing and shoving, of the stench from the bucket, the train reached Auschwitz.

* * *

The train arrived during the night of September 5–6. "Everyone knew immediately where we were," Janny Brilleslijper remembered. It rolled past the *Arbeit Macht Frei* sign, past the watchtowers, the huts, the electric poles. When it pulled up to the platform, a loudspeaker blared: *Alles austreten, alle Bagage hinlegen*—"Everyone out, leave all baggage." Bloeme Emden remembered almost nothing of the ride from Westerbork but never forgot the moment of arrival. The platform was lit by neon lamps that shone a bluish light, turning the sky gray. The lights were so bright that she wondered if they were moons. "We're on another planet," she said to herself. Ronnie van Cleef thought the scene looked "like a science fiction movie."[57]

Women were told to go to one side, men to another, with cars available to assist those who couldn't walk—a direct trip to the gas chamber. "Little men in blue striped suits" ran up to the new arrivals and began hissing at them: *Ihr seid gesund. Lauf.* ("You are healthy. Walk.") "They were trying to warn us," Janny said. "We didn't understand any of it."[58] A woman in her mid-forties thought the Nazi who asked *Kannst du gut laufen?* wanted to know if she could run well—the German verb can mean "walk" or "run"—and answered no. She was selected for the gas chamber.[59]

The story of Auschwitz has been told by survivors—Elie Wiesel, Primo Levi, Tadeusz Borowski, and many others. From their work, as well as from all the other memoirs and histories of Auschwitz, we know a great deal about the camp's operations. There was the barbaric ceremony of selection that new arrivals underwent immediately, with Josef Mengele or another camp administrator sending them "to the left" or "to the right," for immediate murder in the gas chamber or a slower, even more agonizing death in the camp.[60] There was the brutal, often pointless labor: Wiesel, who was around the same age as Anne when he got to the camp, shoveled rock and dug trenches; Levi, trained as a chemist, worked in the rubber factory at Monowitz, a satellite camp that provided slave labor to the German company IG Farben; Borowski, a non-Jewish Pole who occupied a position of greater privilege, unloaded prisoners and their baggage from the cars and took the plunder to "Kanada," the vast storehouse of goods brought to Auschwitz by deportees from all over Europe. There were the daily humiliations and physical torments: the lightweight striped uniform that male prisoners were given to wear in all seasons; the meager rations (officially around 1,700 calories daily, in the form of bread, ersatz coffee, turnip and potato soup, and occasionally meat, but in practice much less); the utter disregard for hygiene and the rampant dysentery that resulted; the wooden bunks with straw mattresses and thin blankets on which the men were made to sleep, two or more to a plank. Perhaps worst of all was the general viciousness: the beatings, the constant threat of the dogs, the daily possibility of being killed by a bullet fired by a guard feeling sadistic or just in a bad mood.[61]

All of this is a faithful representation of the experience of Auschwitz, as far as it can be represented in ordinary language. But the vast majority of the accounts of Auschwitz have been written by men. Although the Nazis intended to exterminate all Jews, they treated Jewish men and women differently: more Jewish women were deported than Jewish men, and more women than men were selected for death in the extermination camps. Women "turned out to be dangerous to the Nazis specifically in their difference from men: in their ability to carry the race," writes Joan Ringelheim, a pioneer in the field of feminist Holocaust studies.[62]

If Anne had survived, she might have written her own memoir of Auschwitz, one just as enduring as the ones we now consider classics. And if she had, our image of Auschwitz—rather, Auschwitz II/Birkenau, the women's camp, which was also the site of the main gas chambers and crematoria—would be a little bit different from what it is today, because of the distinct experience women had in the camp.[63] The experience of children was different still—but virtually all of them were gassed on arrival. In the eyes of whoever conducted the selection for Anne's transport, she was an adult: she passed the initial test and was put into the women's camp together with Margot, her mother, and Mrs. van Pels. "Older girls who could still be expected to be productive as workers could stay with their mothers," remembered Lenie van Naarden, who was also on the transport from Westerbork with Anne.[64]

In reading memoirs of women who survived Birkenau—none of which have achieved the widespread recognition of memoirs by men—one notices many details that are unfamiliar from the Auschwitz of Levi or Wiesel. The women's camp and the men's camp were "different horrors within the same Hell," Myrna Goldenberg, another feminist scholar, has written.[65] To ignore those differences, writes Ringelheim, is "to ignore more than half of the Jewish population who were deported or murdered":

> Jewish men [cannot] stand in for Jewish women as we try to understand their everyday life during the Holocaust, with its terror, loss, escape, hope, humor, friendships, love, work, starvation, beatings, rape, abortions, and killings. Jewish women and men experienced unrelieved suffering during the Holocaust, but Jewish women carried the burdens of sexual victimization, pregnancy, abortion, childbirth, killing of newborn

> babies in the camps to save the mothers, care of children, and many decisions about separation from children. For Jewish women the Holocaust produced a set of experiences, responses, and memories that do not always parallel those of Jewish men.[66]

One primary difference was in the way the female prisoners were clothed. In contrast to the men's striped uniforms, they were given civilian clothing—but without regard to its appropriateness for either the setting or the season. Many were forced to wear clothes that were too tight or otherwise revealing. Bertha Ferderber-Salz, a young mother from Poland who was deported to Birkenau from the work camp Plaszów in 1944, received "a brown silk dress with white spots" that would have fit a woman many times larger than she, its neckline plunging to her waist.[67] Her sister received a practical wool dress, but her sister-in-law got a skirt and pajama jacket small enough for a child. Olga Lengyel, a Hungarian doctor deported to Birkenau in 1944, was given "a formerly elegant [dress] of tulle, quite tattered and transparent, and without a slip. . . . The dress was open in the front down to the navel and in the back down to the hips."[68] All the women's clothes were marked with red paint (some survivors say a red stripe, other say a red arrow) on the back. When the prisoners saw each other so ridiculously dressed, they often burst into laughter.[69]

The Birkenau superintendent reported to the Auschwitz commandant. During the seven weeks that Anne spent in the camp, from September 6 until October 28, the Auschwitz commandant was Josef Kramer, and the Birkenau superintendent was Maria Mandl, known as a "zealous functionary" who "treated prisoners with uncommon cruelty," one scholar of Birkenau writes. Mandl and others "distinguished themselves in their savage treatment of women prisoners. Their brutality was shocking even by Auschwitz standards."[70] The staff was dominated by criminal prisoners and "asocial German women" who were brought to Auschwitz in spring 1942 from Ravensbrück, a women's concentration camp north of Berlin, when the SS expanded Birkenau. Rudolf Höss, who controlled the Auschwitz women's camp until November 1943, later said that "the worst among Ravensbrück prisoners were selected for duty at Auschwitz. In their meanness, coarseness, and baselessness they had no equal among criminal prisoners."[71] Eventually Polish and Jewish women were incorporated into the hierarchy, some equaling the SS in cruelty. The women's barracks were run by a *blokowa*, the equivalent of the male *Kapo;* she was assisted by a *Vertreterin* (representative) and *Schreiberin* (secretary), who wrote and edited the roll call and reports. There were also a doctor, nurses, and half a dozen *Stubendiensten* (orderlies). Camp policewomen were chosen from among the inmates, as well as female firefighters, garbage collectors, and corpse-gatherers.[72]

In fall 1944, when Anne arrived, prisoner registration at Birkenau took place in the "Sauna," a shower room near two of the crematoria. "We saw that huge, black, smoky fire," Janny remembered.[73] Non-Jewish female prisoners were often allowed to keep their hair, but Jewish women were shaved and subjected to what was euphemistically known as "gynecological examination."[74] After a shower (a trickle of cold water that might be supplemented by a Nazi with a hose), some were quarantined for disease on the "visa," an empty square near the perimeter fence. An elderly woman in quarantine with Janny, the wife of a prominent Dutch Communist theorist and politician, died while sitting there in the hot sun. Others remember being quarantined in barracks together with women from all over Europe.[75]

In Auschwitz I—the main camp—prisoners were housed in brick barracks. At Birkenau, which was created in autumn 1941 as a holding pen for Soviet prisoners of war, the barracks were wooden horse stables with beamed roofs instead of proper ceilings and dirt floors that turned to mud when it rained. The initial Soviet prisoners died so quickly that the Nazis were alarmed: those prisoners had been intended to serve as an "asset" to Berlin. The Nazis responded to the "catastrophic conditions" in the camp by increasing its capacity for corpse storage and crematoria.[76]

In summer, the barracks were oppressively hot; in winter, they were freezing, heated only by two iron stoves that were not always operational, owing to difficulties obtaining firewood or coal. Beds—planks lined with horse blankets—were stacked in tiers of three, each holding as many as twelve women. "We called it 'lined up like spoons,'" Ronnie remembered.[77] The wooden frames creaked under the women's weight. Lengyel, who called the bunks "wooden cages," wrote that they sometimes collapsed, causing wounds and broken bones.[78] Without pillows, the women slept with their heads on their fists and all their possessions underneath them, to avoid theft. It was "ghastly" to "suddenly feel a hand under your head, or even worse, a rat," Janny remembered.[79]

The latrines in Birkenau were even more primitive than the barracks. They consisted of a deep ditch with planks thrown across it, on which the prisoners had to squat "like birds perched on a telegraph wire."[80] Each latrine—there were two for each division of the camp, each of which comprised around twenty-eight barracks—was intended to serve thousands of women. "There were feces all over the place. You couldn't put your hands down anywhere, you could hardly put your feet down," Janny remembered.[81] Though it was impossible to maintain any kind of hygiene, some women nonetheless tried to make themselves presentable by using dirt as eyebrow pencil or margarine as face cream. Janny remembered French women who found a piece of mirrored glass and a small comb, which they used to neaten their eyebrows.[82]

The latrines were located in the last row of barracks, a potentially long and treacherous walk. On Ronnie's first night in the barracks, a woman went out to use the latrine and was shot.

She lay outside the barracks all night, moaning; in the morning she was dead. To avoid going out at night, some used as toilets the metal pans designated to hold communal food and drink for the prisoners. In the morning, before roll call, the women grabbed these pans for the distribution of "so-called coffee." "You could ladle some of it out with a cup and drink it," Ronnie remembered. "But then five of you, for example, had to drink from that cup. Then we agreed, 'Remember—three sips for each person,' and then we each had three sips. We stood there watching each other, to be sure that no one took four sips. Then there was some left over. Now everyone could have a fourth sip, because there was still enough."[83]

Anne was often by Ronnie's side, drinking her share from the communal cup of swill. She was "very calm and quiet and somewhat withdrawn," Ronnie said. "The fact that they had ended up there had affected her profoundly—that was obvious."[84] Perhaps these eerily prescient lines from a poem she had written long ago, before she knew hunger, occasionally ran through her mind:

"Quack, quack, quack," said Mistress Chatterback,
Calling her ducklings from the deep.
And up they came, "Cheep, cheep, cheep.
Well, do you have any bread for us,
For Gerald, Mina and Little Gus?"
"Why, yes, of course I do,
A lovely crust I stole for you.
It's all I could find, you'll have to share,
Now please divide it fair and square!"[85]

After the morning roll call, which could last for hours in the cold and rain, the workday began: a lengthy stretch of labor that was physically punishing and often senseless. Janny worked in the weaving mill as well as folding plastic for airplanes and "pulling shoes apart." Lenie and Bloeme remembered dragging stones from one end of the camp to another, while others brought them back. Anne's "work" was likely similar. Unlike Westerbork in summertime, Auschwitz in autumn was gray and damp, the clay soil turning to mud, with no greenery. "There was nothing, nothing that looked alive, no flowers, nothing," said Lenie.[86]

Few memoirs by male prisoners mention Nazis by name. By contrast, many of the women single out Irma Grese, one of the officers who reported to Mandl.[87] Only twenty-two in December 1945, when she was executed for crimes against humanity, she was tall, blond, and elegantly dressed, "with every hair in place," smelling of perfume.[88] She outfitted herself in designer clothing seized from the transports. Lengyel remembered "a sky-blue pea-jacket which matched her eyes," her whip sticking out "jauntily" from the top of her boot.[89] "All the Nazis were in love with her," remembered Arianna Szörényi, a Hungarian-Jewish woman arrested and brought to Auschwitz in summer 1944.[90] Performing selections, Grese "advanced toward the prisoners with a swinging gait, her hips swaying, and the eyes of 40,000 wretched women, mute and motionless, upon her."[91] Clearing the garbage from the officers' kitchen, Ferderber-Salz once found a pile of animal intestines and tore into it, "sucking the raw blood hungrily."[92] Grese happened to pass by and beat her for stealing food. She also forced prisoners to roll in mud. Lengyel wrote that Grese tried to coerce a handsome Georgian prisoner into having sex with her by torturing the girl he loved; she also claimed to have performed an abortion on Grese. "It was dangerous to refuse anything to [her]; yet if the superior authorities learned of her interference with nature, for it was an illegal operation, it would be just as dangerous for us."[93]

In addition to the unimaginable cruelty and brutality that all prisoners suffered, women in Birkenau were subject to uniquely female humiliations. Some, including Lenie, had their periods when they arrived, which made stripping naked even more humiliating. After her turn in the shower, Lenie was furious to discover that another woman had taken her sport shoes and replaced them with pumps. "Period and all," she went naked to complain to a male guard, who made the other woman return them and whipped her. Later a female guard who had noticed her heavy flow surreptitiously gave her a sanitary napkin. Ronnie, who was also menstruating when she arrived, tried to keep her underpants on, but a Nazi hit her on the head and then ripped off her sanitary belt. Menstruation wasn't a problem for long. It has been rumored that the Nazis put something in the women's food to keep them from menstruating, but this doesn't seem to have been true. "It was simply that a woman living below subsistence level doesn't have a period," Janny said.[94]

Nonetheless, women got pregnant in Birkenau. The majority of these pregnancies were the result of rape by Nazis. Women were also raped or coerced into sex by other prisoners, often non-Jews in privileged positions, who promised them food in return for sex; some—Aryan women only—were forced to serve in the infamous brothel in the main camp for Nazis and their guests, known as the *Freudenabteilung*, or "Joy Division."[95] Women who were visibly pregnant on arrival were sent immediately to the gas chamber, but some managed to hide their pregnancies under clothing and made it into the camp. If a baby was delivered in the infirmary, mother and child were both gassed immediately; if the baby was stillborn, the mother was allowed to return to the barracks. For this reason, infirmary workers adopted a policy of euthanizing babies upon birth. "To this day the picture of those murdered babies haunts me," Lengyel writes.[96] Some women were able to conceal their pregnancies till the last moment and labored secretly in the barracks; it was only a matter of time until their babies were discovered. At Bergen-Belsen, Ferderber-Salz encountered a maternity hut filled with pregnant women and nursing mothers, many of whom had been transferred there from Auschwitz. When she asked a midwife what became of the babies, she was told, "Don't ask unnecessary questions."[97]

Like memoirs by men, women's memoirs tend to emphasize themes of hunger and obtaining food, as well as the fear of physical danger. But they also stress the importance of social bonding. Women were likely to come together in groups of two or more, which functioned as surrogate families in which the members shared food, helped one another acquire necessities, and maintained morale. Such comradeship was unusual among men and indeed "conspicuous by its absence," one scholar writes.[98] Giuliana Tedeschi, an Italian-Jewish prisoner, wrote that prison life in Birkenau was "like a piece of knitting whose stitches are strong as long as they remain woven together; but if the woolen strand breaks, the invisible stitch that comes undone slips off among the others and is lost."[99]

The women in these groups worked vigilantly to ensure that none of them would become the dropped stitch. "Camp sisters," or *Lagerschwester*, could be blood relatives or friends: they "accepted responsibility for each other's survival, by sharing food, risking punishments, encouraging each other, and providing physical care," writes scholar Ruth Bondy.[100] Cecilie and Mina Klein, sisters from Hungary, were deported to Auschwitz in summer 1944. "When Mina would tell me, 'Let's end our lives today,' I would persuade her to wait another day, pointing out that the day is almost over and our bread is about to be distributed," Cecilie Klein said later. "Another time I begged her to wait until it gets cold. 'Why end our lives on a sunny day?'"[101] When Ronnie returned to the barracks after a six-week stay in the hospital, other Dutch women pooled their bread rations to acquire a pair of pants for her.[102]

Anne, Margot, and Edith, sometimes joined by other prisoners, formed such a group. "Mrs. Frank tried very hard to keep her children alive, to keep them with her, to protect them,"

Lenie said. But Anne and Margot both struggled in this unforgiving environment. The Polish women in Auschwitz, many of whom had been toughened by weeks or months in the camp, could get away with disobedient acts like skipping the lengthy roll calls. The Dutch women, who had led comparatively pampered lives up till now—"healthy and not yet hungry," said Rachel Frankfoorder—were paradoxically more fragile. "Dutch people melted like snow in the sun," said Lenie.[103]

Anne soon came down with scabies, a rash caused by infestation with the human itch mite; her entire body became covered in spots and sores, and she was sent to the scabies barracks. Witnesses disagree about whether Margot had it too or went with her voluntarily. Edith reacted to being separated from her children with "total despair." She asked Lenie to help her dig a hole under the wall of the scabies barracks. Through the hole, Edith spoke to her daughters and passed her bread ration to them.[104]

At one point, Frieda Brommet and Ronnie were in the scabies barracks with Anne and Margot. Their clothing was taken away from them, and they had to lie naked on the cots together, two women per bunk. Frieda's mother looked out for her daughter and Ronnie, while Edith took care of her own daughters. "We all shared with each other," Ronnie said. One day Frieda and Ronnie discovered a platinum watch hidden in their straw mattress. They passed it through the hole to Edith and Frieda's mother, who used it to buy "a whole loaf of bread . . . and a piece of that cheese that stinks . . . and a piece of sausage." Ronnie also sang to the others to try to keep up their spirits: "That would calm everyone, the Frank girls too."[105]

The worst of Auschwitz's torments may have been the constant slaughter taking place on all sides. On September 15, 1944, ten days after Anne's arrival, all the inmates were forced to stand and watch as two prisoners who had escaped and been caught—a couple in love—were executed. The man, a political prisoner named Edek Galiński, was hanged in the men's camp; the woman, Mala Zimetbaum, was to be hanged in front of the women. As she stood waiting, Mandl, the Birkenau superintendent, made a speech about how prisoners who obeyed would be rewarded with better treatment, while those who broke rules would suffer. Meanwhile, someone slipped Zimetbaum a razor blade, which she used to slash her wrists. According to one account, she slapped Mandl in the face before being taken straight to the crematorium.[106]

Although such public executions were unusual, prisoners were surrounded by death all day long: "carts with corpses, pulled by moving corpses," as well as corpses stacked on carts intended for emptying the latrines. "The emotional shock at the existence of something like that" was something they all felt, Ronnie said. And they saw long lines of men and women—up to 2,000 a day—waiting their turn at the entrance to the gas chambers. "The crematory smoked right before their eyes, and they just watched, knowing exactly what it meant," recalled a prisoner who met some of these women later in Bergen-Belsen.[107]

The women did what they could to support each other in the face of the unremitting horror. The goal of the Nazis was to eradicate the prisoners' humanity: "the disintegration of your personality," said Bloeme Emden. "That didn't work with us, above all because of the mutual support that the members of our group of women gave each other, and because of what we had brought with us in terms of inner strength." Whether they had been in hiding for an extended period or at Westerbork, the Dutch women hadn't been physically conditioned to hard labor and malnutrition the way many women from Eastern Europe had. (All of the Dutch women remembered Westerbork as a paradise in comparison with Auschwitz.) But in many cases, they had spent that time with loved ones, and now they had those memories to draw upon: they talked about holiday meals and other happy moments from the past. "To work it out completely alone—that didn't work," said Lenie. "Even very strong women broke down."[108]

A few prisoners managed to write at the time about their experience in the camp. To the best of my knowledge, all of those who did so were men. Members of the *Sonderkommando*, the "special squad" charged with forcing prisoners into the gas chambers and disposing of their corpses afterward, buried documents testifying to the atrocities near the crematoria.[109] Viktor Frankl, the author of *Man's Search for Meaning*, one of the most famous works about the Holocaust, made notes for his book but lost them while undergoing disinfection. Later, Frankl said that writing, even in a limited way, helped him to rise "above the sufferings of the moment."[110]

There is no evidence that Anne was able to benefit from similar consolation. If she had, we might be reading her memoir today alongside *Night* and *Survival in Auschwitz*. But none of the women who remembered encountering her at Auschwitz seems to have been aware that she was a writer.

8

Corpse
Bergen-Belsen, November 1944–February 1945

> "Death, which you still don't dare look straight in the eye, is very different from what you now think.
>
> Death is good and kind and is just as much a form of the life we love as anything else. How can creation keep renewing herself if she herself does not destroy the old forms?"
>
> —Frida de Clercq Zubli, *The Eternal Song*, quoted in Anne's "Favorite Quotes Notebook"

ON APRIL 15, 1945, the British army liberated Bergen-Belsen. Richard Dimbleby, a veteran BBC war correspondent, reported from the camp the next day. "I find it hard to describe adequately the horrible things I've seen and heard," he began, emotion audible in his voice. As he crossed the barbed-wire fence that led to the camp's inner compound, he was struck by the dust and the smell: "sickly and thick, the smell of death and decay, of corruption and filth." Bodies were strewn along the road. He could see "bony, emaciated faces" at the windows of brown wooden huts—"starving women too weak to come outside, propping themselves against the glass to see the daylight before they died." Less than six feet from a pile of decomposing corpses, four young people were sitting on the ground sharing a morsel of food, as if they were having a picnic.

When Dimbleby entered one of the huts, he was even more shaken by the conditions inside. There was no electricity. The stench of feces and vomit was overpowering. In the darkness, he could make out the convulsions of dying people too weak to rise from the floor. Above the general moaning, he heard the voice of a girl. He stepped over corpse after corpse until he found her.

> She was a living skeleton. Impossible to gauge her age, for she had practically no hair left on her head and her face was only a yellow parchment sheet with two holes in it for eyes. She was stretching out her stick of an arm and gasping something. It was, "English, English. Medicine, medicine." And she was trying to cry but had not enough strength.[1]

The liberated camp held 60,000 prisoners, the vast majority of whom were "acutely ill" or "actually dying of starvation." Thirty thousand more had died in the previous few months. Brigadier Hugh Llewellyn Glyn Hughes, chief medical officer for the British army, called the number of corpses "uncountable." Isaac Levy, a chaplain serving with the British army, tried to compile the names of survivors, but it was "an impossible task . . . some die even as we list them." Some 13,000 survivors of the camp died within three months of liberation.[2]

The army attempted to provide medical aid, but the conditions were beyond anyone's capacity to help. Doctors drank heavily in the evening to blot out the horrors they had seen during the day. "They die on us as soon as we touch them," one said.[3] A doctor who had worked with victims of the Bengal famine advised feeding survivors a mixture of dried milk, flour, and sugar, but they were too starved to digest it. Meanwhile, in a camp storeroom, hundreds of Red Cross food parcels containing canned meat, milk, and cookies, as well as nearly 2,000 cans of Ovaltine, were discovered untouched.[4] The doctors tried supplying nutrients intravenously, but the method was too traumatic for these patients, many of whom had been subjected to Nazi experiments.

The BBC initially held back Dimbleby's radio broadcast about Bergen-Belsen for three days—either because they found it hard to believe or because it was too graphic. They broadcast it only after he threatened to quit. Levy, too, attempted to spread the word about the conditions in the camp. "These are the last relics of European Jewry and we must be with them," he wrote to Rabbi Israel Brodie, chief rabbi of Great Britain. "Belsen is just the beginning, we may yet find more of our brethren in other camps, if and when we arrive in time," he wrote in a letter published in the *Jewish Chronicle*, a London-based Jewish weekly. To his wife, he confessed a darker fear: "I am certain that 90 per cent of those who survive will never be really normal."[5]

In the first few weeks after the camp was liberated, 20,000 corpses were removed from the barracks and the roads. The British forced former SS guards detained in the camp to do the work, using bulldozers provided by the Royal Engineers. Levy and a colleague conducted a burial service and said kaddish, the Jewish prayer for the dead, over the mass graves. "To recite the kaddish over such a heap of emaciated bodies cast helter-skelter into pits, each containing some 5,000 such corpses, seemed to negate the concept of man created in the divine image," he commented later.[6]

Somewhere in the heap, one of the corpses was Anne.

* * *

As the Red Army approached Auschwitz/Birkenau from the East, the Nazis shut down the gas chambers and blew up the crematoria in an attempt to disguise what had taken place there, evacuating the remaining prisoners to camps farther west. At the end of October, they staged a selection to determine which women were still capable of forced labor. Anne and Margot, along with Rachel Frankfoorder and the Brilleslijper sisters, were part of a group of about 1,000 women chosen for transport on or around October 28. They were locked in a barracks for an entire morning, then subjected to another roll call lasting for hours; finally they were put into cattle wagons once again. Edith and Mrs. van Pels remained behind. The Dutch women were "very happy to leave Auschwitz," even for an unknown destination.[7] Nothing, they thought, could be worse than that camp.

This journey was even more difficult than the last. For a trip of four or five days, the women were given a small piece of bread with "a dab of margarine" and one thin blanket apiece, despite the bitterly cold weather. English airmen, who probably thought the train was transporting troops, fired on it regularly; eventually the guards fled. "Everywhere, people were weeping . . . We slept once in a while, but most of the time it was out of the question," Rachel remembered. But when the train finally stopped at Celle, the women felt optimistic. "Oh, we're going to Bergen-Belsen, now that's a good camp," Janny thought. In a downpour of rain and hail, they had to walk five miles from the station to the camp, as the townspeople looked on: "No one lifted a finger to help us."[8] But the area around the camp was beautiful, green and wooded. Some of the women breathed deeply as they walked through the forest, enjoying the scent of nature.[9]

Upon arrival, they were taken to a field where an iron pipe, punctured with holes, spat cold water. "Who had enough courage to get undressed in the ice-cold November wind and wash?" remembered another Dutch woman who arrived from Auschwitz in November 1944, likely on the same transport as Margot and Anne. "We did not have towels, so one couldn't dry oneself.

We didn't even talk about soap. But I felt so filthy and dirty with lice . . . that I plucked up the courage to get completely undressed and give myself a wash in the freezing water."[10]

Occupying an area of about twelve square miles—"a moor with a bush here and there," Janny said—the camp had been established in 1941 for French, Belgian, and Russian POWs. In April 1943, Himmler requisitioned it as a holding pen for a few thousand "exchange Jews"—Jews with foreign papers or other advantages, who could potentially be traded for German POWs being held by the Allies and thus were meant to be kept "healthy and alive." Already the buildings were "dilapidated," with "primitive" sanitary facilities.[11] Between January and September 1944, approximately 4,000 exchange Jews were quartered there—mostly Dutch Jews with exemptions who had come from Westerbork. Hannah Goslar, whose father had bought Paraguayan passports, was transferred there during that period; so was Nanette Blitz, whose family was on the list of Jews eligible for transfer to Palestine.[12] Prisoners were kept in segregated subcamps depending on their nationality and status. The "privileged" prisoners weren't tattooed or shaved and were allowed to wear their regular clothes, albeit with Jewish stars attached; their camp was called the "Star Camp." Hannah and her sister were separated from their father but were able to visit him in the evenings.[13]

At that point—despite punishing work assignments, crowded and unsanitary barracks, and a meager diet—Bergen-Belsen was indeed a "somewhat better camp," as Hannah later said.[14] And some of the Jews actually were "exchanged": around two hundred were sent to Palestine at the end of June 1944, including Mirjam Levie, the Jewish Council secretary who refused to type call-up notices.[15] But things changed drastically starting in September 1944, as the Nazis grew more and more desperate to evacuate prisoners from the front. Inmates were ordered to build huts to house 3,000 women to be transported from Auschwitz in the next few months.

When the transport carrying Anne, Margot, and the other Dutch women arrived, the barracks were not yet finished. Instead, more than a dozen large tents were hastily erected as shelter from the wind and rain. "It looked as if a circus had left them behind," Janny's sister Lien wrote in her memoir.[16] Filthy and hot, the tents "stank like the lion's cage at the [Amsterdam] zoo," Janny said.[17] The women slept on a thin layer of straw or on the bare ground. Hanna Lévy, a Yugoslav prisoner who arrived in the camp in August 1944 and kept a diary there, could hear at night "an oppressive noise that rises up like a black tide from the other side of the barbed wire, mixed with children's sobs, with moans, groans, and complaints." From what she could glimpse of the women from Auschwitz, they looked "dreadful, sick, withered, covered with foul and filthy wounds."[18]

Winter came early to northern Germany. "It freezes, it snows, it hails. Then it thaws again. The mud is indescribable," wrote Abel Herzberg, who was imprisoned in the Star Camp.[19] Within a few days, the tents blew down during a storm. Next the women were moved temporarily to "an old barn piled with rags and old shoes," remembered Lien. It, too, quickly became inundated with mud. Apart from the clothes they were wearing, the women had no protection against the weather. "Why do they want us to live like animals?" Anne asked. "Because they themselves are predators," Janny answered.[20]

Even as other parts of Bergen-Belsen were cleared to create a women's camp, prisoners continued to arrive from camps near the front line by the tens of thousands.[21] Ultimately, around 50,000 people would be murdered in the camp. "Auschwitz was organized hell," Lien wrote, but Belsen was "chaos."[22] The filth and overcrowding in the barracks were overwhelming. To wash, the prisoners had to stand in a bathhouse with gaping holes for windows and doors, "hammered from all sides by gusts of wind," Lévy wrote. Men and women stood together, "cramped, jostled. No point in waiting 'your turn' because there are too many of us and the spigots are always taken—unless, of course, the water is turned off." She no longer cared about bathing next to men: "Sex has no meaning here."[23] Weak from dysentery and other diseases, prisoners relieved themselves wherever they were, unable to reach the latrines. "All we could do was hope we did not get sick in that place," Nanette wrote later.[24]

In December 1944, as Auschwitz was shutting down, the camp's commandant, Josef Kramer, was named commandant of Belsen. He brought with him some of the most infamous staff from Auschwitz, including Irma Grese. Kramer reduced daily rations to a bowl of soup—turnips cooked in water—and a single slice of bread. The entire vat of soup might be sealed and left for two days to spoil before it was served. Food was distributed irregularly, with the lunchtime soup arriving at five or six and the evening meal served in the morning or not at all.[25] At times there was no bread for days. "One of us constantly stood watch for when the food came. You had to jump for it, or it would disappear immediately," Lien wrote.[26]

Because of their poor health, instead of performing harder physical labor, the Frank and Brilleslijper sisters were assigned to rip apart old shoes by hand. Their hands began to bleed and became infected. Lien and Anne had to give up the work, and thus the extra food rations that came with it; Margot and Janny persisted, sharing their food with their sisters. Still, the women grew thinner and thinner. "Anne seemed to consist only of her eyes, great brown eyes with a greenish glint."[27] At some point Auguste van Pels was also transferred from Auschwitz; she joined Anne and Margot in their barracks. Another Dutch woman who shared their barracks thought Mrs. van Pels was Anne and Margot's mother, since "the three always stayed together."[28]

Sometimes, Lien said, Anne was still "the Anne [whom] we

know from the diary, mercurial and full of life."[29] When new transports arrived at the camp, she became animated, hoping to find friends and to learn news of her parents. She and Margot also regularly joined the Brilleslijper sisters to visit a barracks housing Dutch children, caring for them and entertaining them. Sometime in December—it may have been Christmas Day—the prisoners received extra rations: a tiny piece of cheese and jam. Anne, Margot, Lien, and Janny decided to make a party out of it and celebrate St. Nicholas Day, Chanukah, and Christmas all at once. They managed to scrounge up some extra food: a few handfuls of potato peels, which they roasted over an open fire; a bit of sauerkraut; a beet. In one account of the celebration, Anne comes up with a stick of celery; in another, she finds a clove of garlic.[30] "We were all trying our best not to cry, although we were all thinking of our loved ones," Janny remembered.[31] They gathered on their bunks—Anne and Margot occupied the bunk directly below Janny and Lien—to sing sentimental children's songs:

> The sun is taking leave of us
> The evening glow lights up the field
> In sweet repose, the night comes thus
> Without a care to rest we yield.[32]

They dared to imagine, too, what it would be like to go home. Anne pictured a celebratory meal at Dikker and Thijs, one of Amsterdam's fanciest restaurants, famous for oysters, caviar, and lobster.[33] And they told stories. "We thought they must be old stories which we did not happen to know. But now I know that they were stories that Anne had made up herself," Lien remembered. Was Anne recounting the tales she had written in the Annex—"The Wise Old Gnome," "Eva's Dream," or perhaps "Blurry the Explorer," about a teddy bear kept in captivity who longs to see "the big wide world" but meets with violence and danger and ends up performing slave labor? She was modest, telling the others that her father knew much better stories. Margot began to cry at the memory, wondering if he was still alive. Anne answered confidently: "Of course he is alive."[34]

As in Auschwitz, the women had to be constantly vigilant: not just about their physical safety, but also about their mental health. To let down their guard—to stop trying to keep themselves clean, to let their spirits drop—meant death. "In addition to an active form of suicide (by hanging oneself, taking poison, or leaping out a window), there was a passive one, simply losing the will to live," historian Ruth Bondy writes of women in the camps. "As long as there was hope that somebody might need them at the end of the war, the women clung to life."[35] After Edith had been refused selection for the transport, Anne assumed that her mother had been gassed. *Perhaps that is the quickest way to die.* But for a time, she believed that Otto was still alive.

It's not clear what made her abandon that belief. Maybe it was the deterioration in conditions. Between December 1, 1944, and mid-March 1945, 25,000 more prisoners arrived in Bergen-Belsen. By this time bread was even scarcer; in addition to their daily soup, the inmates received only "a teaspoon of butter and a slice of cheese or sausage twice a week, and occasionally so-called 'coffee.'"[36] Nanette, who lost her "privileged" position when her father died and was transferred from the Star Camp to the women's camp, recalled "days when we would not eat at all."[37] Starving people tore up the grass and tried to cook it. When the vats containing soup were brought to the barracks, prisoners sometimes attacked the people carrying them and swarmed to lap up from the ground any drops that spilled. The camp's water supply was cut off for days, and people went insane from thirst. "Washing," one survivor remembered, "meant going into a dark room where the one faucet was and where dead bodies lay in heaps, with rats feasting on them."[38] So many people died at such a rate—five hundred to a thousand per day, according to different estimates—that the crematorium couldn't handle them all. The SS tried burning the bodies on wood soaked with diesel, but Germans in an army training ground nearby complained about the smell. After that, the dead were piled up alongside the barracks or simply left where they were. "We were fifteen thousand prisoners left to our own devices, trying to survive with whatever was made available to us," Nanette remembered.[39]

Sometime that winter, she encountered Anne, who searched the camp for former acquaintances whenever she could. They embraced, tears streaming down their cheeks. Anne told Nanette about having been in hiding, about Auschwitz, and—as Nanette later remembered—about her diary and how excited she had become after hearing Bolkestein's speech on the radio. "We stood there, dreaming about her book being published, about a reality in which she would become a famous writer. . . . Amid all that chaos, we were still capable of dreaming."[40] Nanette met a girl who had seen Edith in Auschwitz and said that she had survived a selection. She passed on the news to Anne, which apparently "renewed her courage."[41]

But in late January or early February, when Hannah Goslar found Anne in the camp, she had lost that courage. Hannah was still in the Star Camp, which was separated from the rest of Bergen-Belsen by a barbed-wire fence stuffed with straw, to prevent prisoners from seeing through it. One day someone told her that Anne was among the group of Dutch women on the other side. That night, Hannah went to the fence and called for her. Mrs. van Pels heard and brought Anne.

More than a year earlier, Anne, safe in the Annex, had dreamed that Hannah was in a concentration camp: *I saw her in front of me, clothed in rags, her face thin and worn . . . I could read in her eyes: . . . Help, oh, help me, rescue me from this hell!*[42] Now, through the fence, Hannah could see only Anne's shadow. Her voice was "fainter, weaker . . . not the boisterous, confident chirp I knew," Hannah wrote later.[43]

"They took my hair," Anne wept to Hannah. She had no warm clothes, only rags. Margot was sick with typhus, too weak to move. Their parents had been gassed. Hannah heard this news with incredulity: she had heard rumors about what went on at other camps, but "organized gassing of people"? That's what happened, Anne said. "Especially for anyone over fifty, like her father. She had seen the curls of crematorium smoke."[44] Hannah told Anne that her own father and sister were still alive. "I have no one," she responded, sobbing. Later, Hannah wondered if knowing Otto was still alive would have helped her muster the will to survive.

Anne asked Hannah to bring her food. "I'll try," Hannah responded, though she had no idea how she would manage it. Over the next few days, she collected food for Anne from other women in the Star Camp, where prisoners could receive parcels from the Red Cross. They met at the fence again, and Hannah whistled her old childhood whistle—the first notes of the Dutch national anthem. When Anne came, she threw the package over. There was a scuffle, then she heard Anne screaming with rage. "A woman has caught it and won't give it to me," Anne wept.[45]

They tried again a few days later. This time Anne caught the package. "Got it!" she called. Hannah thought she sounded "more like her old self."[46] The mother of one of Margot's classmates, in the same subcamp as Hannah, also threw food over the fence to Anne. Anne offered to share it with Janny and Lien, but they told her to keep it for herself and Margot.[47]

Soon after this encounter, Hannah's father died. By the time Hannah had recovered enough to look for Anne again, she was no longer there.

* * *

Typhus was "the hallmark of Bergen-Belsen," said Rachel Frankfoorder. After an incubation period of about a week, it produces severe headaches, muscle pain, high fever, rashes, and delirium; death usually comes within another week. Those suffering from it had "hollowed-out faces, skin over bone." Nanette, who fell sick shortly after liberation and spent two weeks in a coma, called it "a disease as brutal as the SS."[48]

Decades later, Hannah attributed her survival in Bergen-Belsen to her little sister, Gabi, twelve years younger, for whom she was responsible. "I saved her and she saved me," she told an interviewer. "If you were a mother and a daughter, or two sisters or even two cousins, it was a little bit easier." Another young woman who survived the camp remembered that at a moment when she felt ready to give up, she heard her mother's voice in a dream telling her to take care of her younger sister.[49]

In late January or early February, Margot became ill. Anne cared for her, and Janny and Lien brought food as well. "They had the least desirable places in the barracks, below, near the door, which was constantly opened and closed," Rachel remembered. "You heard them constantly screaming, 'Close the door, close the door,' and the voices became weaker every day." On February 7, she and Auguste van Pels were put on a transport to Raguhn, a subcamp of Buchenwald. By that time, both Anne and Margot showed signs of typhus.[50]

Soon Janny and Lien learned that the Frank sisters were in the sick barracks. They urged them not to stay there, but it was too late. Margot "had a high fever and smiled contentedly," Lien remembered. "Her mind was already wandering"—an indication that the disease had progressed to its final stages. Anne, feverish but "friendly and sweet," said to her friends, "Margot will sleep well and when she sleeps I won't need to get up again."[51]

These are the last words of Anne's that anyone recorded. A few days later, Janny and Lien found her body with Margot's. "She stayed on her feet until Margot died; only then did she give in to her illness," Janny said later.[52] They wrapped the corpses in a blanket and carried them to a mass grave.

What might Anne have seen in her last moments? The younger faces of her mother and her sister, bending over her crib with delight. Pim squinting at her from behind his treasured Leica, adjusting the lens. The furry white coat that warmed her as a toddler. Hannah across the classroom at the Montessori school, opening her arms for a hug. Hopscotch on the Merwedeplein, the neighborhood children shouting. Jacqueline pedaling home from the Jewish Lyceum beside her, hair flying in the wind. Presents stacked on the table for her thirteenth birthday, a red-checkered diary somewhere in the pile. Hello Silberberg leaning against the brick wall of her building, waiting for her. The Annex Eight around the kitchen table, sitting down to another meal of kale or beans. Bathing with Margot in the front office. The red high-heeled shoes that Miep managed to find. Bep, cup of soup in hand, putting her head close to share a secret. Peter glancing at her shyly as they studied together. The attic window, Peter by her side, gazing wordlessly together at the horse chestnut tree. Her notebooks and the loose pages of her manuscript spread across the desk she had to share with Pfeffer. *It's an odd idea for someone like me, to keep a diary . . . I have been through things that hardly anyone of my age has undergone . . . Peter hasn't looked at me since yesterday . . . There's in people simply an urge to destroy, an urge to kill, to murder and rage . . . I want to be useful or give pleasure to the people around me yet who don't really know me, I want to go on living after my death!*[53]

Maybe, for her, the story does end differently. She gathers up the papers from her desk and silently descends the stairs. If anyone tries to stop her, she doesn't notice. The bookcase swings open at her touch. Before her lies a meadow full of wildflowers, the meadow she imagined in her stories. A breeze lifts the pages from her hands. She watches as they float out into the world, their destination unknown.

Part 2

"Anne Frank"

9

Author
Otto and the Diary, 1945–1947

I simply can't imagine that the world will ever be normal for us again.

Bussum, the Netherlands, spring 1946. A man walks along a residential street in this quiet canal town east of Amsterdam. His threadbare suit no longer hangs as loosely on his frame as it did a year ago, but the number on his arm reveals to all that he is a survivor of the camps. His eyes are red from weeping, which he still cannot help but do whenever he talks about his family, murdered by the Nazis. Under his arm is a bundle of papers.[1]

He finds the house he's looking for and enters. A Dutch woman is waiting. Like him, she's fifty-seven years old, but the war has prematurely aged her, too. Her husband, a Jewish man named Leon Beek, was exempt from deportation owing to their marriage. He joined the Resistance, working in espionage. Betrayed in January 1943, he was sent to multiple prisons before arriving at Westerbork as an S-detainee, like the Annex Eight.

After more than a year in the camp, he hatched a plan with an officer of the Dutch military police: as soon as the Allied forces were close, the two of them would seize control of the camp and Beek would replace Gemmeker as commandant. But the officer was arrested before they could put their plan into action. Trying to escape with a group of other prisoners, Beek was caught and executed on the dunes outside Westerbork on August 15, 1944, less than a week after the Franks' arrival at the camp.

His widow didn't learn about his death until almost a year later, after liberation. Once a prolific writer, she hasn't written a word since. A stroke has left her paralyzed on her right side. She lives with her son and daughter-in-law, who take care of her. Still, she is "full of fantasy, always adventurous, restless, capricious," her son says later. "Just like some of her protagonists . . . they were her."[2] Within two years, she will be dead.

The visitor tells the woman how much his daughter loved her novels, just like every other teenage girl in the Netherlands. He tells her about the hiding place and shows her the diary—written, she sees, in the form of letters, the same way the heroine of her books did. Even before he tells her, she knows what must have happened to its author. Yes, she says, she will look at the manuscript.

Two weeks later he makes the trip to Bussum again. By now he knows what he wants to do with the book. Still, he is eager to hear her advice.

You must publish your daughter's diary, Setske de Haan—better known by her pen name, Cissy van Marxveldt—tells Otto Frank.

* * *

Liberation came in many different ways. At Bergen-Belsen in April 1945, Janny Brilleslijper watched with "enormous satisfaction" as Josef Kramer, arrested by the British, "was thrown in a jeep" and "kicked in the ass."[3] Nanette Blitz, ill with typhus, was cared for by British nurses; soon she was transferred to a sanatorium near Amsterdam, where she stayed for several years, recuperating from tuberculosis and pleurisy.[4]

As the British approached Bergen-Belsen, the Nazis put any prisoners well enough to travel on transports to camps deeper into Germany. Less than a week before the camp was liberated, Hannah Goslar and her five-year-old sister, Gabi, were forced aboard a transport to Terezín. As they waited on the train platform at Celle, a German soldier sent to escort them—one who had been fighting with the army rather than guarding camps—asked Gabi if she would like a cookie. "What's a cookie?" the little girl replied. The soldier's face crumpled. "Something told me he was only just fully comprehending how dehumanized we had been by his people," Hannah wrote later.[5] As the fronts shifted, their train traveled back and forth for ten days until the Red Army finally liberated it.

By that time, survivors of Auschwitz—including Otto Frank as well as Fritzi Geiringer and her daughter, Eva—had already been trying to get back home for several months. Their circuitous journey first took them east by train through the Soviet Union to Odessa ("Everything blown up," Otto reported). There, waiting to be picked up by the steamship *Monowai*, en route from New Zealand to Marseille, they camped out in a sanatorium on the Black Sea: an abandoned summer palace that had belonged to the tsars, with painted ceilings and elegant parquet floors. The weather was warm, and some of the survivors enjoyed sunbathing on the beaches and exploring the beautiful city, a former naval fortress with distinctive nineteenth-century architecture.[6] Eva was thrilled to receive a toothbrush and toothpaste from an Australian soldier; she hadn't brushed her teeth since Westerbork.[7]

Anne's former classmate Theo Coster, in hiding with a family of non-Jews in the countryside, learned that the war was over on April 17, when he saw a Canadian soldier riding a motorcycle down the road. Albert Gomes de Mesquita, who had once been so embarrassed when Anne tried to explain sexual reproduction to him in front of the entire class, was in hiding with his parents; they heard about the liberation on the radio.[8] Jacqueline van Maarsen was in Amsterdam when the Canadian army finally reached the city on May 7, bearing white bread, chocolate, and cigarettes; her class learned the Canadian anthem in school and sang it to welcome the liberators.[9]

Jacqueline had avoided deportation thanks to the ingenuity of her mother, a Catholic, who managed midway through the war to persuade a Gestapo officer to remove Jacqueline from the register of Jews. In order to be exempted himself, Jacqueline's father—a Jewish man married to a non-Jewish woman—was required to present proof of sterilization as a guarantee against diluting the Aryan race through miscegenation; like many others, he found a doctor willing to falsify the certificate. Jacqueline was able to stop wearing the star and to leave the Jewish Lyceum for an ordinary public school, where some of her classmates were the children of Nazis. She stayed in touch with her old friends, including Nanette and Hannah, until they all eventually went into hiding or were deported with their families. Now she waited for them to return—especially Anne.[10]

The previous nine months, known as the "Hunger Winter," had been a time of almost unendurable hardship in the Netherlands. On September 4, the day after Anne's transport left Westerbork for Auschwitz, the Allies liberated Brussels. As the British army began to advance through the south of the country in mid-September 1944—parts of the Netherlands were initially liberated only to be retaken by the Nazis—Queen Wilhelmina asked Dutch railway workers to go on strike rather than aid the Germans. In response, the Nazis shut down civilian rail transport, using their own employees to run freight trains but refusing to supply food or coal to the Dutch population.[11]

That fall was unusually rainy and cold. In November, the

rivers and canals froze, making it impossible to bring provisions into Amsterdam by barge. "As the winter began, people were becoming as thin as skeletons," Miep Gies remembered.[12] City residents lined up outside bakeries at dawn for the chance to buy a loaf of bread; they scavenged through the frozen garbage that piled up uncollected. Those who still had bicycles could ride into the countryside to trade with farmers for food—or just beg. With fuel also scarce and electricity shut off, Amsterdammers cut down the tall trees that lined the boulevards to use for heat and made lamps out of cotton thread and oil. The weather stayed cold until April. "Toward the end, there was nothing but tulip bulbs and sugar beets to be had," Jacqueline wrote later.[13] (The Dutch proverb *Honger maakt rauwe bonen zoet*—"Hunger makes raw beans sweet"—must have seemed all too apt.) Albert experienced six weeks of no food other than white cabbage with water.[14] The bodies of those who succumbed to starvation lay in the street. Miep later wondered whether she and the other helpers could have come up with enough food to sustain the Annex residents all winter.

After liberation, people celebrated for days. Church bells rang at all hours; streamers flew. Allied planes dropped food packages with butter, cookies, sausages, and more. Within a few days, the electricity went back on. During the Nazi occupation, it had been forbidden to display anything orange, the color of the Netherlands' royal family; now the Dutch planted marigold seeds. Dutch children were sent to Britain on "health holidays" to regain their strength. People began trying to repair the damage accrued under five years of occupation, but supplies were lacking. "Everything was needed, but no one had anything," Miep wrote.[15] For the rest of her life she would be unable to throw away food in any form, even if it was spoiled.

While the Dutch were singing and dancing in the streets to welcome the liberators, Jews in hiding emerged more cautiously—"rubbing eyes that were unused to sunlight, their faces yellow and pinched and distrustful," Miep remembered—to discover, in many cases, that they had lost their entire families.[16] With liberation came the first news footage of the camps, including pictures taken at Bergen-Belsen that came to symbolize the worst depredations of the Nazis. Like the Annex residents and most others in Amsterdam, Jacqueline had heard the rumors about what happened to Jews who were deported east, but she hadn't believed them. "Until I saw the first photographs and film clips of the liberation of the concentration camps with my own eyes, I could not even imagine it," she remembered.[17] Miep could not bring herself to read the stories or look at the photographs. "I needed to do everything I could to keep my optimism about our friends," she wrote later.[18]

Soon the survivors began to return, albeit not many. As would eventually become clear, the Netherlands had one of the highest Jewish death rates—75 percent—in all of Europe. Of a prewar community that numbered around 140,000, only 35,000 remained. Some demographics were hit harder than others: the population of Jews over age fifty and under age sixteen was almost completely wiped out.[19] Lists of camp survivors were posted daily. Jan Gies was assigned to work in Amsterdam's Central Station, greeting the returnees and directing them to sources of aid. The survivors' faces were so shriveled that it was impossible to tell their ages. "I heard it said that where the Jews had looked like everyone else before, now, after what they had endured, those who returned looked different," Miep would write.[20] Jan asked everyone if they had news of the Franks but heard nothing.

On June 3, Otto appeared at their door.

* * *

At liberation, Otto weighed less than 115 pounds. He had "hardly any face left at all, just a skeleton's skull out of which stared pale brown inquiring eyes," Eva Geiringer remembered.[21]

He had survived nearly five months of imprisonment in Auschwitz, plus the torturous journey home.

"Edith is not coming back," Otto told Miep. While still in the infirmary at Auschwitz, he learned that she had died only a few weeks earlier. Hermann van Pels had already been gassed. Peter had gone on the death march, despite Otto's efforts to persuade him to hide in the infirmary. All that was known about Fritz Pfeffer and Auguste van Pels was that they too had been transferred somewhere. "But I have great hope for Margot and Anne."[22]

The next day, he returned to Prinsengracht 263. Three dried brown beans were lying on the floor by the entrance. A huge sack of them had once burst while Peter was hauling it up to the attic.

> *A shower—no a positive hailstorm of brown beans came pouring down and rattled down the stairs. There were about fifty pounds in the sack and the noise was enough to waken the dead. Downstairs they thought the old house with all its contents was coming down on them. It gave Peter a moment's fright, but he was soon roaring with laughter, especially when he saw me standing at the bottom of the stairs like a little island in the middle of a sea of beans! I was entirely surrounded up to my ankles in beans. Quickly we started to pick them up. But beans are so slippery and small that they seemed to roll into all the possible and impossible corners and holes. Now, every time anyone goes upstairs they bend down once or twice in order to be able to present Mrs. v.P. with a handful of beans.*[23]

Otto picked up the beans from the floor, put them in his pocket, and kept them for the rest of his life.[24]

Soon he received a postcard from his mother in Switzerland, telling him that his relatives there—his sister, her husband, and their children—were still alive. He wrote back immediately, outlining his situation in a few sentences: "It is all like a bad dream. . . . I'm not yet normal, I mean that I haven't been able to regain my equilibrium." After the raid on the Annex, the

Gestapo had confiscated all his possessions; apart from what friends had lent him, he had nothing—"no hat, no raincoat, no watch, no shoes." He was still waiting for news of Anne and Margot. "I don't know where they are and I never stop thinking of them."[25] On the page in his datebook for June 12, 1945, Anne's sixteenth birthday, Otto wrote her name, pressing down so hard that the pen nearly broke through the paper.[26]

Otto wrote to Dutch people who had been in Bergen-Belsen, including Nanette, who told him about her encounter with Anne there. He pored over new lists of survivors whenever they appeared and made the rounds of Jews who had already returned. Eva Geiringer remembered him showing up at the apartment where she and her mother were staying, asking if they had seen his daughters. He came to Jacqueline's apartment as well; she was shocked by how thin and sad he looked.[27] There was nothing to do but wait. "Every time there was a knock at the door or footfalls on the steps, all our hearts would stand still," Miep wrote.[28] Some people waited all day at tram stops or train stations for months after liberation, praying that their loved ones would find their way home. Back in Basel, Ida Elias, the mother-in-law of Otto's sister, Leni, stood in front of the family home every morning to wait for the mailman to bring news of her son Paul, who had fled from Germany to France and hadn't been heard from since. Confirmation of his death, in Auschwitz, didn't come for decades, long after Ida died.[29]

Meanwhile, Otto tried to summon the strength to rebuild. "I am back again and try[ing] to start a new life," he wrote to his old friend Nathan Straus.[30] In a few ways, at least, he was lucky. First, he had a place to live with Miep and Jan. Many survivors returned to find that their houses had been plundered during the Hunger Winter, when people stripped buildings for wood. If a house was still standing, it was likely to be occupied by strangers. A seventeen-year-old who lost both his parents was refused entry to his former home by its current occupants, "recipients of privileges from the occupying powers."[31] Theo Coster's apartment somehow survived intact with most of the family's possessions, but they returned to find the kitchen full of rotten food, the smell pervading every room.[32]

Otto was able to recover some of Edith's heirloom furniture from the friends to whom he had entrusted it, but many others found that property they had given to friends or neighbors for safekeeping wasn't returned. A new word was coined to describe those who held on to Jewish goods: *bewariërs*, combining *bewaren* (to keep) and Aryan.[33] The Dutch government-in-exile had cautioned citizens about buying stolen Jewish property, warning that the items would have to be returned after the war. But a Dutch person buying a house that changed hands several times during the war might not be aware that it had once been owned by Jews.

The legal process of restoring Jewish property turned out to be far from straightforward, owing to a series of policies enacted by the Dutch government that may have been well intentioned but were enforced in extremely bureaucratic and legalistic ways, compounding the difficulties for returning Jews. According to the "occupation measures decree," German anti-Jewish regulations were legally deemed to have never been effective.[34] Because of this, bizarrely, Jews who were fortunate enough to reclaim their real estate found themselves liable not only for "ground lease fees," a municipal tax that those who had occupied their homes during the war were unlikely to have paid, but also a penalty for late payment.[35] As the logic went, if the Nazi regulations had never really been in effect, then the rightful property owners had been delinquent in paying their taxes. Similarly, survivors who had held insurance policies found those policies canceled because they hadn't paid their premiums while they were in hiding or in the camps.

In addition to having a place to live, Otto was also lucky

that he had been able to transfer the ownership of his business to Jan Gies and Victor Kugler rather than turn it over to the Nazis; he was able to return to his former place of employment. Most survivors had nothing. There was little recourse for Jews who had complied in 1942 with the Nazi order to deposit their money and other valuables with Lippmann, Rosenthal and Co., a formerly Jewish bank that had been commandeered by the occupiers. Presuming that the owners would not return, the Nazis had put all the deposits into a collective account. Survivors found their assets frozen while the Dutch analyzed the bank records, trying to determine who was entitled to what—a process that took four years. In the meantime, a blunt announcement was made to the creditors: "Very little remains of the jewelry, paintings, gold and silver, fur coats, stamp collections, furniture and the like; these items were disposed of as quickly as possible."[36] The Dutch government did not consider itself responsible for refunding assets stolen by the Nazis; in any event, it did not have sufficient funds. Dutch Jews thus found themselves in an impossible situation. They had almost nothing to live on, but they hesitated to insist too strenuously on the return of their property for fear of arousing old antisemitic stereotypes.

Despite the widespread plunder of Jewish property, the Dutch government refused to differentiate between Jews and non-Jews in distributing aid—another policy that seemed reasonable on its face but had negative consequences for Jews, who were much more in need of help than non-Jews. Even worse, German-Jewish refugees, like Otto, were treated as enemy aliens and did not qualify for assistance. Many of them wound up emigrating to Palestine, which became the state of Israel in 1948.[37] "The laws for people not yet naturalized are a handicap," Otto wrote to Julius and Walter Holländer, Edith's brothers in the United States. But he tried to be philosophical about his situation: "We all have to bear our fate."[38] The Holländers sent him supplies from America, including food and a raincoat—

essential in the Netherlands. Nathan Straus sent $500, telling Otto not to bother acknowledging it or repaying it: "Just forget about it."[39]

Finally, Otto had sympathetic friends. In addition to Miep and Jan, who were willing to share their apartment with him indefinitely, Johannes Kleiman and Victor Kugler had also survived. After being separated from the Annex Eight at Gestapo headquarters, the men were held in various prisons before being transported to Amersfoort, a Nazi concentration camp about thirty miles southeast of Amsterdam. Conditions there were as brutal as those in other Nazi camps: inmates had to surrender their clothes and valuables, submit to tedious and painful roll calls, and perform slave labor on starvation rations. Kugler, worried about Kleiman's chronic stomach ailments, gave him the potatoes out of his soup. Within a few weeks, the Red Cross managed to get Kleiman released on account of his poor health, but Kugler was sent to several other labor camps. Toward the end of the war, when the Nazis were marching prisoners toward Germany, he and another man escaped when their column was attacked by British airplanes. A friendly bicycle shop owner in a nearby town gave him a bicycle to ride home, telling him to return it after the war.[40]

The Dutch treated Nazi sympathizers harshly: women who had fraternized with Germans were humiliated by having their heads shaved publicly, and many collaborators served jail time. Still, antisemitism resurged in the Netherlands, as it did elsewhere in Europe. Many returning Jews found that the city they thought of as their home was not entirely welcoming. Jacqueline had a boyfriend whose friends made antisemitic remarks around her: "Look, there goes a Jew again," they might say, or gossip about a Jew "who had had the nerve to come back and demand the return of the silver which he had entrusted to the neighbors."[41] Greet van Amstel, a poet and painter, overheard someone say about her on the street, "Don't come too close, they probably have lice." Another survivor was cursed at by a fellow passenger on a tram and told, "they forgot to gas you." Dutch newspapers advised Jews to attract as little attention as possible to avoid provoking antisemitism.[42]

Journalist and scholar Renata Laqueur, who would later publish her diary of Bergen-Belsen, found that the Dutch were eager to share the details of their own suffering—"executions, hunger, strikes"—but less so to hear about what had happened to their former neighbors: "We had to tell our story, but we couldn't yet."[43] When Ima Spanjaard, another Dutch survivor, rang a stranger's doorbell on her way home to ask for a glass of water, the person who answered said, "Don't tell me about the camps. . . . Through the entire Hunger Winter all we had was one kilogram of potatoes a week."[44] Jews, understandably, were unsympathetic to their former neighbors' accounts of the Hunger Winter or of German "atrocities" such as commandeering their bicycles. Unable to participate in the collective memory of Dutch suffering, they found themselves once again isolated from those around them as they tried to heal their own terrible wounds. As one Auschwitz survivor said at the time, "The past has been burned away and thinking about the future fills us with despair and fear. We will never really 'return,' we will never really be among the 'others' again."[45]

* * *

In July 1945, poring over a list compiled by the Red Cross, Otto discovered his daughters' names with crosses marked beside them: the universal signifier of death, even for Jewish Holocaust victims. He learned the details of Anne and Margot's last days from Lien and Janny Brilleslijper. Miep remembered hearing him slit open a letter in the Opekta office, then his voice, "toneless, totally crushed," telling her that Margot and Anne were not coming back. She took out the papers she and Bep had gathered from the floor of the Annex, with the red-checkered diary on top, and brought them to Otto. "Here is your daughter's Anne's legacy to you," she said.[46]

Gradually, information trickled out about the fates of the other Annex residents. Pfeffer had been transferred from Auschwitz to Sachsenhausen and from there to Neuengamme, a camp outside Hamburg, where he died in December 1944. Peter survived the death march from Auschwitz and ended up in Mauthausen, where he died in the sick barracks on May 5, 1945, the day that camp was liberated. Exactly what happened to Mrs. van Pels is still unknown. After being transferred in early February from Bergen-Belsen to an airplane factory in Raguhn, a division of Buchenwald, she was put on a transport to Terezín in the beginning of April and is believed to have died en route or shortly after arrival.[47]

Otto dealt with his grief through action. In Auschwitz, separated from his daughters, he had asked a boy in his barracks to call him "Papa Frank."[48] Now he sought comfort in that role, taking a paternal interest in friends of Anne's and Margot's who had returned from the camps. He traveled fourteen hours by truck to Maastricht—trains were not yet running—to visit Hannah and Gabi Goslar, who were recuperating there in a sanatorium, and helped the sisters make their way to family in Switzerland. As a farewell gift, he gave them Dutch coins with the date inscribed on the back to wear as pendants.[49] Within a few years, Hannah immigrated to Israel, where she lived until her death in 2021, at age ninety-three. He also visited Margot's best friend, Jetteke Frijda, who had survived the war in hiding and was entirely on her own.[50] "All this gave me new goals in life," Otto wrote later.[51]

And he rebuilt the connections that the war had interrupted. He became a voluble correspondent, writing lengthy letters to friends and family, a practice he continued for the rest of his life. "Everything seems unimportant, senseless. But life goes on and I try not to think too much and be angry," he wrote to Julius and Walter Holländer. ("We loved Margot and Anne as if they were our own children. Our life is empty now," the brothers wrote upon learning of their nieces' deaths.) To his mother, in Switzerland, he noted that Anne's diary had survived but that he hadn't yet been able to read it. "Perhaps I shall have the force to do so later," he mused in late August.[52]

By the end of September, Otto had finally begun reading Anne's papers. Overwhelmed by his painful memories, he could manage only a few pages at a time. To his family, he expressed amazement at what he found there. "What I read . . . is indescribably upsetting, but still I read it," he wrote to his sister.[53] The Anne he had known was there on the page: intelligent, creative, funny, impudent, independent-minded. She was a gifted writer: her accurate, detailed descriptions of life in the Annex brought "all the details of our cohabitation" back to him, a time that, in retrospect, seemed blessed.[54] "You will hardly believe it, but in spite of the constant strain and tension, the ever-present fear of discovery, we were really happy because we were sharing everything," he wrote to Milly Stanfield, his cousin in England, about those years in hiding.[55]

But there was also an Anne he hadn't known: "completely different . . . [from] the child I had lost," he wrote later. Despite their closeness, there were aspects of her character that she had kept secret from him. He was stunned by her maturity, her capacity for self-criticism, her self-awareness. He had been unaware, too, of her love for nature or the consolation she found in her belief in God.[56] Later, Fritzi Geiringer Frank would say that Otto had "an overwhelming feeling that he had not known his own child."[57]

Perhaps it was his sense that the Anne of the diary was in some ways a stranger that enabled Otto to move as quickly as he did toward the idea of publishing it in some form. *Neither I—nor for that matter anyone else—will be interested in the unbosomings of a thirteen-year-old schoolgirl*, Anne had written in her introduction to Version B.[58] But Otto was convinced that the book had universal appeal, primarily for its account of her coming-of-age journey. "Even if it wasn't Anne who had written it, it would still be so moving," he wrote to his family in Basel.[59]

Otto's desire to share it bordered on compulsion. He typed out extracts from the text and had them translated into German to share with his family. He also produced a typescript in Dutch. "Sometimes he'd come walking out of his room holding Anne's little diary and shaking his head," Miep remembered. "He'd say to me, 'Miep, you should hear this description that Anne wrote here! Who'd have imagined how vivid her imagination was all the while?'"[60] Eva Geiringer remembered Otto showing up at her and her mother's apartment with "a small bundle wrapped up in brown paper and string." Trembling with emotion, he told them how Miep had saved the diary and tried to read passages from it aloud, but kept breaking down in tears.[61] With Jacqueline he shared the letters Anne had written to her from the Annex. *I hope we'll meet again soon, but it probably won't be before the end of the war.*[62]

"Here is your daughter Anne's legacy to you," Miep had told him when she gave him the papers. What Otto did with that legacy is perhaps the most confusing—and contested—aspect of Anne's story.

* * *

Otto sits at his desk in the office at Prinsengracht 263 and opens the red-checkered notebook. Anne's image smiles up at him from the photo she's pasted to the inside front cover: wearing a frilly white blouse, she's sitting at a desk or table, her arms crossed, an open book in front of her. Above it she has written:

Gorgeous photograph isn't it!

And on the facing page:

> *I hope I shall be able to confide in you completely, as I have never been able to do in anyone before, and I hope that you will be a great support and comfort to me.*[63]

He turns the pages. Her handwriting: blocky, childish print; confident cursive. Photographs of her at the beach with Margot, with Edith's mother. Headshots in different poses. A letter he wrote to her in May 1939, just before her tenth birthday, in which he lectured her about being too impulsive: "The main thing is to reflect a little bit and then to find one's way back to the right path," he had instructed her. A birth announcement from family friends.[64]

Time spins backward; she is thirteen again. *On Friday, June 12th, I woke up at six o'clock, and no wonder; it was my birthday.* She's playing ping-pong, eating ice cream, mooning over boys. *It's easy to see that Hello is in love with me.* There are petty dramas with her friends. *In the afternoon Jacque went to [Hannah's] and I was bored stiff.*[65] How much did he know about her life at the time? Did she confide any of this to him? Was he paying attention? Or was he preoccupied—understandably—with his business, the Nazi regulations, the preparations to go into hiding?

Too soon, the move to the Annex. *It's not really all that bad here, for we can cook for ourselves, and downstairs in Daddy's office we can listen to the radio.* He flips past the letters to the characters from *Joop ter Heul*, which must have been a mystery to him. Amid it all, the constant threat from outside. *God knows which of our acquaintances are left.*[66]

Months pass: Pfeffer's arrival, St. Nicholas Day, the new year. *I shall probably be having my period soon.* The unvarying diet: beans, cabbage, potatoes. *Whoever wants to slim [down] should stay in the 'Secret Annex'!* Her frustrations with her mother. *Mummy gave me another frightful sermon this morning; I can't bear them, our ideas are diametrically opposed.* Mr. van Pels's crude jokes; Mrs.

van Pels's flirtations. *Pim, thank goodness, doesn't find her either attractive or funny.* (No one has called him "Pim" in so long.) Her mounting hatred of Pfeffer. *Everything he says about politics, history, geography and other things is such nonsense that I scarcely dare repeat it.* The tensions between the Franks and the Van Pelses, between the adults and the teenagers. *If I talk, everyone thinks I am showing off; when I'm silent they think I'm ridiculous; rude if I answer, sly if I get a good idea, lazy if I'm tired, selfish if I eat a mouthful more than I should, stupid, cowardly, crafty, etc.*[67]

And he sees, on the page, his own shortcomings as a father, and her passionate, unconditional love for him despite them. *Daddy's the only one who understands me occasionally, but generally he sides with Mummy and Margot . . . Daddy did my hair just now with the curling tongs, lovely, isn't it! . . . It's easy for me to picture Mummy dying one day, but Daddy dying one day seems inconceivable to me. It may be very mean of me, but that's how I feel.*[68]

What must it have been like to read all this, knowing that they all were gone, that she was gone?

* * *

In spring 1978, Arthur Unger, a film and television critic for the *Christian Science Monitor,* traveled to Basel to meet Otto and Fritzi. The original purpose of his trip, apparently, was to discuss the possibility of writing a script about Anne and Peter's relationship. But early in the conversation, Unger mentioned Anne's "other writings," thinking of her short fiction. "You mean the first diary?" Fritzi interjected.[69]

Unger, clearly taken off guard, tried to figure out how to phrase his next question. He gave up. "I'm a little confused," he confessed.

Otto, who was then about to turn eighty-eight, told Unger that Anne rewrote her diary. The originals were at the Anne Frank House, but they had copies in Basel, and Fritzi went to get them so that he could explain to Unger what he meant. "Her diary starts childish," Otto said, showing Unger the pages describing her birthday presents and her classmates, the photos she pasted in.

Unger was astonished. "Has this ever been published?" he asked.

No, Otto said. "You can't—the diary would be too long, if you put in all of it." Unger wondered if a scholarly edition would be possible. "Nobody would pay," Otto responded. Anyway, Anne wouldn't have approved. "Because she didn't want things to be published." He pointed out that the first diary starts with her birthday; the revision, with her entry of June 20. "She wanted to leave out all this. And here she writes—rewrites—her whole diary based on this diary."

"She didn't want things to be published," Otto repeated. "Personal things, childish things which she saw as too childish. Sex things. . . . Things like that are left out." His voice rose with emotion. "In publishing I based more or less on this [Version B]." He thumped his fist on the table. "Because that is what Anne wanted."

Unger was still amazed. "That was a major editing job," he said.

"It was very difficult," Otto acknowledged. He continued: "I must work in her sense. So I decided how to do it through thinking how Anne would have done it."

* * *

Nearly twenty years earlier, Otto appeared before a German court to defend the authenticity of Anne's diary. Lothar Stielau, a high school teacher in the northwestern German town of Lübeck—the birthplace of Thomas Mann—had written an article for a local publication in which he alleged that the *Diary* was "hardly more authentic" than the forged diary of Eva Braun and referred to Otto as one of "the profiteers from Germany's defeat." The article came to the attention of someone at Fischer Verlag, the German publisher of the *Diary*, who shared it with Otto.[70]

Shortly afterward, the local culture ministry opened an inquiry to determine whether Stielau—who had joined the Nazi Party and the Stormtroopers in 1932, when he was in his early twenties, and was now district chairman of the local branch of the far-right, nationalist Deutsche Reichspartei (German Reich Party)—had breached his professional obligation as a teacher to maintain political neutrality. When interviewed, Stielau said he believed that Anne Frank had kept a diary but claimed that passages of the original diary had been edited or omitted—which was, of course, true, though he had no way of knowing it. In response, Otto sued Stielau for "libel, slander, insult, defamation of the memory of a dead person and anti-Semitic utterances."[71]

In the legal proceedings for this case, Otto explained—much more circumspectly than he later would with Unger—that in fall 1945, he had prepared a typed version of the manuscript: though he never let the diary out of his sight, he wanted to have more than one copy of it, and he wanted to get parts of it translated into German so that he could share them with family members in Switzerland who could not read Dutch. He then worked with Isa Cauvern, the wife of Albert (Ab) Cauvern, on another typescript, in which he omitted passages that he deemed too personal or offensive.[72] The Cauverns were close family friends of the Franks; it was their daughter's birth announcement that Anne pasted into her diary. Ab Cauvern made some further edits. "In the beginning I changed quite a lot," he told the German newsmagazine *Der Spiegel*, which published a lengthy article about the lawsuit, though he later clarified that he meant only that he had corrected "punctuation, idiomatic, and grammatical errors."[73] Cauvern also added a brief postscript describing Anne's fate: "Anne's diary ended here. On August 4, the

Green Police made a raid on the 'Annex.' In March 1945, two months before the liberation of our country, Anne died in the concentration camp at Bergen-Belsen."[74]

As we know, Otto couldn't publish only the first, unrevised version—in part because, despite Miep and Bep's effort to salvage all the material they could, a big chunk of it was missing: the original notebooks for December 1942 to December 1943. Moreover, as Otto told Unger, it was "childish," full of things Anne hadn't wanted to publish. And Anne's voice had changed over those two years in hiding. The first version, at least the beginning of it, read like the diary of a schoolgirl. The second was written in the voice of Anne that the world now knows: polished, thoughtful, mature.

But he couldn't publish only the second version, either. First of all, Anne hadn't finished recopying and rewriting it. For all the entries dating after March 29, 1944, he had no choice but to work from the rough draft, since Anne had not edited those pages before her arrest. The task of creating a new book out of the two versions was challenging. "It keeps my brains busy every day," he wrote at the time.[75]

In preparing the typescript intended for public view, Otto worked from Anne's edited version (Version B, the loose sheets of paper), but he also added selections from elsewhere—her original diaries (Version A) as well as some of the autobiographical stories from her "Book of Tales"—that struck him as "essential."[76] As we know, the biggest change he made when compiling his version was to reinstate Anne's romance with Peter. "I thought that much of the deleted material was interesting and characteristic," he explained later.[77]

But what, exactly, did Otto leave out? At least one of the typescripts he worked on has been lost, so it's hard to know in some cases which edits were made by him and which by someone else—either Cauvern or editors at Contact, the Dutch publishing house that first published the diary. "As for me," Cauvern told *Der Spiegel*, "I have not deleted a single passage"—which makes it sound like he knew Otto had.

Although Otto was forthcoming about the edits he made at the behest of Contact, such as removing the incident in which Anne asked to touch Jacqueline's breasts, the interview with Unger appears to be the only time he explained at any length the changes he elected to make on his own. As he said in that conversation, he tried to consider "how Anne would have done it." From his vantage point as a survivor himself, Otto imagined what an Anne who had survived the war would have wanted to include in the published version of her diary. Take, for example, her vitriol toward Mr. and Mrs. van Pels. After writing all those pages, Anne had been with Mrs. van Pels in Auschwitz and Bergen-Belsen, where at least one witness commented on how close they were. Otto had seen Mr. van Pels selected for gassing at Auschwitz. And so he softened some of her harshest criticisms while leaving much of their substance. For instance, in an entry about Edith's anger at Mr. van Pels, Anne wrote in the original: *Mummy made the wish—one that cannot come true just now—never to see Mr. vP's face again.* In Version B, she modified *again* to *for a fortnight.* Otto kept this modification and deleted another harsh line from the same entry: ~~*The van Pels motto is: "If we have got enough, then the rest may have some too, but we get the best, we get it first, we get the most."*~~ A reference to Otto being angry because the Van Pelses were cheating the Franks out of meat and other foods became *Daddy is very angry for some reason or other.* Mostly, however, Otto retained Anne's critical remarks—such as one early on about Mrs. van Pels's *awful manners* and *stupidity*—which provide much of the *Diary*'s comic relief.[78]

Otto took out Anne's most vicious comments about Fritz Pfeffer as well, while leaving many of the others. ~~*It is no exaggeration to say that Pf. has a screw loose. We often joke among ourselves at his lack of memory, his opinions and judgment and have many a*~~

~~*laugh when he has just heard completely wrong and mixes everything up.*~~[79] Perhaps Otto was concerned about the feelings of Pfeffer's partner, Charlotte Kaletta, who later was furious at the way Frances Goodrich and Albert Hackett transformed his character in the stage adaptation of the *Diary:* an educated Jew who prayed regularly in the Annex, he was made to appear entirely ignorant of the Chanukah ritual and generally treated as a buffoon. Otto also altered some of Anne's language regarding the helpers and the other Opekta employees: anything that could be perceived as remotely critical about the helpers was removed, along with the reference to the warehouse employee Willem van Maaren's "dark past." And he took out personal information regarding the Voskuijls and others that was not germane to the happenings in the Annex, as well as removing names of people who had been helpful to them (the man who sold Miep vegetables, for instance).

What about Edith? It has become conventional wisdom that Otto removed Anne's criticisms of her mother, but any reader of the *Diary* can see that this is simply untrue. *I hope that Mummy won't ever read "this" or any of the other things,* Anne wrote in the entry in which she said she could imagine her mother's death, but not her father's. Edith could no longer be hurt by her daughter's cruel words. But Otto may have heard about Edith's heroism on behalf of her daughters at Auschwitz, from Rosa de Winter and other survivors, and could imagine that their relationship had changed as a result of being in the camp together. And so, as with the Van Pelses, he took some opportunities to soften Anne's language while leaving the substance of her content: *Mummy is terrible* in one entry becomes *Mummy is tiresome.* Still—for no apparent reason—there are places in which he reinstated cruel lines about Edith that Anne herself removed, such as a lengthy passage about how she felt unable to call her mother by the Dutch endearment "Mams," preferring a more formal address. (The English translation gives this, unfortunately, as "Mumsie"; the American version would probably be "Mommy.") *Though my mother is an example to me in most things she is precisely the kind of example that I do not want to follow,* Anne wrote in her original long entry of January 6, 1944, which she edited heavily in Version B. Otto restored the line that came before this one—*I need my mother as an example which I can follow, I want to be able to respect her*—and removed the rest.[80] "It is a disagreeable feeling to publish things against her mother—and I have to do it," he wrote to Milly Stanfield.[81]

Otto also had to reckon with how Anne had depicted him as a character in the *Diary.* Sometimes his revisions seem intended to show him in a more flattering light. In the entry for November 3, 1943, Anne recounted that Otto had asked Kleiman to bring a Christian Bible so that she could learn about the New Testament. "Do you want to give Anne a Bible for Chanuka?" Margot asked. (We can imagine her skeptical tone.) "Yes—er, I think St. Nicholas Day is a better occasion," Otto answered. Anne finished off the story with a punch line in her own voice: *Jesus just doesn't go with Chanuka.* In the revision, Otto attributed this quip to himself. In addition, as he had done with Edith, he removed some of Anne's more negative comments about him. ~~*I find Daddy's special liking for talk about flatulence and lavatories revolting.*~~ He changed a reference to *the old folks* to *parents.* He removed what appears to be a comment about his own youthful suicide attempt. ~~*Daddy . . . once ran out into the street with a knife in his hand to put an end to it all.*~~ In an entry in spring 1944, Anne made a rare complaint about his impatience. ~~*He has warned me that if I don't do any algebra, I mustn't count on getting extra lessons later.*~~[82] How he must have wished he could give her those extra lessons now.

What about the way Anne depicted herself? She is both the writer of the diary and a character in it. Apart from the romance with Peter, the most substantive change Otto made was to remove Anne's comments on her own creative process. ~~*At long last*~~

~~*after a great deal of reflection I have started my 'Achterhuis,' in my head it is as good as finished, although it won't go as quickly as that really, if it ever comes off at all.*~~[83] He kept her reference to wanting to write a "novel" about the Annex in response to Bolkestein's speech, but gave no sign that the text the reader is holding has any relation to the book Anne intended to publish.

"One can hardly speak of 'censorship' in describing the editing done by this admirable man, who was under no obligation to publish anything at all, who took it upon himself to do so, and who published the important parts," writes critic Philippe Lejeune, who acknowledges his intense sympathy for Otto in his essay about the editing of Anne's diary.[84] This is true: Otto has been unfairly criticized for his changes to the diary by many readers who, failing to do a line-by-line comparison for themselves, repeat the false arguments of others. At the same time, as Lejeune also points out, it is impossible for anyone—including Otto, who acknowledged that he did not recognize the writer of the diary as his daughter—to know what Anne would have intended: not only after the war, but even if she had had more time in the Annex to complete her work. "Who knows but that two weeks later some pages might have been tossed in the wastebasket, or that some entries from the original diary left out by Anne might have found their way back in? Everything was still provisional and in flux," Lejeune writes.[85]

Especially for this reason, it seems to me that the only real mistake Otto made in the process of preparing the diary for publication was not acknowledging the complicated genesis of the printed text. Did he fear that presenting it as anything other than a diary in the most traditional sense—a book of personal reflections written day by day, contemporaneously, without revision—would open it up to being challenged as inauthentic? Could he have failed to realize that Anne's changes to the text had essentially altered its genre from diary to memoir? He had thought Anne was writing a diary; that was how she described it to the others at the time. It looked like a diary, albeit one in the unconventional form of letters to a fictitious character.

But Otto chose to hide his work. After he completed his edits, he had a clean copy prepared to share with several friends who would eventually be instrumental in helping to publish the diary, including historian Annie Romein-Verschoor, who wound up writing an introduction to the Dutch edition, and Kurt Baschwitz, a professor at the University of Amsterdam. Baschwitz told *Der Spiegel* that Otto had shortened the diary "because some passages were too personal," especially those concerning Edith, though he added that he "did not make a scientific comparison between the printed text and the manuscript." (*Der Spiegel* observed that the diary, as published, was about half the length of the total manuscript pages.)

"Anne Frank's story prevents people from reading her diary as a text," Lejeune writes. "The work she began, and that her father finished, bothers readers who are hungry for firsthand accounts and who cannot conceive of editing as anything other than twisting or censoring that account."[86] Although the subtitle of the original Dutch edition of the book identified it as *Dagboekbrieven*, or "Diary-Letters," in the French and German editions the title was changed to *The Diary of Anne Frank* and in English to *Anne Frank: The Diary of a Young Girl.*[87] A form letter the American publisher sent out to readers who inquired about the original diary stated: "The translation (from the original Dutch) is a literal translation, not simply an approximation. There was no editing at all done on Anne's original writing."[88]

A myth was sprouting around the diary that Otto was powerless to stop, even if he had wanted to.

* * *

In her memoir, Miep makes it sound as though Otto was virtually strong-armed into publishing the diary. As she tells the story, Otto mentioned one day at a gathering of survivors that he happened to have Anne's diary, and a man attending asked to read it. This person was so impressed that he wanted to show it to Jan Romein, a leading historian. "Frank was against it, but his friends cajoled and cajoled, and finally Frank said yes," Miep wrote.[89] Romein then wrote—this part is accurate—an article about the diary for *Het Parool.* "By chance a diary written during the war years has come into my possession," Romein began, describing his absorption while reading it. "This apparently inconsequential diary by a child, this 'de profundis' stammered out in a child's voice, embodies all the hideousness of fascism, more so than all the evidence at Nuremberg put together," he pronounced.[90]

After the article appeared, Miep wrote, Romein "began a campaign" to persuade Otto to publish the diary, but Otto remained "adamant in his refusal." Romein and the friend who gave the manuscript to him argued that "it was Frank's duty to share Anne's story with others, that her diary was a war document and very important because it expressed a unique voice of a young person in hiding." They persuaded Otto that he had a "duty to forgo his own sense of invaded privacy." Reluctantly, he "agreed to allow a small, edited edition to be printed."[91]

Perhaps Miep was camouflaging her own discomfort with the publication of Anne's diary. For one thing, she was in it: Anne came up with pseudonyms for the other helpers, but she (and Otto) retained Miep's real name, though not her husband's. In addition to the invasion of her privacy, she may have been concerned that Otto risked attracting too much attention to himself in the fraught postwar climate.

The story of Otto's reluctant publication of the diary in close to its original form—repeated over the years by many others, including Alfred Kazin and Ann Birstein in their introduction to a collected edition of Anne's writing ("it was a Dutch university professor who urged formal publication of the book, and with only very slight excisions by Mr. Frank, *Het Achterhuis* was published")—has endured because it makes sense.[92] A diary, by definition, is not intended to be published; a memoir is. But because the decision was made to present the book as a diary, the fiction that Otto—and, correspondingly, Anne—had not intended to publish it is all but necessary. Here is another reason the truth of the editing process had to be concealed: it sits uncomfortably with this story. The amount of editing Otto did to the diary makes it obvious that he did wish to publish it.

Otto's decision to publish the diary was hardly shocking. A generation of French writers and artists, including George Sand, Delacroix, and Michelet, had been using their diaries, many of which were published posthumously, to reflect on art and literature, their romantic lives, and even sexuality and bodily functions.[93] There was also precedent for publishing a diary by a dead girl: At the time, one of the best-known published diaries was the *Journal of Marie Bashkirtseff*, a Ukrainian artist who died of tuberculosis in 1884 at age twenty-five. The book contained much about her love life, but also her reflections about her art, her desire for fame, her difficulties with her family, her illness, and her fear of death.[94] Anne does not mention reading Bashkirtseff's diary, but it may have been an influence.

Though Otto did spend much of 1945 and 1946 seeking advice from friends on whether to publish the diary, it's clear that he wanted to do so nearly from the start. "Otto felt that Anne's diary should be published, that it was important for children, especially German children," Kurt Baschwitz's daughter remembered.[95] (Baschwitz himself wrote of the diary, "It is the most moving document about that time I know, and a literary masterpiece as well.")[96] Werner Cahn, a friend of Otto's who worked for the publishing house Querido, reinforced his opinion. "He says: Absolutely publish it, it is a great work!" Otto wrote to Alice in fall 1945.[97]

But others were skeptical. "Who's going to read that?" a rabbi to whom Otto turned for spiritual guidance asked in amazement.[98] Nathan Straus, who looked at a preliminary English translation, worried that Otto's judgment of the manuscript was "inspired by affection for his lost little daughter rather than based upon any real merit inherent in a child's diary."[99] When Otto asked Baschwitz's daughter whether she thought the diary would appeal to young people, she told him she wasn't sure—she was uncomfortable with Anne's negativity toward her mother and with the sexual material.

So were a number of publishers. Cahn, acting on Otto's behalf, took the manuscript to Querido and to the German house Fischer Verlag, both of which turned it down. He then shared the typescript with Annie Romein-Verschoor, Jan Romein's wife, who also had no luck persuading a publisher to take it. A reader for the publisher H. Meulenhoff advised publication, but the house voted against it, owing to the diary's intimate subject matter and sexual content. At that point Romein wrote his article for *Het Parool*, which an editorial consultant at Contact saw. The house requested the manuscript, but staff were divided on whether it was appropriate to publish—again because of the "sexual topics," as Otto wrote later.[100] Two staff members later said that passages related to Edith and to menstruation were deleted from the text. Part of the reason for the deletions was that the book was intended as part of a series of short books; as such, it had to fit into an established format. But Otto later claimed that "religious advisers" working for Contact had objected to the material about menstruation, which he did not find offensive and reinstated in translation.[101]

Het Achterhuis: Dagboekbrieven, 1942–1944 was published on June 25, 1947, in an edition of 1,500 copies, with a preface by Romein-Verschoor and a jacket blurb taken from Romein's article. "BOOK," Otto wrote in his datebook. Romein-Verschoor compared the book to Bashkirtseff's diary but claimed it was more authentic, calling it "pure in its conversation with itself, without one disturbing or unspontaneous thought of later readers."[102] The myth of the *Diary*'s creation, now sprouted, was beginning to grow.

In a letter congratulating Otto on the publication of the *Diary*, Jacqueline wrote, "Who knows, someday Anne's book could even become as famous" as Bashkirtseff's. Later, she said she had written that to make him feel good, but she didn't believe it. In fact, she was unsurprised that the first publishers Otto approached found "no particular merit in a young girl's musings" and thought the book would be a "losing proposition." She thought Dutch people wouldn't be interested in reading books about the war so soon afterward.[103] Miep agreed: "Most people wanted to forget the war, to put it behind them and to move on."[104]

Despite a rapturous reception—praising Anne's precocity and literary talent, critics called it "a miracle," "uniquely tragic," a "moral testament"—the book was slow to sell, though it did go into a second printing by the end of the year.[105] Otto sent copies to politicians as well as family and friends. "The book should be read as widely as possible, because it should work for people and for humanity. Speak about it, recommend it to others," he wrote to Anne's onetime boyfriend Hello Silberberg, who had survived the war in Brussels under a false identity.[106] "I don't think it has ever been so difficult in my life to write a letter such as this—even if Anne had not mentioned me in her diary, or if I had never known her, this story would have touched me profoundly," Silberberg wrote back.[107]

The book next appeared, in similarly modest printings, in Germany (*Der Tagebuch der Anne Frank*, 1950) and France (*Le Journal de Anne Frank*, 1950). The German translation was done by Anneliese Schütz, a German refugee to the Netherlands from Berlin who had taught Margot literature before the war and also knew Anne. Otto later judged her as "too old for the job" and her language "pedantic"; Cahn wondered if the translation could have been part of the reason why "well-intentioned German literary circles" sometimes questioned the *Diary*'s authenticity. There were also political problems with the translation. As Schütz later explained to *Der Spiegel*, "A book intended after all for sale in Germany . . . cannot abuse the Germans."[108] Together with Otto, Schütz decided on certain emendations. Quoting the guidelines for Annex life prepared before Pfeffer's arrival, Anne had written that only *civilized languages are permitted, therefore no German;* this was changed to "all civilized languages may be spoken," eliding the fact that the Annex residents took pains to speak to each other in Dutch rather than in German, even though the latter would have been much easier on the adults. Anne's description of Westerbork was cut, as well as the line about the deportees being gassed. *Heroism in the war or against the Germans* was changed to "heroism in the war and in the struggle against oppression." Anne had written that *Germans and Jews are the greatest enemies in the world;* Otto and Schütz emended it to "these Germans and Jews are the greatest enemies."[109] As Otto explained later, "There were other Germans too. . . . We had friends in Germany . . . we knew these could never have been Nazis."[110]

The novelist Hermann Hesse and the sociologist (and Buchenwald survivor) Eugen Kogon both turned down Otto's requests to write a foreword; it was written by Marie Baum, a social scientist whose appointment to teach at the University of Heidelberg, Otto's alma mater, had been rescinded in 1933, since she had one Jewish grandparent. Baum described the book as a depiction of "the inner life of a gifted child" born into "an educated, prosperous German family that fled in 1933 from the onset of the persecution of the Jews," requiring the reader to deduce that the Franks were themselves Jewish.[111] Nonetheless, booksellers were reluctant to display the book in their windows.

Francis K. (Frank) Price, the manager of Doubleday's Paris office, received an advance copy of the French edition from a colleague. The preface, by the Catholic novelist and historian Henri Daniel-Rops, did not impress him. "A child of thirteen writing her diary," Daniel-Rops mused. "Childishness? Dreadful precocity? Neither one nor the other. . . . Anne Frank's daily notations are so modest in tone, so true, that it never occurs to a reader that she might have written them with any 'literary' motive—still less that a 'grown-up' might have revised them."[112] Price judged the book insignificant and told his assistant, Judith Bailey—later Judith Jones, the legendary editor of Julia Child and many others—to reject it.

Bailey found herself drawn in by the photograph of the girl on its cover: dark-haired, slender, with a prominent nose and lively eyes. She opened the book and read for hours. "I, too, became entrapped in those rooms behind the hidden staircase, listening for ominous sounds, caught up in the mounting tensions." The book, she told her boss, was both a remarkable historical document and a uniquely intimate glimpse into the mind of a teenager. Price was dubious: "What? The book by that kid?" But he agreed to send it on to New York.[113]

INTERLUDE

Anne Frank in Ethiopia

In 2005, twenty-year-old Yikealo Beyene sneaked across the border from his native Eritrea into Ethiopia without saying goodbye to his parents. A "young idealist with a big mouth," he had been targeted by the secret police, interrogated, and tortured. "I can never go [back] to Eritrea while the ruling party is still there," he later told an interviewer.[1]

In Ethiopia, along with thousands of other Eritrean refugees, Beyene wound up in a refugee camp. It was hot, dusty, and primitive, but there was a library with a few shelves of tattered books, including a one-volume omnibus that comprised *Robinson Crusoe*, Benjamin Franklin's autobiography, and *The Diary of a Young Girl.* Beyene became an unusual reader of the *Diary:* one who encountered it without already knowing Anne's story, or indeed anything about the Holocaust. Reading it, he came to think of Anne as his friend. As a young man who had known war since infancy, he found her longing for a normal life deeply touching. He thought she would be freed at the end. When he found out the truth, he cried.

Beyene saw it as his mission to share the *Diary* with the children he taught in the refugee camp. He began translating it into Tigrinya, his native language, using a pocket English-Tigrinya dictionary and writing longhand on paper. Spoken by about 10 million people, primarily in Eritrea, Tigrinya is a phonemic language written in Ge'ez script, like Amharic. The project occupied Beyene for much of the two years he spent in the refugee camp.

During those years, camp life became more dangerous. Militant groups threatened the refugees: since military service is compulsory in Eritrea, they were essentially deserters. A friend of Beyene's was kidnapped and nearly beaten to death. Together with others from the camp, Beyene fled to Sudan, but the situation there was hardly safer. He found smugglers to help him make his way to Cairo, but they said he was "not allowed to carry anything, not even a piece of paper." He handed over the translation, as well as his own diaries, but the smugglers refused to give them back. In Cairo, where he stayed in an apartment with about thirty other refugees, he mourned for his lost manuscript.

Cairo was a short-term solution: Egypt had a repatriation agreement with Eritrea. Meanwhile, Libya had signed an agreement with Italy to prevent migration across the Mediterranean. The only way out was to the east. In winter 2008, Beyene joined a group hoping to cross into Israel via the Sinai Desert. His knowledge of Israel was mainly limited to the war in Gaza that was ongoing at the time. But he knew it was the Jewish state. "I was thinking of Anne Frank," he said later. Maybe if he got to Israel safely, he could look up her family.

The truck carrying the refugees arrived at the border in the middle of the night. Beyene crossed a barbed-wire fence and was immediately picked up by Israeli soldiers. "Do you know Anne Frank?" he asked one of them, who was taken aback. "Of course, I know her diary," he responded. But when Beyene asked for help contacting her relatives, the soldier only smiled and offered him some food and water.

The refugees were kept in military barracks for a few days and then dropped off at the bus station in Be'er Sheva, a city in southern Israel. Beyene made his way to Jerusalem, where he found a job as a night watchman at a construction site. When he got his first paycheck, he bought an English-language edition of the *Diary* and started translating it again.

Beyene spent eight years in Israel. He studied psychology in Herzliya, near Tel Aviv, and earned a master's degree. He created an after-school program for underserved children, an Israeli-Eritrean cycling team, and a farming project. But during those years, the Israeli government stepped up pressure on African migrants, some 60,000 of whom entered the country before the construction of a wall on the border with Egypt. For a time, the government encouraged them to leave by giving them cash and a plane ticket—an offer that about 20,000 accepted. The 40,000 who remain are subject to deportation, likely to Rwanda or Uganda. The majority of the refugees are fleeing persecution in their native countries, but Prime Minister Benjamin Netanyahu's government has characterized them as "infiltrators" who promote crime. Some American Jewish organizations, including the Hebrew Immigrant Aid Society, have pressured Israel to change its policy.

In 2016, Beyene married an American and moved to the United States to join her. He now lives in Seattle and speaks regularly on refugee issues. He still hopes to publish the *Diary* in Tigrinya.

10

Celebrity
The Diary in America, 1951–1952

Who besides me will ever read these letters?

THE TWO DECADES OR SO AFTER World War II are often remembered as a golden age of American publishing: "a world where print was still king, and literature was at the center of a nation's culture," as Louis Menand writes.[1] It was also a professional landscape that—unlike academia, law, or medicine—was unusually accessible to Jews. Many publishing houses founded in the early decades of the twentieth century had Jewish publishers or high-level editors, including Alfred A. Knopf, Boni & Liveright, Simon & Schuster, Viking, Random House, Pantheon, Grove Press, and Farrar, Straus. Magazine journalism was less hospitable to Jews; Saul Bellow would recall being interviewed for a job at *Time* magazine in 1943 and being told that as an "outsider" he had no chance—an incident he used in his novel *The Victim*, published in 1947. In the film *Gentleman's Agreement*, which came out the same year, Gregory Peck plays a journalist at a weekly magazine who pretends to be Jewish in order to write about antisemitism—an obvious sign that there were no Jews among his colleagues. But that too began to change by the late 1940s, with Irving Howe's appointment as a book critic for *Time*.[2]

In this climate, Doubleday was an outlier. The largest publishing house in the United States by the early 1950s, its 5,000 employees occupied three full floors at 575 Madison Avenue, a brand-new twenty-five-story glass and concrete office building a few blocks from Central Park. Despite publishing popular Jewish authors such as Leon Uris and Herman Wouk, the firm had a reputation for being unwelcoming to Jewish staff. Leonard Shatzkin, who came to Doubleday as head of research in 1949, was warned by his future boss that he might encounter antisemitism at work. Shatzkin took the job and remained at Doubleday for ten years, but he left when he realized that he would never reach the topmost rung.[3]

Yet it was Doubleday that published the *Diary* after houses much friendlier to Jews—including Knopf, Viking, and Schocken—passed on it.[4] In his incisive study of the role Jews played in postwar American publishing, Josh Lambert notes that many Jewish publishers, sensitive to charges of clannishness or nepotism, strived to avoid appearing to favor Jewish books. In the case of Knopf, the house even published numerous books with anti-Jewish biases, including works by Willa Cather, H. L. Mencken, T. S. Eliot, and Raymond Chandler. Shortly after rejecting the *Diary*, Knopf considered a collection of columns from *Commentary* magazine. Bill Cole, the house's non-Jewish publicity director, argued that the book would be of interest not only to Jews but "even to the *goy polloi*." But Harold Strauss, then editor-in-chief at Knopf, was concerned that Jews wouldn't buy it. "The Jewish market has become quite a good one," he wrote in an internal memo, but only when "a book coincides with one of the major Jewish emotional orientations," such as Israel, the Holocaust, or antisemitism. In addition, he wrote, the book "treats the Jews as separate communities in America; and many Jews are unwilling to think of themselves in that way"—Strauss perhaps among them.[5]

In a 1950 article titled "The Restricted Market"—an allusion to the phrase "restricted clientele," which was advertising code for hotels that excluded Jews and Blacks—the writer Meyer Levin argued that such concerns about Jewish books were preventing the publication of Anne's diary in America. The author of some half-dozen books published in the 1930s, primarily on Jewish themes, Levin also worked as a journalist, with assignments ranging from reporting on the Spanish Civil War to writing film criticism for *Esquire*. His audience, as he told a friend, was "faithful but not too numerous"; he often struggled financially.[6] Part of the reason for his lack of popularity, he came to believe, was that his writing was seen as "too Jewish."[7] An editor asked him to diversify the Jewish characters in one of his novels to make it more representative of America. When he was at *Esquire*, the magazine received complaints that it published too many leftists and Jews. The editors responded by running his pieces under the byline "Paterson Murphy," prompting a quip from Ernest Hemingway, a friend of Levin's: "The hand is the hand of Meyer but the foreskin is the foreskin of Paterson Murphy."[8]

During World War II, Levin became a war correspondent in France; he then served in the U.S. Army's Office of War Information. Reporting from Europe in spring 1945, he witnessed the liberation of the camps. "All week I have been talking to Jews who survived the greatest mass murder in the history of mankind," he wrote in an article datelined "Buchenwald, May 2, 1945." Levin described "remote Polish villages whose mud ruts were filled with human bodies," a German officer "playfully" lining up Jewish children to execute them, a mother holding her baby above her head while dogs tore her apart.[9] He took on the role of lifeline for the survivors, collecting their names and hometowns as well as an address of someone he could contact on their behalf. "Survivors would crowd around his jeep and try to write their names on the hood, on the fenders, until the vehicle was covered with scrawls in Hebrew and Roman characters," Lawrence Graver writes in his chronicle of Levin's ultimate obsession with the *Diary*.[10]

In 1950, Levin, who was then living in Paris, read *Le Journal de Anne Frank*. The book was "one of the most widely and seriously read books in France," Janet Flanner reported in the *New Yorker* in November 1950, describing Anne as "a precocious, talented little Frankfurt Jewess" and praising her "acute analyses of her uncontrollable growing love for . . . Peter (whom she frankly found stupid)."[11] Levin was captivated by the *Diary*'s juxtaposition of adolescent innocence with the persecution of the Jews. Ever since his experience at Buchenwald, he had been possessed by what he later called an "idée fixe": the conviction that what happened to the Jews of Europe must be told. But, as a nonsurvivor, he couldn't do it himself; the best he could manage was "a tangential glimpse." Someday, he hoped, "a teller would arise" from among the persecuted.[12] Here was the teller he had been waiting for.

Levin reached out to Otto Frank to inquire about the *Diary*'s publication prospects in English. Upon learning from Otto that it had been rejected by a long list of British and American publishers, he became incensed. How was it possible that John Hersey, a non-Jew, could easily find a publisher for *The Wall*, his fictionalized account of the Warsaw Ghetto Uprising, while the *Diary*, "a real document" of Jewish suffering, went unread in English? The reasons publishers had given ranged from practical considerations, such as the expense of translation, to subjective ones: the book was "too special," one house had apparently said.[13]

As it happened, the *Diary* had been rejected by many of the same publishers who had also rejected Levin's own memoir, *In Search* (published by Horizon, a small press, in 1950). "Although editors found the manuscript forthright and often moving, they were put off by what they saw as Levin's relentless preoccupation with Jewish victimization and self-hatred, notably his indignation at his own difficulties getting fiction published," Graver writes.[14] Levin, however, did not see it that way. His book, like Anne's, must have been "too Jewish" for the American market.

* * *

When Frank Price, on Judith Bailey's recommendation, brought the *Diary* to the attention of Doubleday's New York office, Otto was also considering an offer from Little, Brown, another primarily non-Jewish house. He had been reluctant to proceed because the publisher wanted motion picture, radio, and television rights, which Otto refused to grant as a matter of principle: he did not want an American movie to be made from the book. "I couldn't bear the thought of some actress playing my Anne," he told Price and Bailey when they met at Doubleday's Paris office, an elegant apartment on a fashionable street near the Eiffel Tower.[15] Price offered terms similar to Little, Brown's: an advance of $500 (the equivalent of around $6,000 in 2024), with Otto retaining adaptation rights.[16] Otto accepted.

In contrast with literary houses like Farrar, Straus or Knopf, Doubleday was considered middlebrow. "I sell books, I don't read them," Nelson Doubleday II, president of the company from 1928 to 1946, was known to say. When he died in 1949, Edna Ferber—one of the company's many best-selling authors—said that his main achievement was "devising schemes for putting books in the hands of the unbookish." Dozens of retail stores promoted and sold Doubleday books; the firm also ran a popular book club for which it printed lower-quality hardcovers to sell at volume. Douglas McRae Black, who took over as president after Nelson Doubleday II, considered publishing "a commerce first and a 'noble calling' second."[17]

Anne's diary was assigned to Barbara Zimmerman, an entry-level staffer who would eventually—under her married name, Barbara Epstein—co-found the *New York Review of Books.* Born in 1928, a year before Anne, she was a recent college graduate whose only previous job had been as a summer camp counselor. Once, when she visited a radio studio to participate in a program on which high school students discussed the *Diary*, the director of the show mistook her for one of the teenagers.[18] People have speculated that the fact that she was assigned the book implied that Doubleday didn't expect much from it.[19] It also seems possible that Zimmerman was given the book because she was Jewish, albeit nonreligious: she and Otto would later exchange Christmas greetings. Another Jewish Doubleday employee, vice president Joseph Marks, also worked on the book. In their correspondence, Otto couldn't get used to the Americanization of Marks's name, routinely spelling it "Marx."[20]

Otto was apparently beloved by everyone he worked with at Doubleday. "He is, without a doubt, one of the sweetest men imaginable," an employee in the Paris office gushed.[21] Both Marks and Price would come to consider him a friend; Price visited the Annex and later spoke movingly about the experience, while Marks and his wife vacationed with Otto and Fritzi years after the *Diary* was published. But Otto's relationship with Zimmerman was exceptional. In 1952 and early 1953, from the months before the *Diary*'s publication through the messy negotiations over its dramatic adaptation, the two were in constant communication. "How much would I like to meet you," he wrote to her early on.[22] Her letters to him are newsy and effervescent, laying out business matters in clear, concise language while showing a tender concern for his health and state of mind. He sent her gifts: Dutch chocolate, an attractive waterproof case for papers and books, a gold pin. When he came to New York in fall 1952 to try to resolve ongoing problems with the dramatic rights, Zimmerman met his boat at the dock. During his visit, they saw each other almost daily and went to the theater and the movies together; when he left, a month and a half later, the first letter he wrote from the ship was to her. Back in Amsterdam, he kept a photograph of her in his office and another at home; she did the same with his photograph. "He's exactly what Anne says of him in the book . . . a really remarkable human being," she wrote to Price.[23]

Zimmerman's superiors at Doubleday made it clear that they considered the *Diary* an exception to the "commerce first, 'noble calling' second" rule; they felt a moral obligation to publish it, but they did not think it would sell. Serialization possibilities were judged "doubtful"; the sales representative in charge of selling serial rights to newspapers—then a crucial driver of sales—confessed later that he wasn't "all that keen" on the book.[24] The first printing was only 5,000 copies, with an advertising budget of precisely zero dollars.[25]

Nonetheless, on the strength of her own powerful attachment to the *Diary*—in one of her early letters to Otto, before the book's success, she affirmed her "great feeling for it"—Zimmerman managed to engineer an impressive sales push.[26] "This is an extraordinary book and one which should have a steady and substantial sale," predicted a memo that went out to sales representatives, likely written by her.[27] The book's striking red dust jacket displayed Anne's picture above the title "Anne Frank: The Diary of a Young Girl" and the tagline "An extraordinary document of adolescence." (Other titles considered were "The Secret Annex," "Families in Hiding," and "Blossom in the Night.") The flap copy noted the "extraordinary conditions" in which Anne had spent two years of her life but emphasized the "compelling self-portrait of a young girl just on the brink of maturity," which illuminated "the critical years of adolescence."

The back cover reproduced a page from the *Diary* in Anne's handwriting in which she quotes Eisenhower on D-Day in English: "This is *the* day." Early copies of the finished book were sent to influential educators, child psychologists, and authors, including Thomas Mann.

The first sign that the book might be something unusual came when the former first lady Eleanor Roosevelt agreed to provide an introduction, which Zimmerman drafted and Roosevelt accepted verbatim. It emphasizes the *Diary*'s uplifting and universal qualities; the word "Jew" does not appear. The book was "one of the wisest and most moving commentaries on war and its impact on human beings that I have ever read," Zimmerman/Roosevelt wrote, but at the same time "makes poignantly clear that ultimate shining nobility of [the human] spirit." Consistent with the Doubleday vision of "putting books into the hands of the unbookish," the introduction emphasizes the book's interest for a general audience: "her diary tells us much about ourselves and about our own children."[28] This language echoes the marketing memo, which notes that the *Diary* "is not preeminently a Jewish book . . . it will equally appeal to a less specialized and larger group of readers." If Jews were reluctant to emphasize their separateness from mainstream American society—and, especially after the Holocaust, understandably so—the *Diary* was a book with the power to convince their non-Jewish neighbors that they were just like everybody else.

Levin, too, participated enthusiastically in the book's marketing. Zimmerman's early letters to Otto often include happy comments about his work on behalf of the *Diary*. "I found Mr. Levin very charming and he has many fine ideas about the book," she reported to Otto in May, after Levin had visited her to offer his help.[29] (Later Zimmerman would remember that a remark Levin made at one of these early meetings had startled her: "He is at present suing a storage warehouse for $100.00, he informed us brightly one day . . . when all of us were in a warm, confiding mood.")[30] In addition to continuing his efforts to sell movie and dramatic rights, which Otto had asked him to take on after their initial meeting, he secured an assignment to review the book for the *New York Times Book Review* and persuaded the editor to allow him extra space. He did so without mentioning that he was acting as Otto's informal agent, a conflict of interest that would cause trouble when discovered.

On Sunday, June 15, *New York Times* readers woke up to the news that President Truman had dedicated the world's first atomic submarine, hailing it as "the forerunner of nuclear power for everyday use." General Dwight D. Eisenhower, a candidate for the Republican presidential nomination, had given a campaign speech in which he disavowed any role in the political decisions made by the Allies at Yalta and Potsdam. Connecticut senator Brad McMahon, also a candidate for president, urged the stockpiling of hydrogen bombs. The price of the Sunday edition was scheduled to increase from fifteen cents to twenty cents the following week, the cost of newsprint having doubled in the years since the war.

And on the cover of the *Book Review*, American readers saw for the first time Anne's soon-to-be iconic image—dark hair pulled back with a barrette, faraway eyes, Mona Lisa–esque half-smile. Levin's review, headlined "The Child Behind the Secret Door," adhered so closely to the talking points laid out in Doubleday's marketing memo that it seems possible Zimmerman had a hand in writing it; perhaps she and Levin discussed its angle at one of their pleasant lunches. Levin described Anne as an ordinary teenager whose feelings were "of the purest universality," her difficult circumstances notwithstanding. "Little Anne Frank," Levin wrote, "spirited, moody, witty, self-doubting," had expressed in her diary "the drama of puberty" in "virtually perfect" form. Despite the gulf between her situation and that of the ordinary American reader, what "overwhelmingly" arose from the book was a sense of "the universalities of human nature." The figures in the *Diary* "might be living next door . . . their tensions and satisfactions are those of human character and growth, anywhere."

There are moments when Levin spoke full-throatedly about what was not yet called the Holocaust: the diarist's voice, he wrote, was "the voice of six million vanished Jewish souls." At the same time, the book was "no lugubrious ghetto tale, no compilation of horrors." Rather, it "simply bubbles with amusement, love, discovery." And was Anne's situation, after all, so different from that of her readers? "Just as the Franks lived in momentary fear of the Gestapo's knock on their hidden door, so every family today lives in fear of the knock of war." What else were all those hydrogen bombs for? But there was no use dwelling in despondency. "Anne's diary is a great affirmative answer to the life-question of people today, for she shows how ordinary people, within this ordeal, consistently hold to the greater human values," Levin concluded.[31]

The cognitive dissonance of the Holocaust, for Jews who did not experience it, lies in understanding both that it could have happened to them and also that it didn't. The Franks *might* have lived next door to American Jews—and indeed, if they had gotten visas, they would have—but in fact they lived across an ocean, and that decided their fate. The American Jewish community in the early postwar years primarily comprised people who had emigrated from Europe between 1880 and 1930 and their descendants; Levin himself was born in Chicago in 1905 to Lithuanian immigrants.[32] It was sheer luck, an accident of destiny, that these immigrants had been spared almost certain death under Hitler. Many of them left behind relatives who perished. For them, the *Diary* served as a profoundly painful reminder of just how lucky they were—and of their obligation, however they may have thought of it, to those who had been less fortunate.

But American Jews made up only a small portion of the *Diary*'s potential readership. The readers who sent the book to the top of the best-seller lists—and the audiences who later packed the house of the Cort Theater night after night to see the Broadway adaptation—came from all walks of life, as the letters they would send to Otto Frank demonstrate. To say that Otto hoped the *Diary* would find its way into the hands of as many people as possible is not to accuse him of being driven only by commercial motives, although the need to earn money naturally played a role in his decision-making. (Remember that he lost everything in the war and was dependent on Miep and Jan for housing afterward; in the years before the *Diary* was published, his letters betray his financial instability.) His motives were also idealistic: he believed in the *Diary* as a beacon to promote international tolerance and peace. But it could have the necessary impact only if its universal qualities, rather than its Jewish qualities, were emphasized. "It is not a Jewish book! So do not make a Jewish play out of it!" he wrote to Levin during their discussions of the adaptation. Still, he continued, "In some way of course it must be Jewish . . . so that it works against anti-Semitism."[33]

Later Levin would rail against Otto for betraying Anne's spirit by authorizing a Broadway adaptation that elided much of the diary's Jewish content. But the seeds of that conflict are evident already in Levin's review. Demonstrating an instinct for how to appeal to a wide readership that he mainly failed to muster for his own work, he downplayed the book's depiction of "life under threat" and described it as "a warm and stirring confession, to be read over and over for insight and enjoyment." Levin concluded prophetically: "Surely she will be widely loved, for this wise and wonderful young girl brings back a poignant delight in the infinite human spirit."

* * *

Phone calls from booksellers began pouring in to Doubleday on the morning of publication day, June 16: four days after what would have been Anne's twenty-third birthday. Although the publisher hadn't run a single ad for *Anne Frank: The Diary of a Young Girl*, reviews published over the weekend—foremost Levin's—had already made it the hit of the summer. The entire first print run sold out before the end of the day. By the end of the week, a second printing of 15,000 copies was nearly gone; a third printing was ordered for 25,000. The Associated Press named Anne author of the week, a major book club featured the book, and a dozen newspapers bought syndication rights, including the *New York Post*, which ran excerpts from the diary daily from June 25 until July 13.[34] Doubleday hastily earmarked more than $3,000 for advertising.[35] "We *do* have a success on our hands, after all the fears and trembling," Zimmerman exulted.[36] In record-breaking heat, she personally made the rounds of bookstores, thrilled to see the *Diary* prominently displayed in the windows. "This has given [me] faith in America," Otto wrote in response to her near daily updates.[37]

Why did Americans respond so powerfully to the *Diary*? In England, the book was unsuccessful enough that Vallentine, Mitchell, its British publisher, took it out of print in 1953. As an editor there explained to Otto, the English public had turned away from books dealing with the "deep and poignant aspects" of the war; since the country had not been occupied, Anne's story "could never be as real to people" there as it was elsewhere in Europe. But Americans, by virtue of being much farther removed, "could perhaps involve their emotions in Anne's story with complete safety," the editor speculated.[38]

America was geographically removed from the theaters of war, but almost all Americans had been involved in some way in the war effort. In his review of the *Diary*, Lewis Gannett, the book columnist for the *New York Herald Tribune*, mentioned his own service: just a few months after the raid on the Annex, he had encountered some of the first Jews returning to Maastricht, who had been hiding in an attic on the Belgian border. He was still in touch with them. "War is hell," a reader wrote to Doubleday. "We found that out on the sands of Omaha Beach" and on "the hedgerows of Normandy. . . . We saw everything but the innermost heart of the young." The *Diary*, he wrote, was that "missing link."[39]

In the pages of the *New York Post*, her words laid out among crime stories, movie listings, and grocery store ads, Anne must have seemed at once familiar and remote: she had experienced something readers could barely imagine, but she sounded like any other teenager. "She admitted she was scarcely Hollywood talent but she did yearn to become a movie star in her own pixy way," the caption beneath one of her photos read.[40] *Post* readers were so eager for more about Anne that the paper commissioned Levin to write three articles about what happened to the Annex residents after the diary ended. The final one, headlined "How Anne Frank Died," ran opposite an ad for Florida vacations in which a woman in a strapless bathing suit and high heels poses seductively by a palm tree.[41]

Broadway producers were also calling Doubleday: Competition over the stage rights was "one of the hottest races in years," the *New York Times* reported.[42] Here there was a complication. At one of their early encounters in Paris, Otto had promised Levin that he could adapt the *Diary*. The details of what happened between them have by now been gone over many times by many people—editors at Doubleday; lawyers representing Levin, Otto, and others; scholars Lawrence Graver and Ralph Melnick, both of whom wrote full-length books about Levin's involvement with the *Diary*—but without achieving much clarity. Otto seems to have agreed that Levin would negotiate with producers for a play and/or film based on the *Diary* and would also have the right to at least take first crack at a play adapting it. Levin promised Otto that if a situation arose "where a production by a famous playwright is possible only if I step aside, I would step aside."[43]

Zimmerman was initially grateful for Levin's involvement—his review was "half the reason for the success," she speculated. (Another publisher remarked that Levin deserved a prize for "the best review of the year.") But the memory of their happy collaboration began to dissipate as she became concerned that he was "screwing the whole deal up." Together with Levin, she, Marks, and Ken McCormick, a longtime editor-in-chief of Doubleday who was now a director of the company, drafted a telegram to Otto asking him to allow Doubleday to act jointly with Levin as his agents for film and theater rights. Otto, who was already starting to worry about how to handle Levin, agreed. "I know that he understands Anne perfectly and therefore I have all confidence in him," Otto wrote to Zimmerman. But he also recognized that anyone who bought the rights would want to choose their own playwright. Was there any way to get around this while still being fair to Levin? The only option was to hope that the play's future producer would approve of Levin as playwright: "Then everything would be easy."[44]

Nothing would be easy—in part because Otto had been deeply mistaken about Levin. Levin may have said that no one other than the survivors could tell their story, but he saw himself as one of them. This was already evident in his report from Buchenwald. Though he immediately grasped that the inmates of the camps had undergone an experience that fundamentally transformed them as human beings, he also felt that after having spent time with the survivors, he shared their unique perspective. Even as he wrote that "no one who has not been through their experience can ever understand them," in the very same breath he asserted: "My mind has become in the faintest way like their minds; I am beginning to understand how they feel."[45]

Just as Levin identified inappropriately with the survivors of Buchenwald, so too did he identify inappropriately with Anne. He referred to his *New York Post* articles as "my sequel to Anne Frank's Diary."[46] Worse, his insistence on defining Anne as the "teller" of the great Jewish tragedy made him unable to see her as anything else. Ironically, the same person who had insisted that Anne's feelings were "of the purest universality" would alienate just about everyone close to him with his belief that Broadway producers, playwrights, and even Otto were conspiring to erase her Jewish identity.

* * *

Before the book went "skyrocketing," Levin must have seemed like a fine choice to adapt the *Diary*. But once producers started suggesting playwrights such as Clifford Odets, Arthur Miller, or Maxwell Anderson, the bar was raised. The Doubleday staff involved weren't convinced that any of these big names were necessarily right for the job: some of the producers interested were "true salesmen of the soul," as Zimmerman put it. But now that her faith in the book had been vindicated, she was convinced that "something very *great* could come out of this as a play."[47] Otto, too, was deeply invested in the question of dramatization from the start, knowing that a play (and the movie that would almost certainly follow) had the potential to reach many more people than the book. "There is no reason of doing things hastily but one should not let matters slip either," he cautioned.[48]

The first dissonant note came early in July, when Levin complained brusquely to McCormick that Marks, who had taken charge of the negotiations, was reneging on Otto's promise to him by encouraging producers interested in the rights to consider other, more famous playwrights. "The only specific instruction from Otto Frank upon this subject is that Meyer Levin be employed as adaptor or collaborator," Levin insisted.[49] In reality, Otto's instructions were far from specific: in the only note he had yet sent to Doubleday on the subject—a cable Levin drafted himself—he wrote that it was his "desire" that Levin be involved "to guarantee [the] idea of [the] book."[50] (Levin was already digging in on the assertion that only he could convey the essence of the *Diary.*) Now Levin charged that Marks was "actively campaigning" to get rid of him, damaging his reputation.[51]

Was Marks biased against Levin? Or was it just that the book, having taken off, was suddenly a much more enticing dramatic property than it had been when Otto initially offered it to Levin? Like just about everything else in this story, it's unclear. "No one who buys the rights wants to have a prescription [for] what he has to do," Otto had admitted.[52] Anderson, for one, maintained—in front of Levin—that he had nothing against Levin but could not work with any collaborator.[53] It's possible that the prejudice against Levin was not personal—at least not yet. The extremely successful marketing strategy for the book had worked strenuously to appeal to an American audience rather than a specifically Jewish one. Although Miller and Odets were both of Jewish descent, both were known for plays on "American" subjects rather than explicitly Jewish ones. But a playscript by Levin, whose work focused almost entirely on Jewish themes, would have the opposite effect.

Marks's take was different from Levin's. Before negotiations had begun, he said, Levin had promised him and McCormick that if a playwright with a much higher standing wished to adapt the *Diary*, he would leave the decision to Doubleday. But after their meeting with Anderson, Levin changed his tune, insisting that no other playwright could "bring to the play what he, Levin, could." As Marks continued to meet with producers, he discovered that some were unwilling to accept Levin at all and that others would work with him only if a collaborator was also involved. Marks and McCormick thus decided that Doubleday should withdraw from the negotiations, leaving Otto and Levin to work out matters between themselves. "Levin, by his own statement, is a pretty fast guy with a lawsuit and . . . has not endeared himself to any of the people with whom he has worked," Marks cautioned.[54] Price and Zimmerman, too, were alienated by Levin's aggressiveness and by his proprietary attitude toward the book. "He is simply a very neurotic case and his activities in this matter would be fascinating for a psychiatrist, but were not a little trying for us," Zimmerman wrote.[55]

The controversy left Otto shaken. Ever since the war, he had suffered from attacks of what he called "nerves," which caused crying jags and fits of uncontrollable trembling. "The war and loss of his family had placed a terrible strain on Otto's emotional and mental well-being," Eva Geiringer, who was at this point about to become his stepdaughter, later wrote.[56] Anytime he experienced significant tension, he risked breaking down. Though the U.S. reception of the *Diary* had been overwhelmingly positive, the excitement of it had brought him to such a state. Now it looked as though he might need to come to New York to take part in the negotiations in person. "I was unable to write these last days and did not feel well at all," he confessed to Zimmerman after learning that Marks had withdrawn.[57] His anxiety lingered for several weeks.

An apparent solution arrived in the form of Cheryl Crawford, an established Broadway producer and co-founder of the Group Theatre. She believed that Levin had "talent" and was willing to give him eight weeks to write a draft. If she liked it, she would produce it; if she didn't, she would hire another playwright and compensate him.[58] Levin appeared to agree that the offer was fair; so did Zimmerman. And if things didn't work out with Crawford, many others were interested.

* * *

Levin gave his own version of what happened next in an undated single-spaced eighteen-page letter, addressed to Anne Frank herself, titled "Another Way to Kill a Writer." He apparently wrote this *cri de coeur* in the summer of 1955, shortly before the Goodrich/Hackett version of the *Diary* opened on Broadway. "Miss Crawford and I seemed to be in accord that a truly faithful adaptation was required, rather than a free adaptation of your diary," Levin wrote to his imaginary Anne. "She even pointed out, as I had already noted, that many scenes contained dialogue that could be transferred intact to the stage, if the scenes could be woven into the dramatic structure. So as to lose no time, I went to work, with a general verbal understanding as our agreement. We hoped to present the play in the fall season while your book was, as they say here, still 'hot.'"[59]

By early October, when Otto arrived in New York, Levin had finished a draft of the play. It's hard to know now exactly what that draft looked like; the only published version that exists, printed privately by Levin in 1967, incorporates revisions he may have made to the text after the Broadway adaptation was produced. But there can be no doubt that it was much more strongly Jewish in theme than Otto had envisioned. It opened with a group of mourners in black raincoats chanting a Hebrew prayer. A narrator popped in throughout to explain context to the audience: the Final Solution, the creation of Auschwitz, the Allied advance.[60]

Crawford read the draft and initially gave Levin a positive assessment. Otto read it too and seemed to be "satisfied with it in rough," Zimmerman told Price.[61] But within a few days Crawford had changed her mind, telling Levin that "emotionally and dramatically it did not touch me sufficiently" and that it adhered too closely to the *Diary*. She gave him only a weekend to revise it.[62] Crawford also suggested that Kermit Bloomgarden, another highly regarded producer who had already expressed his interest in the rights, give a second opinion. Bloomgarden, who had produced Arthur Miller's *The Crucible* and *Death of a Salesman* as well as Lillian Hellman's *The Children's Hour*, responded that "no producer" would want Levin's version. Zimmerman wondered if Crawford was "trying to ease [Levin] out of it." She thought he wouldn't "start trouble," but in fact he did so immediately.[63]

Levin seems to have taken Bloomgarden's response as a personal challenge. He would later claim to have received expressions of interest from multiple producers, including Harold Clurman and Herman Shumlin. Regardless of whether this was true—he may have misinterpreted their remarks—he regarded Crawford's rejection of his script as a breach of their agreement. In a letter to Crawford, he asserted that he no longer considered their agreement binding (in fact, they had not signed a contract) because her objection to his work was rooted not in "dramatic technique" but rather in an "intangible" sense of the play's content. He asked her to release Otto from his obligation to her and allow Levin to seek another producer himself.[64]

In the meantime, at Doubleday's suggestion, Otto had engaged Myer (Mike) Mermin, a lawyer whose offices happened to be located in the same building as the publisher, to represent him in these dealings. Mermin reminded Levin that Otto, who didn't feel capable of making the judgment himself, had agreed to let Crawford assess the script. Levin, who now believed that Crawford "never had any serious intention of accepting a play I wrote," insisted that he had "every moral right" to seek out another producer.[65]

Mermin drew up an agreement allowing Levin one month to find someone from a predetermined list of "top producers" who would commit to producing Levin's script and pay an option fee of $1,000.[66] (The list did not include Shumlin, who was interested in producing Levin's play but was deemed of insufficient standing.)[67] It's clear from the correspondence that—as Levin would later complain—this agreement was designed to get rid of any legal claim he could make to the play. As Zimmerman described it: "Meyer has been given a list of about twelve producers (most of whom . . . will not be interested from the start) . . . to peddle his script [to]." She continued: "They must produce Meyer's script and no other. In other words, no collaborator can be called in." There was "a certain danger" that someone might yet accept the script, but they had to take that chance. "Needless to say, Meyer Levin has behaved disgustingly throughout the whole thing and this is the sop that has to be given him," she concluded.[68]

Despite Zimmerman's strong language, it's hard to disagree with her assessment of Levin's behavior. His breach of protocol in refusing to simply bow out after Crawford rejected his script shocked everyone involved. He also had begun to exaggerate his role in the *Diary*'s success, claiming falsely that he had made the initial connection between Otto and Doubleday.[69] But Levin continued to believe that he had a "moral right" to the material because no other playwright would be able to communicate the authentic voice of the *Diary*. The play should be "as Anne would have written it, were she the playwright. My function, as I see it, or any adaptor's function, would be to do this, and not to inject his own ideas, his own art, his own personality," he wrote to Otto.[70] But he failed to recognize that no one could know how Anne would have written a play based on her diary—or how her ideas might have changed after the war. And while a faithful adaptation was important to Otto, he sought a playwright who would bring "his own art" to the work—precisely the opposite of what Levin proposed.

Otto may also have been spooked by the mounting claims on the *Diary* made by the American Jewish community. A radio play adapted from Levin's script and produced by the American Jewish Congress was broadcast by the CBS program "The Eternal Light" on Rosh Hashanah, shortly before Otto's arrival in New York. (His ship happened to dock on Yom Kippur: "Personally I do not mind, but perhaps I shall not tell . . . others when I arrive," he confided to Zimmerman.)[71] A representative of the Labor Zionist Organization of America was already planning an event connected to the play involving "leading Jewish personalities," with admission tied to the purchase of an Israel bond.[72] While Otto was a strong Zionist and would continue to support Israel throughout his life, he must have quailed at the thought of Anne's *Diary* being made into a Jewish cause, which ran in direct opposition to his own political commitments. Levin's attempts to appeal to his Jewish fellow-feeling—including hosting him for a Shabbat dinner—could only have backfired.

Meanwhile, Doubleday was drawing up a big holiday marketing plan for the *Diary*, which included a special deal for booksellers to encourage them to "order enough copies of *Anne Frank: The Diary of a Young Girl* for Christmas gift-buying."[73] The book was on many reviewers' best-of-the-year lists—"excellent publicity especially for the book as a Christmas gift," Zimmerman assured Otto.[74] While it is hard to picture the *Diary* under the tree on Christmas morning, it is clear from the letters Otto received that non-Jewish readers constituted much, if not most, of the book's audience. When Levin wrote sourly to Otto that "it was our own people who made Anne's book a success here," Zimmerman swooped in to contradict him.[75]

Mermin's compromise brought about its desired result: no producer committed within the designated month. "ALL APPEARS SETTLED," Zimmerman cabled Otto, who had been waiting anxiously for the news.[76] Levin, to her surprise, was "taking it like a lamb . . . perhaps he has become acquainted with the milk of human kindness or humility within the past weeks."[77] Crawford had already begun speculating about whether Carson McCullers, whose play *The Member of the Wedding* (adapted from her own novel) had recently closed after fourteen months on Broadway, might be persuaded to adapt. She had given Doubleday a brief essay about Anne's tales to help place the stories with magazines. Before Levin's month was out, she, Otto, and Price had lunch at the Continental Hotel in Paris. McCullers was in poor health, leaning on a walking stick for support; Otto found her "a sensitive and lovable creature," her expression "nervous," her eyes "restless yet warm."[78] After their meeting, she tore through Anne's diary in three days. "I think I have never felt such love and wonder and grief. There is no consolation to know that a Mozart, a Keats, a Chekhov is murdered in their years of childhood," she wrote to him.[79] Her artistic approach, Zimmerman suggested, would be preferable to a "documentary kind of straight adaptation."[80]

* * *

Levin did not take it like a lamb for long. When the *New York Times* announced that McCullers might adapt the *Diary*, he lost his mind a little. "I should be heartbroken if the material were sold to some producer who would simply appoint any friend of his to write the play or film," he had written to Otto back in July.[81] Now, he believed, this was precisely what had happened. (Crawford and McCullers had a longtime friendship and were rumored to have been romantically involved.)

It's hard to know how Levin would have reacted if the playwright he had been pushed aside to make way for had been Jewish. A later candidate was George Tabori, a Hungarian Jew whose father had died in Auschwitz.[82] But the fact that McCullers was not Jewish seems to have been what sent him over the edge. He fired off angry letters to Crawford, Mermin, Marks, and especially Otto, calling McCullers a "tactless and inappropriate choice" and claiming that he had received phone calls from "absolute strangers" who were dismayed by the *Times* announcement and wondered "whether there was anything that could be done to prevent the book being adapted by a non-Jew."[83] It would be "irresponsible . . . toward the book and toward the public to remain silent" about this travesty, he decided.

"I pity him," Otto told Zimmerman, who agreed that Levin had no factual or legal basis for his grievance.[84] She was particularly annoyed by what she saw as Levin's Jewish chauvinism. He had made it clear that he believed a non-Jew would be "handicapped" in dealing with the *Diary*.[85] Zimmerman vehemently disagreed. "Naturally a Jew will feel in certain ways stronger about the book, but in other ways this might be a disadvantage," she wrote to Otto. At the same time, a non-Jew, while still having powerful feelings about the *Diary*—as McCullers clearly did—would be less inclined to limit the play "to simply Jewish experience." Zimmerman went so far as to say that a non-Jewish adapter would be preferable—an extension of the same argument she had been making about the book from the start: "The wonderful thing about Anne's book is that it is really universal, that it is a book, an experience, for everyone. . . . Just a little objectivity would, on the part of the writer, ensure this very broad appeal."[86] Otto's old friend Nathan Straus, whom Otto asked for his opinion, agreed, adding another revealing point: "there is, to my mind, little doubt but that the play would be much more readily accepted on its merits if it were written by a non-Jew."[87]

Zimmerman also noted that despite Levin's claims to have produced a faithful adaptation of the book, his play failed to recognize the crucial contributions of the helpers, especially Miep, who is a major figure in the *Diary*. In various ways, Levin was oblivious to the roles of women. He underestimated Zimmerman's position at Doubleday, writing later, in his memoir about his Anne Frank obsession, that she had appeared to him in meetings as "mousey and silent."[88] His push to take credit for the U.S. publication of the *Diary* had the effect of erasing Judith Bailey's genius in plucking it from the slush pile. Bailey and Zimmerman both identified with Anne as a young woman—an aspect of her character that Levin downplayed in order to elevate his own connection to her as a Jew. What made him so certain that he, a middle-aged American man, could represent what he called Anne's "authentic voice"? Zimmerman, while apologizing for her "female chauvinism," noted about the choice of McCullers, "The more I think of a *woman* writing the script, the wiser it seems to be."[89]

Levin's tactics grew uglier. He threatened to sue Crawford;

he besieged Otto with mail, alleging that Mermin and Marks had lied to him and that Mermin had turned away producers who were prepared to do the play; he wrote a letter to the editor of *Variety* accusing Crawford of having persuaded Otto to give her the rights under false pretenses.[90] "He is impossible to deal with in any terms, officially, legally, morally, personally," Zimmerman fumed. She considered appealing to Levin's wife, the novelist Tereska Torres (with whom both she and Otto remained on good terms), to make him "stop this needless destruction."[91] Meanwhile, Levin's rhetoric grew increasingly melodramatic. "One doesn't proceed with an execution when the prisoner is proven falsely convicted," he wrote to Mermin, arguing that "new facts" had voided their agreement. To Otto his language was even more outrageous. "Your daughter wrote, 'If my diary goes, I go too.' This is how every writer feels about his work," he wrote.[92]

By February, Crawford already showed signs of hesitation. "With poor Meyer's psychosis, I just don't know what he is likely to do or say next," she wrote to Otto.[93] She felt guilty about having drawn McCullers, with her fragile health, into such a debacle. Her latest production, Tennessee Williams's *Camino Real*, was struggling. (It was "the worst play [Williams] had ever written," Mermin told Otto.)[94] Without a partner, she might not have sufficient funds for the option on the *Diary*. In April, she pulled out, citing her fears of a lawsuit by Levin and the failure of the Williams play: "the temper of the times here is for lighter entertainment."[95] It seemed at first that McCullers might be willing to work on the play with another producer, but soon she changed her mind as well, citing her "wretched" health.[96]

Otto had financial anxieties of his own. Prinsengracht 263 had already become a pilgrimage site for readers of the *Diary;* Kleiman and Kugler, who still worked for Opekta there, would give visitors spontaneous tours of the Annex. Otto learned that the owner wanted to sell the house to a buyer who would tear it down to build a new house on the premises. In order to prevent this—which Otto and others rightly felt would be a tragedy—Kleiman arranged for the business to purchase it. But they soon discovered that the same person had bought the house next door and was planning to destroy it. Without the support of the neighboring building, Prinsengracht 263 was in danger of falling down.[97] During Otto's visit to New York, Marks had suggested that the building be turned into a library or youth center, preserving the Annex for future generations—an idea Otto loved.[98] If a play or film had been on the horizon, he wouldn't have hesitated to fund the preservation of the house. But without a commitment from a producer, he felt he couldn't.

The news that Vallentine, Mitchell planned to take the *Diary* out of print in England after only three years also hit Otto hard. He responded with letters of grievance in a tone not far removed from Levin's, accusing the house of having neglected the book.[99] Though it was experiencing remarkable success elsewhere—including in Japan, where it became a best-seller—Otto may have been picturing an eventual day when the *Diary* would go out of print, silencing Anne's voice forever. Play and film adaptations would stave off that moment. Otto was also experiencing personal troubles: within the space of a few months, his mother died of a stroke and his older brother died suddenly of a heart attack.

Otto's fears about the play did not last long. In August 1953, producer Kermit Bloomgarden announced his intention to take an option on the *Diary*. He had written to Otto about it the previous summer, but Otto had already committed to Crawford. Calling Levin "the least trusted man in America next to McCarthy probably," Zimmerman urged Otto to commit to Bloomgarden quickly before Levin had a chance to scare him away, as he had done with Crawford. "Meyer has a pathological hatred for successful people," she wrote.[100]

Indeed, as soon as word of Bloomgarden's interest was made

public, Levin went on the attack again. In a long and impassioned letter to Bloomgarden, he insisted on the "moral right" to test his play before an audience to determine its stageworthiness. To prevent his play from going forward constituted an injustice against the *Diary* itself. He promised that he wasn't in it for the money, vowing to waive his royalties and assign them to "a memorial for Anne Frank." (Such an offer does not seem to have been made by anyone else involved.) He also threatened to inform any writer who might be interested in working with Bloomgarden of the situation, to forestall "any future complications that might lead to a moral problem for such a writer."[101] "It seems to me that we are no longer dealing with a human being but with some monster," Zimmerman wrote to Otto, calling Levin "completely out of touch with reality . . . brutal, dishonest—thoroughly immoral."[102] But she didn't think a lawyer would take his case, assuring Otto that the worst he could do was annoy Bloomgarden and a future playwright. Nonetheless, Bloomgarden insisted on including a clause in his contract with Otto indemnifying him against any claims made by Levin. Mermin told Otto that any other producer would want the same: no one could predict "what irrational behavior he may indulge in on the fantasy that he is discharging the solemn duty of an artist to his creation."[103]

In December, Mermin told Otto that Bloomgarden had gone to Hollywood to consult on the play with Frances Goodrich and Albert Hackett, a married couple who were established adaptors of screenplays, including *It's a Wonderful Life*. Though they weren't "big names" on Broadway, their movies had been successful, and he recommended that Otto approve them as dramatists.[104] Otto was initially anxious about the idea of "a 'Hollywood' writer for such a serious and delicate subject." But Zimmerman reassured him of Goodrich and Hackett's "warm and good approach": "They are adaptors, mainly, and thus would I feel be very close to the book," she wrote, apparently forgetting that Otto had wanted the play to be its own work of art.[105] Mermin also informed Otto that by now he had racked up legal fees of several thousand dollars owing to the enormous amount of time Mermin had spent dealing with Levin. In consideration of Otto's financial situation, he suggested they apply the $250 Otto would receive when Bloomgarden signed the contract, as well as his next payment of $250, and work out the rest later.[106]

What choice did Otto have? He agreed to allow Goodrich and Hackett to adapt the *Diary*.

INTERLUDE

Ghostly Muse

Ever since the late 1970s, the town of Athens, Georgia, has been a headquarters for the alternative rock scene: the B-52s and R.E.M. got their start here. Home to the University of Georgia, it's known for antebellum architecture, cheap rents, and a downtown packed with places to hear music.[1]

It was probably inevitable that the group of musicians known as the Elephant 6 collective would land in Athens. Jeffery Nye Mangum and Robert Schneider had met some twenty years earlier in elementary school and spent much of their teens and twenties bouncing from place to place, picking up friends and collaborators along the way. In Ruxton, Louisiana, their hometown, they hung out at a combination bar, nightclub, and laundromat called the Fun-O-Mat, where Mangum sometimes used metal coat hangers as drumsticks during performances. In Denver, Mangum lived in a boiler room and a walk-in closet that he believed was haunted. In Queens, he and his collaborators—

now making music under the name Neutral Milk Hotel—lived and worked in the home of bandmember Julian Koster's grandmother, who was "so hard of hearing that it didn't matter how much noise Julian's friends made," journalist Kim Cooper writes. And sometime in 1996 or 1997, Mangum and a few of his collaborators established a base in Athens, settling in a big wood-frame house with an expansive porch on a tree-lined street.

Somewhere along the way, Mangum—a tall, shy man who wore his straight brown hair in a chin-length bob and performed in patterned thrift-store wool sweaters—wandered into a secondhand bookstore and picked up *The Diary of a Young Girl.* He read the book straight through and "spent about three days crying," he later told a journalist. "While I was reading the book, she was completely alive to me," he continued. "I pretty much knew what was going to happen. But that's the thing: you love people because you know their story. . . . Here I am as deep as you can go in someone's head, in some ways deeper than you can go with someone you know in the flesh. And then at the end, she gets disposed of like a piece of trash." After finishing the book, he carried it around with him.

In the Aeroplane Over the Sea, much of which Mangum wrote in the wake of his encounter with the *Diary*, is acknowledged as one of the greatest indie-rock albums of all time. Neutral Milk Hotel was "better than Nirvana, better than Radiohead," one music magazine opines; another compares *Aeroplane* to T. S. Eliot's *The Waste Land.* Its rerelease as part of a vinyl box set in 2023, in honor of its twenty-fifth anniversary, generated a new crop of think-pieces and encomia.

People tend to remember the first time they heard the album, which doesn't sound like anything else. Mangum first played it in public at a house party for other members of the Elephant 6 collective, a loose conglomeration of bands that were all produced by Schneider and shared a similar homemade aesthetic—much of the music was recorded on four-track tape.

"Within a hundred and twenty seconds, everything went silent," Dave Wrathgabar, guitarist for the Elephant 6 band Elf Power, remembered. Sometimes Mangum's twangy voice is backed only by his own guitar; other tracks feature an incongruous blend of instruments—a ghostly, whining musical saw; a brass band of the sort you might hear on the street in New Orleans—all distorted to fuzz. "*Aeroplane* isn't about airtight instrumentation or tricky songwriting . . . but about a remarkable range of feeling put into melody," Taylor Clark writes in *Slate*. A critic who heard Neutral Milk Hotel perform in May 1997 said they "seemed as though they had just emerged from a home studio where they had been locked up for years," which was more or less accurate. The stage held dozens of instruments, including a xylophone missing half its keys and "a beat-up Tibetan prayer board."

The album is a song cycle around the themes of love, loss, and rebirth, haunted by Anne Frank. Mangum would later say that he felt he hadn't written the songs but "just channeled them from somewhere." He stayed up into the early hours, drinking coffee and working, trying to stave off the sleep problems—night terrors, waking dreams, sleepwalking—that plagued him. He liked to play guitar in the bathroom, listening to the echo bounce off the tile walls. The title track, a folksy love ballad that includes the line "Anna's ghost all around," came to him while he was lying in the backyard with his girlfriend at the time, watching the trees. Suddenly he jumped up and exclaimed, "I got a song in my head!" she remembered later.

The years of Anne's birth and death appear repeatedly in the songs, as well as often-cryptic references to her sister and the circumstances of her death. A surreal quality pervades the album. On trips to San Francisco, Mangum and other band members liked to visit a place called the Musée Mechanique, a collection of vintage penny arcade machines, and record sound there. On one visit, trumpet player Scott Spillane noticed a girl who was the "*spitting fucking image* of Anne Frank." He and

Mangum watched her, wondering if they were seeing a ghost. In "Holland, 1945," which incorporates a splice of sound from the Musée Mechanique, Mangum imagines Anne reincarnated as "a little boy in Spain / Playing pianos filled with flames." While writing the songs, he had a recurrent dream that he could use a time machine to save Anne—a fantasy that appears in the song "Oh Comely." In "Two-Headed Boy Part 2," he dreams of her alive and crying.

Aeroplane had an unusual effect on fans. Chris Bilheimer, who did the album design, repeatedly wept when he watched Neutral Milk Hotel perform live. "There was something in Jeff's voice, just the sound of his voice, that encapsulated so many different feelings at the same time," he said later. In a long quest-style profile written without the cooperation of Mangum, who has long rejected nearly all interview requests (including mine), journalist Kevin Griffis interweaves his search for the singer with his own grief about his brother's suicide.* "The album, even as its funereal horns blow, is the sound of transcending death. No, not just transcending it, but finding some underlying joy there," Griffis writes.

The *Aeroplane* tour took a psychic toll on Mangum. He became obsessed with what fans were posting about him on the Internet, searching chat rooms for references to the band. Possibly owing to the stress of his sudden stardom, he had a breakdown, which he described as "the platform of the mind . . . crumbling." "Fan culture can be terrifying," the critic Carl Wilson muses in a piece about the twenty-fifth anniversary album. "Fan idols themselves are symbolically sacrificed even as they are worshipped. Their privacy, humanity, and multidimensionality are ripped away to satisfy the needs of their congregants."

Always reclusive, Mangum became "the Salinger of indie rock," as Clark puts it. He stopped answering the phone, refused

*Jeff Mangum, if you're reading this, I'd still like to interview you.

any contact with the press, and turned down performance opportunities, including an offer to open for R.E.M. during their 1999 tour. He got interested in religion, reading the works of Jiddu Krishnamurthi, a Theosophist philosopher, and spending time in a monastery. His "creative end" was "as dead as Anne's," Cooper concluded in her book about *Aeroplane* in 2005. This judgment was premature: Mangum started performing again sporadically in 2011 and reunited Neutral Milk Hotel for a major tour from 2013 to 2015. Then he vanished again.

Mangum's disappearance from public life stunned his fans, who had their own surreal fantasies about him. One posted online about wanting to build a "hermitage" for Mangum where he could communicate with the world via a tube that connected to a vent, which would then broadcast on the radio. Others imagined he really might have managed to time travel in search of Anne Frank. According to this theory, Mangum went back in time to save her, brought her to Louisiana to pose as his sister, and then married her. One website offers as "evidence" photos from Mangum's high school yearbook in which his sister does bear a resemblance to Anne.

But it's most likely that Mangum simply wants his privacy. He squashed Griffis's efforts to profile him. "I'm not an idea," he wrote to the journalist in an email. "I'm a person, who obviously wants to be left alone. . . . Since it's my life and my story, I think I should have a little say as to when it's told."

11

Ambassador
Into the Infinite, 1955–1959

If we bear all this suffering and if there are still Jews left, when it is over, then Jews, instead of being doomed, will be held up as an example. Who knows, it might even be our religion from which the world and all peoples learn good, and for that reason and that reason only do we have to suffer now. We can never become just Netherlanders or just English or any nation for that matter, we will always remain Jews, but we want to, too.

THE DIARY OF ANNE FRANK opened on October 5, 1955, at the Cort Theater, an imposing building with a neoclassical pillared façade modeled on the Petit Trianon at Versailles and an ornate jewel-box interior. Barbara Zimmerman, by then Barbara Epstein, attended with her husband, the publishing executive Jason Epstein, as well as Joseph and Lillian Marks, Myer and Mildred Mermin, and Nathan and Helen Straus. Afterward, they joined the cast for dinner at Sardi's. "They have made a lovely, tender drama . . . they have treated it with admiration and respect," Brooks Atkinson wrote in his *New York Times* review, crediting not only Goodrich and Hackett but also director Garson Kanin, set designer Boris Aronson, and the cast, especially Joseph Schildkraut as Otto Frank and Susan Strasberg, who made her Broadway debut as Anne.[1] An instant sell-out, the play won all three major theater awards: the Pulitzer Prize, the New York Drama Critics' Circle Award, and the Tony Award. Reviews treated it as not only the theatrical event of the season but also a spiritual experience.[2] Decades later, it's clear that many audience members regarded viewing *The Diary of Anne Frank* as tantamount to witnessing the Holocaust in some form.

Yet in important ways the Goodrich/Hackett play has come to be regarded as a failure. In large part this reflects the influence of a number of more recent critics, among them Cynthia Ozick, who have sharply criticized the playwrights for downplaying the Jewish aspect of Anne's story and transforming her into a figurehead against prejudice, generically and banally understood. In a furious *New Yorker* essay titled "Who Owns Anne Frank?" Ozick, calling Goodrich and Hackett's writing "skilled and mediocre," accused the entire cohort involved with the play—the playwrights, Bloomgarden, and Kanin, potentially in collaboration with Lillian Hellman, an acknowledged Stalinist—of appropriating Anne's words and story to serve their own purposes in litigating "the ancient dispute between the particular and the universal." Though the play had "electrified audiences everywhere"—including in Germany, where it was met with reverent silence rather than applause—Ozick saw it as a crucial component in the campaign to dumb Anne down for mass audiences, namely by stripping the *Diary*'s now-notorious line about people being "good at heart" from its context in a passage about the dangers of war and setting it at the very end of the play, leading audiences to assume it was the final line of the *Diary*. In a tacit acknowledgment of how poorly the adaptation has stood the test of time, playwright Wendy Kesselman was authorized to overhaul it after the publication of the Definitive Edition in the mid-1990s. Her revision was promoted as incorporating material omitted from the *Diary* as originally published, but it also silently emends the most frequently criticized aspects of the Goodrich/Hackett version.[3]

In addition to the "good at heart" line, the other passage that Ozick and her fellow critics singled out as particularly egregious is an alteration of Anne's comment, in her long entry chronicling the break-in on Easter in 1944, about Jewish persecution: *Right through the ages there have been Jews, through all the ages they have had to suffer, but it has made them strong too.*[4] In the play, her character says, "We're not the only people that've had to suffer. There've always been people that've had to . . . sometimes one race . . . sometimes another."[5] (The ellipses, a stylistic tic of Goodrich and Hackett, are in the original; as Francine Prose points out, their Anne "can hardly utter a sentence without pausing to collect her scattered thoughts, none of them especially incisive.")[6] These ludicrous lines, excised from Kesselman's version, infuriated Meyer Levin, who compared them to the Soviet denial of Jewish suffering at Babi Yar. "Why had her Jewish avowal been censored on the stage?" he asks in *The Obsession.*[7]

How could it not have been? The blockbuster reception of the *Diary* was predicated upon its presentation as universal, from the flap copy and the Eleanor Roosevelt introduction to Levin's own review. The play was no different. Otto Frank had made it clear that he did not want a "Jewish play"; neither did Kermit Bloomgarden, who, in notes to Goodrich and Hackett, compared Anne to George Bernard Shaw's Joan of Arc. In his account of the debacle, Ralph Melnick makes much of Hellman's interference, but things might have gone much the same way without her. It was Kanin—an American Jew, as was Bloomgarden—who proposed the "sometimes one race . . . sometimes another" line. Anne's comments about the suffering of the Jews struck him as "an embarrassing piece of special pleading," he told Goodrich and Hackett. Throughout history, people "suffered because of being English, French, German, Italian, Ethiopian, Mohammedan, Negro, and so on. . . . The fact that in this play the symbols of persecution and oppression are Jews is incidental, and Anne, in stating the argument so, reduces her magnificent stature." Instead, Kanin felt, Peter should be "the young one," outraged by the persecution of the Jews, and Anne "wiser," pointing out that different minorities have been oppressed throughout the ages. "At this moment," he concluded, "the play has an opportunity to spread its theme into the infinite."[8]

Reading the correspondence between the playwrights and the others involved—Kanin, Bloomgarden, and especially Otto—is to sense at once Goodrich and Hackett's genuine desire to be faithful to the *Diary* and the extent to which they were out of their league. "We feel very honored and very humbled in approaching the task" of adapting the *Diary*, the playwrights wrote to Otto in December 1953. "We pray that we may be able to capture its quality . . . [and] the spirit and indomitable courage of your daughter." They were reading all the material they could find on what they called, delicately, "the events and conditions at the time the Diary was written." They hoped they could call on him once in a while with questions about "personal matters."[9] In his response, written on New Year's Day 1954, Otto made it clear how high the stakes were for him. Confessing his hesitation about dramatizing the *Diary* at all—"I was afraid that the personal, individual touch which makes the book so vivid and moving might get lost"—he wrote that Eleanor Roosevelt, along with others, had persuaded him that it was his duty "to propagate Anne's ideas and ideals in every manner and to show to mankind whereto discrimination, hatred and persecution are leading."[10]

It's no wonder if Goodrich and Hackett felt intimidated by their task. They were screenwriters for hire, accustomed to jumping from project to project, most of which seem not to have been overly intellectual. Now they were faced with a play that presented "not only great spiritual . . . but technical hazards," as they confided to their agent.[11] Their focus seems to have been on the challenges of structure and stageworthiness rather than substance. Anne had described Mrs. van Pels as coquettish, Pfeffer as a boor, her father as saintly. Now they had to create characters who could embody those attributes onstage. And while Anne would remain at the center, her perspective could not be the only one. In one of the play's most startling lines, during a scene of intense conflict between the Franks and the Van Daans, the Otto character laments, "We don't need the Nazis to destroy us. We're destroying ourselves."[12] Anne never suggests that the adults felt this way about their arguments. But the fact that Otto doesn't seem to have remarked critically on this line implies that it rang true.

Goodrich and Hackett felt great sympathy for Otto's position. A distant cousin of Otto's who was also a friend of theirs had sat in on some of Otto's meetings with Cheryl Crawford in New York and told them how upset Otto had been to hear people "calmly talking about the family and about little Anne as if they were figures of Mr. Frank's imagination, instead of his family, so newly dead."[13] In his communications regarding Schildkraut, Otto notes how difficult it is to write to the actor about "playing 'Otto Frank.'"[14] Later, picturing the technical challenge of the opening scenes—the play begins with Otto's return from Auschwitz and flashes back quickly to the move to the Annex—he wrote: "I appear coming from concentration camp looking [worn out] and badly dressed . . . and there is a very short interval when I have to act, coming from my private home with the family, well dressed and in good condition."[15] He could not think of "Otto Frank" as a character on the stage.

Goodrich and Hackett were innocent enough that, when they received a letter from Levin—"In fairness to yourself as well as to me, I cannot help feeling that you ought to hear about the circumstances surrounding my dramatization of the book," it began—they thought it would be sufficient to send an empathic response telling him that they, too, had once been disappointed when a producer had deemed an adaptation unsatisfactory. In response, he sent them "a FOUR PAGE SINGLE SPACED letter . . . very very bitter."[16] Bloomgarden told them not to answer it, but a few days later, while their agent was meeting with Myer Mermin, Mermin's secretary came in with the evening edition of the *New York Post* open to an ad Levin had placed headlined "A Challenge to Kermit Bloomgarden." "Is it right for you to kill a play that others find deeply moving, and are eager to produce?" Levin had written. He added "a plea" to readers: "If you ever read anything of mine . . . if you have faith in me as a writer, I ask your help."[17] Bloomgarden, who later joked that Levin had challenged him to a duel, was primarily concerned about the effect on Goodrich and Hackett. "This man is a villain—and no further attention or thought should be given to him," he told them.[18]

The playwrights did their homework. They met with a rabbi in Los Angeles, who turned out to be the father of one of Anne's classmates, to go over the Chanukah candlelighting ceremony, which they elevated from a mention in the *Diary*—*Because of the shortage of candles we only had them alight for ten minutes, but it is all right as long as you have the song*—into a major scene in the play.[19] (It was Kanin, the correspondence reveals, who made another of the most-criticized decisions: the substitution of the lilting tune "Oh Hanukkah" for "Maoz Tzur," the stately liturgical poem normally sung after lighting Chanukah candles.)[20] They ordered books about the war against the Jews and the problems of adolescence; they met friends of Otto's who shared artifacts from Amsterdam during the occupation, including the yellow star. Later, they visited Amsterdam and toured the Annex while a photographer recorded details for use in designing the set. Kanin, who stayed overnight in the Annex, noticed that one of the pictures Anne had pasted on her wall was of Ginger Rogers in *Tom, Dick and Harry*, a film he had directed. Goodrich in particular was emotionally affected by the experience. She also was moved by the expressions of support she received from those whom she asked for help: "Everyone has such an affection for Anne."[21]

Otto legally retained the right of approval over the script; he was so "desolate" at having to tell Goodrich and Hackett that he found an early version unsuccessful that he carried his letter around for several days before sending it.[22] But for the most part, they—together with Bloomgarden and Kanin—overruled his critiques. When Otto asked that "Maoz Tzur" be reinstated in the film version, Kanin, Goodrich, and Hackett all insisted the ending of the first act would be "flat as a latke" without the lighter song.[23] Regarding another fictional detail, in which Anne hands out handmade Chanukah gifts to all the residents while wearing a lampshade on her head, Otto conceded that it "could have happened."[24]

In yet another scene Goodrich and Hackett invented, the Hermann van Pels character (known in the play as Mr. van Daan, Anne's pseudonym for him) is caught stealing bread from the kitchen. Otto found it "dramatic and effective" but worried that Mr. van Pels's brother, who lived in New York and would certainly see the play, might be offended.[25] (The playwrights kept the scene.) It's surprising that this was his only criticism of that scene. As poorly as Mr. van Pels comes off, Edith, too, behaves strikingly out of character, threatening to throw the Van Daans out and yelling at Peter, "He's no father to you . . . that man!"[26] Fictional Edith suggests that finding a new hiding place for the Van Daans could be as easy as giving extra cash to Miep, but in reality it would have been shockingly cruel to turn out any of the residents. Still, Otto apparently wasn't troubled by this. Eva Geiringer Schloss, his stepdaughter, would later complain that while Otto never hesitated to invoke Anne's memory while talking to her children, his stepgrandchildren—"Anne would not have done that," he would say when they misbehaved—he rarely mentioned either Margot or Edith, except in connection with Anne.[27] Perhaps Anne was right that the marriage had resembled a business relationship.

Otto was also initially anxious about the way the playwrights represented Pfeffer (Dussel).[28] Made out to be older—he was fifty-three when he went into hiding—he is depicted as ignorant of Jewish customs, such as giving gifts on Chanukah. In reality, he was devout enough to perform his own prayers in the Annex: *One of my Sunday morning ordeals is having to lie in bed and look at Pfeffer's back when he's praying*, Anne wrote, complaining that he spent *a quarter of an hour . . . rocking from his toes to his heels.*[29] Some of his buffoonish interjections seem intended for comic relief. At the end of the bread-stealing scene, which is interrupted by the news that D-Day has started, he exhorts the others to stop fighting: "You're spoiling the whole invasion!"[30] But in general he's a jerk to the other residents, voicing aloud negative comments that Anne makes privately in her diary, such as calling Peter a "clumsy fool."[31] When Miep brings a cake as a New Year's gift to the residents, his snide comment about the Van Daans' greed is another echo of the *Diary:* "Everybody gets exactly the same . . . except Mr. Van Daan always gets a little bit more."[32] But Otto seems to have rationalized his concerns. When Pfeffer's partner, Charlotte Kaletta, later wrote to him in anger about the way the man she loved had been depicted to the world, Otto responded that she shouldn't expect "historical truth" from art.[33]

Some of Goodrich and Hackett's deviations from the *Diary* seem intended to explain its confusing or contradictory elements. The Van Daans, like Dussel, are depicted as Dutch Jews rather than German refugees, which allows for a backstory involving Mr. van Daan's aid to Otto when he first came to the Netherlands—the rationale for the choice of the Van Daans as hiding partners. The play also tries to explain why Anne shared a room with a man her father's age, giving reasons why other configurations wouldn't have worked.

But there are many other changes that will sound discordant to a reader familiar with Anne Frank's story. The prohibition on making noise lasts the entire working day, whereas in reality the residents got a break for lunch, while the workmen were out of the warehouse. (All of the office employees, who worked on the second floor of the building, were aware of the Jews' presence.) Anne receives the diary in the play not for her birthday but as a kind of consolation gift when the family goes into hiding. The residents grow visibly tense every time a car pulls up outside, while Anne mentions anxiety only at hearing footsteps downstairs. In an invented entry in which Anne compares the sounds of the residents' stomachs grumbling to an orchestra—"It only needs Toscanini to raise his baton and we'd be off in the Ride of the Valkyries"—the reference to Wagner of all composers seems insensitive. And when Anne visits Peter in his room, he welcomes her with "a bottle of pop," a gesture that seems intended to make them appear as much like American teenagers as possible even as it negates the circumstances of extreme deprivation in which they found themselves.[34] But it is a measure of Goodrich and Hackett's success that many of the choices they made now feel inevitable: the use of Otto arriving at the Annex after the war as a framing device, Anne's voiceovers as bridges between the scenes, the pattern of tension and relaxation from one scene to the next.

It can probably never be known whether the influence of Hellman, who read the script in multiple versions, was primarily technical or ideological. In *The Obsession*, his memoir about his history with the *Diary*, Levin makes much of the fact that the negotiations over the play coincided with Stalin's Doctors' Plot and alleges that Hellman was the mastermind of a cabal working behind the scenes to promote communist ideology.

Though Hellman was involved in Bloomgarden's negotiations over the *Diary* at an early stage and suggested Goodrich and Hackett (who were her friends) as adaptors, most commentators, including Lawrence Graver, have dismissed Levin's accusation as paranoid raving. Melnick gives more evidence for Hellman's involvement than had been previously known, but not all of it is convincing.[35]

Considering how vehemently Levin insisted on the sanctity of his version of Anne, it's ironic that when he eventually sued Goodrich and Hackett—together with Otto, Bloomgarden, and Crawford—one of the charges was plagiarism. After viewing the play in a pre-Broadway staging in Philadelphia, where it opened on the eve of Rosh Hashanah, he wrote to Otto that it was "very much like the play I wrote . . . except . . . that in my play the characters are more fully and truly developed."[36] It's hard to reconcile his view of the Goodrich/Hackett adaptation as a travesty to Anne's vision with his assertions that the playwrights stole his work. Still, when the case went to trial, Levin's lawyer was able to convince the judge that Kanin, after reading Levin's version, had suggested adding the device of Anne reading from her diary between scenes—thus constituting inadvertent borrowing by Goodrich and Hackett. The playwrights furiously annotated their script to demonstrate that their ideas had come from the *Diary* itself, but they eventually compromised with Levin's lawyer on a statement to the effect that "they had innocently received and made use of suggestions from Mr. Frank and others" which had been taken from Levin's script without their knowledge.[37]

In fact, Levin didn't originate the idea of the voiceovers. A program written by radio and television scriptwriter Morton Wishengrad and presented in November 1952 on NBC's weekly religious series *Frontiers of Faith* featured a voiceover in which Otto read aloud from the *Diary* and Anne's voice joined in, just as in the Goodrich/Hackett version. Wishengrad also structured his script with a framing device in which Otto and Miep return to the Annex. And in Anne's scenes with Peter, she tutors him and talks about God—and also tells him that Christians and Jews both suffer! The series was produced by the Jewish Theological Seminary (JTS), a leading institution of Conservative Judaism. "Beyond its general humanitarian value, this endorsement of greater tolerance and unity exemplifies JTS's approach to promoting Jewish integration into the American mainstream," one critic wrote.[38] Neither Graver nor Melnick mentions Wishengrad's adaptation, which doesn't seem to have been introduced as evidence in the trial.

Levin's *Anne Frank*—at least in the published version available today—is more appealing than it is often given credit for. Though it includes a scene of Anne and Peter discussing the cat's genitalia in which she tells him that "the female sex urge is just as strong as in the male" and quotes the vision of love in Plato's *Symposium*, their romantic relationship is deemphasized. Without overdoing it, Levin manages to convey hints of the ever-present danger, such as Margot overhearing the new owner of the building asking about the rooms above the office. He includes more dialogue between Anne and Margot, giving a stronger sense of their relationship. Comic relief comes largely from Mrs. van Pels, who does "reducing exercises" and speaks French to Peter and her husband.[39]

At the same time, Levin's adaptation makes some odd choices. There is a cringey scene in which Dussel examines Anne for some ailment: "He taps along her spine, draws himself up, and finally administers a tap to her bottom." Anne doesn't hear Bolkestein's speech but is told about it afterward by Otto, who attributes it to the BBC; after a quarrel, she hands him her diary to read. (Before he does, Peter interrupts, warning of thieves.)[40] While the Goodrich/Hackett adaptation erases Bep and combines Kleiman and Kugler into a character called "Kraler," in Levin's the helpers hardly appear—Miep not at all.

In retrospect, many critics have concluded that for all his intemperance and megalomania, Levin was essentially right to represent Anne as more traditionally Jewish than Goodrich and Hackett did. In a review of Graver's book, former *New York Times* drama critic Frank Rich writes that Levin was "prescient about the cultural defanging of Nazi genocide." Recognizing that Otto Frank was glad for his daughter to be "memorialized as an affirmative figure of hope rather than a grim Nazi casualty," Rich argues that Levin's version was both "truer than the Hacketts' to Anne Frank and, with its interpolations of concentration-camp history, more faithful to the specifics of the Holocaust."[41]

But what Rich, Ozick, and others overlook is that Anne, like her father, was not conventionally religious in any way. Despite all the ellipses, Goodrich and Hackett's interpretation of her theology—"Just to believe in something! When I think of all that's out there . . . the trees . . . and flowers . . . and seagulls . . . When I think of these good things, I'm not afraid anymore . . . I find myself, and God"—is pretty accurate.[42] In addition to the Chanukah prayers, her diary contains a single mention of candle lighting on Shabbat (*When I looked into the candle this evening, I felt calm and happy*) and one line about Yom Kippur (*There can't be many people who will have kept it as quietly as we did*).[43] Judaism for her represented an ethnicity and a culture more than a religion—just as it did for many American Jews. Her "Favorite Quotes Notebook," in which she cites at length the non-Jewish memoirist Alice Bretz's distinctly New Testament conception of God ("The essential necessity is friendship with God") and a fictionalized conversation between Galileo and a Church official, makes it clear that her thoughts about God are generically spiritual rather than Jewish or Christian.[44] The nightly prayer she says in German—*Thank you, God, for all that is good and dear and beautiful*—has no direct correlative in Judaism.[45] On her bedroom wall, next to the pictures of movie stars and the royal family, was a cut-out of Jesus's head from

Michelangelo's Pietà.[46] As the scholar Yasmine Ergas observes, "Exploring spirituality introspectively and untrammeled by religious observance, Anne developed beliefs at most loosely related to Judaism."[47]

Not only does Levin's play overemphasize Anne's own devotion to Judaism, it sanctifies the Holocaust itself in a way that anticipates the increasing focus on the catastrophe in American Jewish circles in the late twentieth and early twenty-first centuries. When Anne initially enters the Annex, the character representing Kleiman removes the Jewish star from her coat; she takes it from him and kisses it, as if it were a mezuzah. In addition to "Maoz Tzur" and "El Malei Rachamim," a mourner's prayer recited by Jews from Eastern Europe (and thus almost certainly unknown to the Franks), Levin's play includes the prayer "Ani Ma'amin" ("I believe") and a musical setting of "O Absalom," the biblical verse in which King David wishes his life had been taken instead of his son's.

"The real conspiracy that snared Levin was not that of a few powerful people but the larger cultural current in an America in which audiences wanted feel-good entertainment, Jews wanted to assimilate and the government wanted Germany rebuilt," Rich argues. It was an environment in which Wolcott Gibbs, a theater critic for the *New Yorker*, could characterize the events of the war as ancient history in his review of *The Diary of Anne Frank:* "We remember the terrible facts of the old nightmare and the names of the places—Dachau, Buchenwald, Belsen—that were most hideously involved in it, but the atmosphere is not as easy to recall."[48] The names of the camps may induce less horror in the contemporary reader than Gibbs's easy assumption that "we," a decade later, had largely forgotten the war years.

Yet, as Kanin knew, to point out that something exceptional had happened to the Jews of Europe ran the risk of "special pleading"—an expression that Gibbs happened to use in the very same *New Yorker* piece in reference to a new translation of a baldly political play by the French pacifist writer Jean Giraudoux. If any kind of overt speaking up for one's own identity group constitutes "special pleading," Anne Frank, of all writers, would have earned the right to it. But American Jews of the time, raised on the virtues of assimilation, found the Jewish excesses of someone like Levin—whose persecution obsession would badly damage both his career and his personal life—more dangerous than the depiction of the Holocaust as just another instance of persecution. Even Rabbi Stephen Wise, who had pressured the Roosevelt administration to intervene in World War II on behalf of the Jews and later said he was "almost demented over my people's grief," wrote to Otto after seeing the play in Philadelphia that "the handling of the Jewish angle [was] delicate and in good taste."[49]

Otto did not attend the opening or any other production of the play. He sent a note to the cast in advance of the Philadelphia opening to explain his absence; it was posted on a bulletin board at the theater and distributed among the staff. "You will all realize that for me this play is a part of my life, and the idea that my wife and children as well as I will be presented on the stage is a painful one for me," Otto wrote. Still, in the end, it was most important that the play's message "reach as many people as possible and awaken in them a sense of responsibility to humanity."[50]

* * *

The Diary of Anne Frank ran on Broadway for 717 performances. Many of the cast and crew involved later expressed pride at having been part of such a meaningful and historically significant production, but the stress of the subject matter took a toll, particularly for those with a personal relationship to the material. Eva Rubinstein, who played Margot, was the daughter of the pianist Arthur Rubinstein and Nela Młynarska, a ballerina. In fall 1939, she and her parents came to New York from France on the USS *George Washington,* the last boat carrying Americans out of Europe. It was so full that families were split up, with women and children on one side of the boat and men on the other; four or five people shared a cabin. "It never felt like a plain old play. It really felt like a responsibility," she said later.[51]

Set designer Boris Aronson emigrated to the United States from Russia in 1922. His wife, Lisa Jalowetz Aronson, who worked alongside him but was uncredited, was studying art and theater in Vienna when the Anschluss took place. She ended up in Amsterdam, where she survived the war by passing as Indonesian; hired to work as a nanny, she "hid in the open."[52]

Even those who had no personal connection were deeply affected. "It was unlike anything I had ever experienced, totally absorbing, demanding, and fulfilling," Susan Strasberg later remembered.[53] The daughter of Lee Strasberg, a co-founder of the Group Theatre and director of the Actors Studio, she grew up surrounded by Broadway and Hollywood royalty. She spent weekends at the Kazans' country house, where Marlon Brando was sometimes a guest, and hung out on the beach in Fire Island with Marilyn Monroe, whom she considered a friend. She was already playing small roles in television and film when she was invited to read for Anne Frank. Before her audition, at the Beverly Hills Hotel, Schildkraut called her by the endearment "Suzileh" and recalled having met her as a baby. As she read the last scene—a monologue by Anne featuring the famous line—she began to weep. "Hello, Anne," Schildkraut said when she finished.[54]

Despite the auspicious start to their relationship, Schildkraut and Strasberg clashed on the set. Schildkraut, nicknamed "Pepi," also felt a connection to the material: his father had been a star in the Yiddish theater in New York, where Aronson had worked for him. Schildkraut's wife would later comment on the way her husband took on Otto's mannerisms. But Schildkraut was upset at having to shave his head for the role and complained about being directed to act in a more restrained style than he was accustomed to. He accused Strasberg of deliberately trying to upstage him by stealing scenes, perhaps with her parents' encouragement. (In reality, Strasberg's father was emotionally distant and uninvolved with her work.) "Every other day he threatened to quit, accompanied by torrents of tears, which I later learned he could turn on or off at will," she recalled.[55] In her memoir, she wrote that he sometimes pinched her onstage hard enough to bruise her or otherwise distracted her while she was delivering her lines. She also alleged that he sexually harassed her, entering her dressing room without knocking and opening his mouth one night when she kissed him goodnight. When Strasberg's contract expired, she was replaced by Dina Doron, an Israeli actress.

After the Broadway production closed, Schildkraut, together with most of the other original cast members, stayed on for the year-long national tour, which played in major cities around the country. But the producers felt it was important for Americans who lived in smaller communities to be able to see the play. "We want to go south," Bloomgarden told Steve Press, who played Peter van Daan on Broadway and on the national tour. Kanin had other commitments, so Bloomgarden organized a "bus and truck tour" with Kip Good, another Broadway director. "It would use the story of Anne Frank to teach America about the Holocaust," writes journalist Adam Langer.[56] In fall 1958, they went on the road to cities in Virginia, North Carolina, Ohio, Kansas, Nebraska, Michigan, Alabama, Arkansas, and elsewhere. The cast and crew traveled in a bus that bore a big sign reading "The Diary of Anne Frank," but eventually that was taken down for fear of antisemitism.

"There was always a police presence in the audience to make sure that nothing bad ever happened," Press told Langer.[57]

There was no Jewish population in some of the places they visited; for many in those audiences, cast members were the first Jews they had ever seen. Many colleges and universities still enforced quotas for Jews, and country clubs were restricted. At a lunch with society ladies in New Orleans, Pauline Hahn, who played Anne, realized that "a Jew had never walked into this place before."[58] In the segregated South—they played in Little Rock weeks before public schools were closed down to protest desegregation, and in Shreveport three months before Martin Luther King Jr. spoke there—the cast and crew sometimes had to stay in different hotels.

Once in a while, in response to a line in the play in which Otto asks rhetorically, "Did we start the war?" someone in the audience would call, "Yes, you did." But the vast majority of the audiences were welcoming. People came to see the play and returned the next night with their children or grandchildren. At each stop, they sold copies of the *Diary*—sometimes hundreds. Teachers asked if they could assign the book in class or put on a production of the play in their schools. As Press would later say, the play "opened up this book into a new world."[59]

* * *

While the bus and truck tour wound its way through rural America, Twentieth Century Fox had won a bidding war for the movie rights. George Stevens, director of *A Place in the Sun* and *The Greatest Story Ever Told* (about the life of Jesus), served as director. During World War II, he had been part of the U.S. Army Signal Tour, shooting footage of D-Day and the liberation of concentration camps, including Dachau; some of his film was presented as evidence in the first Nuremberg trials. After the war, he had wanted to make a movie about it, but he "never found the right subject," his son, George Stevens Jr., said later. "He kind of came to feel that *Anne Frank* was his war film."[60]

Schildkraut would reprise his stage role in the film. So would

Gusti Huber, the actress who played Edith, even though disturbing information had turned up about her activities during the war years. Born in Vienna, she had immigrated to the United States in 1946 and married radio executive Joseph Besch, a former captain in the U.S. Army, who claimed she was the first Austrian actress to be cleared by the American military government. While the play was still in rehearsals, Kermit Bloomgarden received a letter from German-American actress and sculptor Lotte Stavisky alleging that Huber was a Nazi sympathizer who had been a personal friend of Goebbels.[61] In interviews with the American press, Huber claimed that she had refused to join the Nazi Party and had once been arrested by the Gestapo for cursing Hitler. According to Herbert G. Luft, a journalist for the *American Jewish Ledger*, this was all fiction. "In 1943, while the real Mrs. Frank remained in constant fear for the lives of her dear ones, Gusti Huber charmed the Germans in a movie entitled 'Gabrielle Dambrone.' . . . In 1944, when the Frank family was shipped off in sealed cars, Miss Huber amused the citizens of the Third Reich," Luft alleged.[62] The only person who seemed to be concerned about this was Meyer Levin, who circulated information about Huber's Nazi past to journalists covering his lawsuit. Huber's bio in the playbill for *Anne Frank* ends in 1938; on her death, in 1993, her *New York Times* obituary was silent on her wartime activities.[63]

Strasberg would not join the cast. Otto apparently wanted Audrey Hepburn, who grew up in the Netherlands during the occupation and saw Anne as her "soul sister," to play the role, but Hepburn declined.[64] Deciding that "it would be better to get a completely new girl," Stevens put his son, George Stevens Jr., in charge of the global search for a new Anne.[65] More than 10,000 hopefuls between the ages of thirteen and eighteen applied; Stevens Jr. interviewed around 3,000 of them. Among the candidates were the dancer Leonora de Heer, who said she had known Anne at Bergen-Belsen; Sabine Sinjen, a German child actress; and Marianne Sarstadt, a Dutch dancer.

Someone on Stevens's team had seen a picture of Millie Perkins, a high school student from New Jersey who worked as a teen model, on the cover of a magazine. "She just seemed like the right person," Stevens Jr. said later. They reached her in the middle of a modeling job in Paris; on the plane to California, she read the *Diary*. "Oh my gosh, this is something wonderful," she thought. She, too, identified strongly with Anne. "Anne Frank could not be told what she could and couldn't think," she said later. "When I read the diary, I said, oh my goodness, I know who she is. Because it was me."[66] Richard Beymer played opposite her as Peter; a few years later, he was Tony in the movie version of *West Side Story*.

Exteriors for the film were shot on location in Amsterdam, though not in the Annex itself, which was recreated for the film on a Hollywood lot. For the bombing scenes, a special contraption was devised to shake the set so that the actors would respond with genuine fear. The set was "monitored" by a former Dutch Resistance fighter, who marveled at "the great lengths [Stevens] goes in order to keep things exactly in the atmosphere of Holland during the war." Among the Resistance fighter's tasks was to stand behind the actors while wearing an SS uniform, to make them act with "shivers down their spine." When a visitor remarked that she had expected a movie shoot to be much noisier, Stevens responded, "The subject is much too delicate for that."[67]

But in some ways the film strayed even further from the historical facts of Anne's life than the play. The film opens with a shot of Otto climbing out of a truck, wearing the striped uniform of a concentration camp inmate. The Annex residents sit watching the bombers with their faces pressed against the window, whereas in reality they kept the windows covered with blackout curtains. The relationship between Anne and Peter is distinctly more physical: the two are depicted kissing passionately and lying in each other's arms. (This, at least, was probably closer to what actually happened.) The penultimate scene, in which Anne and Peter kiss as tires screech outside, is simply excruciating, as is Anne's farewell to her diary: "I must leave you behind," she says in a voiceover. "P.S. Please, please, anyone, if you should find this diary, will you please keep it safe for me, because someday I hope that—" Her voice cuts off, as if Anne had literally been interrupted in the midst of writing.

Shelley Winters won an Academy Award for Best Supporting Actress for her portrayal of Mrs. van Daan, but her performance today seems mannered and melodramatic. Political issues aside, Gusti Huber does a lovely job of portraying Edith, and her German accent feels realistic, especially in contrast with Winters and Lou Jacobi (as Mr. van Daan), who speak like working-class Jews from Brooklyn. Millie Perkins did her best to pronounce the German names correctly—"AH-na," "PAY-ter"—but she can't quite lose her all-American drawl. Winters took it upon herself to teach Perkins about Jewish history and traditions, giving her books to read and talking to her about Anne's religious background.

It's absurd to hear cover-girl Perkins complaining to Beymer that she's not pretty—as one critic has observed, she resembles Audrey Hepburn far more than Anne Frank—but the main problem is that she feels too likeable to be Anne.[68] "The girl we hope to find must be a personality approximation of the young Anne Frank herself," Stevens had announced to the press. "She must be at once appealing, sympathetic, gay and optimistic, thoughtful and sensitive."[69] Anne was all those things, but she was also moody, nosy, critical, and mercurial. Even by her father's account, she was difficult to live with. "Ecstasy, exuberance, brattiness, and even all my silent screams could be exposed," Strasberg wrote about her portrayal of Anne.[70] But there's no anger in Perkins's performance, no sense that her Anne found the exigencies of the Annex anything other than a minor inconvenience to make the best of.

In Stevens's original ending for the film, Anne, wearing a concentration camp uniform (another ahistorical touch), sways eerily, surrounded by mist. This ending, not surprisingly, was resoundingly rejected by test audiences and replaced with the close of the framing device, in which Otto recounts the fate of each resident and concludes of Anne, "She puts me to shame." As numerous critics have pointed out, both play and film center Otto's character far more than the *Diary* does; his presence at the beginning and the end works to authenticate the *Diary* for the audience, and many of the scenes are shown from his perspective.

If the bus and truck tour traveled on wheels, the movie version of *The Diary of Anne Frank* had wings. Joe L. Riddle, who would become a writer for the *Arkansas Democrat-Gazette*, saw the film at age six in Augsburg, Germany, where his father was stationed.[71] The town was some thirty miles from Dachau, and his father took the family to see what remained of the camp. "I still get shivers when I recall that visit," he wrote sixty years later. Across the globe in Jamaica, the movie inspired thirteen-year-old Michelle Cliff to read about the Holocaust and to begin her own diary. "She gave me permission to write, and to use writing as a way of survival," Cliff, who went on to become a major figure in global postcolonial literature, told an interviewer decades afterward.[72]

There can be no doubt that the movie helped to fulfill Otto's stated purpose of bringing Anne's message to an ever greater number of people. But there were also unintended consequences. Shifting the diary from the page to the stage and then the screen disrupts the intimate relationship that exists between book and reader. The Anne who writes is no longer a distinct individual but a role that can—and will—be interpreted by a multitude of actresses. And the "you" to whom her writing is addressed is no longer "Kitty," but an audience, distant and anonymous. As one critic writes, "This universal Anne was open to metaphor for audiences anywhere."[73]

INTERLUDE

Surrogate Father

The stage contains nothing but a desk, a chair, and a microphone. A tall, heavyset man, wearing plain black pants and a black shirt, takes a seat and begins to speak. For the next hour, he becomes Otto Frank. In a stream-of-consciousness monologue, he talks about his daughter, her brilliance, his burden. Sometimes he speaks as if addressing her: "You know your great-uncle?" He croons in a singsong voice, ending a passage with a couplet that rhymes, or nearly does, like "brethren / ignore them." At points he smiles and laughs, but by the end he is grimacing like a mask of tragedy, tears streaming from his eyes. "I have borne your genius like a madman!" he moans. His daughter is "the new Saint Joan, burning at the stake."[1]

But he talks also about things that don't come from Anne's life, or her lifetime: the shooting of a security guard at the United States Holocaust Memorial Museum by a white supremacist in 2009; the dangers faced by migrant families. "Mi amor," he calls her, promising to "float you across the river to safety, keeping La Migra at bay." He mentions "Gutierrez, a poet willing to die for his art." At the end, his heartrending shrieks blend into the sound of a siren as he calls her name: "Anita, Anita."

I'm watching Roger Guenveur Smith, an actor and performance artist, whose one-man *Otto Frank* is the latest in a series of plays he's written and performed channeling historical figures. Through his voice, they speak about their lives, but also about present-day issues that they might have wanted to address, had they been able to. "In this particular international moment, what [Otto Frank] brings to the table is extraordinary, and extraordinarily vital," Smith said in a radio interview in spring 2022. (*Otto Frank* premiered at the Magic Theater in San Francisco in March 2022; I saw a production at the Public Theater in New York City in January 2023.) He's referring specifically to Russia's recently launched war against Ukraine, which is in the process of turning another population into refugees, but it's clear he's thinking of other human rights issues as well. "My Otto speaks to his daughter from beyond her lifetime and beyond his as well," he said.

After graduating from the Yale School of Drama, Smith started his career with the role of Smiley in Spike Lee's *Do the Right Thing* (1989), which he improvised, and went on to work with Lee on a dozen other movies. Some of his other theatrical subjects include Huey Newton, Jimi Hendrix, Bob Marley, and Jean-Michel Basquiat: "a long lineage of historical characters" that he has "tried to bring into the present moment, kicking and screaming," as he puts it. He played Christopher Columbus as "a man still among us, a lounge entertainer with political aspirations." For his portrayal of Frederick Douglass, he dressed in a black leather jacket as an homage to Newton.

While performing as Rodney King in Amsterdam, Smith visited the Anne Frank House. As the father of two daughters, he came away particularly moved by Otto's story. "He's kind of an enigma, even though he lived a long and productive life as a steward of his daughter's work," he says. He pictured Otto wrestling with himself over the *Diary:* "One can only imagine the difficulty with which her father went through those pages. And the great dilemma then of absorbing it for himself and for their surviving family and trying to decide in what way he was going to share it with the world—if he was going to share it with the world at all. . . . He then becomes the purveyor of her brilliance."

Smith, who describes himself as a "history buff," develops his projects through a twofold process of both "intense archival immersion and improvisation." Sitting in the audience at the Public Theater, I could tell he had consumed much of the same material about Anne and Otto as I had; some of his more obscure references must have been lost on most of the other attendees. At the same time, he ranges freely in describing things that did not and never could have happened to Otto or Anne. A director he has worked with describes his performance style as "unique and emotionally intense," employing "spoken word, historical fact and jazzlike riffs, accompanied by a restless physicality."

Otto Frank is scripted, but Smith has spoken at length about his interest in bringing the techniques and style of jazz into theatrical work. For Huey Newton, he "absorbed" his lines "from a comprehensive study of Huey's work and interviews with him," comparing the work to a "song cycle": "We play the same songs every night, but we play them differently," as a jazz musician does. As Smith speaks his lines, composer Marc Anthony Thomas, his longtime collaborator, performs a live score that enhances and dramatizes the monologue. Sometimes they begin with written words, sometimes with Thomas improvising. The music for *Otto Frank* ranges from moody piano to the tinkling sounds of a music box playing "Happy Birthday" to atmospheric sounds like sirens.

I went into the performance knowing almost nothing about Smith or his prior work. It wasn't until after it was over, when I saw Smith under bright lights in the theater lobby, that I realized he was Black. "I would not be the first person one would think of in casting an Otto Frank," he acknowledges. As a light-skinned Black man, he has joked about his ability to blur racial categories: another Black man once came up to him on the street to say that he had seen an ad for Smith's work on television and wondered, "What are they doing having a white boy playing Frederick Douglass?"

Smith strongly resists the idea of categories, period. When a critic once asked him whether he considered his work theater or performance art, he pushed back: "You could call it entertainment. You could call it church. . . . It's all of those things. Why must we compartmentalize?" He applies the same philosophy to himself as a performer. "I will not be relegated into these boxes," he says. "'Ethnic' artists quite often box ourselves. We ethnicize ourselves. It's either this, or it's that, and you've got to be here, or you've got to be there."

"I missed the Jewishness of Otto Frank," the friend with whom I saw the performance confessed to me later. I was reminded of Otto's contradictory instructions to Levin, insisting that *The Diary of Anne Frank* should not be "a Jewish play" while allowing that "in some way of course it must be Jewish . . . so that it works against anti-Semitism." If something is lost when Anne's story migrates into a new political context, can something else be found? Is it possible for Smith's Otto Frank—at once German-Jewish, Black, Mexican—to be both here and there, in his own historical moment and ours; to be himself and also something larger than himself?

12

Survivor
Anne in Fiction

I want to go on living even after my death!

In the sensationalizing language of the *New York Post*, the Broadway play "brought about the reincarnation of Anne Frank—as though she'd never been dead."[1] The crassness of this comment aside, it demonstrates why the cognitive dissonance of seeing his daughters returned to life onstage, as well as his own younger self, was too much for Otto Frank. Theater can indeed give audiences an uncanny sense of resurrection. Jacqueline van Maarsen, who saw the play in Amsterdam, described the experience as seeing "Anne again"; it affected her so powerfully that she was unable to speak afterward.[2] Audiences in Germany were also silent after viewing the play, perhaps overwhelmed by the voice of a Jew returned from beyond the grave to implicitly reproach them.[3]

To make a play out of the *Diary* is to fictionalize it—there can be no other way. And the play, by virtue of its existence, opens the door to other literary possibilities. Otto understood this instinctively: thus his hesitation and anxiety about the dramatic adaptation, the concern he showed over so many of its details, and his own resistance to being turned into a fictional character. By having admitted the possibility of bringing Anne back to life on the stage and screen and thus removing her from the confines of the written *Diary*, the adaptations give others permission to treat her as if she were an imagined figure and resurrect her in their own ways.

Anne now appears in dozens of works of fiction.[4] She may be a major character, as in Philip Roth's *The Ghost Writer* (1979), or one who lurks in the background, as in Richard Lourie's *A Hatred for Tulips* (2007). She might be invoked as a shorthand for the Holocaust, as Norma Rosen does in *Touching Evil* (1959), one of the earliest works of American fiction to treat the subject, or as a patron saint of doomed adolescent love: In John Green's blockbuster *The Fault in Our Stars* (2012), a romance about two teens with terminal cancer, the young lovers travel to Amsterdam and kiss for the first time in the attic of the Anne Frank House. In Stephanie S. Tolan's *The Liberation of Tansy Warner* (1980), the main character works out her feelings about her parents' divorce as she stars in a high school production of *The Diary of Anne Frank*. Adam Langer's *Cyclorama* (2022) tracks a group of students who performed the play in the early 1980s into the #MeToo era, which finds them still reckoning with the actions of the teacher who coached them. The resurrected figures of Peter and Margot feature in novels of their own.[5]

Green's and Tolan's books are classed as young-adult fiction, a genre that took off in the wake of the *Diary* and on which it has been an unrecognized influence, in both its elevation of the voice of a teenage girl and its memoir-in-diaries form. The young-adult novel *Go Ask Alice* (1971), to give just one example, purports to be the found diary of a high school student who becomes a drug addict; it ends abruptly when she overdoses, which the reader is informed of in a postscript that resembles the epilogue to the first edition of the *Diary* ("Anne's diary ends here"). An entire essay could be written on the *Diary*'s impact on this genre.[6]

Here, however, I've chosen to focus on books in which Anne physically appears as a resurrected character: counter-histories in which she survives the Holocaust. As the scholar Hanno Loewy has written, it's not Anne's death that was responsible for her diary's success but the fact that "as one who has historically disappeared . . . she cannot hinder her own ongoing and idealized resurrection."[7] The tension that arises when the fictionally reconstructed Anne encounters her own idealized image offers a startling perspective on the uses that image has served.

* * *

In *The Ghost Writer*, Nathan Zuckerman, a stand-in for the young Philip Roth, imagines introducing a surviving Anne Frank to his parents as his fiancée—an in-your-face comeback to their judgment of him as disloyal to his Jewish identity. In satire as multilayered and pungent as an onion, this sly, brilliant novel wrestles with the assumptions and prejudices of a generation of American Jews; with the obligations of Jewish writers to their community; with the conditions necessary for the creation of art. As such, it seems to be the first book to make use of Anne Frank as a mirror uniquely able to reflect its creator's preoccupations.[8]

Nathan has begun to enjoy some success with his fiction, but personally he is as adrift as the snow that blankets the fields surrounding the house of E. I. Lonoff, a writer of his father's generation whom he has come to visit in the manner of a pilgrimage. Nathan's girlfriend has just broken up with him after his repeated infidelities, and he is embroiled in a battle with his father over a different kind of faithlessness. After reading a story he wrote inspired by a relative's financial and sexual troubles, his father has accused him of playing into the hands of antisemites: "People don't read art—they read about *people.*"[9] Nathan's father has appealed also to a higher authority: Judge Wapter, a scion of the Newark Jewish community, who has written a letter to Nathan with a list of questions that seem intended to provoke.

> If you had been living in Nazi Germany in the thirties, would you have written such a story? . . .
>
> Would you claim that the characters in your story represent a fair sample of the kinds of people that make up a typical contemporary community of Jews? . . .
>
> What set of aesthetic values makes you think that the cheap is more valid than the noble and the slimy is more truthful than the sublime? . . .
>
> Can you honestly say that there is anything in your short story that would not warm the heart of a Julius Streicher or a Joseph Goebbels?[10]

The judge caps his letter with a postscript: "If you have not yet seen the Broadway production of *The Diary of Anne Frank*, I strongly advise that you do so." He and his wife were in the audience for opening night, an "unforgettable experience." Roth expects the reader to be in on his joke: the document cited piously is not the *Diary* but the Goodrich/Hackett adaptation, a denatured facsimile of Anne, which the judge and his wife—like so many others—mistake for the real thing.

Nathan is wrestling with the existential question of how to live as a Jewish writer—an identity in which his birth and upbringing have imprisoned him, but which he accepts, as long as it doesn't have to define him completely. An extraordinarily close reader of the *Diary* who was one of the first to take Anne seriously as a writer, Roth discovers in Anne's thoughts about Jewish identity something of an analogue to his own situation. *We can never become just Netherlanders or just English or any nation for that matter, we will always remain Jews, we must remain Jews, but we want to, too.*[11]

At the same time, in their shame and repression, their obsession with status, their anxieties about how non-Jews view them, Roth sees postwar American Jews as forcing themselves into hiding. As long as they remain in the prison of their identity, they can never achieve their full potential. Just as Anne longs for a time *when we are people again, and not just Jews!* so too does Nathan (read: Roth) wish to be seen not only as a Jewish writer, but as a writer, full stop, without the limiting adjective.[12]

The Ghost Writer presents two possible paths out of this dilemma, neither satisfactory. The first is the life of Lonoff, who is loosely modeled on Bernard Malamud but also contains elements of Chekhov, Flaubert, Henry James, and other creative geniuses of the Western canon.[13] Lonoff has made art out of Jewish life, but he has done so by removing himself from it. "I think of you as the Jew who got away . . . from Russia and the pogroms . . . from Palestine and the homeland . . . from Brookline and the relatives . . . from New York," Nathan says, analogizing the claustrophobia of modern Jewish life in America to a century of persecution.[14] He looks upon Lonoff's literary greatness with something akin to the Zionist pride of his parents' generation: it is a manifestation of Jewish power that will prove to the world that the Jews are a force to be reckoned with.[15] It is also a justification for the work Nathan has been doing, evidence that the stuff of Jewish life—"thwarted, secretive, imprisoned souls"—is an appropriate subject for literature.[16] But the personal costs of this withdrawal are high. Lonoff lives in a remote farmhouse with his non-Jewish wife, Hope, in a state as close to chastity and isolation as married life will permit. (Hope complains, in the novel's penultimate scene, that he hasn't touched her in decades.) He spends his days at his desk, "turn[ing] sentences around."[17] So unsuited is Nathan to this monkish life that when left alone in Lonoff's study for the night, one of the first things he does is masturbate.

The second path is that of Anne Frank, at least as Nathan imagines her. He overhears his host talking with a young woman introduced earlier as a research assistant named Amy Bellette, with whom Lonoff seems to be romantically entangled. Some elements in the conversation, as well as his earlier impression of Amy—a "striking girl-woman," slender and pale, with soft and intelligent eyes—lead Nathan to imagine that she might be Anne Frank.[18] What if Anne had survived Bergen-Belsen and made her way to the United States, believing all her relatives to be dead? (This may be the one false note in *The Ghost Writer:* it's impossible to imagine that a surviving Anne wouldn't have bothered to search for her father.)

As Nathan tells it, Amy/Anne manages to forget about her previous life until discovering, at the dentist's office, an article in *Life* magazine about her father's publication of her diary. After reading the book—she special-orders it from the Dutch publisher—she understands that it derives its power from her death. "Were *Het Achterhuis* known to be the work of a living writer, it would never be more than it was: a young teenager's diary of her trying years in hiding during the German occupation of Holland," Roth writes. "But dead she had something more to offer than amusement for ages 10–15; dead she had written, without meaning to or trying to, a book with the force of a masterpiece to make people finally see."[19] The *Diary* is uniquely able to communicate the experience of Jewish persecution to outsiders. In order for it to retain this power, its author must remain anonymous, even though that means allowing her father to continue to believe she is dead.

Roth has been predictably excoriated by critics who accuse him of crudely exploiting Anne, "the most sacred of Jewish icons."[20] ("Is she Jewish?" Nathan pictures his father asking upon learning he has a new girlfriend.)[21] This simplistic and sanctimonious interpretation fails to appreciate the many levels on which the satire of *The Ghost Writer* works. Consider the scene in which Nathan's father accuses him of disloyalty, which takes place as they walk through the Newark neighborhood where Nathan grew up:

> Here I had practiced my sidearm curve, here on my sled I'd broken a tooth, here I had copped my first feel, here for teasing a friend I had been slapped by my mother, here I had learned that my grandfather was dead. There was no end to all I could remember happening to me on this street of one-family brick houses more or less like ours, owned by Jews more or less like us.[22]

Part of what's at stake for Nathan is precisely what he celebrates in Lonoff's writing: the triumph of recognizing that all this material can be the stuff of literature. But there's something else audible in the phrase "Jews more or less like us," which is almost exactly the way Meyer Levin described the Franks in his *New York Times* review of the *Diary*.[23] The tragedy of the Holocaust as revealed by the *Diary*, as Anne/Amy will later explain, is that it happened even to Jews who were not "pious [and] bearded," Jews like her and her family, who were no different from the "ordinary people" in the audience; that it happened to them simply because they were Jewish.[24] This, she sees, is the genius of the Broadway adaptation: it makes the Franks feel familiar to American Jews.

At the same time, there's nothing distinctively Jewish about Nathan's vision of childhood, with its broken tooth, its early sexual exploration, its personal tragedies; it is universal. The Zuckermans are like other Jews; but they are also, "more or less," like other working-class American families living in the suburbs in the 1950s. Nathan's desire to emphasize his family's commonality with the rest of America rather than their separateness as Jews—to be an "ordinary person," as his father, unconsciously echoing Anne, puts it—is the same desire that spurred German Jews like Otto Frank to lead assimilated lives, drinking in the culture of Goethe and Beethoven as if they were born to it, which they thought they were.

One lesson of the Holocaust is that it may not be possible for Jews to achieve this level of assimilation; the belief that they are accepted by the mainstream culture will always be an illusion. "I can't tell you how strange it felt not to be what I thought I was," playwright Arthur Miller said in a 1947 speech describing his own experiences of antisemitism, which showed him that non-Jewish Americans saw him as different from them in a way he hadn't understood. In reaction, Miller said, he "gave up the Jews as literary material" for reasons similar to the ones Nathan's father suggests: he was afraid that "even an innocent allusion to the individual wrong-doing of an individual Jew would be inflamed by the atmosphere, ignited by the hatred I suddenly was aware of, and my love would be twisted into a weapon of persecution against Jews."[25] This is poignant, but it doesn't solve the problem. If Nathan wants his writing to speak to a larger audience—to "spread its theme into the infinite," as Garson Kanin said in his letter to Frances Goodrich and Albert Hackett cautioning against the play's "special pleading" on behalf of the Jews—then he has no choice but to continue striving to be accepted as part of this larger community.

In accusing him of not having left out "anything disgusting" in his portrayal of Jewish characters, Nathan's father conjures the specter of antisemitism: Gentile readers, he says, will see these stories as being about "kikes and their love of money."[26] Note yet another parallel with Anne: she, too, doesn't shy away from certain "disgusting" elements, such as all the times the residents had to refrain from flushing the toilet all day when strangers were in the office. For her, as for Nathan, the slimy is indeed as truthful as the sublime. Of course, what the *Diary* does leave out, as it must, are the existentially revolting piles of corpses at Bergen-Belsen.

There's a sense, both in this novel and in the story of the

reception of the *Diary* on Broadway, that Jews of Nathan's father's generation felt their children had it too easy. They never experienced real prejudice, the way their parents did in Europe or when they first came to the United States. "I wonder if you fully understand just how very little love there is in this world for Jewish people," Nathan's father says.[27] The persecution of the Jews of Europe, brought to this generation via Anne's *Diary* rather than personal experience, reminds them simultaneously of their privilege and their vulnerability.

Nathan may have to renounce his father in order to become a great writer, just as Anne, in his fictional account, gives up the possibility of contact with Otto to preserve her diary's effect on its audience. Some critics have read Lonoff in *The Ghost Writer* as a substitute father to Nathan. No sooner does Nathan "adopt" Lonoff than he betrays him, too, with the quasi-Oedipal fantasy of seducing Amy/Anne. Considered in Freudian terms, Anne then becomes . . . Nathan's mother?[28] Regardless, the life of a martyr to art is not going to work for him. Nathan doesn't want to live like Lonoff, shut away in his study, renouncing the pleasures of the flesh; in Nathan's adaptation of Isaac Babel's description of the Jewish writer, he is a man with "autumn in his heart . . . spectacles on his nose . . . and blood in his penis."[29]

At the climax of *The Ghost Writer*, all the characters leave the house—another neat duplication of the *Diary*. But the novel leaves open the questions it asks. What *is* a writer's obligation to a community, and is that obligation different for Philip Roth than it was for Anne Frank? We can see something of the way Anne perceived her own obligation in her alteration of the phrase *if people were told* how the Annex residents lived and loved and fought during the war to *if we Jews were to tell*, a change that asserts the authority of Jews over their own narrative.[30] But it's clear that, despite the persecution raging around her, she was innocent of the idea that her depictions of certain Annex residents might play into anti-Jewish stereotypes. If she were alive, would people be telling her that her characterization of Mrs. van Pels, concerned as she is with her money and her possessions, would warm the heart of Goebbels? Is it only in a diary, albeit one intended for publication, that a writer can be truly free of obligations to a larger public? Or does the historicity of the Holocaust—the fact that all Jews were persecuted, whether they were cultured and refined like the Franks or materialistic like the Van Pelses—render the whole discussion moot?

As *The Ghost Writer* forces its readers to realize, in one way the power of the *Diary* is tied to Anne's biography. The reader has to know certain facts in order to appreciate it: that the story it tells is true and that Anne was murdered by the Nazis. But the novel also dramatizes the way in which Anne's death has the effect of severing the book from her life. Without her, it stands alone. Nobody asks for her political opinions or literary endorsements. And nobody asks her to live by the book—as they do for Roth, a Jewish writer in postwar America. Holocaust scholar Lawrence Langer and others have speculated that if Anne had survived the camps, she would have renounced her famous statement about people being truly good at heart.[31] Dead, however, there is nothing she can say to interfere with the *Diary*'s message. Anyone may interpret it however they wish.

* * *

In 2019, the *Harvard Lampoon*, a humor magazine, printed an image of Anne's head Photoshopped onto a cartoonish female body: gigantic fake breasts spilling out of a string bikini top, hands placed suggestively on cocked hips, pierced navel. "Virtual Aging Technology Shows Us What Anne Frank Would Have Looked Like If She Hadn't Died," blared the headline above. The caption on the photo: "Add this to your list of reasons the Holocaust sucked."[32]

The joke was both tasteless and unoriginal, since Roth had provoked scandal with the idea of a sexualized Anne Frank forty years earlier. The sexual component of Nathan's fantasy about Amy/Anne is essential to the shock value of that narrative. Particularly in America, Anne's youth and purity were emphasized in the book's marketing, from its title (*The Diary of a Young Girl*) to the photograph selected for its cover. Reviews of both book and play celebrated her as a "maiden," a "child," a "flower."[33] This insistence on Anne's virginity erases the *Diary*'s drama of her growing awareness of herself as a sexual being.

Nathan's desire for Anne shouldn't be taken literally; it's yet another layer of Roth's satire of American Jewish culture. *The Ghost Writer* was published in 1979, one year after the miniseries *Holocaust* aired on NBC to some 120 million viewers. Just as Nathan masturbates to his fantasy of Amy/Anne undressing for bed, Americans were titillating themselves with stories about the Holocaust while failing to grasp its significance.

But if it is scandalous for Anne to be seen as sexy, it's worse for her to be physically repugnant. In Shalom Auslander's *Hope: A Tragedy*, a very different story of a surviving Anne Frank, she appears as a hideous old crone: her eyes cloudy with cataracts, her skin gray and sallow, her posture bent, her hands "withered" and "skeletal."[34] This horror-trope version of Anne inhabits the attic of the farmhouse where Solomon Kugel has recently moved with his wife, Bree, and their son, Jonah. The house has an odd smell, but the real estate agent persuades him that it's just age.

One night, Kugel hears a tapping noise. Heading up to the attic to investigate, he discovers the old woman typing at a keyboard. When she tells him who she is, at first he takes a sanctimonious tone. "I know Anne Frank died in Auschwitz . . . along with many others, some of whom were my relatives. And I know that making light of that, by claiming to be Anne Frank, not only is not funny and abhorrent but it also insults the memory of millions of victims of Nazi brutality," he lectures her. "It was Bergen-Belsen, jackass," she corrects him. As for the relatives he supposedly lost: "Blow me, said Anne Frank."[35]

Foul in both her language and her habits—instead of using a toilet, she defecates into the heating vents, which transmit the stench throughout the house—the woman exacts a kind of blackmail on Kugel. She refuses to leave until she's finished the novel she's been working on for the past forty years. (The *Diary* is a hard act to follow.) He doesn't dare to tell his wife, fearing her reaction. And so he becomes a Miep-like figure, secretly providing her with food, printer paper, and whatever else she requires. As their tenant demands to use the attic for storage and Bree grows suspicious of her husband's odd habits, Kugel's situation becomes increasingly untenable. Even if she isn't really Anne Frank, he can't throw this fragile elderly woman out of the house. And what if she *is* Anne Frank? Better to suffer the Holocaust himself than to explain that to his mother. "My own son, she would say, ratting out Anne Frank."[36]

In the backstory Auslander gives her, Anne hid in the attic of a German farmer somewhere near Bergen-Belsen after the camp was liberated—and remained there, implausibly, for several years. One day the farmer brought her a newspaper: thousands of people were reading her diary. "I'd forgotten about it by then, to be honest," she says. But when she goes to visit the publisher, he tells her to get lost. As it turns out, a parade of girls have claimed to be her, seeking a share of the royalties. To prove that she isn't a fraud, she tells him about the passages her father edited out—"parts only I, back then, could have known about." Stay dead, the publisher advises. "Nobody wants a live Anne Frank. They want a martyr, they want to know we've hit bottom. That it gets better, because it can't get worse. They want to know that we can rise like a phoenix from our own fiery human ashes."[37]

As sharp as this satire is, *Hope: A Tragedy* does not approach the richness and complexity of *The Ghost Writer.* But it is very, very funny. Much of the humor focuses on the figure of Kugel's mother, a Brooklyn-born and -bred Jew who fabricates absurd stories about being a Holocaust survivor. "That's your grandfather," she told Kugel as a child, pointing to a lampshade. "It says Made in Taiwan," he pointed out. "Well, they're not going to write Made in Buchenwald, are they?" she snapped back.[38] Using the same currency, Anne Frank makes it clear that she knows Kugel won't kick her out: "Because you're Jewish . . . and you feel guilty for *not* suffering atrocities." Indeed, even as the consequences of keeping her secret grow more and more dire, he perseveres.

Hope: A Tragedy appeared in 2012, more than thirty years after *The Ghost Writer*, at the tail end of a boom in Holocaust-related fiction and film. "I was raised with that little kid's face in my face for so many years reminding me that I was going to die, badly, and before my time," Auslander said in a radio interview. "I was advised to never forget, but boy, if I could forget for a minute, I would love to." He makes it clear that his portrait of Anne was motivated not by animosity but by love. Rereading the *Diary*, he said, made him realize, "This kid was cool! . . . She was not going to grow up and be a wallflower." Perhaps in a jab at Roth, he continued, "She was not going to be someone my mother would like if I brought her home on a date." If that girl could see "what became of her and her diary," Auslander came to believe, "she would be somewhat disgusted."[39]

In the novel, Anne Frank says, "I'm sick of this Holocaust shit." Perhaps others were as well. Critics declined to get worked up about Auslander's irreverence toward Anne, praising the book's chutzpah as well as its humor.[40]

Similar to the couples in "What We Talk About When We Talk About Anne Frank," Kugel continually asks people he knows if he and his family could use their attic as a hideout—and is rebuffed. No one else understands how seriously he means this request or why he makes it. "There's a huge part of me that . . . just wants to take my kids and wife in the attic and lock the door . . . because I was raised with that attitude, that the best defense is a good paranoia," Auslander said.[41] Kugel's own paranoia turns out to be justified. Anne Frank may outlive them all.

* * *

Hope: A Tragedy is a farce; its hideous depiction of the surviving Anne doesn't pretend to be realistic. In *Annelies*, the novelist David R. Gillham makes what may be an even bolder choice, imagining Anne had she survived Bergen-Belsen and returned to Amsterdam. In this version of the story, Margot dies, but Anne awakens to find herself alive. Stunned by the face she sees in the mirror—the "dark cauldron eyes," the lice scabs on her skull—she decides to remember herself as "the dark-haired, ugly-duckling type who showed up in the glass above the lavatory sink" in the Annex.[42]

The reader, too, may prefer to remember the Anne of the Annex rather than Gillham's depiction of her. There are touching moments, such as when she steals a roll from the supper table and hoards it for later: "She finds that she can sleep through the night knowing it's there."[43] But this Anne is bitter, snarky, angry, resentful. She smokes; she's promiscuous. She has no interest in going back to school: "After Belsen what can the Pythagorean theorem mean to her?" And she is self-righteous, using her trauma "as if it's a weapon to wield," as Kugler scolds her.[44]

Gillham deserves credit for both his imagination and his courage: an Anne who survived Auschwitz and Bergen-Belsen would not have been the person we know from the *Diary*. She reacts to her own most famous line with horror: "If she had just been stabbed in the chest with a knife blade, she could not have suffered a sharper pain." People still good at heart? The girl who believed that is dead, she tells her father. That part of her didn't survive.[45]

Otto, too, finds that the Anne who returned was "no longer my little kitten. Of course, how *could* you be the same? How could *any* of us *ever* be the same?"[46] Bereft at the loss of his image of her, he holds on to her diary, "all I had left of the Annelies I'd known," without telling her it has survived.[47] This was one of several of Gillham's inventions that didn't convince me. Everything we know about Otto Frank suggests that he could not have kept this important secret from his daughter. And in the absence of proof of Anne's death, why would Miep have given the diary to him at all?

Gillham, who is not Jewish, first came to the *Diary* in his twenties, after reading *The Ghost Writer*, and was startled both by its author's talent and by the strong personal connection he felt to her. The idea for *Annelies* came to him after he read Cynthia Ozick's *New Yorker* essay about Anne, in which Ozick poignantly imagines that she might have become a great fiction writer, "a long row of novels and essays spilling from her fluent and ripening pen." He made a first attempt at the novel, then put it aside, unsure whether he had the skill to tell Anne's story. But a few years later his agent encouraged him to continue.

Gillham worked on the book for more than six years. In addition to reading survivor testimonies and doing other historical research, he traveled to Westerbork and Bergen-Belsen, as well as to sites important to Anne's life: the Franks' former apartment on Merwedeplein, which is now used as housing for writers seeking asylum from persecution; her Montessori school; the bookshop where she picked out her diary; the ice cream shop where she hung out with her friends.[48] The childhood Anne isn't a saint in his book; she sometimes comes across as bossy or obnoxious, as when she tells Margot she wants to be a famous writer, "the kind the world adores."[49] By reimagining Anne's life both before and after the war, Gillham attempts to restore her as a human being.

As I've said, that is my own intention in this book. Perhaps this is why I struggled with Gillham's most counter-historical moments. As a biographer, I typically have trouble reading historical novels, stumbling over the question of where the line between fact and fiction is located. Especially relating to the Holocaust, about which many facts are well known, historical fiction has to make sense within the context of the facts. It can expand the space between those facts, but it cannot replace them entirely.

One example of how this can work is Richard Lourie's *A Hatred for Tulips* (2007), in which Willem, age sixty-five, returns to the Netherlands to visit Joop, the Dutch brother his mother left behind decades earlier when she ran off with a Canadian soldier. (He hates tulips, he explains, because he knows what they taste like: "In the war, at the end, when there was nothing, we ate them.")[50] Joop, it turns out, has been carrying a burden of guilt: he believes he played a role in the betrayal of the Annex. Trying to earn money to appease his abusive father, Joop learned he could make extra income on the side by delivering food in secret to people in hiding. Among the clever connections to reality here is a mention of the jailing of the greengrocer Van Hoeven, whom Anne's readers will recognize as one of Miep's suppliers. As Joop tells it, the crucial tip leading to the raid came from an elderly lady who lived above the grocery store; suspecting that Van Hoeven was up to something, she followed him to Prinsengracht 263. Even if there weren't still uncertainty around exactly what triggered the raid on the Annex, this would be a plausible scenario.

In Gillham's novel, the surviving Anne is the one carrying around a burden: she believes that she killed Margot by pushing her off the bunk they shared in Bergen-Belsen. Margot was coughing, she later confesses to Bep, and she couldn't sleep: "I didn't mean to shove her . . . to shove her so *hard.*" Bep tries to absolve her: "What you just told me you *think* happened . . . you should consider it nothing more than a hallucination," she says. The blame for Margot's death "lands squarely on the men who perpetrated these crimes."[51] This is obviously true, and Anne believes her.

But even if the supposed act was accidental, as Gillham strongly implies, it strikes me as more than a fictional liberty. Once suggested, it can't be taken back or disproved. When I asked Gillham whether it concerned him that readers might mistake the scene for reality, he responded that to do so would misinterpret his book. But there can never be a single correct interpretation of a literary work. Though I believe in the right of a fiction writer to imagine whatever they wish, my own feeling is that the scene trespasses on Anne's memory, not unlike Goodrich and Hackett's transformation of Hermann van Pels into a thief.[52]

Roth brings Anne back to life in order to reflect on issues of Jewish identity as a writer. For Auslander, she's a figurehead for the ways the Holocaust has come to dominate Jewish life in America. Gillham doesn't have an ideological axe to grind with Anne, wishing only to transform her into a believable fictional character. If he's unable entirely to do so, part of the reason may be that we have already done it so well ourselves. Readers already perceive Anne as if she were a figure in a book rather than a real person. To just about everyone, her life is of secondary importance to what we make of it.

* * *

In an old ghost story, a man is presented with a monkey's paw that is said to be cursed: it will grant the bearer wishes, but only at a terrible cost. The original owner tries to throw the paw into the fire, but the man, seduced by its powers, can't resist giving it a try. He wishes for money to pay off the mortgage on his house. The next day his son is killed in a violent accident at work; as recompense, the company offers the sum he needs. After the funeral, the man's wife, insane with grief, insists on using the paw to wish her son back to life. But the thing that knocks on the door is no longer their child in the way they remember him—it's a mutilated corpse.[53]

What makes the story deeply sad as well as terrifying is the way it draws on the universal human longing to defeat death: on some level, we'd be willing to do almost anything to bring a loved one back to life, even in hideously changed form. I wonder if this fable lurks somewhere in the background of Anne's reincarnations, which inevitably contain a touch of horror. In Roth's version, her head is too big for her body; in Auslander's, her ancient body and its functions are portrayed as grotesque; in Gillham's, it's her behavior that's no longer recognizable.[54] The Broadway adaptation, too, resuscitated Anne as something other than she was—perhaps one reason why Otto never wanted to see it. There must have been times when he wished he hadn't taken that particular monkey's paw out of the fire.

Regardless of the reasons why they choose to bring her back, the fiction writers who engage with Anne are ghost writers all, writing for and in her name, albeit without her cooperation or permission. But Anne, too, is a ghost who writes. In *A Hatred for Tulips*, Joop, sneaking into the Annex one night, is spooked by a glimpse of her coming down the stairs in a white nightgown, "floating through the air like a ghost."[55] In Aidan Chambers's *Postcards to No Man's Land*, another young-adult novel, the protagonist is an English teenager who discovers both family secrets and revelations about his own sexuality during a trip to the Netherlands. He goes to pieces after visiting the Annex, where he senses the presence of Anne's ghost: "it was like she was still there."[56]

Eva Geiringer Schloss, Otto's stepdaughter, noted that the lives of Holocaust survivors "always included the ghosts of the people from our original families," but Otto's life did so to an unusual extent. Eva describes the role of the *Diary* in both Otto's life and her mother's as "all-consuming." Together with Fritzi, who was his consultant on business and personal matters as well as his travel companion, Otto spent "practically every waking moment for more than thirty years" managing the business of the *Diary:* corresponding with publishers, adapters, and others who worked on it or wished to; dealing with matters related to the foundations established in Anne's name; responding personally to an unceasing flood of letters from all over the world. "The diary, and Anne's legacy, became his life . . . he had little interest in people who were not interested in 'Anne Frank,'" Eva writes. In addition to comparing the behavior of Eva's children to Anne's, Otto sometimes slipped and called one of the girls by her name.[57] On visits to her grandmother and Otto in Basel, Eva's youngest daughter insisted that Eva sleep in bed with her because she found the house "spooky" and called Basel a "ghost town."[58]

Readers have always wondered whether Anne would have chosen to publish the *Diary* in the same form if she had survived and if she would have gone on to become a great writer. After hearing such a discussion on the BBC in 1953, Otto was puzzled that "this point seems to interest the young people more than the many [issues] which are contained in Anne's book."[59] Indeed, one element these fictional resurrections of Anne have in common is that while she's still a writer, she's a writer who is less successful than the historical Anne Frank, whose book became one of the best-selling nonfiction books of all time. Anne doesn't have to die in order to become a writer. But the extraordinary effect of the *Diary* depends on her death, in a way readers intuitively grasp. As she says in *The Ghost Writer,* "It is too late to be alive now. I am a saint."[60]

INTERLUDE

Family Secret

For decades, Anne was believed to have died sometime in March 1945, perhaps as little as a week or two before the liberation of Bergen-Belsen. But in 2015, researchers at the Anne Frank House conducted a close analysis of the testimony of those who saw Anne and Margot in the camp and determined that both sisters probably died in mid-February at the latest.[1] The news made international headlines.

Chen Drachman, a twenty-eight-year-old aspiring filmmaker, saw one of the news reports. "There was a punctuation error that made it seem like her fate was unknown," she told me over lunch in Tel Aviv, where she and I were both visiting. (Drachman was born in Israel but lives in the United States.) Now in her mid-thirties, she sports closely cropped dark hair and owlish glasses. As a child, Drachman wasn't especially interested in Anne; the first time she tried to read the *Diary*, she was unable to finish it. But she found herself wondering what kind of person Anne Frank, a girl who tried to "carry out ordinary life under completely unordinary circumstances," would be today. Why would she have kept her identity a secret? And what might induce her to give up that secret?

The result is Drachman's first short film, "The Book of Ruth," which premiered in June 2020. It opens with a shot of an elderly woman (played by the remarkable Tovah Feldschuh, her gaze as steely as her hair) working in her garden and singing to herself. She's interrupted by a car pulling up: it's her daughter, son-in-law, and grandchildren visiting for Passover. There are protests that she shouldn't have cooked so much food, good-natured competition over who makes the best matzoh brei, some gentle complaining—"Maybe if you had a phone," the daughter begins, but her mother interrupts: "I don't like it when any random person can find me." In short, it's a warm, ordinary Jewish family scene.

But late that night, the granddaughter, Lizzy (played by Drachman), confronts her grandmother. Why did she abruptly turn off the television when a story about Anne Frank came on? What's the significance of the locket she wears around her neck? "Don't lie—it's just me," she says. "You're her."

"I didn't want it to be a detective story," Drachman told me. "It's a moment in time between a grandmother and a granddaughter around a secret that is quite complex." She has thought deeply about the psychological complications of keeping such a secret, the revelation of which she compares to the experience of coming out. "If you carry a secret for so long, it wears you down. You want to let it go," she says. But if there is a dramatic moment of revelation, we don't see it on camera. Instead, the film cuts to a shot of grandmother and granddaughter sitting on a bench outside, silent, both staring straight ahead rather than at each other. The look on Drachman's face shows that it's as difficult to hear such a secret as it is to reveal it.

In an essay from 2018 titled "Men Explain Anne Frank to

Me," the critic Talya Zax wondered why depictions of the surviving Anne Frank are almost always by men. Noting Anne's own reflections on gender bias—*Of the many questions that have often bothered me is why women have been, and still are, thought to be so inferior to men*—Zax argues that these novels "enter into an odd sort of contest with Frank by claiming to write what she couldn't, on her behalf." In fact, Zax notes, they don't see her as a writer at all. For Roth, she is "an object that American Jews had made sacrosanct"; for Auslander, she is a burden; for Gillham, a PTSD-suffering survivor. Marjorie Ingall, writing in *Tablet*, has stated her discomfort even more strongly: "it feels exploitative for grown men to slobber over Anne, using her as fodder for their own fantasies."

Female artists have produced some of the most interesting works to engage creatively with Anne's legacy, if not with her reincarnation. The Jamaican-American writer Michelle Cliff, born in Kingstown in 1946, found in the *Diary* a way to think about the prejudice around her. "This twelve-year-old Christian mulatto girl, up to this point walking through her life according to what she had been told—not knowing very much about herself or her past . . . this child became compelled by the life and death of Anne Frank. She was reaching, without knowing it, for an explanation of her own life," Cliff writes in *Abeng*, an autobiographical novel in which the adolescent narrator cuts school to watch the movie version of *The Diary of Anne Frank*, just as Cliff once did.

Israeli writer Judith Katzir uses Anne as a touchstone in a novel that chronicles a young teenage girl's love affair with a female teacher. The book's title in Hebrew is *Hineh ani matchilah* or "Here I begin," the first words of Anne's diary in Hebrew; the (unfortunate) English title is *Dearest Anne: A Tale of Impossible Love*. The book is constructed in the form of diary-letters written to Anne by the girl in the novel. Sometimes she compares their situations; she notices, too, that Anne expressed her interest in a girlfriend's breasts ("this doesn't mean that you were a lesbian . . . all it means is that you were sensitive and inquisitive"). But mostly she unburdens herself, sharing every detail of the intensely erotic relationship. Critics have suggested that to reference Anne Frank in such a novel constitutes blasphemy. But it's possible instead to read this story of sexual awakening as bringing life to Anne, allowing her to share vicariously in an experience that she was almost certainly denied.

Perhaps most unexpectedly, director Lisa France's film *Anne B. Real*, with the tagline "Anne Frank meets *8 Mile*," juxtaposes the *Diary* with the life of Cynthia, a Latina teenager who dreams of becoming a rap star, improvising rhymes in front of her bathroom mirror with a toothbrush as a stand-in for a microphone. The family, which includes her older sister's toddler, is crowded into a cramped East Harlem apartment where the electric bill doesn't always get paid; her brother, strung out on drugs, sells her lyrics to a male rapper who passes them off as his own; gun violence assaults the neighborhood and their own lives. Cynthia's father, now dead, gave her a copy of the *Diary* as an example of another creative girl who triumphed despite her dire circumstances, and she turns to it often for comfort and inspiration. The film has some clunky moments, but the characters are charmingly earnest, and France's allusions to Anne's story—including a scene in which the inhabitants of Cynthia's apartment huddle inside, terrified, as her brother bangs furiously on the door—demonstrate her respect for the source.

Part of what makes Drachman's film so moving is the tenderness of its vision. "It's a story about memory, about knowing where you came from, about celebrity culture, the tendency to claim ownership over people and their stories, and also trauma—how different people deal with trauma differently," she told me. Her Anne isn't a sexy coed, a gruesome crone, or a chain-smoking survivor of trauma. She's a real person: a grandmother trying to live out her years in peace with her family.

How we wish, watching it, that Anne could have had this: the cozy house, the Passover seder, the loving granddaughter. "The world made me famous by commemorating the worst thing that ever happened to me," Anne says in the film. "History has forced me to relive my worst nightmares over and over and over again. . . . I just want to be left alone, enjoy my garden. I've paid my dues."

13

Pawn
Anne in the Political World

On a balmy spring evening in Los Angeles, I poked my head inside an unmarked theater, wondering if I had mistaken the date. There were no signs advertising the play I'd come to see, and everyone around me was speaking Spanish. Then I noticed a table piled high with copies of a memoir by a Holocaust survivor, as well as a stack of "Hate has no home here" lawn signs. I was in the right place.[1]

I had come to see *The Diary of Anne Frank—LatinX*, a production by the director Stan Zimmerman featuring actors of Latino heritage. The idea came to Zimmerman in 2018, when the news was filled with stories about the Trump administration targeting for deportation immigrants from Central and South America who had come to the United States illegally. In some cases, these were people who had lived here for decades; they had jobs, houses, and families, including children born in the

United States. For years, the government had looked the other way. Now the rules had changed without warning. Zimmerman saw a CNN feature about a Jewish woman who had signed the lease on a safe house for a migrant family on the run from ICE. "I grew up in a time when the Holocaust was not so far behind me," this woman, whose identity was disguised on camera, told the reporter. "I think there's a strong feeling in the Jewish community: we cannot let this happen. It's our responsibility. What was done to us cannot happen to other people."[2]

In substance, the play that Zimmerman mounted, using Wendy Kesselman's adaptation of the original Goodrich/Hackett script, was identical to the 1997 Broadway production. The only difference was the ethnicity of the majority of the cast. (The small roles of Miep and Kraler, the composite Kleiman/Kugler character, were played by white actors.) The actors transformed into the Annex residents gradually. At the start of the play, dressed in gray hoodies—an item of clothing that appears in some family separation reports—they read clunkily from the script. Midway through Act I, the scripts vanished, and by the start of Act II, the actors were fully inhabiting their roles, in period costume. In honor of the woman featured by CNN, the actress playing Miep initially wore a necklace with a large Jewish star.

I went into this production feeling skeptical. Though I had been horrified by the reports of family separations and the conditions under which the detainees were kept, comparisons of the situation to the Holocaust struck me as imprecise and overheated. But it seemed essential to see a production of the play, which had moved so many people, while I was working on this book. Why not this one? I wasn't sobbing at the end, like a few others in the audience. But I did find the Van Daans both funnier and more loving toward each other than the *Diary* makes them out to be; Edith, too, felt more like a real person. The young actress who played Anne was appropriately sweet and spunky.

Mostly, though, I was distracted by the unresolved political question. During a question-and-answer session after the play, an audience member, her voice filled with emotion, accused Zimmerman and the cast of "appropriating" Anne's story. The defenses given were based in identity politics. The Argentine-born actor playing Mr. van Daan, it turned out, was half-Jewish; his grandfather had been a Holocaust survivor. The play "isn't only about a Jewish family in Holland," he said.[3]

"Do not make a Jewish play out of it!" Otto Frank told Meyer Levin, while nonetheless insisting that "in some way of course it must be Jewish . . . so that it works against anti-Semitism."[4] The Dutch historian Henri van Praag has written of the *Diary*'s power as a modern "cult play," a kind of secular myth that motivates youth "to actions of courage and sacrifice in the service of tomorrow's world," just as religious plays once inspired their audiences to worship.[5] Was Zimmerman's production a useful expansion of the Anne Frank story into a contemporary context? Or was it yet another use of Anne and her diary as a political pawn to be pushed around in ways she never imagined or intended? In the decades since its publication, it has proved challenging for the *Diary* to remain relevant under a variety of political circumstances without losing its power as a document of anti-Jewish persecution.

* * *

From the start, Otto Frank saw the mission of the *Diary* as promoting peace and tolerance, understood in the broadest possible sense. The physical embodiment of this mission is the Anne Frank House, which opened to the public on May 3, 1960. The initial plan was for Prinsengracht 263 to serve as the headquarters of an international Anne Frank Foundation, with a museum, a library, a youth hostel, and space for annual workshops for teachers, behavioral scientists, and others working with adolescents. The foundation would exhibit and publish creative work by students and give out annual awards and fellowships.

As the original prospectus put it, "The name Anne Frank has come to symbolize faith in the good inherent in man and in his capacity to achieve it."[6] The main point, Otto stated, was that the building "should not be a war museum or a shrine, but . . . a place where the post-war generation could seek ways to work for peace."[7]

While the main focus of the museum was always on Anne and the *Diary*, its exhibits also included "material on discrimination, intolerance and an examination of the roads toward peace."[8] But by establishing Anne as a figurehead for "tolerance," a term that can be defined differently depending on the political context, Otto opened the gates for her exploitation in the service of causes that conflict with other interpretations of her legacy.

In 1971, the Anne Frank House hosted the first of a series of exhibitions titled "Nazism in South Africa," created by a joint Dutch and South African student group at the invitation of theologian Hans van Houte, then the director of the House. Inspired by religious leaders who had opposed Nazism, Van Houte hoped to encourage Dutch clergy to stand against apartheid. As scholar Shirli Gilbert describes it, the exhibit "drew direct parallels between the Nuremberg laws and apartheid legislation, and compared the Bantustans"—territories where Black South Africans were forced to live in poverty and deprived of their citizenship rights—"to the Jewish ghettos." After touring the Annex and learning about Anne's life and death, visitors descended the staircase to see a banner that read "Nazism = Apartheid"—a parallel, Gilbert notes, that was "not examined in detail" and for which no historical context was offered. "To people just having toured the Anne Frank exhibition it sinks in straightaway," Berend Schuitema, the leader of the student group that organized the exhibition, said at the time.[9]

Otto, arguing that the two political systems were not comparable, requested that the banner be removed. Still, another exhibition the following year displayed a life-size papier-mâché model of South Africa's prime minister at the time, B. J. Vorster, holding a swastika, and quoted him as saying: "In Italy they call it Fascism; in Germany they call it National Socialism; in South Africa we call it Christian Nationalism." Schuitema, in comments to the press, continued to draw a parallel between the Final Solution and the Bantustan system, which he described as "also a form of extermination," though he later acknowledged that the claim lacked nuance.[10]

Unbeknown to the Dutch activists, however, leaders of the anti-apartheid movement were finding inspiration for their struggle in the Nazi persecution of Jews, though without drawing a direct parallel between their situation and Anne's. As a student activist, Ahmed Mohamad Kathrada (born to Indian immigrants in South Africa in 1929, the same year as Anne) traveled in 1951 to student congresses in East Berlin and Poland. There he visited Auschwitz, which affected him so deeply that he gathered ashes and bone fragments from the ground, put them in a bottle, and brought them back to South Africa. "Auschwitz is arguably the most poignant reminder to mankind of the evils of racism," he wrote later.[11]

In 1962, as the South African government stepped up pressure against anti-apartheid activists, detaining them repeatedly and putting them under severe restrictions, Kathrada went underground. The following year he was arrested in a raid on the headquarters of the military wing of the African National Congress and became one of the accused in the Rivonia Trial, along with Nelson Mandela, Denis Mbeki, and other leaders of the movement. In June 1964, the Rivonia defendants were convicted and sentenced to life imprisonment on Robben Island, a prison more than four miles off the shore of Cape Town. Kathrada was held there for eighteen years.

The prison, which Mandela would later call "another country," was completely cut off from the mainland.[12] In addition to being isolated geographically, prisoners were denied access to newspapers; their books and magazines were censored. The Rivonia prisoners were further separated from the rest of the prisoners. Twenty-five of them were kept in solitary confinement, forced to live in silence and communicate via secret notes. Kathrada, the youngest of the group at thirty-four, became head of the "communication committee," facilitating the circulation of written materials. Prisoners working in the houses of the wardens copied items from newspapers and smuggled them into the prison.

It's not clear exactly how the *Diary* came into the prison; it was likely among the books donated by a library in Cape Town. The Rivonia prisoners passed it among themselves until the pages fell apart, reading it in the evenings after they were locked up. Aside from the Bible, it was the only book Kathrada read in prison. Some prisoners copied the entire book and circulated it as a form of samizdat. Like Anne, Kathrada kept a notebook of inspirational quotations, into which he copied thirteen passages from the *Diary*, including the "good at heart" quote. He included the entire passage, situating Anne's optimism in the context of her fear and despair.[13]

In 1994, the first democratic elections were held in South Africa. Kathrada, who had finally been released from prison five years earlier—he served time in Pollsmoor Prison, near Cape Town, from 1982 to 1989—was elected as a member of parliament, representing the African National Congress. That same year, a traveling exhibition created by the Anne Frank House called "Anne Frank in the World," featuring photographs illustrating the circumstances of Anne's life in Germany, the Netherlands, and in the camps, opened in Cape Town. Mandela gave the opening address, and Kathrada and Mbeki spoke about reading the *Diary* in prison. While acknowledging the historical uniqueness of the Holocaust, they celebrated the *Diary* as a personal inspiration. It "kept our spirits high and reinforced our confidence in the invincibility of the cause of freedom and justice," Mandela said.[14]

In contrast to the dogmatism of the 1971 "Nazism = Apartheid" exhibition, the prisoners on Robben Island appreciated Anne not as a figurehead, but as an individual: a person experiencing extraordinary and extreme circumstances of persecution with whom they could sympathize without the distortions that identification requires. Using the Holocaust more as a "symbolic benchmark" than a "precise historical comparison," as Gilbert puts it, the activists looked to Anne for moral support not only during their struggle but also as they later paved the way toward reconciliation, "invoking the moral gravity of the Holocaust, but avoiding mention of specific opponents or political ideologies." As Tali Nates of the Johannesburg Holocaust and Genocide Center explains, the Holocaust can be a useful starting point for education in tolerance for South Africans precisely because of its historical distance from their specific circumstances. Educators raised under apartheid, Nates writes, can find it "less emotionally charged" to teach about the Holocaust than about their own history.[15]

In addition to what Anne brought to South Africa, the way these activists understood her can help us see the "good at heart" line a little differently. As we know, Ozick and others have denigrated its overemphasis, calling it the naive idea of "a child who continues to hope for a better world" and arguing that it allows a false catharsis that detracts from the brutal reality of Anne's death.[16] Lawrence Langer and Eva Geiringer Schloss have stated confidently that Anne would no longer have believed that people were "really good at heart" after experiencing Auschwitz and Bergen-Belsen.[17]

Kathrada and Mandela saw Anne not as a victim but as "a fighter for human rights."[18] In this light, perhaps we can read the famous quote not as a childishly optimistic effusion but as an act of resistance. To maintain belief in the goodness of humanity when you *see the world being gradually turned into a wilderness* isn't necessarily a sentimental fantasy. It can be a courageous statement of faith in a potentially better future, a future in which democracy might yet win out again even as the thunder approaches and millions suffer. For activists who hope to build such a future for their country, that faith isn't an indulgence—it's a necessity.

* * *

On a visit to Israel in the early 1970s, Otto Frank heard a choir of Japanese students performing a concert in Hebrew. Afterward, he introduced himself, encouraging the group to spread awareness of the Holocaust and promote peace. Had they heard of his daughter's diary? he wondered.[19]

They probably had. The *Diary*, translated into Japanese in 1952 under the title *A Light Ever So Fragile*, had been an enormous success in Japan, selling well over 100,000 copies within a few months of its release and quickly becoming required reading in schools. As in the United States, a cult of celebrity developed around Anne's image: her photograph was displayed in bookstore windows, and "Anne's day" even became a Japanese euphemism for menstruation.[20] More than 30,000 Japanese tourists visit the Anne Frank House every year. The *Diary* has sold more than five million copies in Japanese; it has been adapted into a manga version and an animé movie. It is the "one text that every Japanese child is encouraged to read while growing up," writes Asian studies scholar Sonia Ryang, who recalls reading it herself at age ten.[21]

In Japanese contexts, Anne's name is often linked with that of Hiroshima native Sadako Sasaki, who was two years old when the United States dropped the atomic bomb on her city. After developing leukemia at age eleven, she set the goal of folding one thousand origami cranes before her death, which have now become a symbol of peace. In 1962, a group of activists, including students and Buddhist monks, spent about a year traveling from Hiroshima to Auschwitz, mostly by foot, scattering thousands of paper cranes along the way. Because Japanese people experienced "the bomb and occupation" but also committed "the sin of aggression," they had a "special duty" in promoting world peace, the organizers explained.[22]

The perception of Anne in Japan is inextricably intertwined with the nation's own complicated political history. Some historians argue that the tendency to see Anne as a "symbol of universal forgiveness and forgetfulness" has facilitated a form of "historical amnesia" that allows the Japanese to view themselves as war victims and poses an obstacle to an honest historical reckoning that would include an assessment of their own war crimes. As one scholar writes, the diary became canonical in Japan in part because it enabled "Japanese people to empathize with Anne Frank and see themselves, like her, as innocent victims."[23] Such a reading requires removing Anne from her historical context as a victim of the Axis powers, which, of course, included Japan. A Japanese teenager visiting the Anne Frank House a few years ago, who had read the diary multiple times in its manga version and considered Anne her "soul mate," believed Japan was neutral during World War II.[24]

Makoto Otsuka was one of the students who met Otto Frank in Israel. Disturbed by the Japanese tendency to "sympathize with the girl as war victim and not see the very important background," in 1995 he opened the Holocaust Education Center in Fukuyama City, near Hiroshima.[25] Focusing on children's education, the museum includes a replica of the room Anne shared with Pfeffer and displays objects belonging to the Franks, including a typewriter used by Otto. The garden outside features a sapling from the horse chestnut tree that stood in the courtyard of the Annex and a life-size statue of Anne. With exhibits placed at children's eye level, the museum is intended, as Otsuka once explained, to help young people "think about *why* the Holocaust took place and *what* can be done to prevent such an event from recurring, while, at the same time, not neglecting the tragic aspect of the war which brought so much suffering to Japan."[26] This is obviously a difficult balancing act, since there is tension between the reasons "why" the Holocaust took place and "why" the atomic bomb was dropped on Japan. "One victimhood experience does not cancel out one crime against humanity," Ryang writes.[27]

On a visit to Japan in October 2019, I met with Fumiko Ishioda, the director of the Tokyo Center for Holocaust Research, located in a modest apartment building on a side street in the Meguro district, a residential neighborhood southwest of the city center. The door was adorned with the cute face of a cartoon dog; inside, the office consisted of a narrow room lined with bookshelves stuffed with Japanese-language material on the Holocaust. Ishioda was dressed casually in a white sweater and jeans, her demeanor serious and straightforward. As a child, she told me, all she knew about the Holocaust was that "there was a pretty girl called Anne Frank who died in the war." After a Japanese cult perpetrated sarin gas attacks against civilians in the late 1980s, Ishioda became concerned about the increase in violence among children and teens as a possible precursor to larger-scale hate crimes. "We wanted to explain to kids that Auschwitz didn't happen overnight," she said. For the center's work in tolerance education, which includes outreach to schools, Ishioda travels around with a suitcase donated by the Auschwitz Museum that belonged to a girl named Hana Brady, whose background Ishioda researched, eventually discovering a brother of Hana's who survived.[28]

Ishioda also connects the Holocaust to issues related to Japan, bringing up Japan's invasion of Indonesia (which was at the time a Dutch colony) and enslavement of some 200,000 women mainly from Korea and China as "comfort women"—a topic long taboo in Japanese society. A few months before my visit, the Nagoya District Court shut down the Aichi Triennale, Japan's largest art exhibition, over a statue of a comfort woman created by two South Korean artists. The organizers had received threats of violence, but it was clear that the shutdown was motivated by political reasons as well as safety concerns: the mayor of Nagoya said the statue "tramples on the feelings of Japanese citizens."[29]

Japanese writer and artist Erika Kobayashi has spoken of her encounter, in a ramen shop in New York, with a U.S. Army veteran who had served in Japan in 1953. "Every night he slept with different Japanese girls," Kobayashi said—prostitutes who begged him to bring them back to America. One night he was awakened by the sound of weeping. The woman in his bed was reading the *Diary*.[30] Might she have been a comfort woman during the war who identified with Anne, weeping over her fate as a fellow slave and target of persecution? Or was she engaged in a cross-cultural act of imaginative empathy for a dead Jewish girl half a world away?

* * *

In the past few decades, anti-Zionist writers and activists have increasingly described the treatment of Palestinians by the Israeli government as "apartheid," framing Zionism as a colonial enterprise. Precisely because of her iconicity as a victim of the Holocaust, Anne is often evoked in this context in a way that seems deliberately provocative. An image of Anne wearing a keffiyeh, the scarf that symbolizes the Palestinian cause, was created in 2007 by an artist known as "T" as street art in New York and Amsterdam; it has since spread around the world. In 2019, some Palestinians used it as their social media avatars to protest the Israeli military campaign then taking place in Gaza.

While the image is ambiguous, its apparent intention is to equate Jewish suffering during the Holocaust with the contemporary suffering of Palestinians under Israeli occupation.[31]

In November 2023, in a more nuanced commentary on the Palestinian cause, an Italian street artist known as aleXsandro Palombo created a mural intended to commemorate the massacre of Israeli civilians by Hamas on October 7, 2023. With tears streaming from her eyes, Anne, dressed in a white-and-blue-striped concentration camp uniform, holds an Israeli flag. Next to her stands a Palestinian girl around the same age, wearing a keffiyeh with a Palestinian flag motif. In one hand, she holds a Hamas flag; with the candle in her other hand, she lights it on fire. The image was vandalized almost as soon as it went up, with the images of Anne and the Israeli flag scratched out and the words "Free Gaza" written over them; the Palestinian girl remains.[32]

In the last decade or so, the overlap between antisemitism and anti-Zionism, which can be used as a catch-all term for criticism of Israel but often promotes the destruction of the Jewish state, has become increasingly fraught. People around the world, including American Jews and many Israelis, are sympathetic to the plight of Palestinians and critical of the Israeli government, particularly under prime minister Benjamin Netanyahu. At the same time, ostensible supporters of Palestinian rights often employ antisemitic tropes. In the late 2010s, a Dutch rapper using the moniker "Anne Frank" performed a song called "Free Palestine" and posted tweets supporting Palestinian liberation alongside statements such as "Anne Frank died of typhus so she was never murdered" and "If Taylor Swift were Jewish, I'd gas her personally."[33]

In spring 2023, Roger Waters, the former lead singer in Pink Floyd, performing at an arena in Berlin, projected Anne Frank's name and image onto a gigantic screen and juxtaposed it with that of Palestinian journalist Shireen Abu Akleh, who was shot by the Israel Defense Forces the previous year. The location of Anne's death was listed, along with her so-called crime, "being Jewish," and her sentence, "death." Beneath Abu Akleh's name, the location of death was given as "Jenin, Palestine"; her crime, "being Palestinian"; her sentence, "death."[34] (An IDF investigation determined that the incident was an accident; some maintain that Abu Akleh was deliberately targeted.) Waters's comparison was condemned by Katharina von Schnurbein and Deborah Lipstadt, antisemitism envoys representing the European Union and the United States respectively, and by the Anne Frank Trust UK, one of several philanthropic and educational organizations established in Anne's name around the world, which tweeted that it was "wildly inappropriate to misuse Anne Frank's legacy."[35] Waters, a longtime supporter of the "boycott, divestment, sanctions" (BDS) campaign against Israel, defended his statement as "in opposition to fascism, injustice, and bigotry in all its forms."[36]

In the months following October 7, 2023, which has often been described as the worst single-day massacre of Jews since the Holocaust, this rhetoric has intensified. As of summer 2024, the Israeli military campaign in Gaza, carried out in the form of intensive air strikes as well as ground combat, has resulted in the deaths of tens of thousands of Palestinians, of whom an unknown number—possibly up to one-third—are Hamas combatants. Regardless of the exact figure, it's undeniable and tragic that many civilians have been killed by Israeli bombs; many more have lacked consistent access to food, water, and sanitary facilities. Israel insists that its military does not target noncombatants and that Hamas, which embeds itself within communities and diverts aid intended for civilians, is responsible for the high death toll. Anti-Zionist activists dispute these assertions and claim that Israel is committing genocide—a deliberately incendiary term. At the same time, protests apparently intended to support Palestinian liberation, which gained momentum in spring 2024 on college campuses throughout the United States and elsewhere, often featured explicitly antisemitic rhetoric, including chants of "gas the Jews" and celebration of the October 7 attackers as "martyrs." Some of these protests included incidents in which Jewish students and others were targeted as "Zionists," intimidated, and assaulted.[37]

Today's anti-Zionists define Israel as a "settler colonialist" state, by which they mean a land in which settlers invade or occupy territory, displacing or removing indigenous people. This definition does not account for the deep historical Jewish roots in the region or for the fact that many who fled there—Anne's friends among them—were European refugees from persecution as well as Jews from Arab countries, such as Iraq and Yemen, who met with violence and expulsion both before and after Israel's establishment in 1948. Hello Silberberg, Anne's boyfriend in the summer of 1942, attended meetings of a Zionist club and saw Zionism as a potential lifeline from the Nazis. So did Hannah Goslar, following in the footsteps of her father and grandfather, who had been leaders of the Zionist movement in Germany. After liberation, she immigrated to Israel as soon as she could, even though it meant temporarily leaving her younger sister behind in Switzerland.

Would Anne have joined them, had she survived? In the Annex, Margot talked about wanting to become a maternity nurse in Palestine, a typical occupation for Israeli *chalutzim*, or "pioneers," as the early immigrants called themselves; Hannah ended up following this path.[38] But while it's possible to extrapolate a belief in the need for a Jewish homeland from Anne's comments on Jewish identity—*We can never become just Netherlanders or just English or any nation for that matter, we will always remain Jews*—she never made the connection explicitly. Rather than laboring in the Middle Eastern heat and dust, Anne had visions of *beautiful dresses and interesting people . . . I want to see something of the world and do all kinds of exciting things.*[39] While in hiding, she read a recently published book called *Palestine at the Crossroads* by historian and journalist Ladislas Farago, an account of "Jew and Arab . . . struggling for land which each feels to be rightfully his," but she didn't record her thoughts about it.[40]

During his early life, Otto declined to identify with the Zionist cause.[41] But after the war he became a committed supporter of Israel, the creation of which provided a home for around 200,000 Holocaust survivors who had been languishing in European displaced persons camps for several years after the war ended. (By contrast, around 80,000 survivors were admitted to the United States.) He followed Israeli politics closely and visited the country several times. Though he expressed dismay over the treatment of Palestinians, he felt sympathetic to Zionism as an assertion of Jewish identity and strength in the wake of the Holocaust. "I know that had [Anne] lived through the war she certainly would have been enthusiastic about the Zionist movement and that she would, in her impulsive way, have worked for it," he wrote to Joseph Marks in 1952, thanking him for accepting an award from Hadassah, a major Zionist organization for American women, on Anne's behalf.[42]

No one can know what political beliefs a surviving Anne would have held. But she, too, might well have felt differently about Zionism after the war. The Bergen-Belsen diarist Hanna Lévy-Hass, who initially returned to her native Yugoslavia after surviving the camp, immigrated to Israel in December 1948, though she had previously shown no interest in Zionism. Her daughter, Amira Hass, born in Israel in 1956, has become a well-known leftist journalist who lives in the West Bank and reports on Palestinian affairs in articles that are often deeply critical of the Israeli government.[43]

What we do know is that from the ages of thirteen to fifteen, when many adolescents experience a political awakening, Anne remained largely unpolitical. In the Annex, she asked the helpers to bring her movie magazines, not—as another teenager might have done—political news. She followed the progress of the war along with the rest of the Annex residents, but mostly in the context of her obvious personal stake in it. Gerrit Bolkestein's call for citizens to preserve their war documents is one of the few times she mentions any politician, though she must have listened to their radio addresses regularly.

During her final months in captivity, Anne's thoughts turned more toward political matters. In May 1944, she raged against the financing of war, but stopped short of blaming capitalism for the war. *Why are millions spent daily on the war and not a penny on medical services, artists or on poor people? Why do some people have to starve while there are surpluses rotting in other parts of the world? . . . I don't believe that the big men, the politicians and the capitalists alone are responsible for the war; oh no, the little man is just as guilty, otherwise the peoples of the world would have risen in revolt long ago!*[44] She also showed a burgeoning interest in feminism. A long entry written in June 1944 discusses the ludicrousness of men assuming domination over women because of their physical strength. *Luckily, schooling, work and progress have opened women's eyes . . . many people, particularly women, but also men, now realize for how long this state of affairs has been wrong.* Women require not only independence, but also equal respect to men, she argues—if only because of their bravery in childbirth, which makes them *much more courageous . . . than all the freedom-fighting heroes with their big mouths!*[45]

In January 2024, Holocaust survivors appeared before the Knesset, Israel's parliament, on behalf of relatives, including grandchildren, who were taken hostage by Hamas in the attack the previous October. "This is my second Holocaust," one of them told the politicians.[46] I pictured a ninety-four-year-old Anne among them. Would she have driven Palestinians from Gaza to medical treatment in Israel, like some of the people in the kibbutzim targeted on October 7?[47] Would she support the government's campaign against Gaza, regardless of the human cost, as necessary to preserve Israel's security? Would she live in a settlement on the West Bank, looking out from behind a fence at her Palestinian neighbors? Perhaps, even after living through the violence of the last seventy-five years—the Nakba, the countless attacks on Israel by its neighbors, the occupation, the intifadas, and all the rest—she would still believe that people are *really good at heart.*

* * *

At the Anne Frank House, Anne's red-checkered diary is kept in a glass case on a pedestal, as if it were the crown jewels or a saint's relic. One stormy night, a bolt of lightning shatters the glass. Lines of ink rise from the pages and coalesce into the figure of a slender red-haired girl. Her name is Kitty, and she's confused. What year is it? Why are so many people walking around her house and touching all the things? And where is the girl who brought her to life?

This is the starting point of Ari Folman's *Where Is Anne Frank*, an animated feature film with a companion graphic novel, presented as an attempt to "expand the story's boundaries and connect it to our current world" while making it more accessible to children and teenagers.[48] Wandering around Amsterdam with the diary, Kitty finds her friend's name emblazoned on streets and buildings, but the presence of the refugees cowering in their shadows shows her the world has learned nothing from Anne's story. In an effort to understand what happened to her friend, she follows Anne's footsteps to Westerbork and finally Bergen-Belsen. (She's also running away from the police, who see her as a thief who stole Anne's diary.) There, at a memorial stone for Anne and Margot, she vows to help make "your beautiful dreams come true" by "helping children like you, who still exist all over the world, victims of weapons and hatred."[49]

I'm a fan of Folman's graphic adaptation of the *Diary*, which in general adheres closely to its source, while the images (drawn by David Polonsky) work gorgeously to illuminate what's not said. There are some similar effects here in Lena Guberman's illustrations, especially in the scenes of Auschwitz, which Folman analogizes to the underworld in ancient Greek mythology—an unexpectedly apt comparison, considering that people were stripped of all their belongings before facing Hades, who decided who would stay forever and who would have a chance to move on. If the SS look a little too much like J. K. Rowling's dementors, the visual reference will no doubt resonate with the intended audience.

After the names of refugee families to be deported are read aloud at the shelter, Kitty leaps into action, threatening to destroy the diary unless the deportation of refugees ends and the families are given asylum. "Anne didn't write her diary so that you would idolize her, or name bridges, theaters, schools, and hospitals after her," she declaims from a rooftop.

> The pages themselves are not important. What is important is the message being passed on to the millions of children who read the diary. Do everything you can to save one single soul from harm. To save just one soul, one soul of a child, is worth a lifetime![50]

Anne almost certainly would have endorsed these words. It seems innocent enough: no child should suffer through persecution and war, as she had to suffer. At the same time, the certainty with which the *Diary*'s admirers avow that Anne's "message" for today's world need have nothing to do with antisemitism seems even more shortsighted than it did in the 1950s. Even if those who originally promoted the *Diary* didn't see it as a Jewish book, it's not "special pleading," as Garson Kanin so memorably put it, to point out that something exceptional happened to the Jews of Europe. The fact that the subjects of persecution in the *Diary* are Jewish—not "English, French, German, Italian, Ethiopian, Mohammedan, Negro, and so on"—is not "incidental."

The story's boundaries do not need to be expanded to "connect it to our current world," as Folman claims. Our current world is one in which people can still be killed simply for being Jewish. To consider Anne Frank today to be a Syrian girl, as the *New York Times* columnist Nicholas Kristof wrote in 2016, is to risk losing sight of the real threat that antisemitism still poses—and perhaps always will—to Jews everywhere.

Where is Anne now? "Like God," as a policeman says in *Where Is Anne Frank*, she is everywhere.[51] She is in Soviet Eastern Europe, where state theaters staged productions of the play "to prove conscience" even while entrapping their citizens "in an *achterhuis* of meaningless routine and physical adaptation."[52] She is in North Korea, in the hands of teachers who use the *Diary* to teach their students that "Anne's dream of peace [will] come true" only after America is destroyed.[53] She is in museums: one artist depicts her blurred, without a face, or wearing an Obama t-shirt; another creates stacks of business cards reading "Anne Frank, Author," in different languages—testament to the career Ozick and others imagine she might have had.[54] She is on the tarmac in the Dallas–Fort Worth airport, where a passenger who refused to wear a mask on an airplane during the Covid-19 pandemic compared herself to Anne, saying, "We have to take a stand."[55] She is in a church in San Francisco's Mission District, in a mural of "dancing saints" that includes Shakespeare, Charles Darwin, Malcolm X, and Margaret Mead.[56]

And in some ways, she is still in the Annex. In 2023, a neofascist activist from the United States who claimed to represent a group called the "Goyim Defense League" projected a message alluding to the alleged forgery of the *Diary* on the Anne Frank House.[57] Soccer fans regularly use her image to insult supporters of rival teams via their implied association with a Jew.[58]

The book is a new favorite target of conservative activists in the United States, who seek to have it removed from school libraries and curricula owing to what they deem its explicit sexuality and LGBTQ content.

For the *Diary* to fully realize its potential—not as a bestseller, but as a book that can combat prejudice of all kinds—it must perform the difficult balancing act of being at once universal and particular. Even if it's no longer "only about a Jewish family in Holland," as the Argentinian actor playing Mr. van Daan in Los Angeles rightly argued, the story must always be, on the most basic level, about a Jewish family in Holland. It's possible to draw comparisons with other targeted groups—as the South African activists who drew inspiration from Anne's story did—without ignoring the *Diary*'s original reason for existing. Otherwise, an Anne Frank who is everywhere will ultimately be nowhere.

From the refugee camps of Ethiopia to the towers of Tokyo, the prisons of South Africa to the farms of the American South, Anne Frank has served as friend, inspiration, and truth-teller to millions. Let's remember her also as a teenager behind a locked door, pen and paper at the ready: watchful, indomitable, alive.

NOTES

Introduction: Icon

1. *The Diary of Anne Frank: The Critical Edition*, 216 (July 11, 1942B). Unless otherwise noted, all quotations from the *Diary* are from this edition. To facilitate comparison with other editions, dates (given as month, date, and year) are provided in addition to page numbers.

2. Otto Frank to Barbara Zimmerman, August 14, 1953, Joseph Marks Papers (hereinafter cited as JMP); Paul Jackson, "They Journey to Amsterdam in Search of Anne Frank," *New York Post*, October 23, 1979.

3. Kirshenblatt-Gimblett and Shandler, eds., *Anne Frank Unbound*, 2; Ilana Sichel, "The Japanese Tampon Named After Anne Frank," *Jewish Telegraphic Agency*, January 5, 2016.

4. *Diary*, 694 (July 15, 1944A); Galen Last and Wolfswinkel, *Anne Frank and After*, 13.

5. BBC News, "Row over German High-Speed Train Called Anne Frank," October 30, 2017; Katie Reilly, "Retailers Remove

Anne Frank Halloween Costume After Backlash," *Time*, October 16, 2017; Brooke Leigh Howard, "Rhode Island Restaurant Slammed for Sharing 'Horrific' Anne Frank Meme," *Daily Beast*, updated July 26, 2022; Reuters, "Italy Investigates Anti-Semitic Anne Frank Stickers," October 23, 2017.

6. See, e.g., Blair, *Anne Frank Remembered;* Lindwer, *The Last Seven Months of Anne Frank.*

7. Schjeldahl, "The Dark Revelations of Gerhard Richter." The poster is on display at the Anne Frank House.

8. Michael Tilson Thomas, *From the Diary of Anne Frank/ Meditations on Rilke*, Michael Tilson Thomas and San Francisco Symphony, streaming audio, Naxos Music Library; Grigory Frid, *The Diary of Anne Frank;* Ben-Zvi, Bolshoi Theater Orchestra, streaming audio, Naxos Music Library; "Anne Frank," https://aballetoflife.com/2016/10/19/anne-frank/; Brenda Goodman, "Puppet Show with Dark Tale to Tell," *New York Times*, January 25, 2006.

9. Levin, "The Child Behind the Secret Door." Though it does not appear in the published version, Levin's manuscript of *The Obsession*, his memoir of the affair, contains the following passage: "the appearance of the teller came with the shock of revelation. At once I began to proselytize," quoted in Melnick, *The Stolen Legacy of Anne Frank*, 207.

10. Enzer and Solotaroff-Enzer, *Anne Frank: Reflections on Her Life and Legacy*, 2.

11. See, e.g., Goldstein, "Anne Frank: The Redemptive Myth," in Bloom, *Anne Frank's The Diary of Anne Frank*, 76; Buruma, "The Afterlife of Anne Frank"; Diski, "The Girl in the Attic"; Pommer, "The Legend and Art of Anne Frank," in Bloom; Steenmeijer, ed., *Tribute to Anne Frank*, 8.

12. Steinbuch, "Florida School Yanks Anne Frank Diary for Being Sexually Explicit," *New York Post*, April 10, 2023.

13. *Diary*, 694 (July 15, 1944A).

14. Werner, "Germany's New Flagellants," reprinted in Enzer and Solotaroff-Enzer, 162–64.

15. Kristof, "Anne Frank Today Is a Syrian Girl," *New York Times*, August 25, 2016.

16. Ozick, "Who Owns Anne Frank?" *New Yorker*, September 28, 1997.

17. Rosenfeld, "Anne Frank—and Us: Finding the Right Words," in Enzer and Solotaroff-Enzer, 209.

18. These quotes were gathered from guest books for the dates May 17, 2022, to May 24, 2022.

19. Englander, *What We Talk About When We Talk About Anne Frank*, 29.

20. See, e.g., Nussbaum, "Toward Conceptualizing Diary"; Lejeune, *On Diary;* Paperno, "What Can Be Done with Diaries?"

21. Buruma, "The Afterlife of Anne Frank"; Mulisch, "Death and the Maiden."

22. Tatar, *The Heroine with 1,001 Faces*, xviii.

23. Tatar, 186–87.

Chapter 1. Child

Epigraph: *Diary*, 636 (May 8, 1944A).

1. Westra et al., eds., *Inside Anne Frank's House*, 20–21.

2. Pressler, *Anne Frank's Family*, 50, 19; *Diary*, 636 (May 8, 1944A).

3. *Früher wohnten wir in Frankfurt: Frankfurt am Main und Anne Frank*, 11.

4. Lee, *The Hidden Life of Otto Frank*, 8–9, 15; *Früher wohnten wir in Frankfurt*, 22–23.

5. *Diary*, 636 (May 8, 1944A).

6. Lee, 25–26.

7. In *German Jews: A Dual Identity*, Paul Mendes-Flohr notes that German Jews in the late nineteenth and early twentieth centuries were strikingly devoted to Goethe. "It is said only somewhat hyperbolically that a set of his writings graced every Jewish home and was the standard bar mitzvah and confirmation present," Mendes-Flohr writes. "Many a rabbi wove citations from Goethe into his sermons" (27).

8. Pressler, 55, 69; Lee, 9, 25, 30.

9. Lee, 31; Pick-Goslar, *My Friend Anne Frank*, 71.

10. Anne mentions the joint problem in her diary (179; June 15, 1942A); Schnabel, *Footsteps of Anne Frank*, 58; Pressler, 134.

11. Schnabel, 30, 32.

12. Pressler, 246 and photo insert.

13. Müller, *Anne Frank: The Biography*, 135.

14. Pick-Goslar, 27; Schnabel, 30.

15. Schnabel, 33.

16. Anne's fiction has been published in various collections, including *Anne Frank's Tales from the Secret Annex*, *The Diary of Anne Frank: The Revised Critical Edition*, and *Anne Frank: The Collected Works.*

17. Schnabel, 37–38, 52; Gies, *Anne Frank Remembered*, 46, 39.

18. *Diary*, 226 (July 12, 1942A), 342 (March 10, 1943B), 550 (March 20, 1944A).

19. *Diary*, 223 (July 12, 1942A), 636–37 (May 8, 1944A), 335 (February 5, 1943B).

20. Gies, 56.

21. *Diary*, 260 (September 28, 1942A).

22. Gold, *Found and Lost*, 55–56.

23. Jaldati, *Sag nie, du gehst den letzten Weg*, 420. Later, Lien Brilleslijper (whose given name was Rebekka) went by the name Lin Jaldati.

24. Jaldati, 425. See also Lindwer, 66–74, and Pressler, 220–22.

25. *Diary*, 482 (February 8, 1944A).

26. Blumenthal, "Five Precious Pages Renew Wrangling over Anne Frank," *New York Times*, September 10, 1998.

27. In Anne's entry of December 24, 1943, in Version A (433), she mentions "thinking all the time about Pim, and what he told me last year." In his edit, Otto moved this part of the entry to December 25, 1943, in Version C (433) and clarified: "what he told me about the love of his youth." It is odd that Otto went to such lengths to hide the missing pages when he had already permitted a mention of the affair to appear in the published diary.

28. According to Carol Ann Lee, Otto used the phrase "business arrangement" to describe the marriage to his second wife (23). Lee attributes this information to the nurse who cared for Otto's wife in her old age.

29. The full entry can be found in *The Diary of Anne Frank: The Revised Critical Edition*, 503–4 (February 8, 1944A).

30. Pressler, 87. Straus was then known as Charley; he changed his name to Nathan before embarking on a political career. The precise timing of Otto's studies in Heidelberg is unclear. See also Lee, 9–13.

31. Müller, 253.

32. Pressler, 112.

33. Pressler, 115–19; Lee, 26.

34. Pressler, 140.

35. Lee, 197.

36. Pick-Goslar, 32.

37. *Inside Anne Frank's House*, 20.

38. Schnabel, 36.

39. Pressler, 40, 49; *Früher wohnten wir in Frankfurt*, 7, 10.

40. *Früher wohnten wir in Frankfurt*, 4; Pressler, 123.

41. *Früher wohnten wir in Frankfurt*, 3.

42. Tobias Bünder, "The Story of a Name—Talking About Hertie's Darker Past," *The Governance Post*, August 12, 2016.

43. *Früher wohnten wir in Frankfurt*, 5.

44. Pressler, 122–25.

45. Pressler, 35; Pick-Goslar, 17–18.

46. Galen Last and Wolfswinkel, 12; Pressler, 123.

Chapter 2. Refugee

Epigraph: *Diary*, 416 (November 8, 1943B).

1. Gies, 15; Van Wijk-Voskuijl and De Bruyn, *The Last Secret of the Secret Annex*, 13.

2. Pick-Goslar, 35. Zuider Amstellaan is now called Rooseveltlaan.

3. Schnabel, 49.

4. Pick-Goslar, 25; Gies, 237.

5. *Diary*, 223 (July 12, 1942A).

6. Pick-Goslar, 28.

7. Van Wijk-Voskuijl and De Bruyn, 15.

8. Schnabel, 56.

9. Gies, 56; Schnabel, 59.

10. Pick-Goslar, 46, 43, 33, 66–67.

11. Pick-Goslar, 41.

12. Anne Frank to Alice Frank, undated letter, *Collected Works*, 337.

13. Coster, *We All Wore Stars*, 22.

14. Pick-Goslar, 73.

15. Van Maarsen, *My Name Is Anne*, 76–80, 90.

16. Van Maarsen, 81–82.

17. Van Maarsen, 92.

18. Coster, 51, 102; Gies, 38; Schnabel, 52.

19. Gies, 33, 74.

20. Barbara Ledermann Rodbell, interview by Linda G. Kuzmack, June 12, 1990, digitized recording, United States Holocaust Memorial Museum website, accession number 1990.409.01, https://collections.ushmm.org/search/catalog/irn504687.

21. Ledermann Rodbell, interview; Pick-Goslar, 30.

22. Ledermann Rodbell, interview.

23. Van Maarsen, 51, 61.

24. Moore, *Victims and Survivors*, 58.

25. Coster, 19; Van Maarsen, 51–52.

26. Ledermann Rodbell, interview.

27. Gies, 238.

28. Erika Prins, "Peter van Pels 1926–1945," https://raumdernamen.mauthausen-memorial.org/index.php?id=4&p=137617&L=1.

29. Gies, 47.

30. Müller, 189.

31. Margot Frank to Betty Ann Wagner, April 27, 1940, Rubin, *Searching for Anne Frank*, 14–15.

32. Galen Last and Wolfswinkel, 24–25.

33. Schnabel, 38.

34. Moore, *Victims and Survivors*, 275. See also https://kampwesterbork.nl/en/history/24-history.

35. Presser, *The Destruction of the Dutch Jews*, 406–7.

36. Van Maarsen, 64–65.

37. Schnabel, 58; Daphne Bouman, "Misdadigers-Erfgoed in Amsterdam," https://daphnebouman.com/2019/02/07/misdadigers-erfgoed-in-amsterdam/.

38. Richard F. Shepard, "Anne Frank Letter to Iowa Pen Pal to Be Sold," *New York Times*, July 22, 1988; Rubin, 6–9.

39. Anne Frank to Juanita Wagner, April 29, 1940, *Collected Works*, 338.

40. Margot Frank to Betty Ann Wagner, April 27, 1940.

41. "'That's What I Hope': The Story of Hannah Pick," https://www.youtube.com/watch?v=ZFtj33U3weI.

42. Pick-Goslar, 54; Van Wijk-Voskuijl and De Bruyn, 18.

43. Müller, 115; Pick-Goslar, 56.

44. Holocaust Encyclopedia, https://encyclopedia.ushmm.org/content/en/film/fall-of-rotterdam.

45. Siegal, *The Diary Keepers*, 50, 52.

46. Ledermann Rodbell, interview.

47. Rubin, 25–26, 56–57.

48. Shepard.

49. Rubin, 95.

Chapter 3. Target

Epigraph: *Diary*, 226 (July 1942A [no day]).

1. Bob Moore, "W cieniu Anny Frank," *Zagłada Żydów: Studia i Materiały* 10:384–406. Translation provided by Moore.

2. Moore, *Victims and Survivors*, 42–47.

3. Hillesum, *An Interrupted Life*, 24–25.

4. Ledermann Rodbell, interview; Presser, 10; Wout Ultee, Frank van Tubergen, and Ruud Luijkx, "The Unwholesome Theme of Suicide," in Brasz and Kaplan, eds., *Dutch Jews as Perceived by Themselves and Others*, 325–54; Van Wijk-Voskuijl and De Bruyn, 19; Van Maarsen, 65. For deaths of politicians see, e.g., https://www.encyclopedia.com/religion/encyclopedias-almanacs-transcripts-and-maps/limburg-joseph; https://www.joodsmonument.nl/en/page/227834/michel-joëls.

5. Ledermann Rodbell, interview.

6. Presser, 3–5.

7. Presser, 48.

8. Siegal, 87.

9. Galen Last and Wolfswinkel, 41; Herzberg, *Between Two Streams*, 21.

10. Presser, 16, 222; Moore, *Victims and Survivors*, 55–59.

11. Anne Frank to Alice Frank and Stephen Elias, *Collected Works*, 339; Kohnstam, *A Chance to Live*, 45.

12. Anne Frank to Alice Frank, January 13, 1941, and March 22, 1941, *Collected Works*, 341.

13. Pick-Goslar, 33.

14. Anne Frank, "Lodgers or Tenants," in *Collected Works*, 247–49.

15. Müller, 124, 130–31, 158–61.

16. Nina Siegal, "She Discovered What Happened to 400 Dutch Jews Who Disappeared," *New York Times*, March 16, 2022.

17. Van Maarsen, 69.

18. Coster, 57–58.

19. Siegal, *The Diary Keepers*, 90–91. According to Presser, SS doctor Hans Eisele conducted experiments on at least one of the hostages who was forced to remain in Buchenwald.

20. Presser, 53–54.

21. Siegal, 93.

22. Presser, 54–55.

23. An English edition was also published under the title *Ashes in the Wind: The Destruction of Dutch Jewry* (London: Souvenir Press, 1968).

24. Presser, 539–40. Only nineteen Dutch Jews survived Sobibór (Siegal, 143).

25. Presser, 2.

26. Galen Last and Wolfswinkel, 12.

27. Goldstein, 78.

28. Presser, 101.

29. Presser, 272.

30. Moore, *Victims and Survivors*, 108.

31. Galen Last and Wolfswinkel, 68.

32. Van der Boom, "Een antword aan mijn critici," https://www.groene.nl/artikel/een-antwoord-aan-mijn-critici.

33. Presser, 55.

34. Otto Frank to Nathan Straus Jr., April 30, 1941. Otto addressed Nathan as "Charley," his old nickname. The major sources for Otto's emigration attempt are Breitman and Engel, *The Otto Frank File*, and Adler, *For the Sake of the Children*. Breitman and Engel reprint abridged versions of Otto Frank's letters to Straus; the complete letters are at YIVO. Other sources are noted as relevant.

35. "German Bombs and U.S. Bureaucrats," https://us-holocaust-museum.medium.com/german-bombs-and-us-bureaucrats-how-escape-lines-from-europe-were-cut-off-1b3e14137cc4, accessed September 17, 2023.

36. Müller, 123.

37. George T. Comeau, "Canton's True Tales: A Telegram to 138 High Street," *Canton Citizen*, June 4, 2021.

38. Otto Frank to Nathan Straus Jr., April 30, 1941.

39. Müller, 103.

40. Menand, *The Free World*, 137.

41. Breitman and Engel, 10.

42. Lisa Mullins, "Could FDR Have Saved Anne Frank?" WBUR, June 21, 2019, https://www.wbur.org/hereandnow/2019/06/21/fdr-anne-frank-world-war-ii-visa-quotas.

43. In 1940, Nathan and Helen Straus brought the two-year-old son of a business acquaintance in England, together with his nanny, to live on their estate in Westchester for four years. The son of one of Straus's mother's relatives also came to live with Nathan Sr. and his wife at their home in Mamaroneck. Adler, 96.

44. Breitman and Engel, 33. An exchange of letters between Otto and Nathan in June is missing from the YIVO file but is reprinted in Adler.

45. Coster, 75.

46. Müller, 155.

47. Van Maarsen, 73. In the original, the boys chant "*Jo-den*" (Jews).

48. Schnabel, 57–58.

49. Schnabel, 59; Pick-Goslar, 72, has a slightly different number.

50. Van Maarsen, 74–75. Van Maarsen states the tram's nickname incorrectly; see http://www.amsterdamsetrams.nl/tramjargon/index.htm, accessed April 19, 2024. See also Senay Boztas, "Amsterdam to Mark Role of Tram System in Transportation of Jews to Death Camps," *Guardian*, March 29, 2024.

51. Hondius and Gompes-Labatto, *Absent*, 173, 171.

52. *Diary*, 189 (June 16, 1942A).

53. Hondius and Gompes-Labatto, 73, 94.

54. *Collected Works*, 242.

55. Hondius and Gompes-Labatto, 79, 95, 100.

56. Pick-Goslar, 79.

57. Presser, 259.

58. *Collected Works*, 220, 221, 243.

59. Coster, 73.

60. *Collected Works*, 245.

61. *Diary*, 257 (September 29, 1942B).

62. Some Dutch people joked that *Jood* was an acronym for *Joden Overleven de Ondergang van Duitsland*, "Jews survive the downfall of Germany" (Van Wijk-Voskuijl and De Bruyn, 21).

63. Presser, 120–23.

64. Presser, 125, 127, 258.

65. Coster, 79.

66. *Diary*, 187 (June 15, 1952A). In the *Critical Edition*, Danka is identified only as "J."; her full name is in the *Collected Works*.

67. Hondius and Gompes-Labatto, 144–45.

68. *Diary*, 204, 203 (July 5, 1942B).

69. Hondius and Gompes-Labatto, 144–45; Presser, 136. Hemelrijk survived Sachsenhausen and Buchenwald. After the war, he returned to the Netherlands and continued to teach and translate the classics. See https://www.buchenwald.de/en/geschichte/biografien/ltg-ausstellung/jakob-hemelrijk.

70. Presser, 257.

71. Lindwer, 48; Coster, 14; Presser, 258; Pick-Goslar, 100; Galen Last and Wolfswinkel, 58.

72. Presser, 259.

73. Presser, 259–60.

74. "'That's What I Hope': The Story of Hannah Pick"; Van Maarsen, 100.

75. See https://www.joodsmonument.nl/nl/page/32231/johanna-hermine-biegel, accessed September 17, 2023.

76. Müller, 184.

77. Coster, 177.

78. Antoinette Rainone, "Former Beau Recalls Anne Frank as Riveting, 'Unusually Articulate,'" *Orlando Sentinel*, June 18, 2004.

79. Müller, 184–87.

80. *Diary*, 206 (July 8, 1942A).

81. A sample call-up notice (in Dutch) is available at https://www.annefrank.org/en/anne-frank/main-characters/margot-frank/, accessed September 17, 2023. The translation here is by Sam Garrett.

82. *Diary*, 207 (July 8, 1942A).

83. Diane Daniel, "A Token of Anne Frank's Childhood on View," *New York Times*, February 24, 2014.

84. Gutman and Berenbaum, eds., *Anatomy of the Auschwitz Death Camp*, vii, 7, 10, 16–19; Dwork, *Children with a Star*, 216.

85. Gutman and Berenbaum, 30.

86. Presser, 135–36. Auschwitz, of course, was in occupied Poland, as was the death camp Sobibór, the other potential destination for trains from Westerbork. Perhaps the Nazis considered the camps technically on German territory.

87. Presser, 136–39.

88. Presser, 138.

89. Bolle, *Letters Never Sent*, 75.

90. Presser, 143–46.

91. Presser, 142; Galen Last and Wolfswinkel, 59.

92. Pick-Goslar, 94.

93. Presser, 149.

94. Schloss, *After Auschwitz*, 78.

Chapter 4. Witness

Epigraph: *Diary*, 222 (July 8, 1942A).

1. Gies, 97–98. Detailed photographs of the Annex can be seen in *Inside Anne Frank's House* and on annefrank.org.

2. Van Wijk-Voskuijl and De Bruyn, 32.

3. Gies, 122.

4. Van Maarsen, 96.

5. Gies, 122; Van Wijk-Voskuijl and De Bruyn, 34.

6. Gies, 95.

7. *Diary*, 209 (July 8, 1942B).

8. *Collected Works*, 228.

9. Gies, 98, 102, 104; Van Wijk-Voskuijl and De Bruyn, 34.

10. This story was planted by Hermann van Pels, who came to the Franks' apartment on July 6 after they had left and made a fuss to Goudsmit (sometimes spelled Goldschmidt) over the note with the address. Van Pels pretended to remember meeting a "high-ranking officer" stationed in Maastricht six months earlier who had offered to help Otto. "I think he must have kept his word and somehow or other managed to take Mr. F along with him to Belgium and then on to Switzerland," Van Pels told Goudsmit. "Tell this to any friends who may inquire, don't of course mention Maastricht." Naturally, Goudsmit told everyone. *Diary*, 220–21 (August 14, 1942B); Pick-Goslar, 90.

11. Rainone.

12. Van Maarsen, 97; Pick-Goslar, 92–93.

13. Pressler, 158.

14. Griffioen and Zeller, "The Netherlands: The Highest Number of Jewish Victims in Western Europe," https://www.annefrank.org/en/anne-frank/go-in-depth/netherlands-greatest-number-jewish-victims-western-europe/.

15. Galen Last and Wolfswinkel, 64–67. For "Annex Eight," see *Collected Works*, 231.

16. Dwork, 34.

17. Coster, 85.

18. Dwork, 35–36. Yad Vashem honors three members of the Boogaard family (sometimes also spelled Bogaard) as Righteous Among the Nations.

19. In *Invisible Years*, Daphne Geismar writes about her mother's

abuse by one of the hosts who hid her. Since she never told anyone about the abuse, the family was recognized by Yad Vashem as Righteous Among the Nations. Bart van Es reports a similar story of abuse in *The Cut-Out Girl*, as does Joan Ringelheim in *Women in the Holocaust*, commenting: "[This survivor's] story may not be typical. But if Anne Frank's diary remains the paradigm of hiding, we will never know, because it will be assumed that danger lurked only when Germans located those in hiding" (Ofer and Weizman, eds., *Women in the Holocaust*, 345).

20. *Diary*, 311 (November 17, 1942B).
21. *Diary*, 216 (July 11, 1942B), 313–14 (November 17, 1942B).
22. Gold, 106.
23. *Diary*, 335 (February 5, 1943B).
24. *Diary*, 392 (August 9, 1943B).
25. Van Wijk-Voskuijl and De Bruyn, 55.
26. Gies, 129.
27. Presser, 163–64.
28. Gies, 117.
29. *Diary*, 223 (July 12, 1942A).
30. Gies, 133.
31. *Diary*, 219 (August 14, 1942B). In their play, Goodrich and Hackett attempt to provide a rationale, depicting the Van Pelses as Dutch Jews who helped the Franks when they immigrated to the Netherlands. Edith says to Margot, "I told your father it wouldn't work . . . but no . . . no . . . he had to ask them, he said . . . he owed it to them, he said" (Goodrich and Hackett, *The Diary of Anne Frank*, 54).
32. Gies, 109.
33. *Diary*, 237 (September 21, 1942A).
34. Van Wijk-Voskuijl and De Bruyn, 53.
35. Gies, 107; *Diary*, 233 (September 21, 1942A).
36. *Diary*, 245 (September 25, 1942A).
37. Gies, 123.
38. Gies, 164.
39. *Diary*, 352 (April 1, 1943B),
40. Van Wijk-Voskuijl and De Bruyn, 25, 50.

41. Iskander, "Anne Frank's Reading," in Bloom. Anne copied favorite passages into her "Favorite Quotes Notebook," in *Collected Works*, 357–84.

42. *Diary*, 268 (October 4, 1942A).

43. Unlike Kleiman, Kugler did not tell his wife, who was in poor health, about the eight Jews hiding in the Annex, choosing to bear the stress on his own. Johannes Voskuijl also did not share the information with his wife, Bep's mother, because she was antisemitic.

44. *Diary*, 228 (August 1, 1942A), 226 (July 1942A [no day]), 192 (September 28, 1942A).

45. *Diary*, 237 (September 21, 1942A).

46. *Diary*, 243 (September 25, 1942A), 177 (September 28, 1942A).

47. *Diary*, 244 (September 25, 1942A), 237 (September 21, 1942A), 241 (September 22, 1942A).

48. Berteke Waaldijk, "Reading Anne Frank as a Woman," in Enzer and Solotaroff-Enzer, 332.

49. Soeting, "Dear Diary, Dear Comrade: The Diaries of Setske de Haan, Joop ter Heul and Anne Frank," 191. Waaldijk writes that while Van Marxveldt's work is "not exactly part of the Dutch literary canon, it is no exaggeration to say that almost all women raised in the Netherlands since the 1920s are familiar with her books for girls" (Enzer and Solotaroff-Enzer, 331).

50. Soeting, 190.

51. Van Marxveldt, 34; translation by Sam Garrett.

52. See, e.g., *Diary*, 238 (September 21, 1942A), 252 (September 27, 1942A), 277 (October 14, 1942A).

53. Nigel A. Caplan, "Revisiting the *Diary*," in Bloom, 92.

54. Rachel Feldhay Brenner, "Writing Herself Against History," in Bloom, 62.

55. Gies, 132.

56. Presser, 334.

57. *Diary*, 266 (October 3, 1942A), 267 (October 4, 1942A).

58. *Diary*, 288 (October 26, 1942A).

59. Gies, 48.

60. *Diary*, 303 (November 10, 1942A).

61. For the sake of propriety, Miep also referred to Kaletta as Pfeffer's wife in her memoir.

62. Gies, 135; *Diary*, 310–11 (November 17, 1942B).

63. *Diary*, 682 (June 30, 1944A).

64. *Diary*, 303 (November 10, 1942B). The observation about touching the walls on either side is from Frances Goodrich, "Diary of a Diary," *New York Times*, September 30, 1956.

65. *Diary*, 329 (December 22, 1942B).

66. *Collected Works*, 223.

67. Van Wijk-Voskuijl and De Bruyn, 67.

68. Galen Last and Wolfswinkel, 61–62. For more detail, see Flim, *Het Grote Kinderspel*.

69. *Diary*, 315–16 (November 19, 1942B).

70. *Diary*, 316 (November 20, 1942B).

71. *Diary*, 261 (September 30, 1942A).

72. *Diary*, 321 (December 7, 1942B).

73. Otto Frank to Frances Goodrich and Albert Hackett, February 6, 1954, and September 7, 1955, Goodrich/Hackett Papers (hereinafter cited as GHP).

74. *Collected Works*, 223.

75. *Diary*, 219 (August 14, 1942B).

76. *Diary*, 249 (September 27, 1942A).

77. *Diary*, 306 (May 2, 1943A).

78. *Diary*, 374 (July 23, 1943A).

79. This suggests that Edith wanted another child—another factor that may have contributed to her despondency.

80. *Diary*, 241 (September 22, 1942A). A year and a half later, she was a little less sanguine: "If the war isn't over by September I shan't go to school any more, because I don't want to be two years behind" (*Diary*, 586, April 5, 1944A).

81. *Diary*, 332 (January 13, 1943B), 451 (February 16, 1944A). See Casteel, "Writing Under the Sign of Anne Frank," for a fascinating discussion of the intersections between Holocaust studies and postcolonial studies.

82. *Diary*, 601 (April 9, 1944A). Anne identified so strongly as Dutch that she and Hannah Goslar, when whistling for each other,

used the Dutch national anthem as their personal tune (Pick-Goslar, 26).

83. *Diary*, 416 (November 8, 1943B).

84. Gies, 151; *Diary*, 362 (June 13, 1943B).

85. *Diary*, 390 (August 9, 1943B).

86. *Diary*, 361–62 (June 13, 1943B).

87. Gies, 151.

88. Van Wijk-Voskuijl and De Bruyn, 47.

89. Gies, 168.

90. *Diary*, 366 (July 11, 1943B).

91. Gies, 160.

92. Gies, 153.

93. Siegal, 18. For the teacup photo, see Nina Siegal, "Witnessing the Holocaust," *New York Times*, May 22, 2019.

94. Siegal, *The Diary Keepers*, 241.

95. Ledermann Rodbell, interview.

96. *Collected Works*, 234.

97. *Collected Works*, 241–46.

98. *Diary*, 387 (August 7, 1943B).

99. Van Wijk-Voskuijl and De Bruyn, 63.

100. Otto Frank to Barbara Zimmerman, June 30, 1952, JMP.

101. *Diary*, 587 (April 5, 1944A).

102. *Diary*, 493 (February 17, 1944A). For all the abuse that Mrs. van Pels gets in Anne's diary, this suggests that she took an interest in Anne's writing and encouraged her. Anne cut this entry in Version B; Otto did not reinstate it.

103. *Collected Works*, 293, 289.

Chapter 5. Lover

Epigraph: *Diary*, 444 (January 6, 1944A).

1. *Diary*, 660 (May 26, 1944A).

2. Presser, 212–13; Bolle, *Letters Never Sent*, 17. Jews living elsewhere in the Netherlands had been forced to relocate to Amsterdam starting in September 1940.

3. Wilhelmina, *De Koningin Sprak: Proclamaties en Radio-*

Toespraken van H.m. Koningin Wilhelmina 1940–1945, Christelijk Lektuurkontakt, in association with T. Wever (Driebergen: Franeker, 1985), 74–75. Translation by Tobias Mud.

4. *Diary*, 415 (November 8, 1943B), 410 (October 29, 1943B), 413 (November 3, 1943B); Van Wijk-Voskuijl and De Bruyn, 53.

5. Van Wijk-Voskuijl and De Bruyn, 60.

6. *Diary*, 424 (December 6, 1943B), translation edited slightly.

7. Since Version A is missing for much of this period, counts are partially based on Version B. Anne was more likely to add extra entries when revising than to delete, except for the later entries involving Peter. Philippe Lejeune, noticing the irregular frequency of entries on the loose pages (Version B), wondered if some of the pages might be missing. The Dutch editors of the *Critical Edition* told him that they believed the pages were complete (Lejeune, 249–50).

8. *Diary*, 411 (October 29, 1943B), 422 (November 27, 1943B).

9. *Diary*, 446, 448–49 (January 6, 1944A). Later, Anne would be disappointed to discover that Peter van Pels's cheeks were not *as soft as they look* but scratchy like her father's: *the cheek of a man who already shaves. Diary*, 522 (March 8, 1944A).

10. *Diary*, 305 (January 22, 1944A), 483 (February 12, 1944A).

11. *Diary*, 231 (August 21, 1942B).

12. *Diary*, 516 (March 7, 1944A).

13. Gies, 159.

14. *Diary*, 660 (May 26, 1944A).

15. Prose, *Anne Frank*, 113.

16. *Diary*, 262 (October 1, 1942B).

17. *Collected Works*, 254.

18. *Collected Works*, 256.

19. *Diary*, 426 (December 6, 1943), translation edited slightly.

20. *Diary*, 474 (January 30, 1944A).

21. *Diary*, 441 (November 6, 1944A).

22. *Diary*, 463 (January 24, 1944A).

23. Van Maarsen, 88.

24. Van Maarsen, 95; *Diary*, 443 (January 6, 1944A).

25. *Diary*, 465 (January 24, 1944A).

26. *Diary*, 466–68 (January 24, 1944A).

27. *Diary*, 566 (March 24, 1944A).

28. *Diary*, 483 (February 12, 1944A), 484 (February 14, 1944A), 485–87 (February 14, 1944A).

29. *Diary*, 508–9 (March 3, 1944A), 526 (March 12, 1944A).

30. Lejeune, *On Diary*, 245.

31. Lee, 145.

32. Lee, 146, 149, 152–53.

33. Lee, 153.

34. Pressler, 381.

35. Schloss, 219.

36. *Diary*, 519 (March 7, 1944A), 506 (March 2, 1944A).

37. *Diary*, 443 (January 6, 1944A).

38. Yonah Bex Gerber, "As a Queer Jew, Learning Anne Frank Was Bisexual Is a Game-Changer," *Hey Alma*, June 11, 2019; Julia Diana Robertson, "Omitted: Anne Frank Was Same-Sex Attracted," *The Velvet Chronicle*, November 19, 2021.

39. Andrew Lapin, "'Anne Frank Pornography' Being Banned in Florida, Texas Schools," Jewish Telegraphic Agency, June 13, 2023; Mike Schneider, "Illustrated Anne Frank Book Removed by Florida School," Associated Press, April 10, 2023; Gloria Oladipo, "Texas Teacher Fired for Showing Anne Frank Graphic Novel to Eighth-graders," *The Guardian*, September 20, 2023.

40. *Diary*, 443 (January 5, 1944C).

41. See, e.g., Erin Blakemore, "Censoring Anne Frank," History Extra.com, March 9, 2020.

42. Herbert Mitgang, "An Authenticated Edition of Anne Frank's Diary," *New York Times*, June 8, 1989. Otto kept some of Anne's references to menstruation, including her description of her period as a "sweet secret," and removed others. One example: both Anne and Peter seem to have believed that women lost "1 to 2 liters of blood" during a cycle. Otto removed this inaccuracy but retained the significance of the passage: that Anne and Peter were openly discussing menstruation.

43. *Diary*, 70.

44. *Diary*, 74.

45. Elisheva Jacobson, "Stop Calling Anne Frank Your Bisexual Icon," *Hey Alma*, July 8, 2020.

46. Van Maarsen, 77, 79–82.

47. *Diary*, 446 (January 6, 1944A).

48. *Diary*, 514 (March 6, 1944A).

49. *Collected Works*, 254–55; *Diary*, 607 (April 16, 1944A).

50. *Diary*, 528 (March 14, 1944A), 585 (April 3, 1944A), 638 (May 8, 1944A).

51. *Diary*, 591–95 (April 9, 1944A); Gies, 180.

52. *Diary*, 511 (March 4, 1944A), 561 (March 24, 1944A), 624 (May 2, 1944A).

53. *Diary*, 451 (January 6, 1944A). The fact that Anne didn't experience the same feelings of guilt about kissing Jacqueline demonstrates that regardless of her romantic or sexual feelings, she didn't conceive of the relationship as comparable to one with a boy.

54. *Diary*, 609 (April 17, 1944A), 622 (April 28, 1944A).

55. Though Otto could not have known this at the time, if Anne had been pregnant when she arrived at Auschwitz, it would have meant certain death—visibly pregnant women were immediately selected for the gas chamber.

56. *Diary*, 624 (May 2, 1944A).

57. *Diary*, 630 (May 5, 1944A). Inadvertently demonstrating that she was not quite as grown-up as she thought she was, Anne appended to this entry a humorous poem about cats that she clipped from a newspaper.

58. *Diary*, 549 (March 20, 1944A).

59. *Diary*, 550 (March 20, 1944A).

60. *Diary*, 652 (May 19, 1944A), 507 (March 2, 1944A).

61. *Diary*, 378 (July 29, 1943B).

62. *Diary*, 613 (April 18, 1944A), 499 (February 23, 1944A), 534 (March 16, 1944A).

63. *Collected Works*, 361–63, 383.

64. *Diary*, 577 (March 28, 1944A).
65. *Diary*, 692 (July 15, 1944A).
66. *Collected Works*, 254–56.
67. *Diary*, 625 (May 2, 1944A).
68. *Collected Works*, 383–84.
69. *Diary*, 676 (June 13, 1944A).

Chapter 6. Artist

Epigraph: *Collected Works*, 377.

1. *Collected Works*, 295–96.

2. One exception is Yasmine Ergas, who notes, in a thoughtful essay comparing the diaries of Anne and Etty Hillesum, that "religiosity surfaces throughout fables and short stories animated by Anne's psychological twins: fairies, elves, bears, and little girls. Belief in God repeatedly issues from their voyages in search of self" (Ergas, "Growing Up Banished," 91).

3. *Diary* (Revised Critical Edition), 796.

4. Carson McCullers, "The Fables of Anne Frank," Carson McCullers Collection, Harry Ransom Humanities Research Center.

5. The complete text of Bolkestein's speech in Dutch is available at https://www.annefrank.org/en/anne-frank/the-timeline/entire-timeline/#74. Translation by Sam Garrett.

6. Karl Silberbauer, the Gestapo officer who led the raid on the Annex, later recalled that when he encountered Anne, she looked both prettier and older than she does in that photograph.

7. Gies, 158.

8. *Diary*, 578 (March 29, 1944A). As Nigel Caplan observes, "romance" is a mistranslation of the Dutch word *roman;* like its cognates in French and German, it means "novel" (Caplan, 85). Rachel Feldhay Brenner comments: "In Frank's 'detective story,' the suspense is not evoked by the expected discovery and elimination of a wily criminal. Rather, it generates from the threat of discovery and elimination of the innocent victim" (Brenner, 51).

9. It is clear in the original Dutch that Anne meant not that the story would be amusing, but that it might sound strange to oth-

ers: *Maar nu in ernst het moet ongeveer 10 jaar na de oorlog al grappig aandoen als men vertelt hoe wij als Joden hier geleefd, gegeten en gesproken hebben.* A more literal translation might be: "But seriously, about ten years after the war it might already come across strangely if people were told how we Jews have lived, eaten, and talked here." Translation by Tobias Mud.

10. *Diary*, 578 (March 29, 1944B).

11. *Diary*, 578–79 (March 29, 1944B).

12. *Diary*, 653 (May 20, 1944A).

13. Lejeune, 47.

14. The loose pages are in several different shades—pink, beige, blue, and gray—which has led Lejeune as well as scholar Suzanne L. Bunkers to speculate that Anne may have color-coded them thematically. See Bunkers, "The Complicated Publication History of the Diaries of Anne Frank," in Ben-Amos and Ben-Amos, eds., *The Diary*.

15. Paperno, 573.

16. Nussbaum, 130. See also Ben-Amos and Ben-Amos, as well as Hassam, "Reading Other People's Diaries."

17. Nussbaum, 130.

18. *Diary*, 304 (January 22, 1944A).

19. *Diary*, 226 (July 1942A [no day]). Van Maarsen's memoir suggests that she didn't mean Anne specifically but rather "one is scared to do anything" (Van Maarsen, 94). In the original, the line in Anne's *Diary* is in the first person: *Ik durf niets meer te doen, want ik ben bang dat het niet mag.*

20. *Diary*, 185 (June 20, 1944B). As Caplan points out, Otto moved Anne's long paragraph about anti-Jewish legislation, putting it with the entry for June 20, 1942, but also kept her other mentions of antisemitism. For a reader ignorant about the Holocaust, Anne's hints about persecution make more sense with the explanatory paragraph included. Ergas notes that Anne introduces herself as Jewish almost immediately and talks at length about the persecutions: "To be a Jew, a persecuted Jew, is an essential component of Anne's sense of self: it prescribes the coordinates by which

she locates herself in the world" (88). This was true of Anne in spring 1944, but not two years earlier—a small example of the way the opacity around the diary's provenance has affected the ability of critics to properly interpret it. When Ergas published her essay in 1987, the Critical Edition had not yet appeared in English; thus she had no way to know about Anne's drastic revisions.

21. *Diary*, 198 (June 24, 1942B). Adding her experience with Mr. Keesing allows Anne to introduce the description of herself as "Miss Quack-Quack," a motif she repeated later to illustrate how hard it was for her to stay quiet when strangers were in the building.

22. *Diary*, 204–5 (July 1, 1942B).

23. Prose, 13.

24. *Diary*, 264–65 (October 6, 1942A), 269–71 (October 7, 1942A).

25. *Diary*, 206–8 (July 8, 1942A; July 8, 1942B), 210 (July 9, 1942B).

26. Compare *Diary*, 226 (July 1942A [no day]), with 206–15 (July 8–10, 1942B); Van Wijk-Voskuijl and De Bruyn, 63.

27. *Diary*, 563 (March 24, 1944A).

28. *Diary*, 284.

29. *Diary*, 264–65 (October 6, 1942A).

30. *Diary*, 288 (October 26, 1942A), 272 (October 9, 1942B).

31. For a discussion of this, see Van der Boom, "Een antword aan mijn critici," or Siegal, 392–99. (Neither Van der Boom nor Siegal makes this mistake.)

32. *Diary*, 357 (May 2, 1943A).

33. *Diary*, 258 (September 27, 1942A), 257–58 (September 29, 1942B).

34. *Diary*, 647 (May 11, 1944A).

35. Caplan, 85.

36. Gerrold van der Stroom, "The Diaries, *Het Achterhuis*, and the Translations," in *Diary*, 71. In his *New York Times* review of the *Diary*, Meyer Levin, who almost certainly did not know the circumstances of the book's composition, sensed this. "It is this unfolding psychological drama of a girl's growth, mingled with the physical danger of the group, that frees Anne's book from the hori-

zontal effect of most diaries," Levin wrote. "Hers rises continuously, with the tension of a well-constructed novel."

37. See, e.g., *Diary*, 218 (July 11, 1942B).

38. *Diary*, 645 (May 11, 1944A).

39. Orléans and Forster, *A Woman's Life in the Court of the Sun King*, xxi, xxxiii. Writing to a friend on January 11, 1678, Liselotte wrote: "I am certain that I should amuse Your Grace for at least an hour if I were to tell Your Grace about life here and the things that go on, which one cannot possibly imagine unless one sees and hears them and is in the midst of them" (22). One can hear an echo of this in Anne's "it would be quite funny 10 years after the war if we Jews were to tell how we lived and what we ate and talked about here."

40. *Diary*, 303 (November 10, 1942A; November 10, 1942B).

41. *Diary*, Revised Critical Edition, 377.

42. *Diary*, 279 (October 15, 1942A), 279 (October 20, 1942B).

43. *Diary*, 280 (October 20, 1942B), 333 (January 30, 1943B), 365 (July 11, 1943B), 645 (May 11, 1944A).

44. Caplan, 88.

45. *Diary*, 411 (October 29, 1943B).

46. Fredericks, *How to Read a Journal*. For more on Fredericks and his journal, see Benjamin Anastas, "The Paper Tomb," *New Yorker*, November 8, 2021.

47. Coster, 22.

48. *Diary*, 623 (April 28, 1944A).

49. Respondents to a survey by Philippe Lejeune about diary-keeping used the following metaphors to describe their journals: "Breath—the breath of life—flowing water—island—sheltered harbor—mirror—shattered mosaic—way-markers—laboratory—spinal column—crutch—safety-railing—magic ritual—crooning chant, litany—pen-pusher's occupation—message in a bottle—outlet—digestion—shitting—water-closet—cesspool—pus—masturbation—drug—cigarette—bomb—radioactivity—body—mummies—withered flowers—herbarium" (37).

50. Gies, 22.

51. Paperno, 563.

52. *Diary*, 569 (March 25, 1944A).

53. Lejeune, 42.

54. *Diary*, 693 (July 15, 1944A).

55. *Collected Works*, 263.

56. Quoted in Dan Doll, "British Diary Canon Formation," in Ben-Amos and Ben-Amos, 80. In "Confessions of a Mask," a fascinating essay about journal writing, Nausicaa Renner writes that the journal serves the purpose of allowing a reckoning with one's life. "If we were honest with ourselves," she continues, "all we would write is: My parents, my lovers, death" (https://www.nplusonemag.com/online-only/online-only/confessions-of-a-mask/). These are precisely the subjects of Anne's diary.

57. Virginia Woolf, *The Diary of Virginia Woolf*, vol. 1 (New York: Harcourt Brace Jovanovich, 1977), 266.

58. Quoted by Elizabeth Podnieks, "The Literary Author as Diarist," in Ben-Amos and Ben-Amos, 285.

59. Sontag, *Reborn*, 166.

60. Gies, 186.

61. *Diary*, 180 (June 20, 1942B).

62. Van Wijk-Voskuijl and De Bruyn, 59.

63. *Diary*, 217 (July 11, 1942B), 340 (March 10, 1943B), 343 (March 12, 1943B).

64. *Diary*, 587 (April 5, 1944A).

65. Enzer and Solotaroff-Enzer, 331. See also Anne's entry of April 11, 1944A: *If God lets me live, I shall attain more than Mummy ever has done, I shall not remain insignificant, I shall work in the world for mankind* (*Diary*, 601).

66. *Diary*, 440 (January 6, 1944A). See Lejeune, "How Anne Frank Rewrote the Diary of Anne Frank" (*On Diary*, 237–66), for a detailed analysis of this entry.

67. *Diary*, 438–39 (January 2, 1944B).

68. Caplan, 90–91.

69. *Diary*, 438.

70. *Diary*, 534 (March 16, 1944A), 544 (March 17, 1944A), 548 (March 19, 1944A), and many more.

71. Caplan, 91.

72. *Diary*, 518 (March 7, 1944A).

73. Kathryn Carter, "Feminist Interpretations of the Diary," in Ben-Amos and Ben-Amos, 42.

74. Steedman, *The Tidy House*, 76.

75. *Diary*, 628 (May 3, 1944A), 662 (May 26, 1944A), 678 (June 13, 1944A).

76. *Diary*, 694 (July 15, 1944A).

77. *Diary*, 519–20 (March 7, 1944A). Liselotte von der Pfalz, too, wrote about "the healing powers of nature" (Orléans and Forster, xxv).

78. *Collected Works*, 372, 383.

79. *Diary*, 569 (March 25, 1944A).

80. Gies, 187.

81. Steven E. Kagle makes a similar observation about prison diaries: "It is not the suffering in the prisons that makes these diaries so important for the canon, it is how a diary helped the diarists survive" ("The American Diary Canon," in Ben-Amos and Ben-Amos, 113).

82. Schnabel, 137.

Interlude: The Raid

1. For accounts of the raid, see Harry Paape, "The Arrest," in *Diary*, 21–27; Gies, 193–99; Sullivan, *The Betrayal of Anne Frank*, 3–8.

2. Sullivan, 3.

3. Jules Huf, "Luister, wij interesseren ons niet voor politiek," reprinted in *Groene Amsterdammer*, May 14, 1986.

4. *Diary*, 385 (August 5, 1943A); Paape, "The Betrayal," in *Diary*, 42.

5. *Diary*, 618 (April 25, 1944A).

6. Van Wijk-Voskuijl and De Bruyn, 111; Lee, 324.

7. Van Wijk-Voskuijl and De Bruyn, 132.

8. Sullivan's team cites Otto's and Miep's reluctance to discuss the identity of the betrayer after a certain date as evidence that they suspected Arnold van den Bergh and wanted to avoid making

public the fact that a Jew had betrayed the Annex. But if Otto and Miep believed that Nelly Voskuijl was the betrayer, their reluctance to discuss it can be explained as protecting Bep.

9. The full historians' report is available at https://www.niod.nl/en/news/research-report-book-about-betrayal-anne-frank-based-assumptions-and-lack-historical-knowledge. See also Ruth Franklin, "Beyond the Betrayal," *New York Review of Books*, May 26, 2022.

10. *Diary*, 45.

11. "New Perspective on Anne Frank's Arrest," https://www.annefrank.org/en/about-us/news-and-press/news/2016/12/16/new-perspective-anne-franks-arrest/.

12. *Diary*, 21.

13. *Diary*, 22. One conflicting point in the accounts of the raid is whether Kugler showed the police the bookcase concealing the door to the Annex or they spotted it on their own, which many have read as an indication that they were tipped off to the exact location of the Jews in the building. The former FBI agent working with the "Cold Case Team" pointed out that a mark on the floor in front of the bookcase—a "witness mark," in police lingo—would have indicated, to a detective's trained eye, that it was frequently moved. Thus, even if the police seemed to know exactly where the Jews were hiding, that doesn't mean somebody told them. See https://www.coldcasediary.com/press/.

14. "Reminiscences of Victor Kugler," 359.

15. *Diary*, 595 (April 9, 1944A).

16. Lee, xx.

17. Gies, 194.

18. Gies, 197.

19. Gies, 200.

20. Van Wijk-Voskuijl and De Bruyn, 96.

21. Van Wijk-Voskuijl and De Bruyn, 97.

22. Van Wijk-Voskuijl and De Bruyn, 137–38, 141.

23. Gold, 172. In her later years, when Miep imagined the afterlife, she pictured returning to the Annex. "Perhaps when the time comes for me to join Jan and our friends in the hereafter, I'll

push aside the bookcase, walk behind it, climb the steep wooden stairway, careful not to hit my head on the low ceiling," she wrote in her memoir. In her fantasy, Anne asks once again for the news; her husband leans against the dresser, Peter's cat in his arms; and the others sit around the table, waiting for her (Gies, 264).

Chapter 7. Prisoner

Epigraph: *Diary*, 602 (April 14, 1944A).

1. Presser, 406. For general information on Westerbork, see Presser, 406–64; Galen Last and Wolfswinkel, 75–89.

2. Mechanicus, *Waiting for Death*, 72.

3. Etty Hillesum wrote of a nine-month-old baby, "very sweet, blue-eyed, and beautiful," who wasn't allowed to go outside with the other babies when they were taken out for fresh air because she had a "criminal record" (Hillesum, 337).

4. Hillesum, 253.

5. Presser, 411; Hillesum, 357.

6. Quoted in Presser, 415.

7. Schnabel, 155. Schnabel uses pseudonyms for some of his interviewees; Rosa de Winter is "Mrs. de Wiek."

8. Mechanicus, 216; Hillesum, 245. As an employee of the Jewish Council, Hillesum was permitted to spend extended periods of time in Amsterdam for health reasons.

9. Mechanicus, 7. Mechanicus arrived at Westerbork with broken fingers on both of his hands. A friend reported that the guards at Amersfoort stood on his hands until the bones were crushed, a punishment chosen "because he was a famous journalist, and his hands were the tools of his trade" (Siegal, 213).

10. Presser, 427–28.

11. "'That's What I Hope': The Story of Hannah Pick."

12. Konig, *Holocaust Memoirs of a Bergen-Belsen Survivor and Classmate of Anne Frank*, 15.

13. Ed van Thijn, "Memories of a Hidden Child," in Brasz and Kaplan, 273.

14. Hillesum, 370–72.

15. Galen Last and Wolfswinkel, 85.

16. Mechanicus, 46, 72.

17. Galen Last and Wolfswinkel, 85.

18. Hillesum, 351; Mechanicus, 135.

19. Mechanicus, 73 (translation slightly edited), 168.

20. Hillesum, 257; Mechanicus, 216.

21. Coster, 122.

22. Mechanicus, 25.

23. Mechanicus, 111, 95. See also Boom, "Een antword aan mijn critici," and Moore, *Victims and Survivors*, 222.

24. Mechanicus, 96, 89, 187–88, 234.

25. Mechanicus, 96.

26. Mechanicus, 26–27.

27. Hillesum, 274.

28. Lindwer, 120. Lindwer identifies her as Bloeme Evers-Emden, her married name; for her and others, I have used the names they went by during the time they knew Anne.

29. Lindwer, 52. For more on the Brilleslijper sisters, see Iperen, *The Sisters of Auschwitz*.

30. Otto Frank, "Bitte schreiben Sie," Anne Frank Stichtung (AFS).

31. *Diary*, 668 (June 6, 1944A), 680 (June 23, 1944A).

32. Cohen [*sic*], "The Day I Met Anne Frank," *San Diego Jewish World*, December 8, 2011, https://www.sdjewishworld.com/2011/12/08/the-day-i-met-anne-frank.

33. Gies, 123. Miep found Anne's combing shawl after the raid and kept it.

34. Lindwer, 99.

35. Lindwer, 92.

36. Lindwer, 176.

37. Schnabel, 155.

38. Lindwer, 144.

39. Müller, 301; Lee, 158.

40. Lee, 159.

41. Schnabel, 154.

42. Mechanicus, 133.

43. Hillesum, 338, 225, 340.

44. Mechanicus, 181.

45. In *My Name Is Anne*, Van Maarsen writes that Otto told her after the war that Anne "had gone so far as to declare herself delighted" in Westerbork, "because after two years of being shut in she could finally be outside again, in the sun" (132).

46. Lee, 159.

47. Hillesum, 294.

48. Schnabel, 156.

49. Siegal, 336, 214.

50. Mechanicus, 105.

51. A final transport left for Terezín on September 4, 1944 (Presser, 238, 313, 534).

52. "Laatste trein vanuit Kamp Westerbork vertrok precies 75 jaar geleden," *RTV Drenthe*, September 13, 2019.

53. Presser, 483–84.

54. Dwork, 219.

55. Lindwer, 147, 178, 180.

56. Lindwer, 147–48.

57. Lindwer, 56, 121, 179.

58. Lindwer, 56.

59. Lidia Rosenfeld Vago, "One Year in the Black Hole of Our Planet Earth," in Ofer and Weitzman, eds., *Women in the Holocaust*, 275.

60. Inconsistencies in survivors' testimony demonstrate that the directions were arbitrary: sometimes the group to the right went to the gas chamber, but at other times it was the group to the left.

61. Gutman and Berenbaum, 20–24.

62. Joan Ringelheim, "The Split Between Gender and the Holocaust," in Ofer and Weitzman, 348–49.

63. Birkenau was a complex with multiple sectors. At the time Anne was imprisoned there, the women's camp encompassed sectors BIa and BIb. There were also family camps for Roma (liquidated in August 1944) and Jews from Terezín, as well as several men's divisions.

64. Lindwer, 153.

65. Myrna Goldenberg, "Memories of Auschwitz Survivors," in Ofer and Weitzman, 327.

66. Ringelheim, 346, 350.

67. Ferderber-Salz, *And the Sun Kept Shining*, 136.

68. Lengyel, *Five Chimneys*, 30.

69. Lengyel, 30; Ferderber-Salz, 136. In *Lovers in Auschwitz*, Keren Blankfeld writes that Zippi Spitzer, a graphic designer from Slovakia who was deported to the camp in March 1942, came up with the method of mixing the paint and painting a stripe on the women's clothes.

70. Irena Strzelecka, "Women," in Gutman and Berenbaum, 395–96.

71. Strzelecka, 396.

72. Lengyel, 54–55.

73. Lindwer, 57.

74. Strzelecka, 399.

75. Lindwer, 57, 95.

76. Dwork and van Pelt, *Auschwitz*, 272.

77. Lindwer, 182.

78. Lengyel, 34, 40.

79. Lindwer, 63.

80. Gisella Perl, *I Was a Doctor in Auschwitz*, quoted in Dwork and van Pelt, 268.

81. Lindwer, 64.

82. Lindwer, 98, 58.

83. Lindwer, 151, 182–83.

84. Lindwer, 186.

85. *Collected Works*, 245–46.

86. Lindwer, 62, 124, 154, 156.

87. In some sources, her name is spelled Griese.

88. Grese turned twenty-two during the trial (Lerner, *All the Horrors of War*, 7).

89. Lengyel, 161.

90. Sabina Fedeli and Anna Migotto, dirs., *#Anne Frank—Parallel Stories*.

91. Lengyel, 103.

92. Ferderber-Salz, 149.

93. Lengyel, 202, 161.

94. Lindwer, 151, 181, 63.

95. Ringelheim, 341; Lengyel, 63, 196; Marisa Fox-Bevilaqua, "An Unlikely Tribute," *Haaretz*, January 15, 2015, https://www.haaretz.com/jewish/2015-01-15/ty-article/.premium/how-joy-division-found-inspiration-in-auschwitz/0000017f-dc13-db22-a17f-fcb3b3120000.

96. Horowitz, "Women in Holocaust Literature," in Ofer and Weitzman, 371; Goldenberg, "Memoirs of Auschwitz Survivors," in Ofer and Weitzman, 329; Lengyel, 114.

97. Ferderber-Salz, 159.

98. Goldenberg, 336–37. Other Holocaust scholars reject this interpretation. In "Gendered Suffering?" Lawrence L. Langer argues that there was "little evidence that mothers behaved or survived better than fathers, or that mutual support between sisters, when possible, prevailed more than between brothers." He attributes differences to situational accidents rather than "gender-driven choice" (Ofer and Weitzman, 362). Ringelheim cites Cynthia Ozick's opposition to gender-based analysis of the Holocaust: "The Holocaust happened to victims who were not seen as men, women, or children, but *as Jews*" (348). I find the feminist analyses by Goldenberg, Ringelheim, and others convincing.

99. Tedeschi Brunelli, *There Is a Place on Earth*, 124.

100. Ruth Bondy, "Women in Theresienstadt and the Family Camp in Birkenau," in Ofer and Weitzman, 331.

101. Goldenberg, 331.

102. Lindwer, 185.

103. Lindwer, 153, 96, 149.

104. Lindwer, 155.

105. Lindwer, 192, 187, 189, 191.

106. Blankfeld, 194–95.

107. Lévy-Hass, *Diary of Bergen-Belsen*, 100.

108. Lindwer, 98, 190, 123, 155.

109. Nicolas Chare and Dominic Williams, "How Documents Buried by Jewish Prisoners at Auschwitz Tell the Story of Genocide,"

Slate, February 3, 2016, https://slate.com/human-interest/2016/02/pages-from-the-scrolls-of-auschwitz-buried-by-the-sonderkommando.html.

110. Quoted in Siegal, 433.

Chapter 8. Corpse

Epigraph: *Collected Works*, 479.

1. "Richard Dimbleby Describes Belsen," https://www.bbc.co.uk/archive/richard-dimbleby-describes-belsen/zvw7cqt#:~:text=Richard%20Dimbleby%20was%20the%20first,after%20Dimbleby%20threatened%20to%20resign.

2. Christine Lattek, "Bergen-Belsen," in Reilly et al., ed., *Belsen in History and Memory*, 38, 37; Levy, *Witness to Evil*, 17.

3. Levy, 11.

4. Lattek, 56.

5. Levy, 18, 17, 13.

6. Levy, 11.

7. Czech, *Auschwitz Chronicle, 1939–1945*, 741; "One Day They Simply Weren't There Anymore," Anne Frank House, https://www.annefrank.org/en/downloads/filer_public/08/b3/08b3ff12-d8c1-4964-b9ec-e17a7b035a76/one_day_they_simply_weren.pdf; Lindwer, 100.

8. Hanna Lévy-Hass, a young Yugoslav woman who kept a diary at Bergen-Belsen, described making this trip some six weeks earlier: "The inhabitants of the villages—women in coquettish summer dresses, passers-by on bikes or on foot, all fresh and properly dressed and groomed, with the calm that comes from a normal life engraved on their faces—would stop for a moment and look at us with curiosity . . . and with absolute indifference!" (62).

9. Lindwer, 100, 65, 101, 66.

10. Galen Last and Wolfswinkel, 96.

11. Lindwer, 65; Tony Kushner et al., "Approaching Belsen," in Reilly, et al., ed., 17, 21–22; Lattek, 44–45.

12. Konig, 25.

13. Lindwer, 49.

14. Lindwer, 49.

15. Siegal, 343.

16. Jaldati, *Sag nie, du gehst den letzten Weg,* 420. Translations from this book are mine.

17. Lee, *Roses from the Earth,* 181.

18. Lévy-Hass, 84.

19. Herzberg, 280.

20. Jaldati, 420.

21. Lattek, 56, 59.

22. Jaldati, 423.

23. Lévy-Hass, 88, 101.

24. Konig, 43.

25. Lévy-Hass, 111.

26. Lévy-Hass, 102; Jaldati, 423.

27. Quoted in Lee, *Roses from the Earth,* 183.

28. Lin Jaldati, "Memories of Anne Frank," pamphlet distributed with press materials for DEFA documentary film *Ein Tagebuch für Anne Frank,* Archiv der Akademie der Künste, Berlin, 35; "One Day They Simply Weren't There," 2.

29. Jaldati, "Memories," 37.

30. Jaldati, quoted in Pressler, 221; Jaldati, *Sag nie,* 422.

31. Lindwer, 68.

32. Lindwer, 69. The original is "'t Zonnetje gaat van ons scheiden," https://www.liedjeskist.nl/liedjes_a-z/z-liedjes/t_zonnetje_gaat_van_ons_scheiden.htm. Translation by Sam Garrett.

33. Many former prisoners remember fantasizing about food in the camp. "I would like to read a cookbook just as I used to read pornography," one said (Galen Last and Wolfswinkel, 96).

34. Jaldati, "Memories," 36.

35. Bondy, 321.

36. Lattek, 55.

37. Konig, 56.

38. Moskovitz, *Love Despite Hate,* 35.

39. Konig, 61.

40. Konig, 70.

41. Coster, 74.

42. *Diary*, 422 (November 27, 1943B). Because Version A for this period is missing, the exact timing of Anne's dream is uncertain.

43. Pick-Goslar, 195.

44. Pick-Goslar, 197.

45. Pick-Goslar, 197–201.

46. Pick-Goslar, 202.

47. Jaldati, "Memories," 37.

48. Lindwer, 104; Konig, 74.

49. Aviva Loeb, "Anne Frank's Childhood Friend," *Jerusalem Post*, July 22, 2014; Moskovitz, 35.

50. Lindwer, 104; "One Day They Simply Weren't There," 4.

51. Jaldati, "Memories," 37; Jaldati, *Sag nie*, 425.

52. Lindwer, 73.

53. *Diary*, 180 (June 20, 1942B), 623 (April 28, 1944A), 524 (March 12, 1944A), 628 (May 3, 1944A), 569 (March 25, 1944A).

Chapter 9. Author

Epigraph: *Diary*, 416 (November 8, 1943B).

1. This scene is reconstructed from several sources on Setske de Haan and Leon Beek. The timing of Otto Frank's appointments with De Haan comes from his diary (AFS). Though the exact content of their conversation is unknown, Otto visited De Haan to ask for her opinion on the quality of the diary and whether he should publish it. See Soeting, *Cissy van Marxveldt*, 472; Soeting, "De deemoed voorbij," 37; Soeting, *Lief Dagboek, beste kameraad*, unpaged.

2. Evenhuis, "Joop ter Heul deze winter als minimusical op televisiescherm," *NRC*, August 29, 1968. Translation by Tobias Mud.

3. Lindwer, 77.

4. Konig, 97.

5. Pick-Goslar, 214.

6. Lee, *Hidden Life of Otto Frank*, 168–71.

7. Schloss, 161.

8. Coster, 138, 178.

9. Van Maarsen, 127.

10. Van Maarsen, 103–6, 112–14.
11. Gies, 209.
12. Gies, 213.
13. Van Maarsen, 123.
14. Coster, 95.
15. Gies, 227–28.
16. Gies, 227.
17. Van Maarsen, 128.
18. Gies, 227.
19. Presser, 540.
20. Gies, 228.
21. Lee, 159.
22. Gies, 231–33.
23. *Diary*, 301 (November 9, 1942B). In his edit, Otto would add after the third sentence, in parentheses: "Thank God there were no strangers in the house."
24. Lee, 177.
25. Pressler, 204–5.
26. Lee, 180.
27. Schloss, 169; Van Maarsen, 130.
28. Gies, 233.
29. Pressler, 261.
30. Otto Frank to Nathan Straus, September 24, 1945, quoted in Adler, 92.
31. Galen Last and Wolfswinkel, 127.
32. Coster, 142–43.
33. Setske de Haan, "The Postwar Jewish Community and the Memory of the Persecution in the Netherlands," in Brasz and Kaplan, 409.
34. Aalders, "A Disgrace?" in Brasz and Kaplan, 397.
35. Piersma and Kemperman, "The 'Aryanisation' of Jewish Property in Amsterdam and Its Consequences After World War II," in Bajohr and Löw, eds., *The Holocaust and European Societies*, 321.
36. Aalders, 399.
37. Galen Last and Wolfswinkel, 125.

38. Otto Frank to Julius Holländer and Walter Holländer, August 20, 1945, quoted in Lee, 197.

39. Nathan Straus to Otto Frank, October 25, 1945, AFS. Permission to quote from correspondence of Nathan Straus and Helen Straus courtesy of Straus Historical Society.

40. "Reminiscences of Victor Kugler," 362–69, 382; Gies, 230.

41. Van Maarsen, 128.

42. Galen Last and Wolfswinkel, 128.

43. Galen Last and Wolfswinkel, 127.

44. Piersma and Kemperman, 333.

45. Galen Last and Wolfswinkel, 124.

46. Gies, 234–35.

47. Lee, 195; Gies, 239; "One Day They Simply Weren't There Anymore," Anne Frank House.

48. Testimony of Sal Liema in *Anne Frank Remembered.*

49. Pressler, 232; Lee, 196.

50. "In Memoriam," https://stichting5.rssing.com/chan-9598495/all_p5.html, accessed October 1, 2023.

51. Lee, 195.

52. Lee, 193–98.

53. Pressler, 242.

54. Frank, "Bitte schreiben Sie."

55. Lee, 193.

56. Frank, "Bitte schreiben Sie."

57. Jane Pratt, "The Anne Frank We Remember," *McCall's*, January 1986.

58. *Diary*, 180 (June 20, 1942B).

59. Pressler, 242.

60. Gies, 240.

61. Schloss, 172–73.

62. *Diary*, 243 (September 25, 1942A).

63. *Diary*, 177 (June 12, 1942A).

64. *Diary*, 191, 193.

65. *Diary*, 177 (June 14, 1942A), 203 (June 30, 1942A), 199 (June 30, 1942A).

66. *Diary*, 222 (July 8, 1942A), 266 (October 3, 1942A).

67. *Diary*, 287 (October 18, 1942A), 356 (April 27, 1943B), 233 (August 22, 1942A), 262 (October 1, 1942B), 380 (August 3, 1943B), 333 (January 30, 1943B).

68. *Diary*, 223 (July 12, 1942A), 275 (October 10, 1942A), 267 (October 3, 1942A).

69. Arthur Unger, interview with Otto Frank, State Historical Society of Missouri.

70. *Diary*, 84–86.

71. *Diary*, 84–86.

72. *Diary*, 62–64.

73. "Was schrieb das Kind?" *Spiegel*, March 31, 1959.

74. *Diary*, 64. Anne's date of death was estimated as March for many years, but researchers have determined that she likely died in early February. See "One Day They Simply Weren't There Anymore," Anne Frank House.

75. Lee, 203.

76. *Diary*, 63.

77. Unidentified letter, quoted in Lee, 216.

78. *Diary*, 457–58 (January 15, 1944A and B), 408 (September 29, 1943B), 253 (September 28, 1942B).

79. *Diary*, 421 (November 17, 1943B). In Anne's defense, one of Pfeffer's comments triggering this remark was "Hitler will be forgotten by history."

80. *Diary*, 267 (October 3, 1942A), 501 (February 28, 1944A and C), 440 (January 6, 1944A and C).

81. Lee, 203.

82. *Diary*, 412 (November 3, 1943B), 543 (March 17, 1944A), 635 (May 7, 1944A), 550 (March 20, 1944A).

83. *Diary*, 653 (May 20, 1944A)

84. Lejeune, 263.

85. Lejeune, 260.

86. Lejeune, 265.

87. As the critic Nigel Caplan has pointed out, "Only the Dutch edition used Anne's own title for her book, whereas by calling it a 'diary,' translators and critics have either shied away from the implication that they are dealing with a crafted work of literature,

or (probably unwittingly) have perpetuated Anne's own fiction of a day-to-day journal" (85).

88. Form letter dated February 20, 1953, JMP.

89. Gies, 243.

90. *Diary*, 67.

91. Gies, 243.

92. *The Works of Anne Frank*, 17.

93. Michel Braud, "The Diary in France and French-Speaking Countries," in Ben-Amos and Ben-Amos, ed., 92.

94. Braud, 94.

95. Lee, 203.

96. *Diary*, 64.

97. Pressler, 253.

98. Lee, 205.

99. Lee, 228.

100. *Diary*, 68.

101. *Diary*, 68.

102. Steenmeijer, ed., *Tribute to Anne Frank*, 34.

103. Van Maarsen, 141.

104. Gies, 244.

105. *Diary*, 71.

106. Lee, 217.

107. Rainone.

108. "Was schrieb das Kind?"

109. *Diary*, 313 (November 17, 1942B), 473 (January 28, 1944B), 274 (October 9, 1942B).

110. Arthur Unger interview with Otto Frank.

111. Raphael Gross, "Otto Frank and Anne Frank's Diary," lecture, Leo Baeck Institute, November 29, 2019.

112. Steenmeijer, ed., *Tribute to Anne Frank*, 35.

113. Judith Jones, "Anne Frank Remembered," *Vogue*, December 1997, 178.

Interlude: Anne Frank in Ethiopia

1. Sources for this section include: Yikealo Beyene, "Fleeing Brutality and Genocide, I Was Sure in Israel, Anne Frank's People

Wouldn't Deny Us Refuge," *Haaretz*, February 9, 2018; Yochai Meital, "Out of Africa and Back Again," October 2015, in *Israel Story*, podcast, 8:00, https://www.israelstory.org/episode/out-of-africaand-back-again/; "An Asylum-Seeker's Journeys," *Jewish Independent*, https://www.jewishindependent.ca/tag/yikealo-beyene/.

Chapter 10. Celebrity

Epigraph: *Diary*, 297 (October 30, 1942B [incorrectly dated 1943]).

1. Menand, "Missionary," *New Yorker*, July 31, 2005.

2. Lambert, *The Literary Mafia*, 10–13, 16.

3. Silverman, *Time of Their Lives*, 117–18. Shatzkin hired Charles Harris, Doubleday's second Black employee.

4. Graver, *An Obsession with Anne Frank*, 18.

5. Lambert, 36–38. Despite Strauss's reservations, Knopf published *Commentary on the American Scene*, edited by Elliot Cohen, in 1953.

6. Graver, 2.

7. Levin, "The Restricted Market," *Congress Weekly*, November 13, 1950.

8. Graver, 5.

9. Levin, "Death Factory at Buchenwald Horrible Beyond Description," *Watertown Times*, May 2, 1945, quoted in Melnick, *The Stolen Legacy of Anne Frank*, 2.

10. Graver, 8.

11. Flanner, "Letter from Paris," *New Yorker*, November 11, 1950. Flanner, who may not have read the book, also wrote that Anne was in hiding with "about a dozen" other people and that provisions, books, and news were delivered via a clothespress that, "by a secret mechanism, operated as a door into the annex."

12. Levin, *In Search*, 174.

13. Levin, "The Restricted Market."

14. Graver, 12.

15. Frank Price to Don Elder, March 21, 1951, JMP; Jones, *The Tenth Muse*, 46.

16. Contract memo, JMP.

17. Silverman, 115–16.

18. Barbara Zimmerman to Otto Frank, November 17, 1952, JMP.

19. Helen Epstein, interview by the author, May 3, 2021.

20. Otto Frank to Barbara Zimmerman, August 14, 1953, August 21, 1953, and elsewhere, JMP.

21. Betty Tillett to Barbara Zimmerman, February 25, 1952, JMP.

22. Otto Frank to Barbara Zimmerman, June 6, 1952, JMP.

23. Barbara Zimmerman to Frank Price, October 9, 1952, JMP.

24. Marketing memo, undated, JMP; Silverman, 121.

25. In "The Restricted Market," Levin shrewdly predicted as much: "It is scarcely to be expected that the book will be promoted so as to come to the attention of the large audience that might otherwise be ready for it" (9).

26. Barbara Zimmerman to Otto Frank, June 12, 1952, JMP. Ken McCormick later singled her out as having "worked like hell" to promote the book (McCormick to Judith Bailey, June 20, 1952, JMP).

27. Sales memo, undated, JMP.

28. Weirdly, the introduction also states that the Annex residents were "imprisoned not only by the terrible outward circumstances of war but inwardly by themselves." Reprinted in Steenmeijer, 34–35.

29. Barbara Zimmerman to Otto Frank, May 7, 1952, JMP.

30. Barbara Zimmerman to Frank Price, July 22, 1952, JMP.

31. Levin, "The Child Behind the Secret Door," *New York Times*, June 15, 1952.

32. Graver, 61.

33. Graver, 54.

34. "How Book Reviewers Make a Book a Success," press release, JMP.

35. Memo, JMP.

36. Barbara Zimmerman to Frank Price, June 13, 1952, JMP.

37. Otto Frank to Barbara Zimmerman, June 30, 1952, JMP.

38. Barry Sullivan to Otto Frank, April 2, 1953, JMP. Sullivan

added an emotional postscript: the *Diary* moved him so deeply, he wrote, that he "found it difficult to compose a letter that deals entirely with the merely commercial angle."

39. Howard Roszell to Doubleday, October 3, 1952, JMP.

40. *New York Post*, July 13, 1952.

41. *New York Post*, July 16, 1952. The articles, based on Levin's conversations with Otto, are written in hyperbolic prose and are not reliable sources. The author's note, too, contains exaggerations: it identifies Levin as "an authority on what happened to more than 5,000,000 Jews in Europe during and after the war. As a war correspondent he saw most of the Nazi concentration camps and learned the fate of their occupants."

42. Undated clipping, JMP.

43. Melnick, 20–21.

44. Barbara Zimmerman to Frank Price, June 17, 1952, JMP; Otto Frank to Barbara Zimmerman, June 18, 1952, JMP.

45. Quoted in Melnick, 2.

46. Levin, *Obsession*, 96.

47. Barbara Zimmerman to Frank Price, June 17, 1952, JMP; July 2, 1952, JMP; June 27, 1952, JMP.

48. Otto Frank to Barbara Zimmerman, June 30, 1952, JMP.

49. Meyer Levin to Kenneth McCormick, July 2, 1952, JMP. Permission to quote from the correspondence of Meyer Levin courtesy of the Estate of Meyer Levin.

50. Joseph Marks to Frank Price, July 9, 1952, JMP.

51. Meyer Levin to McCormick, July 2, 1952, JMP.

52. Otto Frank to Barbara Zimmerman, June 18, 1952, JMP.

53. Joseph Marks to Frank Price, July 9, 1952, JMP.

54. Joseph Marks to Frank Price, July 9, 1952, JMP.

55. Frank Price to Joseph Marks, July 16, 1952, JMP; Barbara Zimmerman to Price, July 22, 1952, JMP.

56. Schloss, 225.

57. Otto Frank to Barbara Zimmerman, July 9, 1952, JMP.

58. Cheryl Crawford to Otto Frank, July 9, 1952, JMP.

59. Melnick, 40, 122.

60. Levin, *Anne Frank*.

61. Barbara Zimmerman to Frank Price, October 3, 1952, JMP.

62. Melnick, 51–52.

63. Barbara Zimmerman to Frank Price, October 9, 1952, JMP.

64. Melnick, 55.

65. Melnick, 58, 56. Zimmerman wondered about Crawford's intentions as well. "I expect . . . that she will try to buy him off and try to get the play for her own writer. It may be that this is what she planned to do all along, but wanted the play at any cost" (Barbara Zimmerman to Frank Price, October 9, 1952).

66. Barbara Zimmerman to Frank Price, November 18, 1952, JMP.

67. Barbara Zimmerman to Otto Frank, January 30, 1953, JMP.

68. Barbara Zimmerman to Frank Price, November 18, 1952, JMP.

69. Price, undated memo, JMP.

70. Melnick, 31.

71. Otto Frank to Barbara Zimmerman, August 20, 1952, JMP.

72. Pinchas Cruse to Otto Frank, October 17, 1952, JMP.

73. Doubleday to booksellers, November 10, 1952, JMP.

74. Barbara Zimmerman to Otto Frank, December 8, 1952, JMP.

75. Meyer Levin to Otto Frank, early January 1953, JMP; Barbara Zimmerman to Otto Frank, January 15, 1953, JMP. The same was true in the Netherlands. As Otto wrote to Levin: "It is (at least here) read and understood more by gentiles than in Jewish circles" (Graver, 54).

76. Barbara Zimmerman to Otto Frank, December 29, 1952, JMP.

77. Barbara Zimmerman to Frank Price, December 29, 1952, JMP.

78. Otto Frank to Barbara Zimmerman, November 28, 1952, JMP.

79. Excerpt in Otto Frank to Barbara Zimmerman, November 28, 1952, JMP.

80. Barbara Zimmerman to Frank Price, December 8, 1952, JMP.

81. Melnick, 21.

82. Myer Mermin to Otto Frank, May 21, 1953, JMP.

83. Meyer Levin to Myer Mermin, January 6, 1953, JMP, quoted in Otto Frank to Barbara Zimmerman, January 1, 1953, JMP.

84. Otto Frank to Barbara Zimmerman, January 1, 1953, JMP.

85. Melnick, 30.

86. Barbara Zimmerman to Otto Frank, January 7, 1953, JMP.

87. Nathan Straus to Otto Frank, January 15, 1953, AFS.

88. Melnick, 60.

89. Barbara Zimmerman to Otto Frank, January 16, 1953, JMP.

90. Mermin persuaded the editor not to run Levin's letter. "Otto Frank is an unusually gentle and sensitive person. As you probably know, he has suffered tragic losses, including the deaths of every member of his family. His little girl's diary is the big thing in his life today. He worships her memory and hopes that her story will be a source of good to people all over the world. He would be shocked and deeply hurt by any controversy in the public press arising from his daughter's book" (Myer Mermin to Hobe Morrison, January 26, 1953, JMP).

91. Barbara Zimmerman to Otto Frank, January 15, 1953, JMP.

92. Meyer Levin to Myer Mermin, January 15, 1953, JMP; Levin to Otto Frank, February 7, 1953, JMP.

93. Cheryl Crawford to Otto Frank, February 6, 1953, JMP.

94. Myer Mermin to Otto Frank, March 31, 1953, JMP.

95. Cheryl Crawford to Otto Frank, April 22, 1953, JMP.

96. Carson McCullers to Otto Frank, undated [copy], JMP.

97. Otto Frank to Barbara Zimmerman, August 14, 1953, JMP.

98. Joseph Marks to Myer Mermin, July 9, 1958, JMP.

99. Otto Frank to Sullivan, May 11, 1953, JMP.

100. Barbara Zimmerman to Otto Frank, September 3, 1953, JMP.

101. Meyer Levin to Kermit Bloomgarden, October 19, 1953, JMP.

102. Barbara Zimmerman to Otto Frank, October 20, 1953, JMP.

103. Myer Mermin to Otto Frank, October 20, 1953, JMP.

104. Myer Mermin to Otto Frank, December 11, 1953, JMP.

105. Barbara Zimmerman to Otto Frank, December 15, 1953, JMP.

106. Myer Mermin to Otto Frank, December 11, 1953, JMP.

Interlude: Ghostly Muse

1. This section draws on the following sources: Kim Cooper, *In the Aeroplane Over the Sea;* C. B. Stockfleth, dir., *The Elephant 6 Recording Company* (Elephant Films LLC, 2022); Mike McGonigal, "Dropping in at the Neutral Milk Hotel," *Puncture*, Spring 1998, https://web.archive.org/web/20030423054804/http://neutralmilkhotel.net/puncture3.html, accessed October 1, 2023; Taylor Clark, "The Salinger of Indie Rock," *Slate*, February 26, 2008, https://slate.com/culture/2008/02/jeff-mangum-the-salinger-of-indie-rock.html, accessed October 1, 2023; "Top 100 Albums of the 1990s," *Pitchfork*, https://pitchfork.com/features/lists-and-guides/5923-top-100-albums-of-the-1990s/?page=10, accessed October 1, 2023; Neil Strauss, "Matters of Life, Death and Prevarication," *New York Times*, May 1, 1997; Kevin Griffis, "Have You Seen Jeff Mangum?" *Creative Loafing*, September 4, 2003, https://creativeloafing.com/content-184720-have-you-seen-jeff, accessed October 1, 2023; Wilson, "Are We Finally Ready to See Neutral Milk Hotel for What It Really Was?" *Slate*, March 1, 2023, https://slate.com/culture/2023/03/neutral-milk-hotel-aeroplane-sea-meaning-jeff-mangum.html, accessed October 1, 2023; S. B. Kasulke, "Mangum-Gate 2012 Is the Internet's Conspiracy Theory of the Week," *The Ithacan*, October 22, 2012.

Chapter 11. Ambassador

Epigraph: *Diary*, 600 (April 9, 1944A).

1. Atkinson, "Theatre: 'The Diary of Anne Frank,'" *New York Times*, October 6, 1955.

2. In "Anne Frank from Page to Stage," her essential essay about the dramatic adaptation, Edna Nahshon recounts a conversa-

tion with her son about a friend who attends the 1997–98 revival of *The Diary of Anne Frank* in lieu of a Passover seder (in Kirshenblatt-Gimblett and Shandler, 59).

3. See, e.g., Hammelburg, "A Fresh Look at 'Anne Frank' in Search of the Historical One," *New York Times*, November 30, 1997.

4. *Diary*, 600 (April 9, 1944A).

5. Goodrich and Hackett, *The Diary of Anne Frank*, 168.

6. Prose, 215.

7. Levin, *Obsession*, 30.

8. Garson Kanin to Frances Goodrich and Albert Hackett, November 8, 1954, GHP.

9. Frances Goodrich and Albert Hackett to Otto Frank, December 27, 1953, GHP.

10. Otto Frank to Frances Goodrich and Albert Hackett, January 1, 1954, GHP.

11. Frances Goodrich and Albert Hackett to Leah Salisbury, January 7, 1954, GHP.

12. Goodrich and Hackett, 154.

13. Frances Goodrich and Albert Hackett to Leah Salisbury, January 7, 1954, GHP.

14. Otto Frank to Frances Goodrich and Albert Hackett, February 21, 1955, GHP.

15. Otto Frank to Frances Goodrich and Albert Hackett, September 9, 1955, GHP.

16. Frances Goodrich and Albert Hackett to Leah Salisbury, January 7, 1954.

17. Levin, *Obsession*, 95–96.

18. Kermit Bloomgarden to Frances Goodrich and Albert Hackett, January 18, 1954, GHP.

19. *Diary*, 321 (December 7, 1942B).

20. Melnick, 126.

21. Frances Goodrich and Albert Hackett to Otto Frank, March 20, 1954, GHP.

22. Otto Frank to Frances Goodrich and Albert Hackett, June 14, 1954, GHP.

23. Melnick, 147–48.

24. Otto Frank to Frances Goodrich and Albert Hackett, November 5, 1954, GHP.

25. Otto Frank to Frances Goodrich and Albert Hackett, November 5, 1954, GHP.

26. Goodrich and Hackett, 155.

27. Schloss, 244–45. Clearly Otto's memory was softened by time and circumstance; Anne had often been a difficult child.

28. Jack Gilford, the actor who played Dussel, was subpoenaed by Congress and called before the House Un-American Activities Committee (HUAC) during the run of the play. He sometimes had to miss the Wednesday matinees while testifying before the committee (Langer, *Playing Anne Frank*).

29. *Collected Works*, 239.

30. Goodrich and Hackett, 162.

31. Goodrich and Hackett, 105.

32. Goodrich and Hackett, 117.

33. Nahshon, 69.

34. Goodrich and Hackett, 132, 140.

35. Melnick notes that a few months after the play opened on Broadway, Hellman received a $10,000 check from the Soviet government "for an unspecified reason" (208). His source is Joan Mellen's biography *Hellman and Hammett*. But there is nothing to suggest that Hellman was paid by the Soviets for ideological operations. Mellen suggests that the check represented royalties for recent Soviet productions of Hellman's plays.

36. Melnick, 130.

37. Melnick, 175.

38. Leshi Torchin, "Anne Frank's Moving Images," in Kirshenblatt-Gimblett and Shandler, eds., 97–99.

39. Levin, *Anne Frank*, 46, 20.

40. Levin, *Anne Frank*, 55, 77–80.

41. Frank Rich, "Betrayed by Broadway," *New York Times*, September 17, 1995.

42. Goodrich and Hackett, 168.

43. *Diary*, 508 (March 3, 1944A), 237 (September 21, 1942A). In the Goodrich/Hackett Chanukah scene, Margot remembers ob-

servances past as involving "eight days of presents . . . and each day they got better and better," a very American depiction (87).

44. *Collected Works*, 362, 380–83.

45. 3/7/44A. The Critical Edition gives this in German: "Ich danke dir, für all das Gute und Liebe und Schöne."

46. https://artsandculture.google.com/asset/pieta-pasted-on-the-wall-on-top-of-the-picture-of-the-lane-sisters-afs/6wHmsULE3_jX4w.

47. Ergas, 91.

48. Gibbs, "Amsterdam and Troy," *New Yorker*, October 15, 1955.

49. Otto Frank to Frances Goodrich and Albert Hackett, September 26, 1955, GHP.

50. Otto Frank to cast and crew, September 15, 1955, GHP. Otto initially wrote to Levin that he "could not see" the work as a play; now he literally cannot see it.

51. Langer, "Their Own Secret Annex," in *Playing Anne Frank*, January 31, 2023, https://forward.com/podcasts/playing-anne-frank/.

52. Langer, "Their Own Secret Annex."

53. Strasberg, *Bittersweet*, 53.

54. Strasberg, 51.

55. Strasberg, 56.

56. Adam Langer, "The 'Anne Frank' Road Trip That Transformed America," *Forward*, February 7, 2023.

57. Langer, "Anne on the Road," in *Playing Anne Frank*, February 7, 2023, https://forward.com/podcasts/playing-anne-frank/.

58. Langer, "Anne on the Road."

59. Langer, "Anne on the Road."

60. Langer, "Anne Goes to Hollywood," in *Playing Anne Frank*, February 14, 2023, https://forward.com/podcasts/playing-anne-frank/.

61. Melnick, 125.

62. Feldman, "Anne Frank in America," *American Heritage*, February/March 2005.

63. Marvine Howe, "Gusti Huber, Stage and Film Star and an Anne Frank Lecturer, 78," *New York Times*, July 15, 1993.

64. Liz McNeil, "Why Audrey Hepburn Refused to Play Anne

Frank in the Hollywood Film Despite Pleas from Anne's Dad," *Newsweek*, April 5, 2019, https://people.com/movies/why-audrey-hepburn-refused-play-anne-frank/.

65. Adam Langer, "How Hollywood Found Its Anne Frank," *Forward*, February 14, 2023.

66. Barnouw, *The Phenomenon of Anne Frank*, 50.

67. Langer, "Anne Goes to Hollywood."

68. Barnouw, 50.

69. Langer, "How Hollywood Found Its Anne Frank."

70. Strasberg, 52.

71. Joe L. Riddle, "Six Decades Show Value of The Diary of Anne Frank," *Arkansas Democrat-Gazette*, August 9, 2019.

72. Judith Raiskin and Michelle Cliff, "The Art of History: An Interview with Michelle Cliff," *Kenyon Review*, winter 1993.

73. Torchin, 103.

Interlude: Surrogate Father

1. This section draws on the following sources: *Otto Frank*, performed by Roger Guenveur Smith, Public Theater, New York City, January 18, 2023; Smith, interviewed by Brian Watt, KQED, March 20, 2022; Smith, interviewed by Jim Munson, broadwayworld.com, March 10, 2022; Smith, interviewed by Coco Fusco, *Bomb*, July 1, 1997. A brief excerpt of *Otto Frank* can be viewed at https://www.youtube.com/watch?v=OAGs2XX7mls.

Chapter 12. Survivor

Epigraph: *Diary*, 569 (March 25, 1944A).

1. Barry Gray, *New York Post*, October 9, 1955.

2. Schnabel, 54.

3. Werner, "Germany's New Flagellants," in Enzer and Solotaroff-Enzer, 160; Nahshon, 83.

4. This seems to be primarily an American phenomenon; Anne does not exist in Dutch as a literary figure.

5. See Ellen Feldman, *The Boy Who Loved Anne Frank;* Jillian Cantor, *Margot*.

6. I'm grateful to Sana Krasikov for sharing her thoughts on this subject.

7. Hanno Loewy, "Saving the Child," in Langford and West, *Marginal Voices, Marginal Forms*, 157.

8. Roth considered using Anne Frank to dramatize these ideas as early as 1972, as an early draft of what would become *American Pastoral* demonstrates. Among Roth's working titles for the draft—a monologue by an American Jew contemplating the "liberties and security" he has enjoyed as an American citizen—were "The Diary of Anne Frank's Contemporary" and "Anne Frank in America" (Shostak, 124). At around the same time, he marked up a draft of his own writing with a letter grade and critical comment that he signed "AF," suggesting that he saw Anne as "a kind of aesthetic conscience" (Shostak, 203).

9. Roth, *Zuckerman Bound*, 59.

10. Roth, 66–67. According to Brauner in *Philip Roth*, many of these questions were "lifted almost verbatim from hostile reviews and correspondence that Roth had received," including the one about Goebbels (Brauner, 30). The use of all caps in the document's title, "TEN QUESTIONS FOR NATHAN ZUCKERMAN," is a giveaway.

11. *Diary*, 600 (April 9, 1944A).

12. *Diary*, 600 (April 9, 1944A).

13. As Alan Cooper points out, "Lonoff is also Roth; or, more precisely, half of Roth is Lonoff" (Cooper, *Philip Roth and the Jews*, 182).

14. Roth, 32–33.

15. Speaking of Zionism: Roth sends Anne, in his fictional account, to stay at the Biltmore Hotel, which was the site of a major Zionist conference in 1942 that lent its name to the Biltmore Declaration. The declaration called for the establishment of Palestine as "a Jewish Commonwealth"—a major and aggressive departure for Zionist policy at the time. See Bela Ruth Samuel-Tenenholtz, "Exploring the Vault," E20.

16. Roth, 9.

17. Roth, 12.

18. Roth, 11.

19. Roth, 94.

20. Brauner, 33. For an example of such an obtuse reading, see Shatzky, "Creating an Aesthetic for Holocaust Literature," 109–10. Among other errors, Shatzky writes that Anne died in Auschwitz.

21. Roth, 102.

22. Roth, 57.

23. Zuckerman elsewhere describes his argument with his father as "an old family feud" in which his father "played peacemaker for nearly two years before the opponents ended up shouting in court," a description that sounds strikingly like the conflict between Otto and Levin.

24. Roth, 93.

25. Quoted in Crandell, "Re-Addressing the Past—Arthur Miller's Neglected Speech," 90. Miller was criticized by Mary McCarthy, among others, for de-Judaizing his characters into "a hollow, reverberant universality." Leslie Fiedler referred to Miller's characters as "crypto-Jewish." Later, Miller grew more confident about incorporating Jews into his work, imagining that he would create "a gallery of Jewish characters so powerful in their reality" that audiences would see them as no different from other Americans.

26. Roth, 60.

27. Roth, 60. As Shostak writes, Nathan's "maturation as man and artist revolves around confronting the implications of his displacement as a Jew from what would seem to be the defining moment of twentieth-century Jewish history" (127–28).

28. Lonoff's wife is unaccounted for in this scenario, in what might well be a kind of pun on Kafka's aphorism about humanity: "There is hope [Hope], but not for us." In his essay "I Always Wanted You to Admire My Fasting; or, Looking at Kafka," Roth imagined that Kafka emigrated to America, becoming Roth's boyhood Hebrew tutor and dating his aunt Rhoda. In Roth, *Reading Myself and Others* (New York: Farrar, Straus and Giroux, 1975), 247–70.

29. Roth, *Zuckerman Bound*, 32.

30. *Diary*, 578 (March 29, 1944A, March 29, 1944B).

31. See, e.g., Langer, *Using and Abusing the Holocaust*, 25; Schloss, 106.

32. Derrick Bryson Taylor, "Harvard Lampoon Apologizes for Sexualized Image of Anne Frank," *New York Times*, May 15, 2019. The Anne Frank Trust UK created a more decorous image of an older Anne to honor her eightieth birthday. As Jeffrey Shandler points out, "Besides conjuring Anne Frank as living into old age, the composite photograph also implicitly imagines solving the crime of her murder by undoing it, thereby restoring the diary's 'missing' author to her public" (Shandler, "From Diary to Book," in Kirschenblatt-Gimblett and Shandler, eds., 52).

33. Atkinson; Levin, "The Child Behind the Secret Door"; Romein-Verschoor, preface to *Het Achterhuis*.

34. Auslander, *Hope: A Tragedy*, 23.

35. Auslander, 27.

36. Auslander, 30.

37. Auslander, 59–60.

38. Auslander, 64–65.

39. Mark Lawson, "Anne Frank," April 11, 2012, on *Front Row*, BBC Radio 4, https://www.bbc.co.uk/programmes/b01fjth7, accessed September 17, 2023.

40. See Tova Reich, "Shalom Auslander's 'Hope: A Tragedy,'" *Washington Post*, January 23, 2012; Janet Maslin, "Anne Frank, Still Writing in the Attic," *New York Times*, January 17, 2012.

41. Lawson, "Anne Frank."

42. Gillham, *Annelies*, 99–100.

43. Gillham, 204.

44. Gillham, 147, 193.

45. Gillham, 310.

46. Gillham, 304.

47. Gillham, 304.

48. David R. Gillham, telephone interview by the author, May 4, 2023.

49. Gillham, 63.

50. Lourie, *A Hatred for Tulips*, 6. Published in paperback under the title *Joop: A Novel of Anne Frank*.

51. Gillham, 390–91.

52. In fact, the person who was tormented by guilt after the war was Bep, who believed her sister Nelly had betrayed the Annex Eight to the Gestapo. Later in life, Bep descended into depression and attempted suicide. "That grief will never leave my heart," she told her son (Van Wijk-Voskuijl and De Bruyn, 164). She named her daughter Anne.

53. "The Monkey's Paw" exists in many versions. The original story is by the English author W. W. Jacobs. Stephen King's *Pet Sematary* is a well-known elaboration on the theme.

54. See Rachael McLennan, "Philip Roth's Prosthetic Fictions," in *Representations of Anne Frank in American Literature*, 23–44.

55. Lourie, 144.

56. Chambers, *Postcards from No Man's Land*, 298.

57. Schloss, 239, 244–45.

58. Schloss, 245.

59. Otto Frank to Barbara Zimmerman, March 16, 1953, JMP.

60. Roth, 96.

Interlude: Family Secret

1. Sources: "Anne Frank's Last Months," Anne Frank House, March 31, 2015, https://www.annefrank.org/en/about-us/news-and-press/news/2015/3/31/anne-franks-last-months/, accessed September 18, 2023; Chen Drachman, interview with the author, July 19, 2023; Chen Drachman, dir., "The Book of Ruth," thebookofruthfilm.com, accessed September 19, 2023; Talya Zax, "Men Explain Anne Frank to Me," *Forward*, December 16, 2018; Marjorie Ingall, "Trapped in the Annex," *Tablet*, May 31, 2019; Katzir, *Dearest Anne*, 78; Lisa France, dir., *Anne B. Real* (Rêve Entertainment Group LLC, 2003).

Chapter 13. Pawn

1. The lack of publicity was intentional: productions of *The Diary of Anne Frank* have been targets of antisemitism, including

one in 2019 in Melbourne, Australia, where a swastika was painted on a poster promoting the play.

2. Brooke Baldwin, "New 'Anne Frank' Play Uses Mostly Hispanic Actors," CNN, August 6, 2018, https://www.youtube.com/watch?v=VO3c9PvZxck.

3. I attended the play on April 28, 2023.

4. Graver, 54.

5. Steenmeijer, ed., *Tribute to Anne Frank*, 36, 45.

6. "The International Anne Frank Youth Center," memo, December 15, 1958, JMP.

7. Shandler, 56.

8. Steenmeijer, 114.

9. Gilbert, "Anne Frank in South Africa," *Holocaust and Genocide Studies*, 374.

10. Gilbert, 374–75.

11. Roni Mikel Arieli, "Reading the Diary of Anne Frank on Robben Island," virtual lecture, Holocaust Museum Houston, November 6, 2020, https://www.youtube.com/watch?v=oBrSuMKccjA.

12. Mandela, *Long Walk to Freedom*, quoted in Raymond Whitaker, "Mandela's Prison," *Independent*, December 10, 2013.

13. The full quotation appears on page 155.

14. Gilbert, 378, 366.

15. Gilbert, 379–80, 384.

16. Samuel-Tenenholtz, E15.

17. Langer, "Anne Frank Revisited," in *Using and Abusing the Holocaust*, 25; Schloss, quoted in Ken Burns et al., *The U.S. and the Holocaust*, PBS.

18. Gilbert, 379.

19. Yardena Schwartz, "Just Outside Hiroshima, a Holocaust Education Center Flourishes," *Tablet*, June 14, 2018, https://www.tabletmag.com/sections/news/articles/just-outside-hiroshima-a-holocaust-education-center-flourishes.

20. Sichel, "The Japanese Tampon Named After Anne Frank."

21. Ryang, "Anne Frank in Japan," 1.

22. Eric Margolis, "Two Girls Symbolize the Horrors of War," *Japan Times*, December 28, 2020.

23. Angela Coutts, "Remembering Anne Frank in Japan," *Contemporary Women's Writing*, March 2014, 74.

24. "Why Are the Japanese So Fascinated with Anne Frank?" JTA, January 22, 2014, https://www.haaretz.com/jewish/2014-01-22/ty-article/anne-frank-the-japanese-anime/0000017f-e88d-dc7e-adff-f8ad09300000.

25. Otsuka, "Importance of Holocaust Education in Japan," *Journal of Genocide Research* (1993): 459.

26. Makoto Otsuka, 460.

27. Ryang, 6.

28. Fumiko Ishioda, interview with the author, October 23, 2019.

29. "Aichi Triennale Will Reopen Exhibition with 'Comfort Woman' Statue," *Artforum*, October 1, 2019, https://www.artforum.com/news/aichi-triennale-will-reopen-exhibition-with-comfort-woman-statue-244850/.

30. Robert Rand, "The Diary of Anne," *Tablet*, June 12, 2018.

31. Kirshenblatt-Gimblett and Shandler, eds., 17–18.

32. Shannon Power, "Anne Frank Murals Vandalized in Italy," *Newsweek*, November 13, 2023, https://www.newsweek.com/anne-frank-antisemitism-italy-israel-hamas-1843073.

33. Cnaan Liphshiz, "A Dutch Rapper Said She Chose the Stage Name 'Anne Frank' as a Tribute," JTA, June 26, 2019, https://www.jta.org/2019/06/26/global/a-dutch-rapper-said-she-chose-the-stage-name-anne-frank-as-a-tribute-turns-out-shes-anti-semitic.

34. Gabe Friedman, "Roger Waters Dons SS Uniform in Berlin Show," JTA, June 7, 2023.

35. Beth Harpaz, "Anne Frank Trust Scolds Roger Waters," *Forward*, June 9, 2023.

36. Friedman.

37. See Jonathan Stempel, "NYU Is Sued by Jewish Students Who Allege Antisemitism on Campus," Reuters, November 14, 2023; Andrew Lapin, "'Glory to Our Martyrs' Projected onto Building at George Washington University," *Times of Israel*, October 26, 2023; Ronny Reyes, "Jewish Yale Student Journalist Stabbed in the

Eye with Palestinian Flag During Protest," *New York Post*, April 21, 2024; Celina Tebor, Zoe Sottile and Matt Egan, "Columbia University Faces Full-Blown Crisis as Rabbi Calls for Jewish Students to 'Return Home,'" CNN.com, April 22, 2024.

38. Anne's classmate Theo Coster also immigrated to Israel. In Tel Aviv, a civil servant once questioned whether Theo was a Jewish name. Theo shot back that he had gone to school with Anne Frank. "It was neither here nor there, which I knew perfectly well . . . but I'd predicted the effect of the words correctly" (Coster, 157).

39. *Diary*, 637 (May 8, 1944A).

40. *Kirkus*, June 15, 1937, https://www.kirkusreviews.com/book-reviews/a/ladislas-farago-6/palestine-at-the-crossroads/.

41. Pressler, 35.

42. Otto Frank to Joseph Marks, December [misdated November] 15, 1952, JMP.

43. Hass, afterword to Lévy-Hass, 85–102.

44. *Diary*, 628 (May 3, 1944A).

45. *Diary*, 678 (June 13, 1944A).

46. Ofer Aderet, "'It's Happening Again': Holocaust Survivors Who Lost Family October 7 Speak at Knesset," *Ha'aretz*, January 31, 2024, https://www.haaretz.com/israel-news/2024-01-31/ty-article/.premium/its-happening-again-holocaust-survivors-who-lost-family-october-7-speak-at-knesset/0000018d-5be6-d4f8-a9df-5feef9620000.

47. Astha Rajvanshi, "How Israeli and Palestinian Medical Volunteers Work Across Borders to Save Lives," *Time*, March 8, 2024.

48. Folman, *Where Is Anne Frank*, 156.

49. Folman, 130–31.

50. Folman, 141–42.

51. Folman, 42.

52. Cooper, 205.

53. Rebecca Leung, "If Anne Frank Only Knew," *60 Minutes*, February 26, 2004, https://www.cbsnews.com/news/if-anne-frank-only-knew/.

54. Jac Lahav, "Anne Frank," https://www.jaclahav.com/portrait/2016/10/6/48-jews; Kirshenblatt-Gimblett and Shandler, 258–59; Ellen Rothenberg, "Anne Frank Project," https://www.ellenrothenberg.com/anne-frank-project.

55. Samantha Berlin, "Woman Compares Herself to Rosa Parks After Refusing to Wear Mask on Plane," *Newsweek*, April 1, 2022.

56. "Short Biographies of Some of God's Friends," Saint Gregory of Nyssa Episcopal Church, accessed October 5, 2023, https://www.saintgregorys.org/saints-by-name.html.

57. Andrew Lapin, "US Neo-Nazi Extradited to Netherlands for Projecting Message on Anne Frank House," JTA, September 12, 2023, https://www.timesofisrael.com/us-neo-nazi-extradited-to-netherlands-for-projecting-message-on-anne-frank-house/. The message read "Inventor of the ballpoint pen," a reference to a conspiracy theory alleging that the *Diary* was originally written with a ballpoint pen, which was invented after World War II, and thus is a forgery.

58. See, e.g., Ruairidh Barlow, "Real Madrid Ultras Respond to Atletico Stunt with Disgraceful Anne Frank Poster," *Football Espana*, January 27, 2023.

SELECTED BIBLIOGRAPHY

Adler, Joan. *For the Sake of the Children: The Letters Between Otto Frank and Nathan Straus Jr.* New York: Straus Historical Society, 2013.

Amir, Ruth, and Pnina Rosenberg, eds. *The Diary of a Young Girl.* Critical Insights. Ipswich, Mass.: Salem Press, a division of EBSCO Information Services, 2017.

Arieli, Roni Mikel. "Reading the Diary of Anne Frank on Robben Island." Holocaust Museum Houston, November 6, 2020. https://www.youtube.com/watch?v=oBrSuMKccjA.

Auslander, Shalom. *Hope: A Tragedy.* New York: Riverhead, 2012.

Bajohr, Frank, and Andrea Löw, eds. *The Holocaust and European Societies: Social Processes and Social Dynamics.* London: Palgrave Macmillan, 2016.

Barnouw, David. *The Phenomenon of Anne Frank.* Translated by Jeannette K. Ringold. Jewish Literature and Culture. Bloomington: Indiana University Press, 2018.

Ben-Amos, Batsheva, and Dan Ben-Amos, eds. *The Diary: The Epic of Everyday Life.* Bloomington: Indiana University Press, 2020.

Blair, Jon, dir. *Anne Frank Remembered.* 1995; Culver City, Calif.: Columbia TriStar Home Entertainment, 2004, DVD.

Blankfeld, Keren. *Lovers in Auschwitz: A True Story.* New York: Little, Brown, 2024.

Bloom, Harold, ed. *Anne Frank's The Diary of Anne Frank: Bloom's Modern Critical Interpretations.* New York: Bloom's Literary Criticism, 2010.

Bolle, Mirjam. *Letters Never Sent: Amsterdam, Westerbork, Bergen-Belsen.* Translated by Laura Vroomen. Jerusalem: Yad Vashem, International Institute for Holocaust Research, 2014.

Boom, Bart van der. "Een antwoord aan mijn critici." *De Groene Amsterdammer,* February 6, 2013.

Brasz, Chaya, and Yosef Kaplan, eds. *Dutch Jews as Perceived by Themselves and by Others: Proceedings of the Eighth International Symposium on the History of the Jews in the Netherlands.* Brill's Series in Jewish Studies, v. 24. Leiden: Brill, 2001.

Brauner, David. *Philip Roth.* Manchester: Manchester University Press, 2007.

Breitman, Richard, and David Engel. *The Otto Frank File.* New York: YIVO Institute for Jewish Research, 2007.

Bretz, Alice. *I Begin Again.* New York: McGraw-Hill, 1940.

Buruma, Ian. "The Afterlife of Anne Frank." *New York Review of Books,* February 19, 1998.

Cantor, Jillian. *Margot.* New York: Riverhead, 2013.

Casteel, Sarah Phillips. "Writing Under the Sign of Anne Frank." *Modern Fiction Studies* 60, no. 4 (Winter 2014): 796–820.

Chambers, Aidan. *Postcards from No Man's Land.* London: Random House Children's Books, 1999.

Cliff, Michelle. *Abeng.* New York: Plume (Penguin Group USA), 1995.

Cooper, Alan. *Philip Roth and the Jews.* Albany: State University of New York Press, 1996.

Cooper, Kim. *In the Aeroplane over the Sea.* New York: Continuum, 2005.

Coster, Theo. *We All Wore Stars: Memories of Anne Frank from Her Classmates.* Translated by Marjolijn de Jager. New York: Palgrave Macmillan, 2011.

Crandell, George W. "Re-Addressing the Past—Arthur Miller's Neglected Speech: 'Concerning Jews Who Write.'" *Studies in American Jewish Literature (1981–)* 16 (1997): 86–92.

Czech, Danuta. *Auschwitz Chronicle, 1939–1945.* New York: Henry Holt, 1990.

Diski, Jenny. "The Girl in the Attic." Review of *Diary of a Young Girl*, by Anne Frank, edited by Otto Frank and Mirjam Pressler. Translated by Susan Massotty. *London Review of Books*, March 6, 1997.

Dwork, Debórah. *Children with a Star: Jewish Youth in Nazi Europe.* New Haven: Yale University Press, 1991.

Englander, Nathan. *What We Talk About When We Talk About Anne Frank: Stories.* New York: Vintage, 2013.

Enzer, Hyman Aaron, and Sandra Solotaroff-Enzer, eds. *Anne Frank: Reflections on Her Life and Legacy.* Urbana: University of Illinois Press, 2000.

Ergas, Yasmine. "Growing Up Banished: A Reading of Anne Frank and Etty Hillesum." In *Behind the Lines*, ed. Margaret R. Higonnet, Jane Jenson, Sonya Michel, and Margaret Collins Weitz, 84–96. New Haven: Yale University Press, 1987.

Feldman, Ellen. "Anne Frank in America." *American Heritage*, February/March 2005.

———. *The Boy Who Loved Anne Frank.* New York: Norton, 2005.

Ferderber-Salz, Bertha. *And the Sun Kept Shining.* New York: Holocaust Library, 1980.

Flim, Bert Jan. *Het Grote Kinderspel.* Amsterdam: Stichting Amphora, 2020.

France, Lisa, dir. *Anne B. Real.* 2002; Rêve Entertainment Group, DVD.

Frank, Anne. *Anne Frank: The Collected Works.* London: Bloomsbury Academic, 2019.

———. *The Works of Anne Frank.* Westport, Conn.: Greenwood, 1974.

Frank, Anne, H. J. J. Hardy, David Barnouw, Gerrold van der Stroom, and Arnold Pomerans. *The Diary of Anne Frank: The Critical Edition*. New York: Doubleday, 1989.

Franklin, Sara B. *The Editor: How Publishing Legend Judith Jones Shaped Culture in America*. New York: Simon and Schuster, 2024.

Fredericks, Claude. *How to Read a Journal*. United States: Claude Fredericks Foundation, 2011.

Früher Wohnten Wir in Frankfurt—Frankfurt am Main und Anne Frank. Frankfurt am Main: Amt für Wissenschaft und Kunst der Stadt Frankfurt am Main, 1985.

Galen Last, D. van, and Rolf Wolfswinkel. *Anne Frank and After*. Amsterdam: Amsterdam University Press, 1996.

Gies, Miep. *Anne Frank Remembered: The Story of the Woman Who Helped to Hide the Frank Family*. New York: Simon & Schuster, 1987.

Gilbert, Shirli. "Anne Frank in South Africa: Remembering the Holocaust During and After Apartheid." *Holocaust and Genocide Studies* 26, no. 3 (December 23, 2012): 366–93.

Gillham, David R. *Annelies*. New York: Viking, 2019.

Gold, Alison Leslie. *Found and Lost: Mittens, Miep, and Shovelfuls of Dirt*. London: Notting Hill Editions, 2018.

Goodrich, Frances, Albert Hackett, and Anne Frank. *The Diary of Anne Frank*. New York: Random House, 1956.

Graver, Lawrence. *An Obsession with Anne Frank: Meyer Levin and The Diary*. Berkeley: University of California Press, 1995.

Green, John. *The Fault in Our Stars*. New York: Penguin, 2012.

Gross, Raphael. "Otto Frank and Anne Frank's Diary: The History of a Universal Icon." New York: Leo Baeck Institute, 2019.

Gutman, Israel, and Michael Berenbaum, eds. *Anatomy of the Auschwitz Death Camp*. Bloomington: Indiana University Press, 1994.

Hassam, Andrew. "Reading Other People's Diaries." *University of Toronto Quarterly* 6, no. 3 (spring 1987): 435–42.

Herzberg, Abel J. *Between Two Streams: A Diary from Bergen-Belsen*.

Translated by Jack Santcross. London: I.B. Tauris in association with European Jewish Publication Society, 1997.

Hillesum, Etty. *An Interrupted Life: The Diaries, 1941–1943, and Letters from Westerbork.* Translated by Arnold J. Pomerans. New York: Henry Holt, 1996.

Hondius, Dienke, and Miep Gompes-Lobatto. *Absent: Herinneringen aan het Joods Lyceum Amsterdam, 1941–1943.* Amsterdam: Vassallucci, 2001.

Iperen, Roxane van. *The Sisters of Auschwitz: The True Story of Two Jewish Sisters' Resistance in the Heart of Nazi Territory.* New York: Harper Paperbacks, 2021.

Jaldati, Lin. *Sag nie, du gehst den letzten Weg: Erinnerungen.* Berlin: Der Morgen, 1986.

Jones, Judith. *The Tenth Muse: My Life in Food.* New York: Alfred A. Knopf, 2007.

Katzir, Judith. *Dearest Anne: A Tale of Impossible Love.* Translated by Dalya Bilu. New York: Feminist Press at the City University of New York, 2008.

Kirshenblatt-Gimblett, Barbara, and Jeffrey Shandler, eds. *Anne Frank Unbound: Media, Imagination, Memory.* Bloomington: Indiana University Press, 2012.

Kohnstam, Pieter. *A Chance to Live: A Family's Journey to Freedom.* Sarasota, Fla.: Bardolf, 2006.

Konig, Nanette Blitz. *Holocaust Memoirs of a Bergen-Belsen Survivor and Classmate of Anne Frank.* Amsterdam Publishers, 2018.

Lambert, Joshua. *The Literary Mafia: Jews, Publishing, and Postwar American Literature.* New Haven: Yale University Press, 2022.

Lane, Margaret. *The Tale of Beatrix Potter: A Biography.* London: Warne, 1946.

Langer, Adam. *Cyclorama.* New York: Bloomsbury, 2022.

———. *Playing Anne Frank.* Produced by the Forward. https://forward.com/podcasts/playing-anne-frank/.

Langer, Lawrence L. *Using and Abusing the Holocaust.* Bloomington: Indiana University Press, 2006.

Langford, Rachael, and Russell West, eds. *Marginal Voices, Marginal*

Forms: Diaries in European Literature and History. Amsterdam: Rodopi, 1999.

Lee, Carol Ann. *Roses from the Earth: The Biography of Anne Frank*. New York: Viking, 1999.

———. *The Hidden Life of Otto Frank*. New York: Viking, 2002.

Lejeune, Philippe. *On Diary*. Translated by Katherine Durnin. Honolulu: Published for the Biographical Research Center by the University of Hawai'i Press, 2009.

Lengyel, Olga. *Five Chimneys*. London: Granada, 1981.

Lerner, Bernice. *All the Horrors of War: A Jewish Girl, a British Doctor, and the Liberation of Bergen-Belsen*. Baltimore: Johns Hopkins University Press, 2020.

Levin, Meyer. "The Child Behind the Secret Door." *New York Times*, June 15, 1952.

———. *The Obsession*. New York: Simon and Schuster, 1973.

———. *In Search: An Autobiography*. New York: Horizon Press, 1950.

Levin, Meyer, and Anne Frank. *Anne Frank: A Play*. New York? M. Levin, 1972.

Levy, Isaac. *Witness to Evil: Bergen-Belsen, 1945*. London: Peter Halban in association with the European Jewish Publication Society, 1995.

Lévy-Hass, Hanna. *Diary of Bergen-Belsen*. Translated by Sophie Hand. Minneapolis: Consortium Book Sales, 2009.

Lindwer, Willy. *The Last Seven Months of Anne Frank*. Translated by Alison Meersschaert. New York: Pantheon, 1991.

Lourie, Richard. *A Hatred for Tulips*. New York: Thomas Dunne, 2007.

Maarsen, Jacqueline van. *My Name Is Anne, She Said, Anne Frank: The Memoirs of Anne Frank's Best Friend*. Translated by Hester Velmans. London: Arcadia, 2007.

McLennan, Rachael. *Representations of Anne Frank in American Literature: In Different Rooms*. New York: Routledge, 2017.

Mechanicus, Philip. *Waiting for Death: A Diary*. Translated by Irene R. Gibbons. London: Calder and Boyars, 1968.

Melnick, Ralph. *The Stolen Legacy of Anne Frank: Meyer Levin, Lillian*

Hellman, and the Staging of the Diary. New Haven: Yale University Press, 1997.

Menand, Louis. *The Free World: Art and Thought in the Cold War.* New York: Farrar, Straus and Giroux, 2021.

Mendes-Flohr, Paul R. *German Jews: A Dual Identity*. New Haven: Yale University Press, 1999.

Moore, Bob. *Victims and Survivors: The Nazi Persecution of Jews in the Netherlands*. New York: Arnold, 1997.

Moskovitz, Sarah. *Love Despite Hate: Child Survivors of the Holocaust and Their Adult Lives*. New York: Schocken, 1983.

Mulisch, Harry. "Death and the Maiden." *New York Review of Books*, July 17, 1986.

Müller, Melissa. *Anne Frank: The Biography*. Translated by Rita and Robert Kimber. New York: Metropolitan, 2013.

Nussbaum, Felicity. "Toward Conceptualizing Diary." In James Olney, ed., *Studies in Autobiography*. New York: Oxford University Press, 1988.

Ofer, Dalia, and Lenore Weitzman, eds. *Women in the Holocaust*. New Haven: Yale University Press, 1998.

Orléans, Charlotte-Elisabeth, and Elborg Forster. *A Woman's Life in the Court of the Sun King: Letters of Liselotte von Der Pfalz, Elisabeth Charlotte, Duchesse d'Orléans, 1652–1722*. Baltimore: Johns Hopkins University Press, 1984.

Ozick, Cynthia. "Who Owns Anne Frank?" *New Yorker*, October 6, 1997.

Paperno, Irina. "What Can Be Done with Diaries?" *Russian Review* 63, no. 4 (2004): 561–73.

Pick-Goslar, Hannah. *My Friend Anne Frank*. New York: Little, Brown, 2023.

Pozorski, Aimee L., ed. *Roth and Celebrity*. Lanham, Md.: Lexington, 2012.

Presser, Jacob. *The Destruction of the Dutch Jews*. Translated by Arnold J. Pomerans. New York: Dutton, 1969.

Pressler, Mirjam. *Anne Frank's Family: The Extraordinary Story of Where She Came From*. Translated by Damion Searls. New York: Anchor, 2012.

Prose, Francine. *Anne Frank: The Book, the Life, the Afterlife*. New York: HarperCollins, 2009.

Reilly, Joanne, et al., ed. *Belsen in History and Memory*. London: F. Cass, 1997.

"Reminiscences of Victor Kugler—the 'Mr. Kraler' of Anne Frank's Diary, as told to Eda Shapiro." *Yad Vashem Studies* 13 (January 1, 1979): 353–85.

Renner, Nausicaa. "Confessions of a Mask." *n + 1*, December 30, 2019.

Roseman, Mark. *The Past in Hiding*. London: Allen Lane, 2000.

Rosen, Norma. *Touching Evil*. Detroit: Wayne State University Press, 1990.

Roth, Philip. *Zuckerman Bound: A Trilogy and Epilogue, 1979–1985*. New York: Library of America, 2007.

Rothstein, Edward. "Anne Frank: The Girl and the Icon." *New York Times*, February 25, 1996.

Rubin, Susan Goldman. *Searching for Anne Frank: Letters from Amsterdam to Iowa*. New York: Harry N. Abrams, 2003.

Ryang, Sonia. "Anne Frank in Japan." *Transnational Asia* 2, no. 1 (May 9, 2019). https://doi.org/10.25613/w7jm-37rx.

Samuel-Tenenholtz, Bela Ruth. "Exploring the Vault: Jewish Ethnicity and Memory in Philip Roth's 'The Ghostwriter.'" *Shaanan* 9 (2004): E7–E26.

Schjeldahl, Peter. "The Dark Revelations of Gerhard Richter." *New Yorker*, March 16, 2020.

Schloss, Eva. *After Auschwitz: A Story of Heartbreak and Survival by the Stepsister of Anne Frank*. London: Hodder & Stoughton, 2013.

Schnabel, Ernst. *The Footsteps of Anne Frank*. Translated by Richard and Clara Winston. Harpenden, Herts.: Southbank, 2014.

Shatzky, Joel. "Creating an Aesthetic for Holocaust Literature." *Studies in American Jewish Literature (1981–)* 10, no. 1 (1991): 104–14.

Shostak, Debra. *Philip Roth—Countertexts, Counterlives*. Columbia: University of South Carolina Press, 2004.

Siegal, Nina. *The Diary Keepers: World War II in the Netherlands, As*

Written by the People Who Lived Through It. New York: HarperCollins, 2023.

———. "She Discovered What Happened to 400 Dutch Jews Who Disappeared." *New York Times*, March 16, 2022.

Silverman, Al. *The Time of Their Lives: The Golden Age of Great American Book Publishers, Their Editors, and Authors.* New York: Open Road Integrated Media, 2016.

Soeting, Monica. "Dear Diary, Dear Comrade: The Diaries of Setske de Haan, Joop Ter Heul and Anne Frank." *European Journal of Life Writing* 7 (August 1, 2018): CP183–99.

———. "De deemoed voorbij: Cissy van Marxveldt en haar rebellenclub." *De Paralelduiker* 13 (2008): 23–37.

———. *Cissy van Marxveldt: Een biografie.* Rijksuniversiteit Groningen, 2017.

———. *Lief Dagboek, beste kameraad: Cissy van Marxveldt in England.* Bloemendaal: Schaep14, 2017.

Sontag, Susan. *Reborn: Journals and Notebooks, 1947–1963.* New York: Farrar, Straus and Giroux, 2008.

Steedman, Carolyn. *The Tidy House: Little Girls Writing.* London: Virago, 1982.

Steenmeijer, Anna G., Otto Frank, and H. van Praag. *A Tribute to Anne Frank.* Garden City, N.Y.: Doubleday, 1971.

Strasberg, Susan. *Bittersweet.* New York: Putnam, 1980.

Stroom, Gerrold van der. "The Diaries, *Het Achterhuis*, and the Translations." In *The Diary of Anne Frank: The Critical Edition.* New York: Doubleday, 1989.

Sullivan, Rosemary. *The Betrayal of Anne Frank: A Cold Case Investigation.* New York: Harper, 2022.

Tatar, Maria. *The Heroine with 1,001 Faces.* New York: Liveright, 2021.

Tedeschi Brunelli, Giuliana. *There Is a Place on Earth: A Woman in Birkenau.* Translated by Tim Parks. New York: Pantheon, 1992.

Tolan, Stephanie S. *The Liberation of Tansy Warner.* New York: Scribner, 1980.

Westra, Hans, and Anne Frank House, eds. *Inside Anne Frank's*

House: An Illustrated Journey Through Anne's World. Woodstock: Overlook Duckworth, 2004.

Wijk-Voskuijl, Joop van, and Jeroen de Bruyn. *The Last Secret of the Secret Annex: The Untold Story of Anne Frank, Her Silent Protector, and a Family Betrayal.* New York: Simon and Schuster, 2023.

Wolf, Diane L. *Beyond Anne Frank: Hidden Children and Postwar Families in Holland.* Electronic resource. Berkeley: University of California Press, 2007.

ACKNOWLEDGMENTS

EARLY ON IN THIS PROJECT, a historian told me bluntly that the area of Anne Frank studies is a "crowded field." First and foremost, I want to acknowledge my debt to all those who have written about Anne Frank and her world, especially Carol Ann Lee, Melissa Müller, and Francine Prose, authors of three previous biographies. I drew on the work of many other scholars, from experts on the Holocaust in the Netherlands to brilliant critics of literature and art inspired by Anne. To all of them, I express my deep appreciation for their work.

Ron Leopold and Gertjan Broek welcomed me to the Anne Frank House in Amsterdam and facilitated my research there. At the Anne Frank Fonds in Basel, Barbara Eldridge generously granted me access to and permission to quote from Otto Frank's papers. As always, archivists are a biographer's heroes: the staff at YIVO, Columbia University's Rare Books Library, the Wisconsin Historical Society, and the Simon Wiesenthal Center were especially helpful.

I was honored with a residency at the Maison Dora Maar in summer 2022, a time of great productivity. Thank you to Gwen Strauss and her wonderful staff for the haven they have created.

Tobias Mud, a talented artist who proved to be an indispensable researcher, was on board for "the strangest book ever written about Anne Frank," as I described it to him. Tobias scoured Dutch archives and other resources in his patient, creative, and speedy efforts to answer all my questions, from the menu at Dikker & Thys to the routes of Amsterdam tramlines.

The members of my biography writing group—Patricia Auspos, Betty Boyd Caroli, Barbara Fisher, Dorothy O. Helly, and Melissa Nathanson—read and commented on every page of my manuscript, as did Rebecca Donner, a brilliant biographer and generous friend. Arnon Grunberg, my dear friend of many years, and Josh Lambert also offered very helpful comments on individual chapters. Throughout the research and writing, numerous friends shared thoughts and ideas about Anne Frank; thanks especially to Sana Krasikov and Martha Hodes for their insights. I'm grateful also to my newsletter readers, who often shared their own perspectives on Anne. My friends in the Bunker, your advice is without peer.

I gave preliminary talks about this book at the Women Writing Women's Lives seminar, Stanford University, American University, and Fordham University. Thank you to the organizers as well as to the audiences who showed up and asked challenging questions. I've been an active participant in Biographers International Organization and have benefitted enormously from the camaraderie and collegiality at their annual conference. The New York Institute for the Humanities remains my favorite place to have lunch in Manhattan.

I'm grateful to Steve Zipperstein, Ileene Smith, and Anita Shapira at Yale Jewish Lives for their faith that I could write this book, and to Steve especially for his encouragement throughout the process and his thoughtful edits. Heather Gold and Elizabeth Sylvia deserve special mention for their care and dedication during production.

As my agent, Sarah Burnes has been my tireless champion and

cheerleader for twenty years. I don't know where I would be without her business acumen and wise counsel.

Finally, thank you to my family, who gamely switched gears to Anne Frank after enduring my years of obsession with Shirley Jackson. Sam and Ren listened to my ideas and offered their invaluable perspectives. Ariel will soon be old enough to read the *Diary;* sometimes, while writing about Anne, I saw her face. Since we met, my husband, Joseph Braude, has been my partner in everything, including this book.

INDEX

Abeng (Cliff), 320
Abu Akleh, Shireen, 334–35
African National Congress, 327, 328
Ahlers, Tonny, 159
Alfred (Hannah Goslar's boyfriend), 74
Alfred A. Knopf publishing company, 241, 242
Amstel, Greet van, 217–18
Amsterdam Jewish Council, 47, 48, 53–54, 60, 160, 166
Andersen, Hans Christian, 88
Anderson, Maxwell, 255, 256
Anne B. Real (film), 321
Annelies (Gillham), 312–15, 316, 320
Arnon, Yakov, 64
Aronson, Boris, 274, 287
Aronson, Lisa Jalowetz, 287
Aryanization, 30, 50
Asscher, Abraham, 47, 55, 66, 73
Atkinson, Brooks, 273
Auschwitz, 10, 25, 52, 94, 113–14, 165; evacuation and liberation of, 80, 194–95, 197; operations at, 179–80; origins of, 54; public executions at, 189–90; structure of, 71–72, 183; women in, 180–88
Auslander, Shalom, 11, 309–12, 314, 315, 316, 320

Bailey (Jones), Judith, 237, 245, 263
Baschwitz, Kurt, 231, 233
Bashkirtseff, Marie, 233, 234–35
Basquiat, Jean-Michel, 296
Baum, Marie, 236
Bayens, Thijs, 159–60
Beadle, John, 149
Beek, Leon, 207–8
Bellow, Saul, 241
Bełżec, 54, 167
Bergen-Belsen, 7, 10, 25, 165, 171, 187–88, 192–203, 208–9
Bergh, Arnold van den, 160
Besch, Joseph, 290
The Betrayal of Anne Frank (Sullivan), 160

Beyenc, Yikealo, 238–40
Beymer, Richard, 291, 292
Biegel, Miss (biology teacher), 65, 69
Bilheimer, Chris, 201
Biltmore Declaration, 391n15
Birstein, Ann, 232–33
Black, Douglas McRae, 246
Blankfeld, Keren, 372n69
Blitz, Nanette, 67, 203, 208–9, 210; Anne recalled by, 36; in Bergen-Belsen, 196, 198, 200, 201, 214; in Westerbork, 168, 170
Bloch, Alfred, 35
Bloemendal, Betty, 94
Bloomgarden, Kermit, 258–59, 265–67, 274–76, 278, 282, 288, 290
"Blurry the Explorer" (Anne Frank), 130, 199
Boethius, 5–6
Bolkestein, Gerrit, 131–32, 134, 135, 201, 230, 283, 338
Bondy, Ruth, 188, 200
Bonger, Willem Adriaan, 45
Boni & Liveright publishing company, 241
Boogaard, Johannes, 81
Boom, Bart van der, 54–55
"The Book of Ruth" (film), 319, 321–22
"Book of Tales" (Anne Frank), 23, 226
Borowski, Tadeusz, 179, 180
Boswell, James, 149
Brady, Hana, 332
Brando, Marlon, 287
Braun, Eva, 224
Brauner, David, 391n10
Brenner, Rachel Feldhay, 362n8
Bretz, Alice, 126, 138, 284
Brilleslijper, Lien, 195, 197, 218; Anne recalled by, 198; Edith Frank recalled by, 175; in Westerbork and Bergen-Belsen, 25, 173, 179, 198, 202, 203
Brilleslijper, Marianne (Janny), 174, 175, 178, 187, 218; in Auschwitz, 179, 183, 184, 185; in Bergen-Belsen, 25, 195–99, 202, 203, 208; Edith Frank recalled by, 175
Brodie, Israel, 194
Brommer, Frieda, 178, 189
Browning, Elizabeth Barrett, 154
Buchenwald, 51, 203, 254
Bunkers, Suzanne L., 363n14
Burney, Fanny, 154
Buruma, Ian, 13

Cady's Life (Anne Frank), 144
Cahn, Werner, 233, 234, 236
Campbell, Joseph, 13
Camino Real (Williams), 264
Canada, 169
Caplan, Nigel, 147, 153, 154, 362n8, 363–64n20, 379–80n87
Carver, Raymond, 9
Cather, Willa, 242
Cauvern, Albert ("Ab"), 225–27
Cauvern, Isa, 225
Chambers, Aidan, 316
Chandler, Raymond, 242
Chekhov, Anton, 303
Chełmno, 54
Child, Julia, 237
The Children's Hour (Hellman), 258
Clark, Taylor, 270, 271
Cleef, Ronnie van, 175, 178, 179, 184–85, 187, 190
Cliff, Michelle, 293, 320
Clurman, Harold, 259
Cohen, David, 47–48, 55, 64, 66, 67–68, 73
Cohn, Vera, 174
Cole, Bill, 242
Columbus, Christopher, 296
"comfort women," 332–33
The Consolation of Philosophy (Boethius), 5–6
Contact publishing company, 226–27, 234
Cooper, Kim, 269, 272
Coster, Theo, 38, 51, 62, 209–10, 215, 397n38
Crawford, Cheryl, 257, 258–59, 261–65, 277, 282

Creizenach, Theodor, 29
The Crucible (Miller), 258
Cuba, 59, 60, 169
Cyclorama (Langer), 300

Dachau, 30, 167, 285, 289, 293
Daniel-Rops, Henri, 237
Danka (Anne's classmate), 67
Dante Alighieri, 69
Darwin, Charles, 341
Dearest Anne (Katzir), 320–21
Death of a Salesman (Miller), 258
Delacroix, Eugène, 233
The Destruction of the Dutch Jews (Presser), 52–53
Dettmann, Joseph, 157, 158, 161
Deutsche Bahn, 4
"The Diaries, *Het Achterhuis*, and the Translations" (van der Stroom), 118–19
The Diary of Anne Frank—LatinX (play), 323–24
The Diary Keepers (Siegal), 101
Dickens, Charles, 86
Dimbleby, Richard, 192–93, 194
Diski, Jenny, 6
Dominican Republic, 57
Do the Right Thing (film), 296
Doron, Diana, 288
Doubleday, Nelson, II, 245–46
Doubleday publishing company, 237, 242, 245–48, 251–56, 261
Douglass, Frederick, 296, 298
Drachman, Chen, 318–19, 321–22
Dreyfus, Alfred, 31
Dwork, Debórah, 81
dysentery, 180, 198

Ehrlich, Max, 169
Eichmann, Adolf, 46, 71, 72
Eisenhower, Dwight D., 248, 249
Elias, Buddy, 22
Elias, Erich, 30, 56
Elias, Ida, 214
Elias, Paul, 214
Eliot, T. S., 242
Elizabeth II, queen of Great Britain, 76
Emden, Bloeme, 173, 179, 185–86, 190
Englander, Nathan, 8, 9
Enzer, Hyman A., 5
Epstein, Barbara (Zimmerman), 246–49, 252, 254–67, 273
Epstein, Jason, 273
Ergas, Yasmine, 285, 362n2, 363–64n20
Eritrea, 238–39
Es, Bart van, 354–55n19
Esquire, 243
Ethiopia, 238–39
"Eva's Dream" (Anne Frank), 103–4, 131, 199
Eva's Youth (van Suchtelen), 88

"The Fairy" (Anne Frank), 130
Farago, Ladislas, 337
Farben, IG, company, 72, 180
Farrar, Straus publishing company, 241
Fault in Our Stars (Green), 300
"Fear" (Anne Frank), 104
Feldschuh, Tovah, 319
Ferber, Edna, 245
Ferderber-Salz, Bertha, 182, 186, 187–88
Fiedler, Leslie, 392n25
Fischer Verlag, 225, 234
Flanner, Janet, 244
Flaubert, Gustave, 303
"The Flower Girl" (Anne Frank), 104
Folman, Ari, 339–40, 341
The Forsyte Saga (Galsworthy), 87–88
France, Lisa, 321
Frank, Alice Stern (paternal grandmother), 20, 21, 27, 30, 265
Frank, Anne (Annelies Marie): in the Annex, 79–86, 93–94, 102–3, 222; attraction to girls imputed to, 116, 119; in Auschwitz, 188–89; in Bergen-Belsen, 195, 198–203; as blank slate, 5–9; bookishness of, 86; boyfriends of, 35, 69–70, 108–9, 111–12, 117–18, 120–28; cats fancied by, 33, 39; death of, 7–8, 203, 218, 226, 318; de-Judaization of, 5–6; Dutch citizenship desired by, 132; eating

Frank, Anne (*continued*)
habits of, 85; father idealized by, 23–24, 223, 277; father's business viewed by, 49; as feminist, 338; in fiction, 300–317; fictional writings of, 23, 103–4, 129–30, 144; friends of, 34–36, 37; future plans of, 97–98, 199; as icon, 2–4, 330–42; ill health of, 21–22, 101; independence from mother asserted by, 152–53; irony employed by, 145; at Jewish Lyceum, 63–65, 103, 107, 133; Margot contrasted with, 23–25, 123; misconceptions of, 11, 15; mother's depressive behavior noted by, 84; mythological parallels with, 13–15; parents' marriage criticized by, 26–27, 280; perceptiveness of, 92; personal improvement stressed by, 149; physical appearance of, 99–100, 101; politics slighted by, 337–38; prayer resisted by, 85; as reader, 87–91, 99; resilience of, 95, 96; sexual maturation of, 110; short temper of, 106; spirituality of, 110, 126, 155–56, 176, 177, 220, 284–85; talkativeness of, 65–66; Peter van Pels and, 108–9, 111–12, 117–18, 120–28, 153–54, 175–76; wartime viewed by, 155, 173–74
—diary: Anne's writing of, 88–89, 90–92, 107; as best-selling book, 2, 116, 250–52, 265, 317; changing authorial voice in, 135–47, 149–53; editing and rewriting by Anne, 118, 136–38, 154–55; epistolary form adopted for, 88–91, 106; original documents found by Miep and Bep, 12, 163, 221, 226; Otto's editing of, 112, 113, 117–18, 119, 224–33, 346n27; pseudonyms used in, 2, 3, 12, 232; Version A and Version B, 11–13, 114, 118, 133, 134, 136–37, 139–42, 144–47, 149–50, 151, 152–54, 226, 346n27, 358n102, 359n7; Version C (first published version, *Het Achterhuis: Dagboekbrieven, 1942–1944*), 12, 13, 26, 147, 231, 234–35, 346n27; Version D ("the Definitive Edition"), 13, 116, 274; version published in English (*Anne Frank: The Diary of a Young Girl*), 12, 117, 231, 242, 247–48, 251–52; version published as the Critical Edition (*The Diary of Anne Frank: The Critical Edition*), 11, 26, 89, 113, 118, 143, 144, 343n1
—diary, later adaptations of: for Broadway theater (as *The Diary of Anne Frank*), 251, 253–67, 273–75, 286–87, 298, 299; movie version of, 289–94

Frank, Edith (Holländer; mother), 21, 22, 30, 50, 56, 59, 144; Anne reproved by, 26; in the Annex, 79, 161; in Auschwitz, 25, 181, 188–89, 195; daughters' intimacy with, 28–29; death of, 62, 213; depressive behavior of, 84–85, 151; *Diary*'s criticism of, 228–29; emigration to Netherlands of, 31; favoritism of, 23; future plans of, 97; Germany recalled by, 39; marriage of, 27–28; protectiveness of, 151–52; prudishness of, 110; in stage version of the *Diary*, 279; in Westerbork, 175

Frank, Elfriede Geiringer ("Fritzi"; second wife of Otto Frank), 115, 176, 209, 220, 223, 246, 316–17

Frank, Helene (Leni; aunt), 21, 27, 30, 80, 214

Frank, Herbert (uncle), 21, 30

Frank, Margot Betti (sister), 19, 21, 26, 30, 48, 60, 69, 99, 144, 204; Anne contrasted with, 23–25; Anne's

sexuality viewed by, 124–25; in the Annex, 79, 103, 161; in Auschwitz, 181, 188–89; in Bergen-Belsen, 195, 200, 201, 203; death of, 218, 318; deportation summons for, 70–71, 140–41; Germany recalled by, 39; industriousness of, 22, 23, 37, 86; at Jewish Lyceum, 63–64
Frank, Michael (paternal grandfather), 20, 21, 27
Frank, Otto ("Pim"; father), 2–3, 21, 30, 34–35, 43, 143–44, 204, 282; amiability of, 24, 151; Anne's fairy tales viewed by, 130; Anne's sexuality viewed by, 123–24; in the Annex, 79, 161; and anti-apartheid movement, 326–27; in Auschwitz, 113–14; as businessman, 49, 50, 77; defamation suit filed by, 225; *Diary* edited by, 7, 10, 12, 26, 112, 113, 114, 117–19, 147, 152, 153–54, 224, 226–31, 233, 236, 317; in *Diary*'s film version, 291, 292; *Diary*'s publication secured by, 207–8, 220–21, 232, 233–34, 244–49, 252; *Diary*'s stage adaptation and, 253, 255–57, 260–67, 276, 279–80, 286, 299–300, 325; early years of, 20; emigration from Germany to Netherlands, 31; emigration from Netherlands to United States sought by, 55, 56, 59–62; English spoken by, 59; foundation planned by, 325–26; Levin's harassment of, 264; after liberation, 209, 212–13, 215–20; marriages of, 27–28, 115; military service of, 27, 162; one-man show about, 295–98; postwar finances of, 251, 264–65; punctiliousness of, 152; as storyteller, 22–23; as tutor, 86; in Westerbork, 173–74, 175; and Zionism, 31, 337
Frank, Robert (uncle), 21, 30
Frankenstein (Shelley), 14
Frankl, Victor, 191
Frankfoorder, Rachel, 174–75, 178, 189, 195, 202, 203
Fredericks, Claude, 148
Frijda, Jetteke, 219
Fünten, Ferdinand aus der, 66, 165

Galiński, Edek, 190
Gannett, Lewis, 252–53
Garbo, Greta, 76
Galsworthy, John, 87–88
Geiringer (Frank), Elfriede ("Fritzi"), 115, 176, 209, 220, 223, 246, 316–17
Geiringer (Schloss), Eva, 115, 257, 316, 329; after liberation, 209; Otto Frank recalled by, 212, 214, 221, 279–80; Westerbork viewed by, 176
Geiringer, Heinz, 75, 115
Geismar, Daphne, 354–55n19
Gemmeker, Albert, 167, 169–70, 208
Gentleman's Agreement (film), 241–42
German National People's Party, 29
German People's Party, 29
The Ghost Writer (Roth), 11, 300, 301–9, 313–16, 317, 320
Gibbs, Wolcott, 285–86
Gies, Jan, 12, 50, 212, 216, 217; Anne's independence viewed by, 25; Annex raid and, 162, 163; Annex visited by, 78, 82, 83, 122; Jews hidden by, 100; in Resistance, 93
Gies, Miep, 39, 77, 94, 101, 108, 121, 156, 204, 217, 263; Anne and Margot viewed by, 23, 24–25, 36; Anne's intensity recalled by, 150; Anne's papers discovered by, 12; Annex raid and, 161–64; Annex visited by, 78–79, 82–84, 86–87, 92, 93, 95–96, 99, 100, 157; as diarist, 148; *Diary*'s publication viewed by, 231–32, 235; Edith's pessimism recalled by, 85; frugality of, 37; "Hunger Winter" recalled by, 211; after liberation, 211–12, 214, 218–19, 221; River

Gies, Miep (*continued*)
District recalled by, 32; in stage version of *Diary*, 280
Gilbert, Shirli, 326, 329
Gilford, Jack, 388n28
Gillham, David R., 11, 312–15, 316, 320
Giraudoux, Jean, 286
Go Ask Alice (Beatrice Sparks), 300
Goebbels, Joseph, 290
Goethe, Johann Wolfgang von, 6, 51, 86
Gold, Alison Leslie, 24–25
Goldenberg, Myrna, 181
Gomes de Mesquita, Albert, 65, 81, 210, 211
Good, Kip, 288
Goodrich, Frances, 95, 228, 266–67, 273–84, 306, 314
Göring, Hermann, 45, 92
Goslar, Gabi, 34–35, 203, 209, 219
Goslar, Hannah, 34, 38, 74, 79–80, 107, 196, 204, 210, 219; Anne recalled by, 35, 148; in Bergen-Belsen, 201–3, 209; deportation of, 102; during German invasion, 41–42; at Jewish Lyceum, 64, 65, 68, 69, 103; Margot recalled by, 22, 23; as Zionist, 336
Goslar, Hans, 34, 37
Goslar, Ruth, 34, 37, 79, 85, 123
Goudsmit, Mr. (subletter), 79, 91
Goudstikker, Jacques, 45
Graver, Lawrence, 244, 245, 253, 282, 283, 284
The Greatest Story Ever Told (film), 289
Green, John, 300
Grese, Irma, 186, 198
Griffis, Kevin, 271, 272
Grimm, Brothers, 88
Grove Press, 241
Guberman, Lena, 340

Haan, Setske de (Cissy van Marxveldt), 36, 90, 144, 207–8, 356n49, 376n1
Hackett, Albert, 95, 228, 266–67, 273–84, 306, 314
Hadassah, 337
Hahn, Pauline, 289
Harsányi, Zsolt, 156
Hartog, Lena, 159
Harvard Lampoon, 308
Hass, Amira, 337
Hass, Hanna (Lévy-), 197, 198, 337, 374n8
Hassel, Elisabeth, 168
A Hatred for Tulips (Lourie), 300, 314, 316
Heer, Leonora de, 290–91
Hellman, Lillian, 258, 274, 275, 281–82
Hemelrijk, Jaap (Jakob), 67
Hemingway, Ernest, 243
Hendrix, Jimi, 296
Hepburn, Audrey, 290
The Heroine with 1,001 Faces (Tatar), 13–14
Hersey, John, 244
Herzberg, Abel, 46, 48, 166–67, 197
Herzl, Theodor, 31, 35
Hesse, Hermann, 236
Hiatt, Jack, 58
The High School Times of Joop ter Heul (van Marxfeldt), 90
Hillesum, Etty, 45, 167, 170, 172, 176–77, 362n2
Himmler, Heinrich, 72, 196
Hitler, Adolf, 7, 29, 30, 51
Holländer (Frank), Edith. *See* Frank, Edith (Holländer; mother)
Holländer, Julius (uncle), 56, 58, 60–61, 216, 220
Holländer, Rosa (maternal grandmother), 37, 56, 59
Holländer, Walter (uncle), 56, 58, 216, 220
Holocaust (television series), 309
Hope (Auslander), 309–12, 314, 315, 316, 320
Höss, Rudolf, 183
Houte, Hans van, 326

Howe, Irving, 242
Huber, Gusti, 290, 292
Hudson, Henry, 74
Huf, Jules, 158, 159
Hughes, Hugh Llewellyn Glyn, 193

I Begin Again (Bretz), 126, 138
An Ideal Husband (Wilde), 4, 127–28
Ingall, Marjorie, 329
In Search (Levin), 245
In the Aeroplane Over the Sea (Neutral Milk Hotel), 269–72
Ishioda, Fumiko, 332
Israel, 7, 216, 239–40, 330, 333–35, 338–39. *See also* Palestine
It's a Wonderful Life (film), 266

Jacobi, Lou, 292
Jacobs, W. W., 394n53
James, Henry, 303
Japan, 330–33
Jewish Theological Seminary (JTS), 283
Jewish Weekly, 47, 53, 66, 194
Jews: Anne's diary on persecution of, 13, 44, 67, 92, 94–95, 133, 136, 137, 138, 141–43, 236, 244, 273, 275–76, 302, 307–8, 336; Frank family as, 21, 27, 31, 162, 250, 305–6; in Frankfurt, 29; in hiding, 53, 80–83, 105–6, 157, 158, 159, 211–12; Nazi deportation of, 40, 47–48, 54, 71, 72–73, 80, 162, 165–66, 171–72, 196; Nazi persecution of, 50–51, 66–67, 101–2; Nazi regulations and, 38, 44, 48–49, 50, 62, 66, 210, 216; Nazi slaughter of, 51, 52, 67, 72, 158, 180, 212; in Netherlands, 31, 37, 38, 39, 45–47, 48, 52, 53–54, 62–63, 105–6, 131–32; post-Holocaust, 8–9, 215, 216, 217–18; refugees from Germany, 45, 56–57; in United States, 27, 241–43, 248, 250, 289, 301, 303, 305, 306–7, 336; Zionism and, 31, 336
Jones, Judith (Bailey), 237, 245, 263
Joop ter Heul series (van Marxveldt), 90–91, 97, 120, 144
Judaism: Anne and, 284–85

Kafka, Franz, 392n28
Kagan, Steven E., 367n81
Kaletta, Charlotte, 93, 228, 280
Kanin, Garson, 273–76, 278–79, 282, 285, 288, 306, 340
Kathrada, Ahmed Mohamad, 327, 328, 329
Katzir, Judith, 320–21
Kazin, Alfred, 232–33
Keesing, Aaron, 65–66, 69, 103, 137
Kesselman, Wendy, 274–75, 324
Kindertransport, 45
King, Martin Luther, Jr., 289
King, Rodney, 297
King, Stephen, 394n53
Kleiman, Johannes, 3, 82, 90, 103, 159, 163, 173, 229, 283; Anne's view of, 87; Annex envisioned by, 77; Annex raid and, 158, 161, 162; ill health of, 106, 121, 139; after liberation, 217, 264–65
Klein, Cecilie, 188
Klein, Mina, 188
Knopf, Alfred A., publishing company, 241, 242
Kobayashi, Erika, 333
Kogon, Eugen, 236
Komen, Cornelis, 101–2
Kormann, Max, 169
Koster, Julian, 269
Kramer, Josef, 182, 198, 208
Krishnamurthu, Jiddu, 272
Kristin Lavransdatter (Undset), 156
Kristof, Nicholas, 7, 341
Kugler, Victor, 3, 50, 122, 216, 283; Annex raid and, 158, 161, 163, 173; Annex visited by, 77, 82, 87; after liberation, 264; Nazis escaped by, 217
Kupers, Toosje, 71
Kuperus, Hendrika, 63, 148

Lambert, Josh, 242
Landmann, Ludwig, 30
Langer, Adam, 288, 300
Langer, Lawrence L., 308, 329, 373n98
Laqueur, Renata, 218
Ledermann, Barbara, 37–38, 42, 45–46, 102
Ledermann, Susanne ("Sanne"), 37–38, 41, 46, 66
Lee, Carol Ann, 159
Lee, Spike, 296
Lejeune, Philippe, 113, 134, 230, 231, 359n7, 363n14
Lengyel, Olga, 182, 184, 186, 187
Levi, Primo, 179, 180
Levie, Mirjam, 73, 196
Levin, Meyer, 253, 275, 277–78, 290, 325; boorishness of, 5, 244–45, 254–60, 262–65, 286; *Diary* reviewed by, 249–50, 251, 252, 254, 305, 364–65n36; *Diary* stage adaptation by, 253–60, 263, 283–85; entrepreneurism of, 248–49; Hellman criticized by, 281–82; Jewish themes stressed by, 245, 251, 260–63, 284–85; women slighted by, 263; as writer and journalist, 243
Levine, Harry, 58
Levy, Isaac, 193, 194
Lévy(-Hass), Hanna, 197, 198, 337, 374n8
The Liberation of Tansy Warner (Tolan), 300
Linnaeus, Carl, 87
Lippmann, Rosenthal & Co. (bank), 50, 216
Lipstadt, Deborah, 335
Liselotte von der Pfalz (Elizabeth Charlotte, Duchess of Orléans), 145
Liszt, Franz, 87
Little, Brown publishing company, 245
Loewy, Hanno, 301
Louis XIV, king of France, 145
Lourie, Richard, 300, 314
Luft, Herbert G., 290
Maaren, Willem van, 158–59, 228
Maarsen, Jacqueline van, 40, 51–52, 62–63, 69, 77, 80, 212, 299; Anne's friendship with, 35–36, 88–89, 110–11, 119–20, 133, 151, 204; antisemitism encountered by, 217; deportation avoided by, 210; *Diary*'s publication viewed by, 235; "Hunger Winter" recalled by, 211; religious background of, 38
Malamud, Bernard, 303
Malcolm X, 11, 341
Mandela, Nelson, 327, 328–29
Mandl, Maria, 182, 186, 190
Mangum, Jeffery Nye, 268–72
Mann, Thomas, 224, 248
Man's Search for Meaning (Frankl), 191
Maria Theresa, empress of Austria, 87
Marks, Joseph, 246, 254, 255–56, 262, 264, 265, 273, 337
Marks, Lillian, 273
Marley, Bob, 296
Marxveldt, Cissy van (Setske de Haan), 36, 90, 144, 207–8, 356n49, 376n1
Matthews, Birdie, 41, 42
Mauthausen, 51, 52, 55, 72, 73
Mayerson, Augusta, 58, 60, 61
Mead, Margaret, 341
Mendes-Flohr, Paul, 345n7
Mbeki, Denis, 327, 328
McCormick, Ken, 254, 255, 256, 382n26
McCullers, Carson, 130, 261–63, 264
McMahon, Brad, 249
Mechanicus, Philip, 166–72, 176, 177
Meijer, Jaap, 63–64
Melnick, Ralph, 253, 275, 282, 283
The Member of the Wedding (McCullers), 261
Menand, Louis, 241
Mencken, H. L., 242
"Men Explain Anne Frank to Me" (Zax), 319–20

Mengele, Josef, 180
Mermin, Mildred, 273
Mermin, Myer (Mike), 259, 261, 262, 264, 266, 267, 273, 278
Messersmith, George, 57
Metamorphoses (Ovid), 14
Michelangelo Buonarroti, 285
Michelet, Jules, 233
Miller, Arthur, 255, 256, 258, 306
Mitgang, Herbert, 118
Młynarska, Nela, 286–87
Monroe, Marilyn, 287
Montessori, Maria, 33
Mooyaart-Doubleday, Barbara, 10, 119
Moritz (great-uncle), 21
Mulisch, Harry, 13
Müller, Melissa, 26, 159
mythology, 340; Anne compared to figures in, 13–15; Anne's interest in, 99, 147; of the *Diary*, 231, 235, 325

Naarden, Lenie van, 175, 181, 185–87, 189, 191
Nates, Tali, 329
National Refugee Service, 58–59, 61
"Nazism = Apartheid" (exhibition), 326–27, 329
Netanyahu, Benjamin, 240, 334
Neutral Milk Hotel (band), 269–72
Newton, Huey, 296
New York Post, 252, 253, 254
New York Review of Books, 246
New York Times Book Review, 249
Nin, Anaïs, 150

The Obsession (Levin), 281
Odets, Clifford, 255, 256
onderduikers (Jews in hiding), 81
Opekta (pectin company), 30, 31, 49, 77, 228, 264
Otto Frank (play), 295–98
Otsuka, Makoto, 331–32
Ovid, 14
Ozick, Cynthia, 7, 274–75, 284, 313, 329, 341, 373n98

Paape, Harry, 160
Palestine, 171, 196, 333–34, 335–36. *See also* Israel
Palestine at the Crossroads (Farago), 337
Palombo, aleXsandro, 334
Pantheon publishing company, 241
Paperno, Irina, 149
Paradiso (Dante), 69
Peck, Gregory, 241–42
Pectacon (spice company), 39, 49
Pels, Auguste van, 95, 97, 122, 123, 125, 143, 152, 213, 219; Anne's changing views of, 126, 227; Anne's writing viewed by, 104; Annex raid and, 161; in Auschwitz, 181, 195; in Bergen-Belsen, 198, 203; flirtatiousness of, 85, 86, 222–23, 277; volatility of, 85
Pels, Hermann van, 77, 82, 137, 227, 279, 314; in the Annex, 85, 97, 143, 222; death of, 113–14, 213; in spice business, 39, 49
Pels, Peter van, 98, 118, 149, 151, 204, 213; as Anne's boyfriend, 10, 111–15, 120–28, 175–76, 244; Anne's initial feelings toward, 86, 108; in the Annex, 79, 109–10, 143; in Auschwitz, 113–14; death of, 219
Pepys, Samuel, 149
Perkins, Millie, 291, 292–93
Pfeffer, Fritz, 2, 82, 95, 96, 112, 204; Anne's view of, 93–94, 102–3, 145, 227–28, 277, 280; in the Annex, 79, 92; argumentativeness of, 106, 110; death of, 219; fiancée of, 93, 97, 160; meddlesomeness of, 123; in stage version of the *Diary*, 280
Philomela, Greek myth of, 14
Pippin, Jennifer, 117
A Place in the Sun (film), 289
Plato, 283
Polonsky, David, 340
Pomosin-Werke, 50
Postcards to No Man's Land (Chambers), 316

Praag, Henri van, 325
Praag-Sigaar, Nanette van, 94
Press, Steve, 288, 289
Presser, Jacob: deportation of, 73; *The Destruction of the Dutch Jews*, 52–53, 55; Holocaust chronicled by, 40, 46, 52, 75, 83; on Nazis' ineptitude, 53; as teacher, 65, 67–69, 73–74
Pressler, Mirjam, 13, 89–90
Price, Francis K. (Frank), 237, 245, 246, 256–57, 258
Prose, Francine, 109, 125, 138, 275

Random House publishing company, 241
Renner, Nausicaa, 366n56
Rich, Frank, 284, 285
Richter, Gerhard, 4
Riddle, Joe L., 293
Rimbaud, Arthur, 14
Ringelheim, Joan, 181–82, 354–55n19, 373n98
Rivonia Trial (South Africa), 327–28
Rogers, Ginger, 76, 279
Rogers, Edith, 57
Romein, Jan, 232, 234
Romein-Verschoor, Annie, 231, 234–35
Roosevelt, Eleanor, 248, 275, 276
Roosevelt, Franklin D., 55, 57
Rosen, Norma, 300
Rosen, Willy, 169
Rosenfeld, Alvin, 7–8
Roth, Philip, 11, 300, 301–9, 314, 315, 316, 320
Rowling, J. K., 340
Rubinstein, Arthur, 286
Rubinstein, Eva, 286
Ryang, Sonia, 330, 332

Sachs, Bernard, 55
Saint Joan (Shaw), 275
Sand, George, 233
Sarstadt, Marianne, 291
Sasaki, Sadako, 330
Schiff, Peter, 39, 107, 123, 153
Schildkraut, Joseph, 274, 277, 287–89
Schiller, Friedrich, 19, 86
Schloss, Eva (Geiringer). *See* Geiringer (Schloss), Eva
Schneider, Robert, 268, 269
Schnurbein, Katharina von, 335
Schocken publishing company, 242
Schuitema, Berend, 326–27
Schütz, Anneliese, 235–36
Schumann, Robert, 68
Seyss-Inquart, Arthur, 48
Shandler, Jeffrey, 393n32
Shatzkin, Leonard, 242
Shaw, George Bernard, 275
Shelley, Mary, 14
Shostak, Debra, 392n27
Shumlin, Herman, 259
Siegal, Nina, 101
Silberbauer, Karl, 156–59, 161, 162
Silberberg, Helmuth ("Hello"), 69–70, 79, 108, 136–40, 204, 235, 336
Sinjen, Sabine, 291
Simon & Schuster publishing company, 241
Smith, Roger Guenveur, 296–98
Sobibór, 52, 54, 69, 80, 165, 167, 170
Solotaroff-Enzer, Sandra, 5
Sonnemann, Leopold, 29
Sontag, Susan, 150
Spanjaard, Ima, 218
Spillane, Scott, 270–71
Spitzer, Zippi, 372n69
Stanfield, Milly (cousin), 20, 56, 220, 229
The Star-Gazer (Harsányi), 156
Stavisky, Lotte, 290
Stevens, George, 289, 290, 292–93
Stevens, George, Jr., 289, 290–91
Stielau, Lothar, 224–25
Stilgenbauer, Kathi, 22, 39
Strasberg, Lee, 287
Strasberg, Susan, 274, 287–88, 290, 292
Straus, Helen, 55, 58, 61, 273
Straus, Nathan, Jr., 56, 214, 217, 263, 273; *Diary*'s merit questioned by, 234; family background of, 27; as Franks' prospective sponsor, 58–61; in public service, 55

Straus, Nathan, Sr., 27
Strauss, Harold, 242–43
Stroom, Gerrold van der, 118–19
Suchtelen, Nico van, 88
suicide, 46, 69, 158, 200
Sullivan, Rosemary, 160
Symposium (Plato), 283
Szörényi, Arianna, 186

Tabori, George, 262
Tatar, Maria, 13–14
Tedeschi, Giuliana, 188
Thackeray, William Makepeace, 87
Terezín (Theresienstadt), 162, 165, 171
Thijn, Ed van, 94, 168–69
Thomas à Kempis, 6
Thunberg, Greta, 11
Tietz brothers, 30
Tilson Thomas, Michael, 5
Time, 241, 232
Tolan, Stephanie S., 300
Tolstoy, Leo, 6
Tom, Dick and Harry (film), 279
Torres, Tereska, 264
Touching Evil (Norma Rosen), 300
Truman, Harry, 249
Twisk, Pieter van, 159–60
typhus, 7, 202–3

Undset, Sigrid, 156
Unger, Arthur, 223–24, 227
Uris, Leon, 242

Vallentine, Mitchell publishing company, 252, 265
Veen, Gerrit van der, 40
The Victim (Bellow), 241
Viking publishing company, 241, 242
Vorster, B. J., 327
Voskuijl, Bep, 33, 86, 94, 99, 100, 121, 140–41, 151, 158, 159, 204, 283; Anne's papers discovered by, 12; Anne's temper recalled by, 106; Annex raid and, 161, 162, 163; Annex visited by, 79, 82–83, 95–96, 103
Voskuijl, Johan, 82, 85, 96, 158, 159
Voskuijl, Nelly, 159

Waaldijk, Berteke, 152, 356n49
Wagner, Betty Ann, 41–43
Wagner, Juanita, 40–43
Wagner, Richard, 281
Wagner, Robert F., 57
The Wall (Hersey), 244
Wannsee Conference (1942), 72
Waters, Roger, 334–35
Werner, Alfred, 6–7
Westerbork (transit camp), 10, 28, 75, 92, 105, 190; in Anne's diary, 141–43; conditions at, 141–43, 166–68; deportations from, 171–72, 178; Nazi takeover of, 165–66; origins of, 39–40, 166; punishment block of, 174–75; religious services at, 170; school and orphanage at, 168; work at, 169, 174
"What We Talk About When We Talk About Love" (Carver), 9, 311
"What We Talk About When We Talk About Anne Frank" (Englander), 8–9, 311
Where Is Anne Frank (animated film), 339–40, 341
Wiesel, Elie, 179, 180
Wiesenthal, Simon, 158
Wijk-Voskuijl, Joop van, 159
Wijsmuller-Meijer, Gertruida (Truus), 45
Wilde, Oscar, 4, 87, 127–28
Wilhelmina, queen of the Netherlands, 39–40, 42, 106, 210
Williams, C. K., 5
Williams, Tennessee, 264
Wilson, Carl, 271
Winter, Judy de, 178
Winter, Rosa de, 167, 175–76, 178
Winters, Shelley, 292
Wise, Stephen, 286
"The Wise Old Gnome" (Anne Frank), 129–31, 199
Wishengrad, Morton, 282–83

women, 90, 128, 263, 356n49; Anne's writing on, 151, 152, 155, 320, 338, 360–61n42; hiding in the Annex, 121, 133, 151; Japan and, 332–33; Nazi deportations and, 59–60, 172, 178, 180; in Nazi camps, 10, 71, 92, 141–42, 168, 174, 179, 180–83, 184, 186–91, 192–93, 195, 197, 198, 200, 202, 361n55, 373n98; Nazi sympathizers and fraternizers, 217; and storytelling, 13–14, 90, 149, 150
Woolf, Virginia, 150
Wouk, Herman, 242
Wrathgabar, Dave, 270

Yevtushenko, Yevgeny, 5

Zax, Talya, 319–20
Zimetbaum, Mala, 190
Zimmerman (Epstein), Barbara, 246–49, 252, 254–67, 273
Zimmerman, Stan, 323–25
Zionism, 64, 70, 260–61, 333–36
Zubli, Frida de Clercq, 129, 192
Zyklon B, 72

Jewish Lives is a prizewinning series of interpretive biography designed to explore the many facets of Jewish identity. Individual volumes illuminate the imprint of Jewish figures upon literature, religion, philosophy, politics, cultural and economic life, and the arts and sciences. Subjects are paired with authors to elicit lively, deeply informed books that explore the range and depth of the Jewish experience from antiquity to the present.

Jewish Lives is a partnership of Yale University Press and the Leon D. Black Foundation. Ileene Smith is editorial director. Anita Shapira and Steven J. Zipperstein are series editors.

PUBLISHED TITLES INCLUDE:

Abraham: The First Jew, by Anthony Julius
Rabbi Akiva: Sage of the Talmud, by Barry W. Holtz
Ben-Gurion: Father of Modern Israel, by Anita Shapira
Judah Benjamin: Counselor to the Confederacy, by James Traub
Bernard Berenson: A Life in the Picture Trade, by Rachel Cohen
Irving Berlin: New York Genius, by James Kaplan
Sarah: The Life of Sarah Bernhardt, by Robert Gottlieb
Leonard Bernstein: An American Musician, by Allen Shawn
Hayim Nahman Bialik: Poet of Hebrew, by Avner Holtzman
Léon Blum: Prime Minister, Socialist, Zionist, by Pierre Birnbaum
Louis D. Brandeis: American Prophet, by Jeffrey Rosen
Mel Brooks: Disobedient Jew, by Jeremy Dauber
Martin Buber: A Life of Faith and Dissent, by Paul Mendes-Flohr
David: The Divided Heart, by David Wolpe
Moshe Dayan: Israel's Controversial Hero, by Mordechai Bar-On
Disraeli: The Novel Politician, by David Cesarani
Alfred Dreyfus: The Man at the Center of the Affair, by Maurice Samuels
Einstein: His Space and Times, by Steven Gimbel
Becoming Elijah: Prophet of Transformation, by Daniel Matt
Becoming Freud: The Making of a Psychoanalyst, by Adam Phillips
Betty Friedan: Magnificent Disrupter, by Rachel Shteir
Emma Goldman: Revolution as a Way of Life, by Vivian Gornick

Hank Greenberg: The Hero Who Didn't Want to Be One, by Mark Kurlansky
Peggy Guggenheim: The Shock of the Modern, by Francine Prose
Ben Hecht: Fighting Words, Moving Pictures, by Adina Hoffman
Heinrich Heine: Writing the Revolution, by George Prochnik
Lillian Hellman: An Imperious Life, by Dorothy Gallagher
Herod the Great: Jewish King in a Roman World, by Martin Goodman
Theodor Herzl: The Charismatic Leader, by Derek Penslar
Abraham Joshua Heschel: A Life of Radical Amazement, by Julian Zelizer
Houdini: The Elusive American, by Adam Begley
Jabotinsky: A Life, by Hillel Halkin
Jacob: Unexpected Patriarch, by Yair Zakovitch
Franz Kafka: The Poet of Shame and Guilt, by Saul Friedländer
Rav Kook: Mystic in a Time of Revolution, by Yehudah Mirsky
Stanley Kubrick: American Filmmaker, by David Mikics
Stan Lee: A Life in Comics, by Liel Leibovitz
Primo Levi: The Matter of a Life, by Berel Lang
Maimonides: Faith in Reason, by Alberto Manguel
Groucho Marx: The Comedy of Existence, by Lee Siegel
Karl Marx: Philosophy and Revolution, by Shlomo Avineri
Louis B. Mayer and Irving Thalberg: The Whole Equation, by Kenneth Turan
Golda Meir: Israel's Matriarch, by Deborah E. Lipstadt
Menasseh ben Israel: Rabbi of Amsterdam, by Steven Nadler
Moses Mendelssohn: Sage of Modernity, by Shmuel Feiner
Harvey Milk: His Lives and Death, by Lillian Faderman
Arthur Miller: American Witness, by John Lahr
Moses: A Human Life, by Avivah Gottlieb Zornberg
Amos Oz: Writer, Activist, Icon, by Robert Alter
Proust: The Search, by Benjamin Taylor
Yitzhak Rabin: Soldier, Leader, Statesman, by Itamar Rabinovich

Ayn Rand: Writing a Gospel of Success, by Alexandra Popoff
Walther Rathenau: Weimar's Fallen Statesman, by Shulamit Volkov
Man Ray: The Artist and His Shadows, by Arthur Lubow
Sidney Reilly: Master Spy, by Benny Morris
Admiral Hyman Rickover: Engineer of Power, by Marc Wortman
Jerome Robbins: A Life in Dance, by Wendy Lesser
Julius Rosenwald: Repairing the World, by Hasia R. Diner
Mark Rothko: Toward the Light in the Chapel,
by Annie Cohen-Solal
Ruth: A Migrant's Tale, by Ilana Pardes
Menachem Mendel Schneerson: Becoming the Messiah,
by Ezra Glinter
Gershom Scholem: Master of the Kabbalah, by David Biale
Bugsy Siegel: The Dark Side of the American Dream,
by Michael Shnayerson
Solomon: The Lure of Wisdom, by Steven Weitzman
Steven Spielberg: A Life in Films, by Molly Haskell
Spinoza: Freedom's Messiah, by Ian Buruma
Alfred Stieglitz: Taking Pictures, Making Painters, by Phyllis Rose
Barbra Streisand: Redefining Beauty, Femininity, and Power,
by Neal Gabler
Henrietta Szold: Hadassah and the Zionist Dream,
by Francine Klagsbrun
Leon Trotsky: A Revolutionary's Life, by Joshua Rubenstein
Warner Bros: The Making of an American Movie Studio,
by David Thomson
Elie Wiesel: Confronting the Silence, by Joseph Berger

FORTHCOMING TITLES INCLUDE:

Hannah Arendt, by Masha Gessen
The Ba'al Shem Tov, by Ariel Mayse

Walter Benjamin, by Peter Gordon
Franz Boas, by Noga Arikha
Bob Dylan, by Sasha Frere-Jones
George Gershwin, by Gary Giddins
Ruth Bader Ginsburg, by Jeffrey Rosen
Jesus, by Jack Miles
Josephus, by Daniel Boyarin
Louis Kahn, by Gini Alhadeff
Mordecai Kaplan, by Jenna Weissman Joselit
Carole King, by Jane Eisner
Fiorello La Guardia, by Brenda Wineapple
Mahler, by Leon Botstein
Norman Mailer, by David Bromwich
Robert Oppenheimer, by David Rieff
Rebecca, by Judith Shulevitz
Philip Roth, by Steven J. Zipperstein
Edmond de Rothschild, by James McAuley
Jonas Salk, by David Margolick
Stephen Sondheim, by Daniel Okrent
Susan Sontag, by Benjamin Taylor
Gertrude Stein, by Lauren Elkin
Sabbatai Tsevi, by Pawel Maciejko
Billy Wilder, by Noah Isenberg
Ludwig Wittgenstein, by Anthony Gottlieb